Microsoft® Excel® Workbook

2nd Edition

by Paul McFedries
Greg Harvey, PhD

A Wiley Brand

Microsoft® Excel® Workbook For Dummies®, 2nd Edition

Published by: **John Wiley & Sons, Inc.,** 111 River Street, Hoboken, NJ 07030-5774, www.wiley.com

Copyright © 2022 by John Wiley & Sons, Inc., Hoboken, New Jersey

Published simultaneously in Canada

For general information on our other products and services, please contact our Customer Care Department within the U.S. at 877-762-2974, outside the U.S. at 317-572-3993, or fax 317-572-4002. For technical support, please visit https://hub.wiley.com/community/support/dummies.

Wiley publishes in a variety of print and electronic formats and by print-on-demand. Some material included with standard print versions of this book may not be included in e-books or in print-on-demand. If this book refers to media such as a CD or DVD that is not included in the version you purchased, you may download this material at http://booksupport.wiley.com. For more information about Wiley products, visit www.wiley.com.

Library of Congress Control Number: 2021950990

ISBN: 978-1-119-83215-7 (pbk); ISBN: 978-1-119-83216-4 (ePDF); ISBN: 978-1-119-83217-1 (ePub)

SKY10031849_120721

Contents at a Glance

Table of Contents

Introduction

Microsoft Excel is one of the most powerful and sophisticated software programs available today. That power and that sophistication mean Excel can do some extraordinary, just-this-side-of-miraculous things, but they also mean that Excel comes with a learning curve. Sure, you can get productive with Excel amazingly quickly, but if you want to do more than just scratch Excel's surface, then you need to get comfy with many of the program's deeper — and more useful — features.

Sounds like a plan, right? But what's the best way to get to know this wider Excel landscape? Well, consider what you might do when you arrive in a city you've never visited. One way to get the feel for the place would be to wander the streets willy-nilly. Nothing wrong with that, but it will probably mean your knowledge of the city is scattershot and skin-deep. If you want to really get to know the place, then you need a guidebook that tells you what's worth seeing, how to get there, and what to do when you arrive.

Excel is no different. To really get to know the vast "city" of Excel, clicking commands and cells at random won't get the job done. Instead, it's much better to take a few guided tours that tell you what features are worth learning, how to find those features, and how to use them. This gives you the practical, hands-on experience you need to really learn what Excel can do.

About This Book

As its name suggests, *Microsoft Excel Workbook For Dummies* is designed to give you the kind of hands-on experience with all the major aspects of the program you need to start using the program for business or home with a degree of confidence and efficiency. As you'd expect from this type of book, the workbook is primarily composed of questions and exercises that give you plenty of opportunities to experience the purpose and benefits of Excel's many features.

It's my hope that as a result of doing the exercises in this workbook, you'll not only be in firm command of the basic skills necessary to work with confidence in Excel, but also have a good idea of the overall power of the program and what you can do with it.

Conventions Used in This Book

By convention, all the text entries that you type yourself appear in bold. When it comes to instructions in the exercises throughout the workbook, you'll notice two conventions:

» Ribbon commands often follow the sequence of the tab, command button, and drop-down menu option. For example, the command Home ⇨ Format ⇨ Column Width means that you should select the Home tab, followed by the Format command button, and then finally the Column Width option on the menu that appears.

» Ribbon hot keys are often given following the Ribbon command sequence. For example, Alt+HOW selects the Home tab, followed by the Format command button, and then the Column Width option, entirely from the keyboard.

» Filenames in the exercises are shown in full, including their filename extensions as in Exercise3-1.xlsx or Spring Furniture Sales.xlsx. Keep in mind, however, that the display of filename extensions may be turned off on your computer and, in that case, the filenames appear in file lists without their filename extensions as in Exercise3-1 and Spring Furniture Sales.

One other convention that you'll notice used throughout the text is the display of the names for Excel Ribbon commands, Quick Access toolbar buttons, and dialog box options in the title case, wherein all major words are capitalized except for prepositions. The title case is used to make these names stand out from the rest of the text. Often, however, especially in the case of dialog box options, Microsoft does not always follow this convention, preferring to capitalize only the first letter of the option name.

Foolish Assumptions

I assume that you're a new user of Microsoft Excel motivated to learn its essentials either for work or at home.

To complete most of the exercises in this workbook, you only need to have Microsoft Excel installed on a computer running a version of Microsoft Windows 10 or 11. And it doesn't matter whether you obtained Excel with a Microsoft 365 subscription or an Office 2021 purchase; this book covers the core functionality of both flavors of Excel. For some of the printing exercises, you will benefit from having a printer installed on your system (although you can complete most of their steps and get the gist of the lessons without actually printing the sample worksheets).

Beyond the Book

Some extra content for this book is available on the web. Go online to find the following:

>> **The examples used in the book:** The downloadable practice files that come with this workbook are an integral part of the workbook experience. These files contain the practice material that you need to complete most of its exercises. You can find these here:

www.wiley.com/go/excelworkbookfd2e

>> **Cheat Sheet:** Besides what you're reading right now, this book also comes with a free access-anywhere Cheat Sheet that provides a handy reference for Excel's hot keys. To get this Cheat Sheet, go to www.dummies.com and type **Microsoft Excel Workbook For Dummies Cheat Sheet** in the Search box.

Icons Used in This Book

Icons are sprinkled throughout the text of this workbook in high hopes that they draw your attention to particular features. Some of the icons are of the heads-up type, whereas others are more informational in nature:

EXAMPLE

This icon indicates the start of a question-and-answer section in the workbook.

HINT

This icon indicates a hint that can help you perform a particular step in the exercise.

TIP

This icon indicates a tidbit that, if retained, can make your work somewhat easier in Excel.

REMEMBER

This icon indicates a tidbit that is essential to the topic being discussed and is, therefore, worth putting under your hat.

This icon indicates a bit of trickery in the topic that, if ignored, can lead to some sort of trouble in your spreadsheet.

WARNING

Where to Go from Here

This workbook is constructed such that you don't have to start working through the exercises in Chapter 1 and end with those in Chapter 24. That being said, it's still to your benefit to complete all the exercises within a particular chapter, if not in a single work session, at least in a short time period.

If you're a real newbie to Excel and have no experience with any of the earlier versions of the program, I urge you to complete the exercises in Part 1, Chapters 1 through 5, before you take off in your own direction. The exercises in this part are truly fundamental and are meant to give you a strong foundation in the basic features that all Excel users need to know.

Please keep in mind that I designed the exercises in this workbook to work with my Excel companion book, *Excel All-In-One For Dummies*. It can therefore provide you with additional information about the Excel features you're using either at the time you go through the workbook exercises or afterwards. To facilitate this crossover usage, I have, wherever possible, used the same example files in the exercises of this workbook as you see illustrated and explained at length in the larger book.

Whatever you do next and wherever you go in this workbook, just be sure that you enjoy yourself!

1
Building Worksheets

IN THIS PART . . .

Navigate the commands on the tabs of the Excel Ribbon and on the File menu in the Backstage View.

Customize the Quick Access toolbar and Excel Ribbon.

Perform basic data entry chores.

Format worksheet cells.

Print worksheet data.

Edit your worksheet data.

Chapter **1**

Getting Familiar with the Excel Interface

f the proverbial journey of a thousand miles begins with a single step, what should be the first step on your new Excel journey? You can take lots of possible directions, but might I humbly suggest a tour? Nothing exhaustive, mind you; just a quick look at the most basic elements of the Excel program window. Does that sound too elementary? You'd be surprised. One of the secrets of Excel proficiency and efficiency is knowing where to find the command, feature, or setting you want to work with next. Sure, maybe you really *want* to waste precious time clicking aimlessly around the Excel interface until your blood boils and jets of steam blast out of your ears. Hey, it's your life. But my guess is that doesn't sound appealing to you, not even a little. So: A tour it is, then.

To that end, the exercises in this first chapter are designed to get you familiar with the Excel interface. After doing these exercises, you should be comfortable with all aspects of the Excel window and the command structure and ready to do all the rest of the exercises in this book.

Launching Excel

Excel is one of the primary application programs included as part of Microsoft Office. To get proficient with Excel, you need to be familiar with all the various ways of launching the program.

Q. How many ways are there to start Excel?

A. You should be familiar with the two main methods:

- Click Start and then click Excel in the All Apps list. If you're using Windows 11, you need to first click the Start menu's All Apps button and then click Excel.

- Double-click an Excel workbook file in any folder on any drive to which your computer has access.

Q. Are there quicker ways to launch Excel?

A. Yes, you can use two other methods:

- If you see an Excel icon pinned to the Start menu, click that icon.

- If you see an Excel button pinned to the Windows taskbar, click that button.

Try It

Exercise 1-1: Pinning Excel to the Windows Start Menu and Taskbar

In Exercise 1-1, you pin Excel both to the Windows Start menu and to the Windows taskbar and then launch Excel using each of these two methods:

1. Click Start and then locate Excel in the All Apps list (remember to first click All Apps if you're running Windows 11).

2. Right-click Excel and then click Pin to Start.

   Windows adds a pinned tile for Excel to the bottom of the Start menu.

3. In Windows 11, click Back to return to the main Start menu, right-click the pinned Excel icon, and then click Move to Top.

   Windows moves the pinned Excel tile to the top-left corner of the Start menu.

4. Right-click the pinned Excel tile on the Start menu and then click Pin to Taskbar.

   Windows adds a pinned Excel button to the taskbar.

5. If you don't like where Windows pinned the Excel button, click and drag it to the left or right to your preferred location.

   Windows moves the pinned Excel button along with the mouse pointer and you can drop the button in your preferred position.

6. Practice launching Excel by clicking the pinned Excel Start menu tile and then exiting the program. Then launch Excel again, this time by clicking the pinned Excel button on the Windows taskbar.

   You can leave Excel running for Exercise 1-2.

Identifying the Parts of the Excel Window

When you launch Excel by opening the Windows Start menu and clicking Excel, the Home tab of Excel's Backstage view appears. Click the Blank Workbook thumbnail to start a fresh workbook, which contains a single worksheet named Sheet1.

Before you can start using Excel, you must be familiar with its window. Figure 1-1 shows you the Excel window as it appears when you launch a new workbook. Note the names of the different parts of the window before you perform Exercise 1-2.

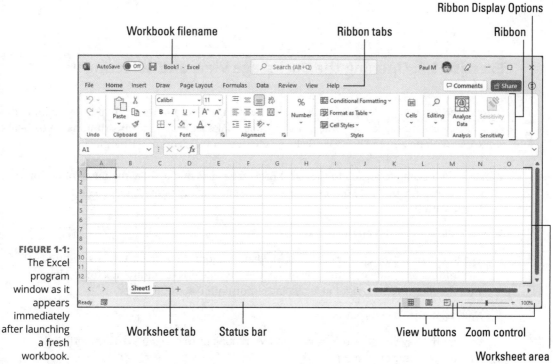

FIGURE 1-1: The Excel program window as it appears immediately after launching a fresh workbook.

EXAMPLE

Q. What are the primary functions of the commands located on the File menu in the Excel Backstage View?

A. To open, close, save, print, and share your Excel workbook files as well as to modify the Excel program options.

Q. What's the primary function of the Ribbon in Excel?

A. To group related Excel commands together and give you quick and easy access to these commands.

Q. What is the primary function of the Quick Access toolbar?

A. To enable you to quickly select Excel commands that you use all the time without having to open the File menu or use the Ribbon commands.

Selecting Commands in the Backstage View

Clicking the File tab opens the Excel Backstage view with a menu of options that appears down the left side. Almost all the commands on this menu are related to actions that affect the entire file, such as saving and printing. If you prefer, you can open this view and access the menu by pressing Alt+F (F for File) instead of clicking the File menu.

When you select any of the major options on the Backstage view — Home, New, Open, Info, Save, Save As, and so on — panels appear that bring together further related and commonly used options on the left side along with pertinent information on the right.

Try It

Exercise 1-2: Opening the Backstage View and Selecting Its Buttons

In this exercise, you get familiar with Excel's Backstage view and its commands by opening the Backstage view and selecting some of its buttons. Make sure that Excel is running and a blank workbook with its empty Sheet1 worksheet is active on your computer monitor.

1. Click the File tab to switch to the Excel Backstage view and display the menu of buttons (Home through Options) on the left side of this screen. By default, Excel selects the Home button.

2. Click the Info button on the menu.

   The Info screen now appears to the immediate right of the Info button (see Figure 1-2). The Info screen is divided into two areas: the left side offers commands for working with the file, while the right side displays information about the file.

3. Now, click the Save As button.

   You use the Save As screen to save a new workbook or to save an existing workbook with a new name or location.

4. Click Browse.

   Excel opens the Save As dialog box where you can modify the name, location, and type of Excel workbook file before saving a copy of it.

5. Press the Esc (Escape) key on your keyboard to close the Save As dialog box.

6. Click the Share button.

   Excel closes Backstage view and opens the Share dialog box, which enables you to share workbook files with co-workers and clients.

7. Press Esc to close the Share dialog box.

8. Press Ctrl+P (the shortcut key for printing in Excel).

   Excel opens the Backstage view and displays the Print panel where you can preview the printout (when there's data in your worksheet that can be printed) and change several print settings. Because you selected the Print panel from an empty worksheet, the message, "We didn't find anything to print" appears on the right panel where the first page of the workbook's print preview normally appears.

9. Press Esc to return to the normal worksheet view and then press Alt+FT.

   Doing this selects the Options command in the Backstage view, which in turn, opens the Excel Options dialog box. This dialog box contains all the options for changing the Excel program and worksheet options. These options are divided into categories General through Trust Center.

10. Make sure the General category is selected, use the Office Background list to select a background pattern, and then click OK to put the new setting into effect.

FIGURE 1-2:
The Excel Backstage view with the Info button selected.

Selecting Commands from the Ribbon

The Excel Ribbon contains the bulk of all the commands that you use in creating, editing, formatting, and sharing your spreadsheets, charts, and tables. As shown in Figure 1-1, normally the Ribbon is divided into the following tabs: Home, Insert, Page Layout, Formulas, Data, Review, and View. There's also a Help tab for accessing the Excel Help system. If you're using a touchscreen PC, you also see a Draw tab.

The commands that appear on each tab are then further divided into groups containing related command buttons. Also, many of these groups contain a dialog box launcher button that appears in the lower-right corner of the group. Clicking this button opens a dialog box of further options related to the group.

Exercise 1-3: Selecting Commands from the Ribbon

In Exercise 1-3, you practice selecting commands from the Ribbon. Make sure that Excel is running and an empty Sheet1 worksheet is active on your computer monitor.

1. Click the Formulas tab to displays its commands.

   Note that the commands on the Formulas tab are divided into four groups: Function Library, Defined Names, Formula Auditing, and Calculation.

2. Press the Alt key.

   Note the access-key letters that now appear on the File menu, title bar, and the Ribbon tabs.

TIP

   If you prefer selecting Excel commands from the keyboard, you'll probably want to memorize the following access keys for selecting these tabs:

   > Home tab: Alt+H
   >
   > Insert tab: Alt+N
   >
   > Draw tab: Alt+JI
   >
   > Page Layout tab: Alt+P
   >
   > Formulas tab: Alt+M
   >
   > Data tab: Alt+A
   >
   > Review tab: Alt+R
   >
   > View tab: Alt+W
   >
   > Help tab: Alt+Y2

3. Press W to display the contents of the View tab and then press VG to deselect the Gridlines check box and hide the worksheet gridlines.

4. Select the Gridlines check box to redisplay the gridlines in the worksheet.

   As you may have noticed, the Ribbon takes up quite of bit of screen space that is otherwise used to display worksheet data. You can take care of this by setting Excel to minimize the Ribbon each time you select one of its commands to display only the tab names.

5. Click the Ribbon Display Options button (pointed out earlier in Figure 1-1) and then click Show Tabs Only.

   Excel immediately minimizes the Ribbon to display only the tab names. Click a tab to display its buttons. Excel minimizes the Ribbon to its tab names once again after you select a tab's commands or click outside the Ribbon.

6. Click Data on the minimized Ribbon.

   Excel expands the Ribbon to display all the Data tab buttons.

7. Click anywhere in the worksheet area to minimize the Ribbon once again.

   The only problem with this minimized Ribbon arrangement is that the temporarily expanded Ribbon covers the first three rows of the worksheet. This makes it very difficult to work with data at the top of the worksheet. For that reason, as well as to help you get comfortable with unfamiliar Ribbon commands, you'll work with the Ribbon expanded at all times in all remaining exercises in this workbook.

8. To return to having Excel display the entire Ribbon full-time, click any tab, click the Ribbon Display Options button and then click Always Show Ribbon.

   The Ribbon now remains fully displayed at all times as you select any of its tabs and buttons without ever obscuring any part of the worksheet display.

Adding a custom tab to the Excel Ribbon

Excel enables you to customize the Ribbon by creating a custom tab to which you can then add your own groups of commands. When you create a custom tab, Excel automatically assigns an available hot key to it.

Try It

Exercise 1-4: Adding a Custom Tab to the Excel Ribbon

In Exercise 1-4, you practice adding a custom tab to the Ribbon. Make sure that Excel is running and an empty Sheet1 worksheet is active on your computer monitor.

1. Choose File ⇨ Options (Alt+FT) to open the Excel Options dialog box and then click the Customize Ribbon option.

   Alternatively, right-click any part of the Ribbon and then click Customize the Ribbon.

   Excel displays the Customize the Ribbon panel in the Excel Options dialog box. This panel is divided into two list boxes: Choose Commands From on the left side and Main Tabs on the right side (see Figure 1-3).

2. In the Main Tabs list box, click View to select it (be sure to click just the name View and not its check box) and then click New Tab.

   Right below the View tab, Excel inserts a new tab with the generic name New Tab (Custom), which includes a new group with the generic name New Group (Custom). This custom tab and group appear between the View tab and the Developer tab in the Main Tabs list box.

3. Click New Tab (Custom) in the Main Tabs list box to select it and then click the Rename command button.

   Excel opens the Rename dialog box where you can replace the generic New Tab display name with a descriptive name.

4. Replace New Tab by typing Misc (for Miscellaneous) in the Display Name text box and then click OK.

   Misc (Custom) now appears in the Main Tabs list box sandwiched between View and Developer.

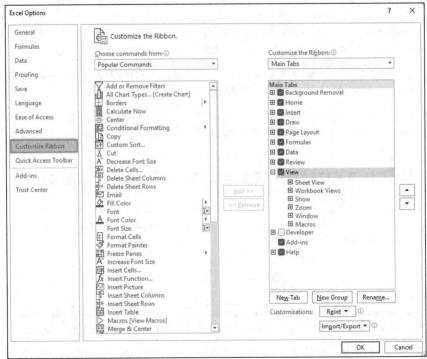

FIGURE 1-3:
The Excel
Options dialog
box with the
Customize
Ribbon option
selected.

Adding commands to groups on your custom tab

After you add a custom tab to the Excel Ribbon, you can then start adding the commands you want to appear on this tab. Just as with the standard Ribbon tabs, the commands you add to your own custom tab are arranged in groups. When you first create a custom tab, it contains only a single tab — named New Group (Custom) — into which to add your commands. You can, however, add other groups to the custom tab using the New Group command button as well as give these groups their own descriptive names using the Rename command button.

Try It

Exercise 1-5: Adding Commands to a Custom Tab

In Exercise 1-5, you practice adding commands to the custom tab you added to the Ribbon in the Exercise 1-4. Before you start this exercise, make sure that the Excel Options dialog box is still open with a Misc (Custom) tab appearing in the Main Tabs list box between View and Developer.

1. Click the New Group (Custom) listing under Misc (Custom) in the Main Tabs list box to select it and then click the Rename button.

   Excel opens the Rename dialog box where you can replace the generic New Group name with your own descriptive name.

2. Replace New Group by typing **Data Form** in the Display Name text box and then clicking OK.

   Data Form (Custom) now appears as the sole group on the Misc custom tab in the Main Tabs list box. Now, you're ready to add the Form command button to the Data Form group that you can use later when completing some of the exercises in Chapter 17.

3. Use the Choose Commands From drop-down list to select Commands Not in the Ribbon.

   Excel now displays an alphabetical list of commands that are not currently on the Ribbon.

4. Click the Form button in this Commands Not in the Ribbon list and then click Add.

   Excel adds the Form button under the Data Form (Custom) group in the Main Tabs list box.

5. Click OK to close the Excel Options dialog box.

   The custom Misc tab you just created now appears at the end of the Excel Ribbon.

6. Click the Misc tab.

   The Misc tab is selected, displaying its sole Form button in the single Data Form group.

7. Click the Home tab to select it.

Selecting Commands on the Quick Access Toolbar

As its name implies, the purpose of the Quick Access toolbar is to give you speedy access to a few Excel tools. That sounds great! So why is the Quick Access toolbar hidden by default in the latest versions of Excel? Good question. The Quick Access toolbar used to appear in the Excel title bar (although you could change that position), so perhaps Microsoft figured the title bar was getting a tad overcrowded. Microsoft did keep the AutoSave switch and the Save button in the title bar, but these are no longer part of the Quick Access toolbar. (Also, Microsoft moved the Undo and Redo buttons to the Home tab.)

If you want to use the Quick Access toolbar, your first chore is to display it.

Displaying the Quick Access toolbar

To get the Quick Access toolbar onscreen, use any one of the following methods:

>> Right-click any part of the Ribbon and then click Show Quick Access Toolbar.

>> Click Ribbon Display Options (see Figure 1-1) and then click Show Quick Access Toolbar.

>> Choose File ➪ Options (or press Alt+FT) to open the Excel Options dialog box, click Quick Access Toolbar, select the Show Quick Access Toolbar check box, and then click OK.

Customizing the Quick Access toolbar

The Quick Access toolbar appears as a strip below the Ribbon and starts off with just the Customize Quick Access Toolbar button, pointed out in Figure 1-4 that, when clicked, opens a pull-down menu. The options on this pull-down menu enable you to quickly customize the buttons that appear in the Quick Access toolbar. In addition, you can change the placement of the Quick Access toolbar by moving it up so that it appears immediately above the Ribbon.

Try It

Exercise 1-6: Customizing the Quick Access Toolbar

In Exercise 1-6, you practice customizing the contents and position of the Quick Access toolbar using options that appear on the Customize Quick Access Toolbar menu. Make sure that Excel is running and an empty Sheet1 worksheet is active on your computer monitor.

1. Click the Customize Quick Access Toolbar button and then click Show Above the Ribbon.

   The Quick Access toolbar with its Customize Quick Access Toolbar button now appears immediately above the Ribbon.

2. Click the Customize Quick Access Toolbar button and then click Show Below the Ribbon.

   The Quick Access toolbar returns to its default position below the Ribbon.

3. Click the Customize Quick Access Toolbar button and then click New.

   Excel adds the New button to the Quick Access toolbar so that you can click it to create a new, blank workbook.

4. Repeat Step 3 to add the Open, Quick Print, and Spelling buttons to the Quick Access toolbar. If you're using Excel on a touchscreen device, also add the Touch/Mouse Mode button, which enables you to quickly switch into Touch mode for easier touch access to the Ribbon commands.

Use the ScreenTips attached to each button to verify that you've correctly added the New, Open, Quick Print, and Spelling buttons (as well as the Touch/Mouse mode button, if applicable) to the Quick Access toolbar, noting the shortcut keys listed.

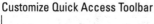

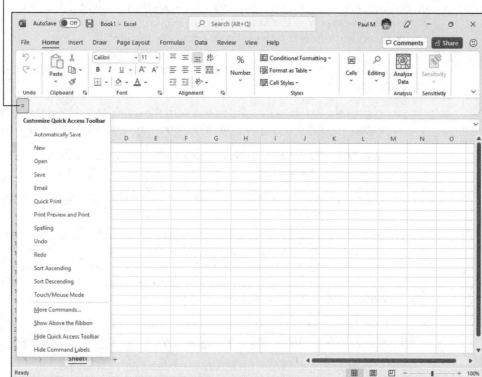

Adding more commands to the Quick Access toolbar

When customizing the command buttons on the Quick Access toolbar, you aren't limited to the selection of commands that appear on the Customize Quick Access Toolbar pull-down menu. Using command options that appear in the Excel Options dialog box, you can add buttons for any of the commands that appear on the Ribbon as well as some Excel commands that remain completely unavailable until you add them to the Quick Access toolbar.

Exercise 1-7: Using the Excel Options Dialog Box to Add Commands to the Quick Access Toolbar

In Exercise 1-7, you practice customizing the contents of the Quick Access toolbar using commands that appear in the Excel Options dialog box. Make sure that Excel is running and an empty Sheet1 worksheet is active on your computer monitor.

1. Click the Customize Quick Access Toolbar button and then click the More Commands option on its menu.

    Excel opens the Excel Options dialog box with the Quick Access Toolbar tab selected (see Figure 1-5). This dialog box contains two list boxes:

    - The Choose Commands From list box on the left where you select the commands to add to the toolbar

    - The Customize Quick Access Toolbar list box on the right, showing the buttons on the toolbar and their order

    To add a new command to the toolbar, you select it in the Choose Commands From list box and then click the Add button. To reorder the buttons on the toolbar, you click its command button in the Customize Quick Access Toolbar list box and then click the Move Up or Move Down buttons (with the black triangles pointing up and down, respectively) until the selected button is in the desired position.

2. Click the drop-down button on the Choose Commands From drop-down list box and then click the Commands Not in the Ribbon option on its drop-down menu.

    The Choose Command From list box now contains only command buttons that are not found on the various tabs of the Excel Ribbon.

3. Click the AutoFormat command option in the Choose Commands From list box (the one with the lightning bolt on top of a small table) and then click the Add button.

    The AutoFormat command option is now listed at the very bottom of your Customize Quick Access Toolbar list box, indicating that it is now the last button on the Quick Access toolbar.

4. Repeat Step 3 to add the AutoFilter and Draw Borders command options to the Quick Access toolbar.

    Next, you want to modify the order in which the command buttons appear on your customized Quick Access toolbar so that they appear in this order arranged in three groups:

    - Open, Quick Print, and New File

    - AutoFormat, AutoFilter, and Draw Borders

    - Spelling and Touch/Mouse Mode (if you're using it)

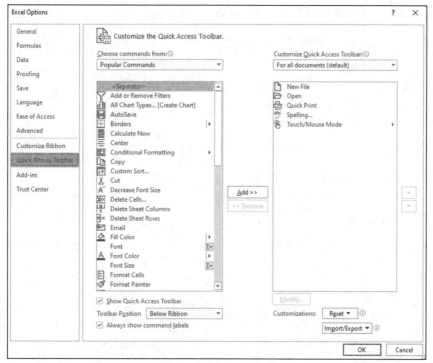

FIGURE 1-5:
The Excel Options dialog box with the Quick Access Toolbar option selected.

5. Click the Open command option in the Customize Quick Access Toolbar list box to select it and then click the Move Up button (the one with the black triangle pointing upward) until Open is the first command in this list.

6. Use the same technique to move the New File command button up until it appears below the Quick Print button.

7. Use the Move Down button to move the Spelling and Touch/Mouse Mode buttons so that they now appear in the same order below the Draw Borders button.

   The command buttons for your customized version of the Quick Access toolbar now appear in the correct order in the Customize Quick Access Toolbar list box in the Excel Options dialog box. The only other thing you need to do is to divide them into groups by adding a vertical bar called a separator.

8. Click the New File command option in the Customize Quick Access Toolbar list box to select it and then click the Separator option at the very top of the Choose Commands From list box to select this option. Click the Add button.

   Excel inserts a separator between the New File and AutoFormat buttons in the Customize Quick Access Toolbar list box.

9. Use this same technique to add a separator between the Draw Borders and Spelling buttons in the Customize Quick Access Toolbar list box.

   Your customized Quick Access toolbar now contains three groups of command buttons created by the two separator options that appear after the New File button and the Draw Borders button.

10. Click OK to close the Excel Options dialog box.

Check the buttons on your customized toolbar against those shown in the toolbar in Figure 1-6.

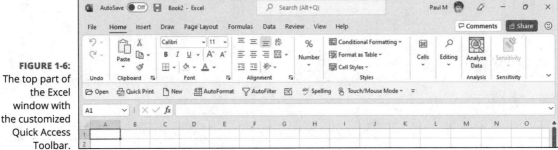

FIGURE 1-6:
The top part of
the Excel
window with
the customized
Quick Access
Toolbar.

IN THIS CHAPTER

» Starting with a blank workbook

» Moving around the workbook

» Selecting cell ranges in a worksheet

» Doing simple data entry in a worksheet

» Using AutoFill to create data series and copy formulas

» Saving the spreadsheet as an Excel workbook file

Chapter **2**

Entering the Worksheet Data

G etting Excel off the ground (which I covered in Chapter 1) is a necessary first step, but you end up with a blank worksheet staring you in the face. Now what? Ah, that's where you put on your hat that says, "Data Entry." *Data entry* refers to filling in Excel's worksheet cells with labels, numbers, dates, and whatever other data you need to get the job done. Data entry is the bread and butter of any worksheet you create or edit. As a result of doing the exercises in this chapter, you get plenty of practice in launching Excel, moving around a new worksheet, the many aspects of doing data entry, and, most importantly, saving your work.

Opening a New Workbook

Each time you launch Excel (using any method other than double-clicking an Excel workbook file icon), you see the Start screen, which is like a scaled-down version of the Backstage view that I talk about in Chapter 1. You see buttons for Home, New, and Open, as well for Account, Feedback, and Options. Use Home to create a blank workbook (by clicking the Blank Workbook thumbnail) or to open a recent file; use New to create either a blank workbook or create a new workbook from one of Excel's many template files; use Open to launch an existing workbook file.

For now, click the Blank Workbook thumbnail either in the Home screen or the New screen. The blank workbook that Excel creates is given the temporary filename Book1 (subsequent blank workbooks are named Book2, Book3, and so on). If you want to start work on a spreadsheet in another workbook, click the New command button on your customized version of the Quick Access toolbar (assuming that you performed Exercise 1-6 in Chapter 1).

When Excel opens a blank workbook, the new workbook follows the Blank Workbook template (which controls the formatting applied to all its blank cells). You can also open new workbooks from other, specialized templates or from a workbook that you've already created. To do this, choose File ➪ New or press Alt+FN. Excel opens the Backstage view's New screen where you can search for a template to use. Figure 2-1 shows the templates that appear when you run a search using the word **personal**.

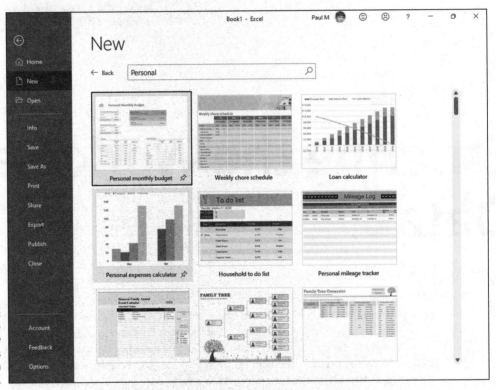

FIGURE 2-1: The Backstage view's New screen enables you to search for a template.

EXAMPLE

Q. What's so special about an Excel template file?

A. A template is a particular type of Excel file designed to automatically generate new workbooks that use both its data and formatting. Each time you create a new workbook based on a template, Excel opens a copy of the template file rather than the original (by appending a number to the template's original filename). Excel template files use the filename extension .xltx to differentiate them from regular Excel workbook files that carry an .xlsx filename extension.

Q. How do you create templates out of your own Excel workbook files?

A. Build a spreadsheet in a new or existing workbook file. To this spreadsheet add all the required text and data, calculating formulas, and formatting required in all the files you will generate from its ensuing template. Choose File ⇨ Save As and then click Browse. In the Save As dialog box, select Excel Template (*.xltx) in the Save As Type drop-down list box and edit the filename (without removing the .xltx filename extension) before you click the Save button.

Exercise 2-1: Opening a New Workbook from the Blank Workbook Template

In Exercise 2-1, you launch Excel (if it's not already running) and then open a new workbook (Book2). Switch back to Book1 (notice the change in the Excel program title bar) and then close the workbook. Notice what happens to Book2 when you close Book1. Leave Book2 open for the next exercise.

HINT

To switch from Sheet1 of Book2 and make Sheet1 of Book1 active, hover the mouse pointer over the Excel taskbar button and then click the Book1 thumbnail that appears above the button. To switch back to Book2, hover the mouse pointer over the Excel taskbar button and then click the Book2 thumbnail that appears above the button. To close a workbook file, choose File ⇨ Close or press Alt+FC.

1. If necessary, launch Excel and then click Blank Workbook. In the program title bar, note that Book1 is the current workbook file.

2. Choose File ⇨ New or press Alt+FN.

   Excel opens the Backstage view's New screen.

3. Click the Blank Workbook thumbnail.

   Excel creates a new workbook file, indicated by Book2 in the program title bar. Hover the mouse pointer over the Excel taskbar button and note the appearance of Book1 and Book2 thumbnails above the Excel button.

4. Press Alt+Tab to make Book1 active. Hover the mouse pointer over the Excel taskbar button and then click the Book2 thumbnail that appears above the button to make Book2 active.

   You can use either method to switch between open Excel workbook files.

5. With Book2 still active (indicated by Book2 in the program title bar), choose File ⇨ Close or press Alt+FC.

   Excel closes Book2 and returns you to Book1. Note that the program would have prompted you to save changes to Book2 before closing it if you had made any data entries in the worksheet. Leave the Book1 workbook open for the next exercise.

Exercise 2-2: Open a New Workbook File from a Template File

In Exercise 2-2, you open a new workbook from the Personal Monthly Budget template installed with Excel.

1. Choose File ⇨ New or press Alt+FN.

   Excel opens the Backstage view's New screen.

2. Click Budgets in the Suggested Searches section and then click the Personal Monthly Budget thumbnail.

   Excel displays a preview and description of this template.

3. Click Create.

   Excel downloads a copy of the Personal Monthly Budget template and then creates a new workbook from that copy. The new workbook's temporary name is Personal Monthly Budget1. This template is all set for you to start editing its values.

4. Choose File ⇨ Close to close the Personal Monthly Budget1 workbook file. If you made any changes to the file, you can click Don't Save in the alert dialog box that appears if you don't want to save changes to this file.

   Excel returns you to your Book1 workbook file that you leave open for the next exercise.

Moving Around the Workbook

The key to doing both data entry and data editing in any Excel worksheet is selecting the cell or cells you want to fill or modify. Selecting a cell almost always entails moving the cell cursor (or pointer) to another part of the current worksheet. Sometimes, it also involves activating a different worksheet in the workbook file.

Excel gives you plenty of choices in techniques for moving the cell cursor, some of which use the mouse and others of which use the keyboard.

Moving within the displayed area

Here's a summary of the most important ways to move the cell cursor to a different cell within the area of the worksheet that's currently displayed onscreen:

>> Click the cell with the white-cross mouse pointer.

>> Press the arrow keys until the cell cursor is in the cell.

>> Click the Name box at the beginning of the Formula bar, enter the reference of the target cell (by column letter and row number as in D12), and press Enter.

Exercise 2-3: Moving the Cell Cursor in a Displayed Area of the Worksheet

For Exercise 2-3, make sure Sheet1 of the blank workbook, Book1, is active before you start practicing moving the cell cursor to different cells in the displayed area using the mouse, arrow keys, and Name box:

1. Move the cell cursor to cell F9 with the mouse.

2. Move the cell cursor to cell C13 using just the down arrow and left arrow keys.

3. Move the cell cursor to cell A1 using the Name box.

REMEMBER

You can always move the cursor to cell A1 (also known as the Home cell) of any active worksheet simply by pressing Ctrl+Home.

Moving to a new area of the worksheet

Many times you have to make cell entries in areas that aren't currently displayed in the active worksheet. One of quickest ways to do this is by entering the reference of the cell you want to go to in the Name box. You can also use any of the following techniques to scroll to new parts of the current worksheet:

» To scroll up and down a window's worth of worksheet rows, press Page Up or Page Down or click the blank area above or below the scroll box in the vertical scroll bar.

» To scroll left and right a window's worth of worksheet columns, click the blank area to the left or right of the scroll box in the horizontal scroll bar.

» To scroll right and left an entire window at a time, press Alt+Page Down and Alt+Page Up, respectively.

» To quickly scroll through rows or columns of the worksheet, hold down the Shift key as you drag the scroll box up or down in the vertical scroll bar, or left and right in the horizontal scroll bar.

» If you use a mouse with a wheel button, scroll up and down the rows of the worksheet by rotating the wheel button forward (to scroll up) and backward (to scroll down).

» If you use a mouse with a wheel button, pan through the rows and columns of the worksheet by clicking the wheel button and then dragging the triangular mouse pointer in the direction you want to scroll.

REMEMBER

Scrolling is not the same as selecting! After scrolling to a new part of the worksheet in view, you still have to select a cell by clicking in it to set the cursor in it.

Exercise 2-4: Moving the Cell Cursor to Unseen Parts of a Worksheet

In Exercise 2-4, you practice moving the cell cursor to cells in the same worksheet that are not currently displayed on your screen.

1. Move the cell cursor to cell C125 with the Name box on the Formula bar.

   Type c125 in the Name box and then press the Enter key.

2. Move the cell cursor to cell CA125 using the horizontal scroll bar.

   Hold down the Shift key as you drag the scroll box in the horizontal scroll bar to the right until column CA appears and then click cell CA125 to put the cell cursor in it.

3. Move the cell cursor to cell CA63560 using the vertical scroll bar.

   Hold down the Shift key and drag the scroll box in the vertical scroll bar down until row 63560 appears and then click cell CA63560 to put the cursor in it.

4. Move the cell cursor directly to cell A1 (the Home cell) in a single operation.

   Press Ctrl+Home.

HINT

Hold down the Shift key to scroll quickly through columns and rows by dragging the scroll box in the horizontal or vertical scroll bar. After scrolling into view the region with the cell you want to select, you still need to click in the cell to select it.

Q. What's the most efficient way to move between ranges of data that are spread out across a worksheet?

A. Use the Ctrl key in combination with any of the four arrow keys to jump from occupied cell to occupied cell in a particular direction.

Exercise 2-5: Moving the Cell Cursor Using the Ctrl and Arrow Keys

In Exercise 2-5, you practice moving the cell cursor around a blank worksheet and between data entries with the Ctrl key and the arrow keys in Sheet1 of Book1.

1. Press Ctrl+→, Ctrl+↓, Ctrl+←, and Ctrl+↑ in succession to jump the cell cursor from one corner to the next of the entire Sheet1 worksheet.

   The first time you press Ctrl+→, the cell cursor jumps from cell A1 all the way to cell XFD1. When you next press Ctrl+↓, the cursor jumps from cell XFD1 all the way down to cell XFD1048576. When you then press Ctrl+←, the cursor jumps all the way left to cell

A1048576, and from there all the way back up to cell A1 when you press Ctrl+↑. All this corner-to-corner jumping happens because no occupied cells are in a particular direction, so the cursor jumps right to the cell on each border of the worksheet.

2. Move the cell cursor to cell A18, type **Testing**, and press Ctrl+Home. Next, press Ctrl+↓.

   The cell cursor stops in cell A18 rather than A1048576 because A18 has content (the label Testing).

3. Move the cell cursor to cell AB18, type **Testing** again, and then press Home. Now, press Ctrl+←.

   This time, the cell cursor stops in cell AB18 rather than XFD18 because AB18 now has content.

4. Press the Delete key and then press Ctrl+← to move to cell A18. Then, press the Delete key again, this time followed by Ctrl+Home.

   Both entries in cells A18 and AB18 are deleted and the cell cursor is back in the home cell, A1.

Moving to a different sheet in the workbook

Each new workbook you start automatically includes one blank worksheet that you can fill with data. If you need more space for a particular spreadsheet, you can add additional worksheets by clicking the Insert Worksheet button (+) that appears immediately following the last sheet tab in the workbook or by pressing Shift+F11. If you want all new workbooks you open to have more worksheets, open the Excel Options dialog box (Alt+FT), make sure the General tab is displayed, and then enter a new value in the Include This Many Sheets text box.

TIP

Each sheet in a workbook is automatically given the next available numeric name, such as Sheet1, Sheet2, and the like, but you can replace these generic names with something descriptive: Double-click the tab you want to rename and then type the new sheet name. Note that the name can't be longer than 31 characters, can't be the same as an existing worksheet name, and can't include the following characters: / \ ? * : [ ]. When you're done, press Enter. You can also color-code a sheet tab by right-clicking it, clicking Tab Color on the shortcut menu, and then selecting the color square on the pop-up palette.

Of course, you must know how to move between the sheets to be able to add and edit data in them. The most direct way to select a new worksheet is to click its sheet tab, although you can also press Ctrl+Page Down to select the next sheet and Ctrl+Page Up to select the previous sheet.

If you add so many worksheets to your workbook that their sheet tabs can't all be displayed at one time, you can use the Tab scroll buttons to the immediate left of the sheet tab to bring into view the tabs you want to select. You can also display more tabs by reducing the width of the horizontal scroll bar (by dragging to the right the split bar that appears when you position the mouse pointer on the vertical bar at the beginning of the scroll bar).

Exercise 2-6: Practice Moving the Cell Cursor to Different Sheets of the Same Workbook

In Exercise 2-6, you practice moving the cell cursor to specific cells in different worksheets of the workbook named Book1, which should be open in Excel.

1. Click the New Sheet icon (+) twice to create worksheets named Sheet2 and Sheet3.

2. Move the cell cursor to cell J10 on Sheet2.

   If used in a formula on another worksheet, this cell reference is indicated as Sheet2!J10.

3. Select cell M21 on Sheet3.

   When you move the cell cursor to a cell, you, in essence, select that cell. If you were to refer to this cell in a formula on another worksheet, this cell would be designated as Sheet3!M21.

4. Select cell J10 on Sheet3 and then click the Sheet2 sheet tab to activate it.

   If you're ever not sure which worksheet you're currently working in, check out the tabs. The tab of the active worksheet is shown underlined and in boldface type.

5. Rename Sheet1 to Spring Sale.

   The easiest way to rename a worksheet is to double-click its tab, type the new name, and then press Enter. Leave the Book1 workbook with the renamed tab open for the next exercise.

Selecting Cell Ranges

When entering, editing, or formatting a single cell, you first move the pointer to the cell as you practiced in the earlier exercises. You can also enter the same data as well as do the same type of editing and formatting in a bunch of cells at one time, but to do so, you must first select the cells where all this is going to happen.

Most of the time when selecting multiple cells in a worksheet, you select a block of cells of so many rows high and so many columns wide. Such a block is known as a *cell range* (or, usually, just a *range*) in the parlance of spreadsheet software.

A range is most often described by the reference of its first and last cell (that is, the cell in the upper-left corner and the cell in the lower-right corner of its block, respectively). When written, this *range address* is separated by a colon as in B15:F20, for a six-row and five-column range whose first cell is B15 and last cell is F20. To select this range, you have three methods you can use:

>> Move the cursor to cell B15 and then drag over and down (or down and over) to cell F20.

>> Click cell B15, hold down the Shift key, then click cell F20.

>> Click cell B15, hold down the Shift key, then use the ↓ and → keys to move the cursor to cell F20.

Excel, however, does not limit you to selecting a single range for data entry, editing, or formatting. You can select as many ranges (even those as small as a single cell) by holding down the Ctrl key as you add a new range to the cell selection.

REMEMBER

Always think of the Shift key when you want to select a single range of cells and the Ctrl key when you want to select more than one range at one time.

EXAMPLE

Q. How do you select ranges that include complete rows and columns of the active worksheet?

A. Click the letter of the column or the number of the row whose cells are to be selected in the column and row header, respectively. To select multiple columns or rows, drag through their column letters or row numbers if they're consecutive, or click their column letters or row numbers as you hold down the Ctrl key if they are non-consecutive. Press Ctrl+A or click the box at the junction of the column and row header with the folded corner icon to select all the columns and rows in the active worksheet (in other words, the entire worksheet).

Q. How do I select the same ranges that span different worksheets of the active workbook?

A. Click the tab of the first worksheet and then hold down Shift as you click the last sheet before you select the range or ranges on the active sheet.

Try It

Exercise 2-7: Practice Assigning Fill Colors to Selected Ranges

In Exercise 2-7, you practice assigning different fill colors to ranges you select in the Spring Sale worksheet of Book1. You can assign these fill colors directly from the Ribbon, using the Fill Color drop-down button in the Font Group.

1. Drag the Zoom slider on the right side of the Status bar to the right until you've increased the magnification of the worksheet to 200%.

   Increasing the magnification of the worksheet display makes it easy to work on a particular section.

2. Drag through the range A2:E2 to select this range; in the Home tab's Font group, click the Fill Color drop-down button and click the White, Background 1, Darker 5% square in the drop-down color palette.

   This square is the one located in the first column of the palette, the second row down.

3. Select the ranges A3:A9 and B3:E3 as a single cell selection and then assign Light Blue as the fill color by selecting its square on the Fill Color palette.

   The Light Blue color is located fourth from the end of the row of Standard Colors in the Fill Color drop-down palette.

4. Select the range B4:E9 and then assign Yellow as the fill color for this range before you position the cell cursor in cell A1 (Ctrl+Home).

   The Yellow fill color is also located in the row of Standard Colors in the Fill Color drop-down palette.

Making Cell Entries

As you may already be aware, Excel recognizes only two types of cell entries: text (label) and numeric (or value). Numeric cell entries are those that consist solely of numbers or calculable formulas. Text entries are those that consist of all letters or a combination of letters, numbers, and punctuation.

Anything you enter into a cell or cell selection is immediately analyzed as either being a number or text entry. Because Excel automatically left-aligns all text entries and right-aligns all numeric ones, you can usually tell immediately how your entry has been classified by noting how it's aligned in its cell.

When you make a numeric entry in a worksheet, Excel not only right aligns the value in its cell, but also assigns whatever numeric format is associated with the number you enter. For example, if you include a dollar sign ($) before the number, Excel applies the Currency format. If your number doesn't specify a numeric format and no numeric format was previously applied to the cell, then Excel uses the General number format. In this format, only significant digits are displayed. This means that all trailing zeros after the decimal point are dropped. Also, if the number you enter contains more digits than can fit within the current column width, Excel automatically converts the value to scientific notation (as in 5E+11 for 500,000,000,000).

Sometimes you have to override Excel's number/text assignment to obtain the desired cell entry. A good example of this is a zip code or numeric part or item number that begins with one or more zeros, as in 00105. If you try to enter this zip code into a cell by typing its five digits, Excel interprets it as a numeric entry and retains only the value 105 in the cell. To retain the leading zeros, you need to force the entry to be recognized as text by typing an initial apostrophe, as in '00105 (this apostrophe does not appear in the cell, although you can see it on the Formula bar).

Entering data in a single cell

Most cell entries are made by typing from the keyboard (although Excel also supports voice and digital ink entry). After typing the characters, which appear both in the cell and on the Formula bar, you must still complete the entry.

REMEMBER

Any time prior to completing the cell entry, you can press the Esc key to clear the cell of all characters you typed there.

EXAMPLE

Q. How many ways are there to complete an entry in the current cell?

A. You should be familiar with all these methods:

- Click the Enter box on the Formula bar (the one with the check mark).

- Press the Enter key.

- Press one of the arrow keys.

- Press Tab, Shift+Tab, Home, Ctrl+Home, Page Up, Page Down, Ctrl+Page Up, Ctrl+Page Down or, any of the other cursor-movement key combinations.

TIP

Click the Enter box on the Formula bar when you want the cell cursor to remain in the cell where you just made the entry (so that you can format the cell in some fashion). Press Enter when you want to move the cell cursor to the next row to make another entry.

Try It

Exercise 2-8: Practice Entering Data in a Simple Table

In Exercise 2-8, you practice doing data entry for the simple Spring Sale Markdowns table shown in Figure 2-2. You make these data entries in the cells that you colored in Exercise 2-7.

1. Enter the table title Spring Sale Markdowns in cell A2.

2. Enter the column headings in row 3 as follows:

   - Code in cell A3

   - Description in cell B3

   - Retail Price in cell C3

   - % Discount in cell D3

   - Markdown in cell E3

3. Enter the code numbers in column A as follows (don't forget how to override Excel and enter these codes as text entries by prefacing each of them with an apostrophe):

   - 02-305 in cell A4

   - 02-240 in cell A5

   - 04-356 in cell A6

   - 01-234 in cell A7

   - 03-003 in cell A8

   - 01-240 in cell A9

4. Enter the furniture descriptions in column B as follows:

- 36-inch round table in cell B4
- 72-inch rectangular table in cell B5
- 76-inch hutch in cell B6
- Side chair in cell B7
- Armchair in cell B8
- Armoire in cell B9

5. Enter the retail prices of the furniture in column C as follows:

- 1250 in cell C4
- 1400 in cell C5
- 2500 in cell C6
- 350 in cell C7
- 500 in cell C8
- 1750 in cell C9

6. Enter the discount percentages in column D as follows:

- 25% in cells D4, D5, and D6
- 15% in cells D7 and D8
- 25% in cell D9

Choose View ⇨ View Side by Side to check your completed spreadsheet table against the one in Solved2-8.xlsx. (Open this workbook in the Chap2 folder inside the Excel Workbook folder that you've downloaded to your computer or OneDrive.)

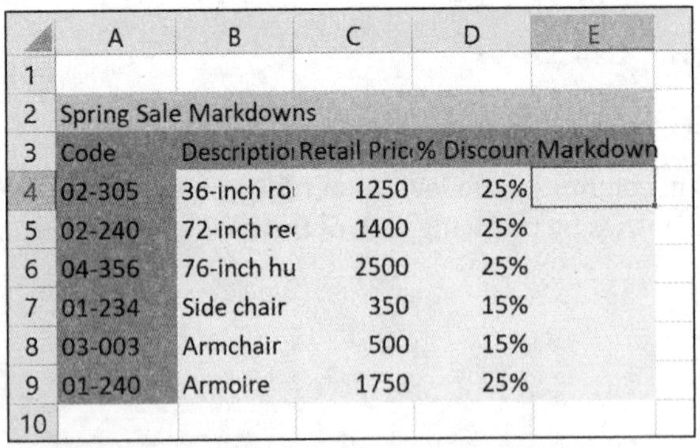

	A	B	C	D	E
1					
2	Spring Sale Markdowns				
3	Code	Descriptio	Retail Pric	% Discoun	Markdown
4	02-305	36-inch ro	1250	25%	
5	02-240	72-inch re	1400	25%	
6	04-356	76-inch hu	2500	25%	
7	01-234	Side chair	350	15%	
8	03-003	Armchair	500	15%	
9	01-240	Armoire	1750	25%	
10					

FIGURE 2-2:
The new Spring Sale table after completing the initial data entry.

Entering data in a range

Sometimes you want to make the same entry in several different cells in the same worksheet. To do this, select all the cells and ranges, type the entry, and then press Ctrl+Enter to both complete the entry you make in the active cell and simultaneously insert the entry into all the other selected cells.

Filling in a data series with the fill handle

The tiny black square in the lower-right corner of the cell cursor is known as the fill handle. The fill handle is your key to the AutoFill feature that enables you to fill in a continuous range either with the same entry or with a data series (such as Monday, Tuesday, Wednesday, and so on, or 101, 102, 103, and the like).

To create a series that increments by a specified amount (such as every day, every other minute, every third month, every tenth widget), enter the first two entries in the series, select those two cells, and then drag the fill handle in the direction you want the series to appear (down or to the right are the most common directions).

TIP

With some sequential series, you can get away with entering just the first value, then using the fill handle to create the rest of the series. For example, to create a series of months, type the first month (such as **January** or **Jan**) and then drag that cell's fill handle. Similarly, to create a series of weekdays, type the first weekday (such as **Monday** or **Mon**) and drag that cell's fill handle.

TIP

Instead of filling in a data series with AutoFill, you can force Excel to copy the entry you've made in the current cell by holding down the Ctrl key as you drag the fill handle. Excel indicates that it copies rather than fills a range by displaying a tiny plus sign to the side of the fill handle mouse pointer.

Try It

Exercise 2-9: Creating a Series of Entries with the Fill Handle

In Exercise 2-9, you practice making the same data entry in multiple ranges and using the fill handle to create various data series in its Sheet1.

1. Make Sheet2 of Book1 active.

2. Select cell A1 and the ranges D3:F3 and B4:B6.

3. Enter today's date, following the date format dd-mmm-yyyy (for example, 25-Dec-2022).

HINT

Don't forget to hold down the Ctrl key when you're selecting the three ranges in the cell selection.

Be sure to complete the current date entry into all the cells of the selection by pressing Ctrl+Enter.

4. Use AutoFill to create a data series with all twelve months in the range A8:A19 starting with January.

5. Use AutoFill to create a data series with the names of all the days of the week in range D8:J8 starting with Monday.

6. Use AutoFill to create a data series with hours from 8:00 AM to 8:00 PM in range C10:C22.

7. Use AutoFill to create a data series in range E10:H10 containing the headings Qtr1, Qtr2, Qtr3, and Qtr4.

8. Use AutoFill to create a series in range E12:E21 containing 1st Team, 2nd Team, 3rd Team, and so on all the way up to 10th Team.

9. Use AutoFill to create a data series in range G12:L12 that contains the name of every other month starting with November in G12 and ending with September.

HINT

Don't forget that you need to indicate the every-other-month increment to Excel (by entering January in cell H12 and then selecting the range G12:H12) before using the fill handle to create the data series.

10. Use AutoFill to copy the data entry New Budget in the range G14:G19.

Copying a formula with the fill handle

AutoFill is not only useful for filling in a data series or copying a static data entry to a continuous range, but also for copying a formula across a row or down a column of a data table. When you copy a formula, Excel automatically adjusts the column and row references in the copies so that they refer to the right data.

REMEMBER

Excel automatically uses the so-called relative column and row cell references in all formulas you create. If you ever need to override this so that all or part of a cell reference is not adjusted in the copied formulas, enter a $ (dollar sign) before the cell's column letter or row number. (You can have Excel do it for you by pressing F4 while building the formula on the Formula bar.)

Try It

Exercise 2-10: Copying Formulas with the Fill Handle

In Exercise 2-10, you complete the Spring Sale table by entering the formula that calculates the amount of the markdown in cell E4 and then using AutoFill to copy that formula down the range E5:E9.

1. Switch to the Spring Sale sheet of Book1 and then move the cell cursor to cell E4.

2. Type = (equal sign) to start the formula for calculating the sale price of the 36-inch round table.

   Remember that all Excel formulas start with the equal sign.

3. Click cell C4 and then type * (asterisk) before you click cell D4.

   Remember that Excel uses the asterisk (*) as the sign of multiplication. Your formula should now read =C4*D4 on the Formula bar.

4. Click the Enter button on the Formula bar and then drag the fill handle of the cell cursor in cell E4 down to E9.

Excel inserts the formula in the cell. The formula =C4*D4 appears in the Formula bar and the calculated markdown amount of 312.5 appears in cell E4. As soon as you release the mouse button after dragging the fill handle, Excel makes adjusted copies of the original formula in the range E5:E9.

5. Use the Side by Side feature to check your results against those in the Spring Sale table shown in Solved2-10.xlsx in the Chap2 folder.

Saving the Spreadsheet Data in a Workbook File

Now all that remains to do is to save the spreadsheets you created while performing the exercises in this chapter before exiting Excel.

TIP

If you ever experience a program crash or power interruption that prevents you from saving your work in Excel, click the Recover Unsaved Workbooks button on the Backstage view's Open screen (Alt+FO). Excel displays your unsaved workbook in an Open dialog box. After opening the unsaved workbook file (by selecting its filename in this dialog box and then clicking the Open button), you can then save your worksheet by following any of the saving techniques outlined in Exercise 2-11.

The first time you save your spreadsheet in a workbook file, the Save This File dialog box appears giving you the opportunity to rename the file (replacing the Book1, Book2 monikers with something more descriptive) in the File Name text box, and indicate the folder in which it should be saved in the Choose a Location drop-down list box. After that, you can use the Save command to save all additional changes to the same file without opening any dialog box.

REMEMBER

Excel uses an XML (eXtensible Markup Language) default file format (indicated by the .xlsx extension to the filename). If you need to create a workbook file that users of older versions of Excel (97-2003) can open and use, you need to save your workbook in the older Excel file format (indicated by the .xls filename extension). To do this, you choose File⇨ Save As and select Excel 97-2003 Workbook (*.xls) on the Save As Type drop-down list in the Save As dialog box.

TIP

Excel saves the current position of the cell cursor in the worksheet when you save its workbook. Therefore, always position the cursor in the cell you want to be current when you next open the workbook for editing before doing the final save of your work session.

Q. How many ways do you know for saving changes to your workbook file?

A. You should be familiar with all these methods:

- Click the Save button (the one with the disk icon) in the Excel title bar.

- Choose File ➪ Save or press Alt+FS (File ➪ Save As or Alt+FA, and then click Browse, if you want to open the Save As dialog box again so that you can rename or save a copy in a new folder).

- Press F12 (Shift+F12 to open the Save This File dialog box).

Try It

Exercise 2-11: Saving a Workbook File

In Exercise 2–11, save the Spring Sales table in a new Excel Practice folder inside the Documents folder on your hard disk:

1. With the Spring Sales table displayed onscreen, select cell A2.

2. Choose File ➪ Save As (Alt+FA), and then click Browse.

    Excel opens the Save As dialog box.

3. Click Documents in the left pane and then click New Folder on the toolbar of the Save As dialog box; type Excel Practice to replace the generic New Folder name, press Enter, and then click Open.

    The new folder name, Excel Practice, now appears at the top of the Save As dialog box.

4. Replace Book1.xlsx in the File Name text box by typing Spring Furniture Sale.

5. Click Save.

6. Close the Spring Furniture Sale workbook by choosing File ➪ Close (or Alt+FC).

Chapter **3**

Formatting the Worksheet

E xcel offers many ways to format a worksheet, but most of your formatting chores will involve changing the look of cells in the worksheet. The formatting you assign a cell not only affects the cell's current contents but it also affects any content you subsequently enter into the cell. The exercises in this chapter give you a chance to practice widening and narrowing the columns and rows of a worksheet to suit the formatting and contents of its cells. In addition, you discover a full array of techniques for assigning formatting to cells in worksheets, using features found on the Home tab of the Ribbon as well as the Format Cells dialog box.

Resizing Columns and Rows

In all new workbooks, the columns of its worksheets are a standard 8.43 characters or 64 pixels wide and all the rows are 15 points or 20 pixels high. You can, if you need, change this default column width for an entire worksheet by clicking its sheet tab to select it and then, on the Home tab, choose Format⇨ Default Width command (Alt+HOD). In the Standard Width dialog box that appears, type the new default width (in characters) in the Standard Column Width text box and then click OK.

Note that Excel does not provide any way for setting a new row height default in a worksheet. The 15-point default value is universal for all worksheets you deal with unless you manually override this height. This is probably because Excel always automatically increases the height of all rows to suit the formatting of its cell entries. Column widths, on the other hand, are automatically widened only under certain circumstances (when applying certain AutoFormat styles and building tables with later versions of Excel).

HINT

You can cajole Excel into doing all the work for you by using AutoFit, which automatically adjusts a column's width to accommodate its widest entry or a row's height to accommodate its tallest entry. The quickest way to run AutoFit on a column is to double-click the right border of the column's header; alternatively, place the cell cursor somewhere in the column and choose Home ⇨ Format ⇨ AutoFit Column Width (or press Alt+HOI). To AutoFit a row, double-click the lower border of the row's header; alternatively, place the cell cursor somewhere in the row and choose Home ⇨ Format ⇨ AutoFit Row Height (or press Alt+HOA).

Making column widths suit the data

Resizing columns to suit the data they contain is one of the most common formatting tasks you perform in creating and editing a spreadsheet.

REMEMBER

You need to widen a column in a worksheet whenever it contains one or more cells with numerical data that have too many digits to be displayed in the current column width (indicated by a string of #### signs in the cells) or text data with characters cut off (because they spilled over into cells in columns to the immediate right that were then truncated by entries made in the adjacent column).

EXAMPLE

Q. How many ways exist for resizing columns in a worksheet?

A. You should be familiar with all the following methods:

- Drag the column's right border in the column header to the left (to narrow) or right (to widen). To resize several columns at once, drag through their column letters in the header or Ctrl+click them before dragging the right border of one of them.

- Double-click the column's right border in the column header to resize it with AutoFit. To resize several columns at once, drag though their column letters in the header or Ctrl+click them before double-clicking the right border of one of them.

- Select the column or columns to resize and then choose Home ⇨ Format ⇨ Column Width (or press Alt+HOW) to open the Column Width dialog box. Enter the new width (in characters) in the Column Width text box and then click OK.

- Select the cell range or selection whose columns need resizing and then choose Home ⇨ Format ⇨ AutoFit Column Width (or press Alt+HOI). Excel widens or narrows the columns in the cell selection to display all the digits and text in the cells in the selection.

- Select the column or columns to resize to standard column width (of 8.43 characters) and then choose Home ⇨ Format ⇨ Column Width (or press Alt+HOW) to open the Column Width dialog box. Type 8.43 in the Column Width text box and then click OK.

Exercise 3-1: Changing Column Widths in a Worksheet Table

In Exercise 3-1, you practice changing the column widths in your Spring Sale Markdowns table.

1. Launch Excel and then open the Spring Furniture Sale.xlsx workbook you created in the exercises in Chapter 2 and saved in the Excel Practice folder. If you didn't do these exercises, open the Exercise3-1.xlsx file in the Chap3 subfolder inside the Excel Workbook folder.

   If Spring Furniture Sale.xlsx is not listed as one of the documents in the right-hand pane of the Recent Workbooks pane in the Backstage View (opened by clicking the File menu or pressing Alt+F), choose File⇨ Open, and select the Exercise3-1.xlsx file in the Chap3 subfolder inside the Excel Workbook folder.

2. Use the AutoFit feature to widen Column B containing the furniture descriptions and Column D containing the discount percentages sufficiently so that none of these descriptions are cut off.

3. Drag the right border of Column C to the left. As you drag the border, Excel displays a banner that tells you the new column width in characters and pixels. Drag the column border until the column is 34 pixels wide and then release the mouse button (note the appearance of ### indicators in all but two cells in Column C). Next, use AutoFit to widen Columns C so that its entries are displayed.

4. Use the Column Width dialog box to set column E to a width of 10 characters or 75 pixels.

5. Narrow column A to 7.14 characters or 55 pixels wide (use any method that works).

6. If you've been modifying your Spring Furniture Sale.xlsx file, click the Save button on the Quick Access toolbar or press Ctrl+S to save your changes. If you've been modifying the Exercise3-1.xlsx file, choose File⇨ Save As or press F12 to open the Save As dialog box and then rename Exercise 3-1.xlsx as Spring Furniture Sale.xlsx in the File Name text box. Then, designate the Excel Practice folder inside the Documents library as the file location before you click Save.

Manipulating the height of certain rows

You don't find yourself having to resize the rows of a worksheet all that much. Most of the time, Excel does all the work for you by automatically resizing them just right to accommodate any and all formatting changes you make to their cells.

About the only time you might want to increase the height of a row on your own is when you want to increase the space between the contents of one row and the contents of the row immediately above without going through the trouble of inserting a blank row as a spacer between them.

EXAMPLE

Q. What are the two ways you can manually modify the height of selected rows in a worksheet?

A. You should be familiar with these methods for changing row height:

- Drag the lower border of the number of the row to modify in the row header either up (to shorten the row) or down (to heighten the row). To modify multiple rows at one time, select the rows (by dragging through or Ctrl+clicking their row numbers in the row header) and then drag just the lower border of one of the selected rows.

- Select the cell range or selection whose row heights need resizing and then choose Home ⇨ Format ⇨ AutoFit Row Height (or press Alt+HOA). Excel adjusts the row heights in the cell selection to fit the tallest entry in each row.

- Position the cell cursor in any one of the cells in the row to be modified (or, to modify multiple rows at one time, select the rows), and then choose Home ⇨ Format ⇨ Row Height (or press Alt+HOH) to open the Row Height dialog box. Enter the number of points in the Row Height text box and then click OK.

Try It

Exercise 3-2: Changing Row Heights in a Worksheet

In Exercise 3-2, you practice modifying row height in the Spring Furniture Sale workbook.

1. Increase the height of Row 2, containing the table title, to 26.25 points or 35 pixels by dragging the row's border.

   As you drag the row border, Excel displays a banner that tells you the current row height in points and pixels.

   Note how the spreadsheet title sinks down when the row height is increased.

2. Restore the height of Row 2 to its original height with AutoFit Row Height.

Cell Formatting Techniques

Cell formatting can run the gamut from changing the font, color, attribute, or alignment of a cell entry to the color, borders, and protection status of the cell itself. You can accomplish most of the formatting in a typical spreadsheet with the command buttons on the Home tab of the Ribbon. The rest you can accomplish with the options available on the various tabs of the Format Cells dialog box.

REMEMBER

The first rule of formatting is to remember to select all the cells that need formatting before you click the desired button either on the Home tab or on one of the tabs in the Format Cells dialog box.

Formatting cells with the Ribbon's Home tab

The Home tab of the Ribbon contains eight groups with lots of command buttons for formatting your spreadsheets:

- **Undo:** Includes the Undo button for reversing one or more of your most recent actions, as well as the Redo button for reapplying one or more actions that you reversed with Undo.

- **Clipboard:** Cutting, copying, and pasting data into new locations in a worksheet as well as the Format Painter for picking up the formatting from one cell and copying it to others.

- **Font:** Changing the font, font size, font attributes, font color, and fill color.

- **Alignment:** Changing the alignment and orientation of entries in a cell range as well as wrapping entries on different rows and merging cells.

- **Number:** Assigning the most popular number formats to cell ranges.

- **Styles:** Assigning conditional formatting, formatting a cell range as a table, and applying styles to a cell range.

- **Cells:** Inserting and deleting cells as well as formatting the widths of worksheet columns and the heights of rows.

- **Editing:** Doing a variety of tasks, including creating statistical formulas (that sum, average, count, and the like) values in a range of cells; filling out a range with a series of entries; clearing the contents, formats, and so forth in cells; sorting and filtering data lists; and finding and selecting particular worksheet cells.

Try It

Exercise 3-3: Applying the Format as Table Option to Your Markdowns Data Table

In Exercise 3-3, you practice formatting the sale furniture markdowns data table in the Spring Sale worksheet of the Spring Furniture Sale workbook using the Merge & Center and Format as Table command buttons on the Home tab of the Ribbon.

1. Center the title of the markdown table in cell A2 over the range A2:E2 and make it bold.

HINT

   Select the range of cells over which you want to center the text that's entered in the first cell of the range (the range A2:E2 in this case), and then click the Merge & Center button in the Alignment group. Click the Bold button in the Font group to make the centered title bold.

   Next, you want to remove all the fill colors assigned to the markdowns table so that you can then format the range as a table.

2. Select the table's cell range A3:E9 and then click the Fill Color drop-down button in the Font group and click No Fill on the drop-down menu.

   Excel removes all the fill colors from this cell range. You will now format this cell range as a table. Doing this makes it possible for you to instantly change its formatting using

Excel's Table Styles gallery. This gallery uses the Live Preview feature that lets you preview any table style in the gallery in the table in your worksheet before you apply the style to the table's cell range.

3. Click the Format as Table button in the Styles group and then click Table Style Light 1 (the first one in the first row) of the drop-down palette.

You must select an initial table format from the Table Styles gallery and specify the cell range of the table before you can use Live Preview to see how any of the other table formats in the gallery suit your table. Note that the Create Table dialog box not only displays the range address of the cell range that it selects in the worksheet (indicated by the dashed border) but also automatically selects the My Table Has Headers check box.

REMEMBER

When the My Table Has Headers check box is selected, Excel automatically considers the data entries in the first row of the cell range as the column headings of the table (to which it adds drop-down buttons called AutoFilter buttons). If you deselect the My Table Has Headers check box, Excel inserts an additional row in your table with generic column headings such as Column1, Column2, and so forth.

4. Click OK in the Create Table dialog box without making any changes to its settings.

Excel adds AutoFilter buttons to the column headings in row 3 of the table — Code, Description, Retail Price, and so on. (You find out how to use these buttons to sort and filter your data in Chapter 17.) It also applies the Table Style Light 1 style (with the alternating lightly banded rows) to your markdown table.

Now, you can have some fun using Excel's Live Preview feature to see how your table would look if you were to apply one of the many other styles in the Table Styles gallery to its data. Note that the end of the Ribbon now contains an additional Table Design tab. You can use the command buttons on the Table Design tab to select a new table style as well as to customize the one currently selected.

REMEMBER

This Table Design tab and the others like it that you'll encounter as you work with different objects in Excel worksheets are referred to as contextual tabs. A contextual tab and all its command buttons appears at the end of the Ribbon only as long as you select the object (a formatted table, in this case) to which its options can be applied.

5. Click cell A2 containing the table title in the Spring Sale worksheet to select it.

The moment you select a cell outside of your formatted data table, the contextual Table Design tab and its command buttons immediately disappear from the Ribbon. To bring this contextual tab and all its options back, all you have to do is select a cell in the data table.

6. Click cell A3 with the column heading Code to select this cell.

The Table Design tab immediately reappears at the end of the Ribbon. You can use Live Preview to preview your markdown table in some of the other styles in its Table Styles gallery.

7. Click the Design tab and then in the Table Styles gallery, position your mouse pointer (but don't click) on the thumbnail of each of the other four or so styles (Table Style Light 2, Light 3, and so on) that are normally displayed in the Table Styles group to the right of the Table Style Light 1 thumbnail.

As you mouse over each thumbnail in the gallery, Excel's Live Preview displays the data in your markdown table in that style. These few light styles whose thumbnails are currently displayed in the Tables Styles gallery on the Ribbon are not, however, your only choices.

8. Click the More button (the button with the line and the downward pointing triangle) located in the lower-right corner of the Table Styles gallery to expand the gallery and then experiment by mousing over the different Medium and Dark styles. (You have to use the scroll bar to display the thumbnails of the Dark table styles.)

   Previewing a style in the gallery is not the same as selecting it. To apply a new style, you must click the thumbnail after previewing it.

9. Format your markdowns table with Table Style Medium 23 in the Table Styles gallery.

   Note that the thumbnails displayed in the single row of the Table Styles gallery on the Ribbon changes to display currently selected Medium 23 style as well as other Medium styles in its row. You can use the Up and Down buttons that appear above the More button at the end of the gallery to display rows above and below the current one without expanding the gallery so that it obscures cells in the worksheet.

10. Use the Save As command on the File menu or press Alt+FA to save your changes to the workbook under the new filename, Spring Furniture Sale Table Format.xlsx.

   Be sure that you don't change the folder (you want to save this version in the Excel Practice folder on your hard drive) or the type of file when you rename it in the Save As dialog box. Append Table Format to the main filename before you click Save.

Try It

Exercise 3-4: Customizing the Table Formatting for Markdowns Data Table

In Exercise 3-4, you practice customizing the table formatting applied to the Spring Sale Markdowns table of your Spring Sale worksheet in the Spring Furniture Sale Table Format workbook. Check the program title bar to be sure that the Spring Furniture Sale Table Format workbook is the one open and active in Excel. If you didn't complete Exercise 3-3, open the Exercise3-4.xlsx file in the Chap3 subfolder of your Excel Workbook folder.

1. Click the Table Design tab at the end of the Ribbon to display its command buttons.

WARNING

   If your Ribbon doesn't have the Table Design tab, this means that none of the cells of your formatted Spring Sale Markdowns table is currently selected. Remember that Excel only adds contextual tabs for an object on the Ribbon when that object is selected in the worksheet. Click one of the cells in your markdowns table to display the Table Design contextual tab.

2. In the Table Style Options group, select the Last Column check box.

   Excel displays the calculated markdowns for each item in Column E in boldface type.

3. In the Table Style Options group, select the Total Row check box.

   Excel now adds a total row in row 10 of your data table with a formula in cell E10 that totals the markdown amounts in column E. This feature is very useful when you need totals to appear at the bottom of your data table. However, it makes no sense here because the markdown amounts are not cumulative.

4. In the Table Style Options group, deselect the Total Row check box to remove the Total row from your data table and then rename the data table by clicking Table1 under Table Name in the Properties group and replacing it with the name Markdowns.

   Now you're ready to further customize the Markdowns table by formatting some of its contents using command buttons on the Home tab.

5. Select the values in the cell ranges C4:C9 and E4:E9. Next, click the Home tab and click the Accounting Number Format button in the Number group.

   Excel adds a dollar sign and two decimal places to all the values in these two cell ranges. Now experiment with the Decrease Decimal and Increase Decimal buttons in the Number group.

6. Click the Decrease Decimal button in the Number group twice to remove all the decimal places from the values in the selected cell ranges and then click the Increase Decimal button twice to bring the decimal places back.

   Now try changing the number formatting for the selected cell ranges.

7. Click the Comma Style button in the Number group to change the number formatting from Accounting to Comma Style.

   The Table Styles gallery is not the only feature to use Live Preview. This feature also works when you want to assign a new font or font size to a cell selection.

8. Select the entire data table as a cell selection (A3:E9) and then click the Font Size drop-down button in the Font group. Highlight larger and smaller font sizes in this list with the mouse before you click 10 to make 10 point the new font size.

   Note that each time you highlight a new size on the Font Size drop-down list, Excel displays all the table data not obscured by the list itself in the new font size.

9. Click the Font drop-down button and highlight different fonts in the drop-down list before you click Arial to make it the new font.

   Each time you highlight a new font on the Font drop-down list, Excel displays all the table data not obscured by this list in the new font.

10. Use the Borders button in the Font group to add a border around all the cells in the cell selection (A3:E9).

HINT

To draw a border around a block of cells, select its cell range (A3:E9 in this case), and then click the Borders drop-down button in the Font group of the Home tab. Click the All Border option on the Borders drop-down list (the one divided into four quadrants).

Next, you're going to remove the AutoFilter buttons that Excel automatically adds to the row containing the column headings of a table when you select a table style with the Format as Table button on the Home tab. (You only need these AutoFilter buttons when you intend to sort or filter the table's data, which you don't need to do here, and, besides, you can always bring these buttons back should you need them later.)

11. Click A3 to select it and then click the Sort & Filter button in the Editing group of the Home tab and, finally, click Filter on its drop-down menu.

    Excel removes all the AutoFilter buttons from all the cells in row 3 of your markdowns table.

    Use the View Side by Side feature (View⇨View Side by Side) to check your fully formatted table against the one entered on the Spring Sale sheet in the workbook file Solved3-4.xlsx, located in the Chap3 Folder in your Excel Workbook folder.

12. When your work checks outs, click cell A1 and then choose File⇨Save As or press Alt+FA to save your changes to the workbook under the new filename, Spring Furniture Sale Cust Format.xlsx.

    Be sure that you don't change the folder (you want to save this version in the Excel Practice folder on your hard drive) or the type of file when you rename it in the Save As dialog box. Replace Table with Cust in the main filename before you click Save. Leave the Spring Furniture Sale Cust Format.xlsx workbook open in Excel for the next exercise.

`Try It`

Exercise 3-5: Using the Format Painter and AutoFormat Features

In Exercise 3-5, you practice using the Format Painter and AutoFormat buttons to format a cell range. The Format Painter button in the Home tab's Clipboard group enables you to pick up all the formatting you've already assigned a cell in the worksheet and apply this formatting to a range you select. The AutoFormat button, which you added as part of customizing the Quick Access toolbar in Chapter 1 is not normally a part of Excel. This button enables you to use an earlier table formatting feature (available in Excel 97-2003) to apply complex formatting to data tables in a single operation.

1. Click cell A3 containing the first column heading, Code, in the markdowns data table and then click the AutoFormat button on the Quick Access toolbar.

    Excel opens an AutoFormat dialog box that contains a list box with samples of various table formats you can apply to your table arranged in two columns. Scroll down the list to see all the table formats available.

2. Click the Classic 3 sample in the AutoFormat dialog box and then click OK.

    Excel immediately applies the Classic 3 table format with its vivid blue coloring to all the data in your table (cell range, A3:E9).

3. With cell A3 still selected, click the Format Painter button (the one with the paintbrush icon) in the Clipboard group of the Ribbon's Home tab.

    A marquee (of marching ants) now appears around the border of cell A3, indicating that the formatting applied to this cell will be copied to whatever cell or cell range you select next.

4. Use the Paintbrush mouse pointer to click cell A2 containing the table title to select this cell and simultaneously copy the formatting from cell A3 to it.

   Excel immediately applies the dark blue fill and bold white font color to the title in cell A2. Unfortunately, the program also applies the Align Text Right formatting while at the same time removing the merge you applied to cells A2:E2.

5. Select the cell range, A2:E2, and then click the Merge & Center button in the Alignment group of the Home tab before you increase the size of the title font to 14 points using the Font Size button in the Font group.

   Excel converts the range A2:E2 into a super-cell in which it now horizontally centers the table title.

6. Save your formatting changes to this table in a new workbook file named Spring Furniture Sale Classic 3.xlsx in your Excel Practice folder and then close the workbook file.

Formatting cells with the Format Cells dialog box

You can use the Format Cells dialog box to gain more control over your cell formatting compared to what you can do using the Home tab's Font, Alignment, and Number groups. This extra formatting control includes applying any number formats other than the Ribbon's standard Accounting, Percent, and Comma number as well as applying custom alignment angles not available from the Orientation button's drop-down list. In the Format Cells dialog box, you can also use the options on the Font tab to select more font attributes; the Fill tab to apply patterns along with fill-in colors for cell backgrounds; and the Protection tab to change locked or hidden status of cells that goes into effect as soon as you protect the worksheet. (See Chapter 18 for details.)

TIP

When you click one of the dialog box launcher buttons that appear in the lower-right corners of the Home tab's Font, Alignment, and Number groups, Excel opens the Format Cells dialog box with the respective Font, Alignment, and Number tabs selected. You can also open the Format Cells dialog box by pressing Ctrl+1 or by choosing Home ➪ Format ➪ Format Cells (or Alt+HOE).

The options on the Number tab for applying the various and sundry number formats that Excel has to offer as well as for creating your own custom number formats is possibly the most important one in the Format Cells dialog box (see Figure 3-1). This tab organizes the ready-made number formats by category from General, the default for all cells in a new worksheet that retains only significant digits, to Custom, where you can create your own number formats. Here's a quick rundown on the other ten categories of number formats that you will probably use more often:

>> **Number:** Applies a number format to numeric entries in which you determine the number of decimal places to display, whether to use the comma as a thousands separator, and the appearance of negative numbers (either with a negative sign or enclosed in parentheses in black or red).

- ≫ **Currency:** Applies a number format to numeric entries in which you determine the currency symbol (the dollar sign is the default), the number of decimal places to display, and the appearance of negative numbers (either with a negative sign or enclosed in parentheses in black or red).

- ≫ **Accounting:** Applies a number format to numeric entries in which you determine the currency symbol (the dollar sign is the default) and the number of decimal places to display (the difference between Accounting and Currency is that Accounting always uses two decimal places and aligns the currency symbol and decimal points in their cells).

- ≫ **Date:** Applies a date format for numeric entries that Excel recognizes as representing dates of the year (because it was entered following one of these date formats).

- ≫ **Time:** Applies a time format using either a 12- or 24-hour clock for numeric entries that Excel recognizes as representing times of the day (because it was entered following one of the time formats).

- ≫ **Percentage:** Displays a numeric entry as a percentage with a percent sign and the number of decimal places you designate.

- ≫ **Fraction:** Applies a fractional number format for the decimal places in your numeric entries.

- ≫ **Scientific:** Applies scientific notation to numeric entries by applying an exponent and the number of decimal places you designate.

- ≫ **Text:** Formats numeric entries as though they were text entries.

- ≫ **Special:** Formats numeric entries following the styles for Zip Code, Zip Code + 4 (with leading zeros retained), Phone Number (with parentheses added to the first three digits as the area code and dashes between the third and fourth digits of the next seven indicating the prefix and main number), or Social Security Number (with dashes between the third and fourth, and fifth and sixth digits of the nine-digit number).

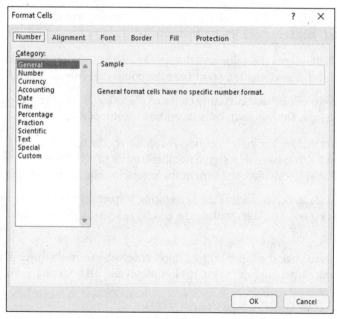

FIGURE 3-1:
The Number tab of the Format Cells dialog box gives you access to a wide variety of number formats.

Exercise 3-6: Practice Formatting Various Values with the Format Cells Dialog Box

In Exercise 3-6, you practice formatting different types of values using some of the number formats found in the Format Cells dialog box.

1. Open a new workbook (Book2) by clicking the New button you added to the Quick Access toolbar or by pressing Ctrl+N, and then rename Sheet1 Number Formats and use it to practice applying the following number formats using the Number tab on the Format Cells dialog box.

2. Format the cell range B2:B5 in the blank Number Formats sheet using the Currency number format with two decimal places, the dollar sign, and negative values set in red parentheses in the Format Cells dialog box.

When you assign a number format to a blank cell range, any values later entered in those cells pick up that number format rather than the General format.

REMEMBER 3. Enter the following values in the cell range:

- 1234.75 in cell B2
- 23500 in cell B3
- -1450.5 in cell B4
- 100.345 in cell B5

Note how Excel automatically adds the Currency format using the parameters you selected in the Format Cells dialog box, including enclosing the negative value -1450.5 in parentheses without a minus sign and displaying the value in red.

4. Apply the Text format to cell B7 from the Format Cells dialog box and then enter 200.25 in this cell and select cell B7, if necessary.

Note how Excel left-aligns the value and the appearance of the alert drop-down button (the diamond with the exclamation point near the upper-left corner of cell B7).

5. Create a formula in cell B7 that currently contains the value 200.25 formatted with the Text format that adds the values in cells B4 and B5 together (=B4+B5).

Uh-oh. Instead of adding the cells together, Excel inserts the text of the formula =B4+B5 into cell B7. You have to assign a number format to cell B7 and re-create the formula to get Excel to calculate the sum of the values in cells B4 and B5.

6. With the cell cursor in cell B7, select the Accounting format on the Number tab of the Format Cells dialog box and then replace the text by re-creating the formula to add the values in cells B4 and B5.

This time when you click the Enter button, Excel enters the formula into cell B7, displaying the calculated answer ($1350.16) in the cell and =B4+B5 on the Formula bar.

7. Enter the date 02-15-2022 in cell B9.

   Note how Excel automatically converts this entry to 02/15/2022.

8. Format cell B9 with Date format on the Number tab of the Format Cells dialog box that follows the pattern March 14, 2012.

   Excel displays the date entered into cell B9 as February 15, 2022.

9. Format cell B9 with General number format, this time by clicking the Number Format drop-down button in the Number group on the Home tab and then clicking General at the top of its drop-down list.

   Note the appearance of the date serial number 44607 indicating that this date represents the 44,607th day since the dawn of the twentieth century.

10. Choose Home ⇨ Undo or press Ctrl+Z to restore the previous date formatting.

    Excel restores the previous date format and February 15, 2022 reappears in cell B9.

11. Enter the number 00401 in cell B11 and then format it with Special Zip Code format on the Number tab of the Format Cells dialog box.

    Note that Excel immediately drops the preceding two zeros when you complete the cell entry in B11 (so that only 401 appears) and then redisplays them the moment you apply the Zip Code format to the value.

12. Enter the number 4155551122 in cell B13 and then format it with the Special Phone Number format.

    Note how Excel parses the number into area code, prefix, and main number by formatting it as (415) 555-1122.

13. Enter the number 20012551 in cell B15 and then format it with the Special Social Security Number format.

    Note how Excel formats the value as the Social Security Number 020-01-2551.

14. Open the Solved3-6.xlsx workbook file in the Chap3 folder of your Excel Workbook folder and use the Side by Side feature to check your formatted values against those in its Number Formats sheet.

15. When everything checks out, click cell A1 and then save your practice workbook in your Excel Practice folder under the filename Number Formatting Practice.xlsx and then close the workbook file.

Try It

Exercise 3-7: Modifying the Alignment of Labels in a Spreadsheet

Between the command options in the Alignment group of the Ribbon's Home tab and those on the Alignment tab of the Format Cells dialog box, Excel gives you almost total control not only over the horizontal alignment of cell entries (that is, between the left and right borders of their columns) but also over vertical alignment (between the top and bottom borders of their rows) and the orientation (direction of the text with regard to a horizontal baseline at 0 degrees). In addition, its Text Control options (Wrap Text, Shrink to Fit, and Merge Cells) enable you to accommodate longer cell entries to restricted column widths.

In Exercise 3-7, you practice modifying the alignment of various labels in the markdowns data table using both the command buttons in the Alignment group of the Home tab and the options on the Alignment tab of the Format Cells dialog box (Ctrl+1). To do this exercise, you need to open your Spring Furniture Sale Cust Format.xlsx saved in your Excel Practice folder.

1. Click the File menu and then click Spring Furniture Sale Cust Format.xlsx in the Recent Workbooks list on the Recent Workbooks panel in the Backstage View to open the file in Excel.

   If this filename is not listed in your Recent Workbooks list, choose File⇨Open, open your Excel Practice folder, select the Spring Furniture Sale Cust Format.xlsx file icon, and click the Open button.

2. Select cell A2 in the Spring Sale worksheet and then increase the height of row 2 from the default 15 points (20 pixels) to 30 points (40 pixels).

   It's not until you increase the row height that you really notice the bottom vertical alignment of text in its cell.

3. Click the Middle Align button in the Alignment group of the Ribbon's Home tab to change the vertical alignment of the table title in cell A2 from bottom to middle.

   Excel moves the title of the table up in its super-cell so that the text is now vertically centered between the cell's top and bottom borders.

4. Italicize the table title using the Italic command button in the Font group of the Home tab of the Ribbon and then increase the size of the table title from 11 points to 16 points using the Font Size button's drop-down list.

   The title of the table is now nicely emphasized in the super-cell created out of the cell range A2:E2.

5. Select the cell range B4:B9 containing the furniture descriptions and then click the Wrap Text command button on the Home tab. Next, narrow Column B to 15 (110 pixels) and use AutoFit to increase the height of rows 4:9 to accommodate the wrapping of the text in cells B4 and B5.

HINT

To select rows 4:9 in the worksheet, click 4 in the row headings column and then drag down to row 9. To apply AutoFit to the selected rows, double-click the lower-right border of the heading for row 9.

When you use the Wrap Text button, Excel automatically wraps the text to other lines in the selected cells whenever you narrow their columns sufficiently that their text can no longer be displayed all on a single line.

6. Select the cell ranges A4:A5 and C4:E5 and then click the Top Align command button in the Alignment group on the Home tab to change the vertical alignment of their data entries from bottom to top.

Excel aligns the data entries in the cell ranges A4:A5 and C4:E5 with the top line of the wrapped furniture description text entries in cells B4 and B5.

7. Select the cell range A3:E3 and then change the orientation of their column headings from 0 degrees to 60 degrees counterclockwise, and then increase the height of row 3, if necessary, so that all the text in the now diagonal column headings are displayed.

HINT

The Orientation button in the Alignment group of the Home tab only supports rotating the text clockwise or counterclockwise 45 degrees. To rotate the text up or down any other number of degrees, you need to open the Alignment tab of the Format Cells dialog box. Entering positive numbers in the Degrees text box on the Alignment tab of the Format cells dialog box moves the orientation of the text up, counterclockwise to the baseline; whereas entering negative numbers in the Degrees text box moves the text orientation down, clockwise from the baseline.

8. Remove the fill color from the merged, super-cell A2 by selecting the merged cell A2 and then clicking the No Fill option on the Fill Color button's drop-down list.

Next, you need to convert the A2 super-cell back into separate cells and return the title text back to its default bottom vertical alignment.

9. Unmerge cell A2 and return it to the bottom vertical alignment before you use AutoFit to return the height of the row to its default.

HINT

- To unmerge a super-cell and convert it back into the original block of individual cells, select it and then click the Merge & Center button on the Ribbon's Home tab.

- To restore bottom vertical alignment, click the Bottom Align button in the Alignment group of the Ribbon's Home tab.

Finally, you are going to move the table title from cell A2 to the home cell, A1.

10. Click cell A2 and then click the Cut button in the Clipboard group of the Home tab. Click cell A1 and press the Enter key.

When you press Enter, Excel pastes the table title in cell A1.

Use the Side by Side feature to check the changes you've made to the formatting of your markdowns table in the Spring Sale worksheet against those shown in that worksheet in the Solved3-7.xlsx workbook file located in the Chapter 3 folder of the Excel Workbook folder.

11. When everything checks out, close the Solved3-7.xlsx workbook file and save your alignment changes in the Spring Furniture Sale file in a new workbook called Spring Furniture Sale Aligned.xlsx located in your Excel Practice folder. Then, close the new workbook.

Using cell styles

Excel enables you to assign complex formatting to selected cells of a worksheet with just a few clicks. The program's Cell Styles gallery gives you access to a variety of predefined cell styles that you can try on for size with Live Preview before assigning to the current cell selection.

Exercise 3-8: Practice Applying Cell Styles

In Exercise 3-8, you practice applying the predefined cells styles to cell ranges from the Cell Styles gallery. For this exercise, open a completely unformatted version of the markdown data table you've been using.

1. Click the Open button on your customized Quick Access toolbar (or press Ctrl+O) to display the Backstage view's Open panel, and then click Browse. In the Open dialog box, click Documents Library in the left-hand pane before you double-click the Excel Workbook folder icon followed by the Chap3 folder icon in the main area. Finally, double-click the Exercise3-8.xlsx file icon.

   Excel opens the Exercise3-8.xlsx workbook file that contains an unformatted version of the now very familiar markdowns table.

2. Click cell A2 and then click the Cell Styles command button in the Styles group on the Ribbon's Home tab.

   Excel displays the Cell Styles gallery divided into various sections: Good, Bad, and Neutral; Data and Model; Titles and Headings; Themed Cell Styles; and Number Format.

3. Position the mouse pointer on the Heading 1 style sample, the first one in the Titles and Headings section of the Cell Styles gallery. Highlight the samples of the other title styles in this row and then click the Heading 4 sample to assign it to cell A2.

   Note how Live Preview shows how the title, Spring Sale Markdowns, that's entered in cell A2 looks in each of the heading styles as you highlight their samples in the Cell Styles gallery.

4. Select the cell range A3:E3 containing the table's column headings and then preview how these headings look with the samples in the Data and Model section of the Cell Styles gallery before applying the Note cell style to this range.

   Excel applies the Note cell style to the range A3:E3 so that these cells now use this Data and Model style's borders and light shading.

5. Select the cell range A4:E9 with the table's data and then apply the Input cell style to this cell selection.

   Excel applies the Input cell style to the range A4:E9 so that these cells now use this Data and Model style's font color, borders, and shading.

6. Select the cell ranges C4:C9 and E4:E9 containing the table's values and then apply the Currency cell style to this cell selection.

Excel applies the Currency cell style to these two ranges so that the values in these cells now use this Number Format style's dollar signs, commas, and two decimal places.

7. Click cell A1 and then save your cell style formatting changes to this version of the workbook under the filename Spring Furniture Sale Cell Styles.xlsx in the Excel Practice folder on your computer's hard disk. Then, close the workbook file.

Using conditional formatting

Conditional formatting enables you to create cell formatting that Excel applies only when a condition or a series of conditions that you define go into effect in the worksheet. Conditional formatting is useful when you want to apply a special type of formatting (such as a red fill color or underlining) to a cell to alert you when the cell's value reaches a particular (high or low) value. In Excel, you can also use conditional formatting to apply different colored data bars, color scales, and icon sets to a range of values to instantly visualize their relative values.

Try It

Exercise 3-9: Practice Applying Conditional Formatting to a Target Cell

Exercise 3-9 gives you practice applying conditional formatting to a particular cell in a spreadsheet so that the cell formatting changes depending upon the value that the cell currently contains.

1. Open the Exercise3-9.xlsx workbook located in the Chap3 subfolder inside your Excel Workbook folder.

   You use its Income Statement to practice applying conditional formatting to a particular cell in an Income Statement spreadsheet so that Excel changes the cell formatting when the value in this cell is greater than, less than, or exactly equal to an anticipated value.

2. Select cell B10 containing the formula for calculating the total operating income or loss and then, in the Home tab's Styles group, click the Conditional Formatting drop-down button.

   Excel opens the Conditional Formatting drop-down menu.

3. Choose Highlight Cells Rules⇨Greater Than.

   Excel opens a Greater Than dialog box that contains two boxes: a text box on the left that currently contains the value 99,440 currently in cell B10; and a drop-down list box on the right that contains the style, Light Red Fill with Dark Red Text.

4. Type **100000** (1 and five zeros) in the text box on the left and then select Green Fill with Dark Green Text as the formatting to use in the drop-down list box on the right, and click OK.

   Excel now automatically formats any value in cell B10 that is greater than 100,000 with a green fill color and dark green font color.

5. Use the same technique to assign a conditional format to cell B10 that formats this cell with Yellow Fill with Dark Yellow Text when its value is less than 100,000.

HINT

Choose Highlight Cells Rules⇨Less Than and then enter **100000** in the text box. Select Yellow Fill with Dark Yellow Text in the drop-down list box in the Less Than dialog box, and click OK.

Note that Excel applies this dark yellow text on yellow fill to cell B10 because the Operating Income (loss) cell, B10, currently contains a calculated value below 100,000.

6. Assign a third conditional format to cell B10 that formats the cell with a custom format that uses a dark blue font color against a light blue fill color with a dark cell border when its value is equal to 100,000.

HINT

After entering 100000 in the text box, select Custom Format at the bottom of the drop-down list box in the Equal To dialog box (opened by selecting Highlight Cells Rules⇨Equal To on the Conditional Formatting button menus). In the Font tab of the Format Cells dialog box, click the Dark Blue square on the Color palette, the Outline preset on the Border tab, and a light blue square on the Fill tab, and click OK twice to close both open dialog boxes.

7. Reduce the Product Costs in cell B6 from the current –12,175 to –2175.

Note that as soon as you change this value, Excel applies your dark green text on a green fill color to cell B10 because the Operating Income (loss) in this cell has risen to 109,440 so that the calculated value now meets the greater than 100,000 condition.

HINT

To replace an existing entry with a new entry, select the cell and enter the new entry as though the cell were still blank.

8. Replace the Revenues value in cell B3 from the current 150,250 with 140,810.

Excel now applies the custom conditional formatting to the calculated value in cell B10 because it now contains the anticipated value of 100,000 exactly.

Use the Side by Side feature to check your Income Statement with conditional formatting against the one shown in Solved3-9.xlsx located in the Chap3 subfolder of your Excel Workbook folder.

9. When everything checks out, click cell A1 and then save your work as a new workbook called Income Statement Conditional Format.xlsx in your Excel Practice folder inside Documents on your hard disk, and then close the workbook.

Try It

Exercise 3-10: Practice Applying Conditional Formatting to a Range of Values

In Exercise 3-10, you practice using Excel's conditional formatting to apply different data bars, scales, and icon sets to a cell range containing a series of sequential values. These colored data bars and scales and icon sets that you apply then call attention to the relationship between the values in this sequence.

1. Open a new blank workbook and then position the cell cursor in cell C1. Then enter the value 1 in cell C1. Be sure to complete the cell entry by clicking the Enter button on the Formula bar so that the cell cursor remains in cell C1.

   Now you use the Fill handle to create a sequential series of numbers in column C.

2. Hold down the Ctrl key as you drag the fill handle down column C until you reach cell C12 and the ScreenTip says 12.

   Now, use the fill handle to create a descending series of values in this column that ends with 0 in cell C24.

3. Enter 11 in cell C13 and then select cells C12 and C13. Next, drag the fill handle in cell C13 down column C until you reach cell C24 and the ScreenTip says 0.

   Note that you don't have to hold down the Ctrl key to create this descending sequential series because cells C12 and C13 are selected as a range and these cells show Excel how to model the series by decreasing each cell by 1.

4. Select the cell range C1:C24. Then click the Conditional Formatting button in the Styles group of the Ribbon's Home tab and highlight Data Bars on the Conditional Formatting drop-down menu.

   Excel displays a Data Bars continuation menu with thumbnails of the various colored data bars that you can assign to your cell selection. You can use Live Preview to see how these colors look in your worksheet before you select them.

5. Highlight each of the different colored data bar thumbnails in the Data Bars continuation menu before you click the Gradient Fill Purple Data Bar thumbnail to assign it to the cell range C1:C24.

   Next, you'll use the fill handle to create a range of temperatures from 0 to 120 degrees that increases sequentially in 10-degree increments. Then you'll use Excel's Conditional Formatting to assign the Red – Yellow – Green Color Scale to this cell range.

6. Use the fill handle to create a range that begins with 0 in cell F15 and 120 in cell R15 incremented by 10 in each succeeding cell to the right.

HINT

   Enter 0 in cell F15 and 10 in cell G15. Then, select the cell range F15:G15 and drag the fill handle to the right until you reach cell R15 and the ScreenTip says 120.

7. Use the Conditional Formatting button on the Home tab to assign the Red – Yellow – Green Color Scale to the cell range F15:R15 after using Live Preview to see how the range would look in all the other color scale combinations.

   Finally, you'll use the fill handle to create a cell range containing a series of percentages ranging from 0% to 100% that increases sequentially by 10% in each succeeding cell. Then, you assign the Three Traffic Lights (Unrimmed) Icon Set to this cell range.

8. Use the fill handle to create a range that begins with 0% in cell F20 and 100% in cell P20 incremented by 10 percent in each succeeding cell to the right.

   Now, play with the different Icon Sets before selecting the Three Traffic Lights (Unrimmed) set for cell range F20:P20.

9. Use the Conditional Formatting button on the Home tab to assign the Three Traffic Lights (Unrimmed) Icon Set to the cell range F20:P20 after using Live Preview to see how the range would look in all the other icon set combinations.

   Use the Side by Side feature to check your conditionally formatted ranges against those in Sheet1 of the Solved3-10.xlsx workbook file located in the Chap3 folder inside your Excel Workbook folder.

10. When your work checks out, select cell A1 and then save your workbook in your Excel Practice folder under the filename Conditional Format Practice 2.xlsx and then close the workbook file.

Hiding Columns and Rows

Excel enables you to hide entire columns and rows in your worksheet. You can use this facility to conceal sensitive data (such as salaries and the like) in worksheets that are used in formula calculations but that are not for everyone's eyes.

Hiding columns and rows is a lot like modifying their width and height (in fact, if the truth be known, a hidden column is just one whose width is reduced to zero and a hidden row one whose height is shrunk to zero): Select the column or columns to hide and then in the Home tab's Cells group, choose Format ⇨ Hide & Unhide ⇨ Hide Columns (Alt+HOUC) or select the row or rows to hide and choose Format ⇨ Hide & Unhide ⇨ Hide Rows (Alt+HOUR).

TIP

You can also quickly hide a column or row by right-clicking its header and then selecting Hide on its shortcut menu.

To redisplay concealed columns, select the columns on either side (left and right) of the hidden columns and then choose Format ⇨ Hide & Unhide ⇨ Unhide Columns (Alt+HOUL). To redisplay concealed rows, select the rows on either side (above and below) of the hidden rows and then choose Format ⇨ Hide & Unhide ⇨ Unhide Rows (Alt+HOUO). Excel then redisplays all the formerly hidden columns or rows.

EXAMPLE

Q. Is there any way to hide individual cell entries in the worksheet rather than entire columns and rows?

A. Although Excel does not provide a command for hiding individual cells or cell ranges, you can accomplish this by creating a Custom number format on the Number tab of the Format Cells dialog box and then applying this custom number format to selected cells from this dialog box. To create this Custom number format, click Custom in the Category list box and then click any of the formatting codes in the Sample list box on the right. Replace its codes with three semicolons in a row with no spaces in between (;;;) before you click. Be aware, however, that applying this ;;; Custom number format hides only the entries as they appear in the worksheet itself but does nothing to cloak their appearance on the Formula bar when the cell cursor is in them. This limits the usefulness of this method to the distribution of printed copies of the spreadsheet because all the entries in electronic copies are vulnerable via the Formula bar.

Exercise 3-11: Practice Hiding Columns and Rows

1. Open the Exercise 3-11.xlsx workbook file located in the Chap3 folder of your Excel Workbook folder. Use its twelve-month Regional Income table to practice hiding columns and rows.

2. Hide the column ranges B:D, F:H, J:L, and N:P and then put the cell cursor in cell A1 so that only columns A, E, I, M, Q, and R are displayed at the far left of the Income Analysis worksheet.

3. Select the column range A:Q and then choose Format⇨Hide & Unhide⇨Unhide Columns on the Ribbon or press Alt+HOUL. Click cell A1 and then verify that all the erstwhile hidden columns of the spreadsheet are redisplayed.

4. Hide the row ranges 4:8, 12:16, and 20:24 and then scroll up to verify that only rows 1, 2, 3; 9, 10, 11; 17, 18, 19; and 25 are displayed at the top of the Income Analysis worksheet.

5. Select the row range 3:25 and then redisplay all the hidden rows by choosing Format⇨Hide & Unhide⇨Unhide Rows or pressing Alt+HOUO. Click cell A3 and then verify that all the missing rows are now redisplayed in the worksheet.

6. Close the Exercise 3-11.xlsx workbook file without saving your changes and exit Excel.

» Using Page Break Preview to adjust the paging

» Adding readymade and custom headers and footers to a report

» Adjusting various page and print settings

» Printing all or portions of a workbook

Chapter 4

Printing Worksheet Reports

You probably won't have to print your worksheets very often, but when you do, you'll want to make your printed Excel reports easy to read and well organized. The exercises in this chapter give you a chance to practice printing many types of worksheet reports using Excel's Page Layout view, Page Break Preview, headers and footers, and Print Titles features. Don't worry if you don't have access to a printer while completing these exercises: In almost all cases, you can use Excel's Print Preview feature in the Backstage view's Print panel to get an idea of how the report will appear on the printed page.

Previewing Pages in the Worksheet and Backstage View

In the regular worksheet view, Page Layout view is your first line of defense against wasting paper on useless reports that contain bad page breaks. For example, you want to avoid page breaks that separate columns and/or rows of the worksheet from data that needs to appear together on a page. When printing the document from the Excel Backstage view, the Print panel also shows you the pages of the report as well as enables you to change basic print settings before sending the report to your printer.

In Page Layout view in the regular worksheet, Excel turns on the display of the horizontal and vertical rulers in the border area and shows representations of the pages in the worksheet area. The depictions of each page include the page's margins, any headers or footers you've assigned (including an area to click if you haven't assigned a header or footer and decide you want to), as well as the worksheet data. You can then use the Zoom slider on the Status bar to zoom in and out on the pages by increasing and decreasing the screen magnification to ensure that none of the data is being printed on the wrong pages.

TIP

In the Print panel in the Backstage view, Excel shows a preview of each page of the printed report with the margin space and any headers or footers you add, more or less as they'll appear in the printout.

Try It

Exercise 4-1: Previewing the Pages in Page Layout View and the Print panel

In Exercise 4-1, you practice using Page Layout view and the Print panel in Excel's Backstage view to check out the paging of an Income Analysis worksheet. You then use this sample Income Analysis worksheet in later printing exercises in this chapter.

1. Open the Exercise4-1.xlsx workbook file in your Excel Workbook folder.

    Excel opens the Income Analysis worksheet that shows regional sales data by month and quarter for one year.

2. Click the Page Layout button on the program's Status bar (that's the middle button of the three that appear immediately to the left of the Zoom slider below the worksheet area).

    Excel switches to Page Layout view indicated by the appearance of the rulers in the worksheet headings area above and to the left of the worksheet; the page representation in the worksheet area, including margins and headings; and the current page and total page indicator on the Status bar.

    You can also switch into Page Layout mode by choosing View➪Page Layout on the Ribbon or pressing Alt+WP.

3. Drag the Zoom slider on the Status bar to the left and click the Zoom Out button (the one with the minus sign) until the screen magnification is reduced until you can see the page depictions for two or three pages including the top rows of the worksheet.

4. Use the vertical scroll bar to scroll down the Income Analysis worksheet until you can see the bottom margins of the pages for the lower rows of the Income Analysis worksheet (pages 2, 4, and 6).

REMEMBER

By default, Excel numbers pages down the rows of data in your worksheet and then to the columns to the right. Thus, the pages in this 10-page report are 1, 3, 5, 7, 9 in the top row of pages proceeding left to right and 2, 4, 6, 8, and 10 in the row of pages below.

Note the top part of the blank pages that are not part of the printed report below pages 2, 4, 6, 8, and 10 (indicated by the Click to Add Data indicators).

5. Use the Zoom slider to return the screen magnification to 100%.

The quickest way to do this is by clicking the center marker of the slider.

6. Press Ctrl+Home to select cell A1 in the Income Analysis worksheet and then click the Normal view button on the Status bar.

You can also select the normal worksheet view by choosing View⇨Normal on the Ribbon or by pressing Alt+WL.

7. Choose File⇨Print or press Ctrl+P to open the Backstage view's Print panel.

On the right side of the Print panel, Excel displays the first of the ten pages in the report.

8. Click the Show Margins button in the lower-right corner of the Print panel to the immediate left of the Zoom to Page button (in the very corner of the panel) to display the report margins in the print preview.

9. Click the Next Page button (the one with the triangle pointing right) once.

Excel displays the columns and rows of data that will print on the second page of the report.

10. Click the Zoom to Page button to zoom in on the second page.

Excel zooms the page to full size while adding scroll bars so that you can scroll now hidden data into view.

11. Click the Previous Page button (the one with the triangle pointing left) and then click the Back button at the top of the Backstage view screen (or press Esc) to return to the regular worksheet.

12. Close the Exercise4-1.xlsx workbook file without saving changes.

Adjusting Page Breaks

While Page Layout view alerts you to all sorts of potential problems in the printed report by showing you everything on the page as it will print, Page Break Preview only shows you where the page breaks occur. Page Break Preview does this by drawing lines between columns and rows in the worksheet that indicate the limits of each page in the report. You can then manipulate the page breaks by dragging these page break indicators to new columns and rows.

Exercise 4-2: Using Page Break Preview to Fix Bad Page Breaks

In Exercise 4-2, you practice using Excel's Page Break Preview view to first identify and then fix page break problems in a report created from another version of the Income Analysis worksheet you first worked with in Exercise 4-1.

1. Open the Exercise4-2.xlsx workbook file in the Chap4 folder located in the Excel Workbook folder.

    Excel opens another, slightly different version of the Income Analysis worksheet you used in Exercise 4-1.

2. Click the Page Break Preview button on the Status bar (the one on the right of the three buttons grouped together to the left of the Zoom slider).

    Excel displays page breaks as dark blue dotted lines between worksheet columns and rows. The program also displays the page numbers in the center of each page and automatically reduces the magnification of the screen to 60% of normal. Note that there are now 12 pages in this report.

3. Scroll down the pages and then fix the first bad page break that occurs between rows 40 and 41.

    Here, the page break automatically placed between rows 40 and 41 separates the Regional Ratio Analysis heading in row 36, the month headings in row 37, and the Gross Profit on Sales heading in row 38 on pages 1, 3, 5, 7, 9, and 11 from the actual regional analysis data on pages 2, 4, 6, 8, 10, and 12.

HINT

To fix this bad page break, you need to drag the page break line between rows 40 and 41 up so that the break now occurs between rows 35 and 36. The Regional Analysis Heading and all the other headings associated with the percentage data will be printed together on pages 2, 4, 6, 8, 10, and 12 of the report.

4. Scroll up until you can see the headings in row 2 of the worksheet. Adjust the page break between pages 1 and 3, and 2 and 4 so that all the Qtr 1 income figures are printed on pages 1 and 2 of the report.

HINT

To fix this bad break, drag the page break line between columns D and E to the right one column so that the break now occurs between columns E and F, putting all the Qtr 1 figures together on pages 1 and 2.

5. Adjust the page break between pages 3 and 5, and 4 and 6 so that all the Qtr 2 income figures are printed on pages 3 and 4 of the report.

HINT

To fix this bad break, drag the page break line between columns J and K to the left one column so that the break now occurs between column I and J, putting all the Qtr 2 figures together on pages 3 and 4.

6. Adjust the page break between pages 5 and 7, and 6 and 8 so that only the Qtr 3 income figures are printed on pages 5 and 6 of the report.

Note that after taking care of all the bad page breaks in the original report the total number of pages is reduced from 12 to 8 pages.

7. Put the worksheet into Page Layout view and then use the Zoom slider and the scroll bars to check the layout and content of all eight pages of the report.

    Make sure that all the quarterly data will now print together on their respective pages.

8. Click the Page Layout tab on the Ribbon and then click the Page Setup dialog box launcher button to open the Page Setup dialog box.

    The Page Setup dialog box opens with the Page tab selected.

9. Click the Margins tab in the Page Setup dialog box and then select the Horizontally and Vertically check boxes in the Center on the Page section before you click OK.

    Excel centers the headings and data on each page of the report between the left and right, and top and bottom margins.

10. Remove the check mark from the Print check box under the Gridlines heading on the Page Layout tab.

    This removes the column and row gridlines from the printed report.

    You can also deselect and select this particular Print check box by pressing Alt+PPG.

REMEMBER

You continue to see the worksheet gridlines in the Page Layout view even after you remove the check mark from the Print check box. To make sure that the worksheet gridlines will not appear in your printed report, you need to switch to Print Preview mode. Print Preview enables you to examine each page of the report.

11. Choose File ⇨ Print or press Ctrl+P to open the Print Preview pane on the Print panel.

    Note that the gridlines no longer appear on the first page of the report in the Print Preview area.

12. Preview all eight pages of the final report using the Next Page and Previous Page buttons. You can also enter the desired page number into the Current Page text box and press Enter.

13. When you've checked all the pages, click the Print button to print the report if you have access to a printer; otherwise, press Esc or click the Back button to exit the Backstage view.

    Now all that's left to do is to return the worksheet to Normal view.

14. Click the Normal button on the Status bar and then save your changes in a new file named Income Analysis Report.xlsx in your Excel Practice folder, and then close that workbook.

Adding Headers and Footers

Excel enables you to add information in the top margin (called a header) and the bottom margin (called a footer) of each page (or every other page) of your printed reports. The program supports two types of headers and footers: prefabricated headers and footers that print only stock information such as the current page number, date, and name of the worksheet, and custom headers and footers that enable you to mix this type of stock information with information of your own.

To add a custom header or footer to a report, you insert codes that retrieve information about the report or workbook file that you can mix with your own text (such as the company or department name) in one of three sections:

» Left section for information to be aligned against the page's left margin

» Center section for information to be centered between the left and right margins

» Right section for information to be aligned against the page's right margin

EXAMPLE

Q. What is the easiest way to add a new prefabricated header and footer to my report?

A. Put the worksheet into Page Layout view (by clicking the Page Layout button on the Status bar) and then click the left, center, or right section of the header or footer area at the top or bottom of the first page (indicated by the Add Header and Add Footer messages). Finally, in the Header & Footer contextual tab, click the Header button or the Footer button and select the type of header or footer text you want to insert.

Q. Can I customize a prefabricated header or footer?

A. Yes, you can: Click the section containing the prefab header or footer you want to customize in Page Layout view. Then, to insert custom text or codes, type the text or click the appropriate command button in the Header & Footer Elements group of the Header & Footer contextual tab.

Try It

Exercise 4-3: Adding a Header and a Footer to a Worksheet Report

In Exercise 4-3, you practice adding both a header and footer to a report generated from a version of the Income Analysis worksheet that you've been working on throughout this chapter. This report will have an alternating header that changes the placement of the current page number depending on whether the page is odd or even and a standard footer that is printed on every page.

1. Open the Exercise4-3.xlsx workbook file in the Chap4 folder located in Excel Workbook folder.

   Excel opens a version of the Income Analysis worksheet you used in Exercise 4-2 without any headers or footers defined.

2. Put the Income Analysis worksheet into Page Layout view by clicking the Page Layout button on the Status bar. Click the Add Header text and then press the Tab key to position the insertion point in the right-hand header section.

Excel sets the insertion pointer or cursor at the right edge of this section (all text in this section is right-aligned).

3. Type **Page** and press the spacebar once. Then, in the Header & Footer contextual tab's Header & Footer Elements group, click Page Number.

   The right section of the header now contains the text you typed, Page, followed by the code, &[Page], which calculates and returns the current page number.

REMEMBER

When inserting codes in a custom header or footer, you need to insert spaces between the codes and any custom text you type if you don't want the code and custom text to all run together. To change the font or assign an attribute to the codes or text you add to a section of a custom header or footer, drag through them to select them, and then click the appropriate button in the Home tab's Font group.

4. Press the spacebar, type **of**, and press the spacebar again. In the Header & Footer contextual tab's Header & Footer Elements group, click Number of Pages.

   The right-hand section of the header now contains the following combination of custom text and codes: Page &[Page] of &[Pages].

5. Click cell A1 to select it.

   As soon as you click out of the right-hand header section, Excel replaces the codes so that your custom header on the first page of the report now reads Page 1 of 6.

6. Click the right-hand section of the header area once again. In the Header & Footer contextual tab's Options group, select the Different Odd & Even Pages check box.

   The Odd Page Header indicator appears right above the left-hand section of the header area, indicating that the custom header you've defined will appear only on odd-numbered pages of the report.

7. Scroll down the worksheet until you can see the top margin area of page 2 of the report (indicated by the heading, Regional Ratio Analysis, in cell A36 right below the empty top margin).

   You will now create the same custom header for a second page except that this even-page header will appear in the left-hand rather than the right-hand header section.

8. Click the left-hand section of the header area right above cell A36 and then use the Page Number and Number of Pages buttons in the Header & Footer Elements group to create the same header: Page &[Page] of &[Pages]. Then, click cell A36 to de-select the left-hand section of the header area.

   The even-page header for the second page of the report now reads Page 2 of 6.

   Next add a prefabricated footer.

9. Scroll up, if necessary, until you see the Add Footer text. Click this text and then, in the Header & Footer contextual tab, click the Footer button in the Header & Footer group. Click the menu item from the list, near the bottom of the Footer button's menu, that displays "Prepared by" followed by your name, the current date, and then the page number (as in "Prepared by Paul McFedries 8/23/2022, Page 1").

Excel places this text in the center section and the page number in the right-hand section of the footer.

10. Click the right-hand section and delete the Page &[Page] code by pressing the Delete key.

Note that the footer with my name and the date is an odd-page footer that prints only on the odd pages of the report. You need to copy this footer to the second page so that it is also printed on the even pages.

11. Select the stock footer text and &[Date] code in the odd-page footer, press Ctrl+C to copy this information to the clipboard. Then, click the center section of the footer area on the second page below row 81 and then press Ctrl+V to paste this same information in as the even-page footer.

The same footer information now appears in the center section of the even-page footer at the bottom of the second page of the report.

12. Click cell A81 and then preview the pages (Ctrl+F2) to make sure that the page number appears aligned with the right margin on all odd-numbered pages and aligned with the left margin on all even-numbered pages and that the footer appears centered on all pages.

13. If the header and footer check out, exit the Backstage view by pressing Esc or clicking the Back button. Select cell A1, return the worksheet to Normal view, and then save the changes to Exercise4-3.xlsx workbook file with the name Income Analysis-HeaderFooter.xlsx in your Excel Practice folder. Then, close the workbook (Ctrl+W).

Adding Print Titles to a Report

In Excel reports, you use Print Titles to print the column and row headings from the worksheet on every page. If you don't bother to add Print Titles to multi-page reports, only the first pages of the report contain the headings that identify the related data, and your readers have no way of identifying the data on the later pages of the report.

Try It

Exercise 4-4: Adding the First Worksheet Column as the Print Title for a Report

In Exercise 4-4, you practice adding column A of the Income Analysis worksheet as the print title for a printed report. You do this so that the row headings in column A appear on all the pages of the report.

1. Open the Exercise4-4.xlsx workbook file located in the Chap4 folder in the Excel Workbook folder on your hard disk.

In this version of the Income Analysis worksheet, all the bad page breaks have been fixed. However, because the report lacks any print titles, the row headings entered in column A of the worksheet appear only on its first two pages.

2. Open the Print panel in the Backstage view (Ctrl+F2) and use its print preview pane to review each of its eight pages to verify that the row headings in column A appear only on pages 1 and 2.

When pages 3 through 8 are printed, the reader will have no references with which to identify the financial data.

3. Click the Back button at the top of the Backstage view or press Esc.

Excel returns you to the Income Analysis worksheet.

4. Choose Page Layout⇨Print Titles or press Alt+PI.

Excel opens the Page Setup dialog box with the Sheet tab selected. This tab contains a Print Titles section where you can define rows of worksheet data to repeat at the top of each printed page as column headings, and columns of worksheet data to repeat on the left side of each printed page as row headings.

5. Click the Columns to Repeat at Left text box in the Page Setup dialog box and then click column A in the worksheet to select it (indicated by a dotted border around the column).

HINT

Click the Collapse Dialog Box button to the immediate right of the Columns to Repeat at Left text box if the Page Setup dialog box obscures column A of the worksheet, making it difficult to click the column and select it. Then, after clicking column A, click the Expand Dialog Box button on the right side of the collapsed dialog box to expand and restore its display.

Excel inserts the absolute column range reference $A:$A in the Columns to Repeat at Left text box.

6. Click the Print Preview command button at the bottom of the Page Setup dialog box. Then, preview each of its now 10 pages in the Print panel to verify that the row headings in column A appear on every page of the report.

Repeating the row headings in column A of the worksheet on each printed page has increased the total number of pages from 8 to 10.

7. Go to page 3 of the report in the Print Preview window and zoom in on this page by clicking the Zoom to Page button (in the bottom-right corner of the Print panel, it's the rightmost button).

8. Click the Show Margins button (in the bottom-right corner of the Print panel, it's the second button from the right) to display the margins.

Excel now displays margin and column markers at the top of the page 3 preview (see Figure 4-1). You can drag these markers to manipulate and change the margin settings and/or column widths.

9. Use the vertical scroll bar to display the top margin and column markers. Then position the mouse pointer on the first column marker that immediately follows the left margin marker (the column marker between the first and second columns). When the mouse pointer becomes a double-headed arrow, drag the marker slightly to the right and then release the mouse button.

When you release the mouse button, Excel shows as many letters as the new width accommodates. Continue to adjust the column marker in this manner until all the letters in Income are displayed in the first column of page 3.

10. Reduce the preview to full page (by clicking the Zoom to Page button a second time) and then check its pages to make sure that the complete worksheet title will be printed on all pages.

Next, you need to remove the margin markers from the worksheet display and the gridlines from the printed report.

11. Click the Show Margins button to hide the margin markers. Click on Page Setup below the Printer Settings in the left pane of the Print panel, and then click the Gridlines check box on the Sheet tab of the Page Setup dialog box to remove its check mark and then click OK.

12. Exit the Backstage view, and then with cell A1 selected in the regular worksheet, save the changes to the Exercise4-4.xlsx workbook file with the name Income Analysis-PrintTitle.xlsx in your Excel Practice folder. Then, close the workbook (Ctrl+W).

FIGURE 4-1: Displaying the column and margin markers in the Print Preview pane of the Print panel.

Modifying the Print Settings for a Report

Regardless of what type of printer you use, Excel has a number of default print settings that it automatically puts into effect when you first print a worksheet. These print settings include

- >> Portrait Orientation rather than Landscape Orientation for the printing (so that the printing runs with the shorter width of the page rather than with the longer length)

- >> Printing at 100% of normal size

- >> Print quality medium (on printers that support different print quality modes)

- >> Letter (8.5 x 11 inch) paper size

- >> Top and bottom margins of 0.75 inch

- >> Left and right margins of 0.7 inch

- >> Header and footer margin of 0.3 inch (with no header or footer defined)

- >> No printing of the column and row gridlines that define the cells in the worksheet

- >> No printing of the column letters and row numbers associated with the cells within the print area in the worksheet

- >> No printing of the comments attached to cells included in the print area (see Chapter 5 for more on comments)

- >> Printing of error values returned by formulas as they appear in the worksheet (see Chapter 6 for more on error values)

- >> Paging order down the rows of the print area and then across the columns

- >> Printing a single copy of all the pages generated from a print area that includes all the data in the active worksheet(s)

REMEMBER

You can change the most commonly used print settings with the options found on the left pane of the Print panel in the Backstage view (Ctrl+P). These print settings include those related to which printer to use, what part of the workbook or worksheet to print, whether to print on one or both sides of the paper, printing multiple copies, switching the orientation of the printing, selecting a new paper size, modifying the margins, and applying scaling to the pages. You can access all other print settings using the tabs found in the Page Setup dialog box. (Click Page Setup below the Printer Settings in the left pane of the Print panel.)

Many times you may find that you can solve minor paging problems in a report on the Print panel by modifying the orientation of the printing, the margin settings, and, as a last resort, the scaling.

If your intention is to produce a facsimile of the worksheet for reviewing its data, you should include the worksheet gridlines and column and row headings in the printout. To do this, you select the Page Layout tab on the Ribbon and then make sure that the Print check box under Gridlines and the Print check box under Headings are both selected (indicated by a check mark) in the Sheet Options group. If you also want to print the comments, click the Sheet Options group's dialog box launcher button to open the Page Setup dialog box and display the Sheet tab. Select the At End of Sheet or As Displayed on Sheet (Notes Only) option on the Comments and Notes drop-down list box, and then click OK.

Exercise 4-5: Modifying Various Print Settings for a Report

In Exercise 4-5, you practice changing different print settings for a report including changing the orientation of the printing from portrait to landscape and using the Scale to Fit option.

1. Open the Exercise4-5.xlsx workbook file in the Chap4 folder in the Excel Workbook folder.

   This CG Media sales workbook opens with the Total Sales worksheet displayed. This worksheet is quite wide as it tracks the monthly sales with quarterly totals for different types of media for an entire year.

2. Switch to Page Layout view (Alt+WP) and use the worksheet scroll bars to check out the pages for a report that prints all the data in the Total Sales worksheet in the default portrait mode.

   Because this worksheet uses more columns than rows, the printed report might be easier to read if you switched the orientation of the printing to landscape.

3. Choose Page Layout⇨Orientation or press Alt+PO and then select the Landscape option on the drop-down menu.

   Excel immediately switches the printing orientation and redraws the page depictions in Page Layout view. Note how many more columns of data fit on the first page of the report in this print orientation.

4. Use the horizontal scroll bar to check out the page breaks for printing the report in landscape mode.

   Note that the third page now contains an "orphaned" column with the annual total sales. You can fix this bad page break using the Width option located in the Scale to Fit group on the Ribbon's Page Layout tab.

5. Click the Width drop-down button in the Scale to Fit group and then click 2 Pages on its drop-down menu.

   Note that when you select 2 Pages for the Width setting, Excel immediately scales the printing size down to 97% now shown in the Scale combo box. Note also that the Scale combo box remains grayed out (unavailable) whenever you set either the Width or Height options in the Scale to Fit group to any other setting besides Automatic.

TIP

Using the Scale to Fit Width and Height options on the Ribbon's Page Layout tab to constrain the printing to a particular number of pages rather than using the Scale option to set a specific scaling percentage is often a much more effective way to eliminate pages with orphaned columns or rows of data.

6. Switch back to Normal view (Alt+WL). Then, click the Qtr1 sheet tab to make this worksheet active and then switch the view back into Page Layout for this sheet (Alt+WP).

   Note that the bad page break for this worksheet report orphans the first quarter totals by printing them on the second page separated from all the supporting monthly sales data printed on the first page.

7. Fix the bad page break by changing the orientation of this worksheet to Landscape so that the quarterly totals are no longer orphaned and all the first quarter sales data print together on the first and only page of the report.

   Next, you need to add a header to the one-page report.

8. Add a header to the report that prints the name of the worksheet (Qtr1) in its left-hand section, the word Confidential in its center section, and the current page number (Page 1) in its right-hand section.

   Finally, you need to add gridlines and the column and row headings to the printout of the first quarter sales data on the first page.

9. Turn on the printing of the column and row gridlines, and the row and column headings in the printed report.

HINT

To display the gridlines, you need to select the Print check box under the Gridlines heading in the Sheet Options group of the Ribbon's Page Layout tab (Alt+PPG). To display the row and column headings, you select the Print check box under Headings in this same group (Alt+PPH).

10. If you have access to a printer, print the Qtr1 worksheet; otherwise, switch back to the Total Sales worksheet and then save the workbook as CGMedia-PrintSettings.xlsx in your Excel Practice folder before you close the workbook.

Printing All or Part of the Workbook

As noted in the previous section on default print settings, the print area that defines which ranges are included in the printout consists of whatever worksheet or worksheets that you've selected at the time of printing. Often you need to reduce the print area to just a range of cells within the active worksheet or to increase it to include the data on all the sheets in the entire workbook. The exercises in this section give you practice in printing not only print areas of different sizes but also printouts that include the contents of formulas in the worksheet (as opposed to their calculated values) and charts that you've created. (See Chapter 15 for practice on charting worksheet data.)

TIP

If you want to print all the data on the active worksheet using the print settings currently in effect for that sheet, click the Quick Print button you added to the Quick Access toolbar in Chapter 1: Excel then sends the print job directly to the default printer without ever opening the Print dialog box.

Printing a range

Often you only need to print a particular range on the active worksheet (as opposed to all the data on the sheet). To print only a range, select the range in the active worksheet and then choose File ⇨ Print (or press Ctrl+P). In the Print panel, use the first drop-down list under Settings to select Print Selection. When you click Print, Excel includes just the selected range in the printout.

TIP If you have a range with data that changes often, you might need to print the range regularly. In that case, name the range and use either the Formula bar's Name box or the Go To feature (as covered in Chapter 5) to quickly select the range for printing.

Try It

Exercise 4-6: Printing a Range of Cells in a Worksheet

In Exercise 4-6, you practice printing just the range of cells in a worksheet containing the quarterly and annual sales totals without the embedded clustered bar chart that accompanies the data.

1. Open the Exercise4-6.xlsx workbook file in the Chap4 folder in the Excel Workbook folder.

    The Quarterly Sales worksheet in the Exercise4-6.xlsx workbook file opens. In this sales worksheet, all the columns with supporting monthly sales figures are hidden so that only the quarterly totals and yearly total are now displayed. They appear above the clustered bar chart that is created from these quarterly sales figures.

2. Select the cell range A1:R15 in the Quarterly Sales worksheet and then open the Print panel in the Backstage view, by choosing File➪Print or pressing Ctrl+P.

    The Print panel opens with the Print Active Sheets option selected.

3. Click the first drop-down list under Settings and then choose Print Selection from the drop-down list.

    Verify that only the CG Media – Quarterly Totals sales range, and not the embedded clustered bar chart immediately beneath it in the Quarterly Sales worksheet appears in the print preview.

    Next, you will change the orientation of the printing from the default portrait to landscape.

4. Click the fourth drop-down list under Settings and then choose Landscape Orientation from the drop-down list.

    The print preview now shows the page in a landscape orientation.

5. If you have access to a printer, print this worksheet by clicking the Print button; otherwise, just close the Print panel (Esc), select cell A1 and then save the workbook as CGMedia-PrintSelection.xlsx in your Excel Practice folder before you close the workbook.

Printing the entire workbook

Printing all the data in the entire workbook is a snap: Open the Print panel (File➪Print or Ctrl+P) and then use the first drop-down list under Settings to select Print Entire Workbook before sending the print job to the Printer by clicking the Print button.

Q. How can I print data on multiple worksheets without printing the entire workbook?

EXAMPLE

A. Select the tabs for all the worksheets in the workbook that contain data you want printed (remember to Ctrl+click to select multiple sheet tabs) before sending the job to the printer.

Try It

Exercise 4-7: Printing All the Sheets in a Workbook

In Exercise 4-7, you practice printing an entire workbook containing worksheets with annual sales data for four years (2019 through 2022) as a single report. This report will contain a single header and footer:

1. Open the Exercise4-7.xlsx workbook file in the Chap4 folder of the Excel Workbook folder.

   This worksheet contains a history of four past years of CG Media annual sales data (2019 through 2022) that you'll print in a single report.

2. Open the Print panel in the Backstage view (Ctrl+P) and then replace Print Active Sheets with the Print Entire Workbook option under Settings.

   Excel displays the first page of a 12-page report in the print preview area on the right side of the Print panel.

3. Check out all 12 pages of the report in the Print Preview window.

   Note that the gridlines are turned on in pages 10, 11, and 12 that print the 2019 annual sales data.

   Next, you need to remove the gridlines from the printed pages for 2019 sales data on pages 10, 11, and 12.

4. Display page 10 in the print preview and then click Page Setup in the left side of the Print panel to open the Page Setup dialog box. Then deselect the Gridlines check box on the Sheet tab and click OK.

   Note that pages 10, 11, and 12 no longer shows gridlines.

   Now, you need to add a header and footer to each worksheet that identifies it in the printed report. The header will be a custom one that displays the name of the worksheet in the left-hand section and the word, Confidential!, in the right-hand section. The footer will be a standard one that prints the current page number and the total page number as in Page 1 of 12.

5. Close the Backstage view (press Esc or click Back) and then click the Page Layout view button on the Status bar.

6. Click Add Header in the header area and then click in the left section. Next, choose Header & Footer⇨Sheet Name to insert the &[Tab] code. Click the right-hand section and then type the text, Confidential!, into this section. Finally, click the Footer button on the Ribbon and click the Page 1 of ? option on its drop-down menu to insert these codes for this prefab footer.

   In the custom header for the Sales 2022 worksheet at the top of the page, Sales 2022 appears aligned with the left margin and Confidential! appears aligned with the right. The prefabricated footer at the bottom reads Page 1 of 3.

7. Following the technique outlined in Step 6, assign the same type of custom header and prefab footer to the Sales 2021, Sales 2020, and Sales 2019 worksheets in the Exercise4-7.xlsx workbook.

   Next, you need to take care of the orphaned data on the third page of each of the four worksheets in the workbook. You do this by changing the orientation of the printing, if need be, and then using the Scale to Fit Width option.

8. Click the Sales 2022 sheet tab and then click the Landscape option on the Orientation button's drop-down menu on the Ribbon's Page Layout tab. Then, click the 2 Pages option on the Width button's drop-down menu in the Scale to Fit group.

   Immediately following the Ready indicator, the Status bar should now read Page 1 of 2.

9. Following the technique outlined in Step 8, reduce the number of printed pages from three to two for Sales 2021, Sales 2020, and Sales 2019 worksheets in the Exercise4-7.xlsx workbook by changing the orientation of the printing from portrait to landscape.

   Immediately following the Ready indicator, the Status bar should now read Page 1 of 2 when you selected each of the three Sheet tabs, Sales 2021, Sales 2020, and Sales 2019.

10. Once again open the Print panel (Ctrl+P) and then use the first drop-down list under Settings to select Print Entire Workbook.

    Excel displays the first page of what is now an eight-page report in the print preview.

11. If you have access to a printer, print this eight-page report; otherwise, just close the print panel, select cell A1 on the Sales 2022 sheet and then save the workbook as CG Media 2019-2022 PrintWorkbook.xlsx in the Excel Practice folder before you close the workbook.

Printing charts in the worksheet

Charts that you create from the data in your worksheets are either embedded in the same worksheet that contains the data or on a separate Chart sheet (see Chapter 15). Embedded charts are printed as part of the worksheet unless you select just the data ranges they're created from as the print selection. Note, however, that charts placed on their own Chart sheets are not printed unless you select their sheets as part of the print selection.

When you print a chart placed on its own Chart sheet, Excel adds a Chart tab to the Page Setup dialog box. The Chart tab contains options for printing the chart draft quality and/or in black and white instead of color. You get experience using these options in Exercise 4-8.

Exercise 4-8: Printing a Chart in a Report

In Exercise 4-8, you practice printing a clustered bar chart that has been added to a workbook on its own chart sheet.

1. Open the Exercise4-8.xlsx workbook file in the Chap4 folder of the Excel Workbook folder.

   This workbook contains two worksheets: Quarterly Sales and Clustered Bar Chart.

2. Click the Clustered Bar Chart sheet tab to display the bar chart and activate its sheet. Then, click the Print Preview and Print button if you added it to the Quick Access toolbar in Chapter 1 or press Ctrl+P.

   You can also open the Print panel by choosing File⇨Print.

   Note that Excel automatically selects landscape as the printing orientation for the chart and scales the chart so that it prints full-size on the page.

3. Click Page Setup in the Print panel to open the Page Setup dialog box.

   Note that the Page Setup dialog box now contains a Chart tab, which replaces the Sheet tab.

4. Click the Chart tab in the Page Setup dialog box and then select the Print in Black and White check box.

TIP

   You use the Print in Black and White option to print an initial printout of a chart for proofing in black and white even when you're printing it with a color printer. That way, you can check the chart before you print it in color so that you don't waste any colored ink.

5. Click the Header/Footer tab in the Page Setup dialog box and then click the Custom Footer button.

   Excel opens the Footer dialog box, which divides the custom footer into three sections: Left, Center, and Right. Note that the cursor is automatically positioned in the Left section.

6. Click the Insert Date button to insert the &[Date] code into the Left section. Then, click the Center section and click the Insert File Name button to insert the &[File] code in the center section. Finally, click the Right section and then click Insert Sheet Name button to insert the &[Tab] code in the Right section before you click OK.

   The custom footer in the Footer drop-down list box now contains the current date, the filename, and sheet name.

7. Click OK to close the Page Setup dialog box.

   The previewed page with the chart now contains your three-part custom footer.

8. If you have access to a printer, print the chart from the Print Preview window; otherwise, close the Print panel and then make the Quarterly Sales sheet active. Save the workbook as CG Media Quarterly Totals - ChartSheet.xlsx in the Excel Practice folder and then close the workbook.

Printing the worksheet formulas

When you print a worksheet, Excel prints the entries exactly as they appear in their cells of the worksheet. As a result, when you print a section of worksheet that contains formulas, the printout shows only the results of the calculations performed by the formulas, not the formulas themselves. In addition to a printout showing the results, you may also want to print a copy of the worksheet showing the formulas by which these results were derived. You can then use this printout of the formulas when double-checking the formulas in a worksheet to make sure that they are designed correctly.

TIP

To help you identify the cell reference of each formula in your printout, be sure to include the gridlines and column and row headings as part of the printout like you do in Exercise 4-9.

Try It

Exercise 4-9: Printing Worksheet Formulas in a Report

In Exercise 4-9, you practice getting a worksheet ready to print with its formulas, gridlines, and column and row headings displayed.

1. Open the Exercise4-9.xlsx workbook in the Chap4 folder of the Excel Workbook folder.

   The Schedule sheet of this workbook contains a target production schedule for various part numbers with monthly quotas for an entire year.

2. In the Formulas tab's Formula Auditing group, click the Show Formulas button (or press Alt+MH).

   Excel displays all the formulas in the cells of the Schedule worksheet. Note that the table title in cell A1, Target Production Schedule, is now truncated to Target Production (the remainder of the heading no longer spills over into the adjacent cells in row 1 even though these cells are empty).

3. Press Ctrl+` (accent grave) to turn off the formula display and return to the normal worksheet display.

HINT

   The ` key (accent grave) is located on the key with the ~ (tilde) usually located to the immediate left of the 1 key on the top row of the QWERTY keyboard.

   Ctrl+` is a toggle key combination: The first time you press it, it turns on the formula display and the second time turns it off.

4. Press Ctrl+` again, this time to turn the formula display back on and then click the Page Layout view button on the status bar. Click the Page Layout tab where you change the following settings with their respective command buttons:

   - Change the orientation of the printing from portrait to landscape with the Orientation button.

   - Add the gridlines and the row and column headings to the printout with the Print check boxes under Gridlines and Headings in the Sheet Options group.

- Make the rows $1:$2 the Rows to Repeat at Top and column $A:$A the Columns to Repeat at Left with the Print Titles button in the Page Setup group.

Now you need to check the pages in print preview.

5. Use the print preview on the Print panel in the Backstage view to check the three pages of the report.

   Note that each of the three pages contains the row and column print titles you assigned.

6. Exit the Backstage view by pressing Esc or clicking Back. Then switch to Page Break Preview view.

   In Page Break Preview view, you will repaginate the report so that there are four pages, each with the months of a quarter: Jan through Mar on Page 1, Apr through Jun on Page 2, Jul through Sep on Page 3, and Oct through Dec (along with the annual totals) on Page 4.

7. Move the page markers so that Page 1 contains only Part No. column along with the Jan, Feb, and Mar production quota columns; Page 2 only the Apr, May, and Jun columns; Page 3 only the Jul, Aug, and Sep columns; and Page 4, only the Oct, Nov, and Dec quota columns along with Total column that includes the grand total formulas.

   The page breaks of the report now divide the production quota figures into four quarters.

8. Return the worksheet to Normal view and then return to the print preview on the Print panel to check the pages of the report.

   Each page should have the row and column print titles along with the row and column headings to help you identify which cell contains what formula.

9. If you have access to a printer, print the worksheet report showing the formulas; otherwise, close the Print panel and hide the display of the formulas in the cells before you save the workbook as Target Schedule -formulas.xlsx in your Excel Practice folder.

Chapter 5

Modifying the Worksheet

Some of your worksheets might require little or no editing after you complete them because your model does the job you created it to do. Conversely, many of your worksheets might need frequent or constant revisions because they require new data or because the existing data changes regularly. Whatever modifications your worksheets need, it's essential that you know all the standard Excel editing techniques. In particular, it's vital to know how to change one part of a worksheet without disturbing the rest of the worksheet contents and without breaking any formulas or other dynamic aspects of the model. The exercises in this chapter give you a chance to practice all aspects of basic editing, including locating the workbook file to open, finding the area in the worksheet that needs editing, and making all the necessary editing changes.

Finding and Identifying the Region That Needs Editing

As you're already aware, an Excel worksheet represents an extremely large space in which to work. Often the biggest challenge in editing a worksheet is just finding and identifying the ranges in the worksheet that need revising. To help you locate the range you want to edit, you can use the following three features to good advantage:

>> **Zoom:** Get an overview of the worksheet and its ranges by zooming out on the worksheet (that is, by reducing the Zoom magnification); get a close-up view of a particular range in the sheet by zooming back in on the worksheet (that is, by increasing the Zoom magnification).

>> **Freeze Panes:** Prevent the rows and columns containing the column and row headings from scrolling so that these headings remain visible at all times while you're scrolling through their data entries.

>> **Custom Views:** Name and save a combination of different worksheet display settings (including frozen panes and various magnification settings) so that you can put them into effect by selecting them.

Q. What is the range of zoom settings I can select for my worksheet display?

EXAMPLE **A.** You can set the worksheet display magnification setting anywhere in the range of 10% to 400% of normal by doing any of the following:

- Drag the Zoom button in the Zoom slider on the Status bar to the left to decrease the magnification percentage or to the right to increase it.

- Click the Zoom In or Zoom Out buttons at either end of the Zoom slider to increase or decrease magnification respectively in 10% increments.

- Click the Zoom Level button located to the immediate right of the Zoom slider that displays the current percentage to open the Zoom dialog box. In the Zoom dialog box, you can select the 200%, 100%, 75%, 50%, 25%, or Fit Selection options or enter the value of the new magnification percentage directly into the Custom option's text box in single-degree increments.

Try It

Exercise 5-1: Creating Custom Views in a Worksheet

In Exercise 5-1, you practice creating custom views of a worksheet that use different zoom magnification settings and panes that freeze specific rows and columns on the screen. By saving custom views you create as a part of a workbook file, you can restore their screen settings in a jiffy by selecting the custom view.

1. Open the Exercise5-1.xlsx workbook file in the Chap5 folder in your Excel Workbook folder.

   This workbook contains a version of the Income Analysis worksheet that you can use to practice creating and selecting custom views.

2. Use the Zoom slider to reduce the screen magnification of the Income Analysis worksheet to 50%.

3. Click the Zoom Level button (that now reads 50%) that's to the immediate right of the Zoom In button (the one with the plus sign) on the Zoom slider to open the Zoom

dialog box. Click the Custom option button and type **45** in the Custom option's text box before you press Enter.

At a magnification setting of 45% of normal, you can now see all the data entered in the Income Analysis worksheet.

4. Change the screen magnification percentage back to 50% and then select the cell range J20:M25 by carefully dragging through this range in the worksheet. Click the Zoom Level button to open the Zoom dialog box and then click the Fit Selection option button before you press Enter.

Excel responds by setting the magnification to something over 200% so that all of the cells in the selected range J20:M25 are visible in the display. Note, however, that without the row and column headings, it's impossible to identify these entries in this range.

5. Put the cell cursor in cell A1 (Ctrl+Home) and move it to the empty cell B3. Then, choose View ⇨ Freeze Panes ⇨ Freeze Panes or press Alt+WFF.

Because the cell cursor is in the row immediately beneath the one with the table's column headings and the column immediately to the right of the one containing the row headings, Excel draws a horizontal line between rows 2 and 3 and a vertical line between columns A and B indicating the limits of the frozen panes. Any entries above the horizontal line and to the left of the vertical line remain on-screen as you scroll through their columns and rows.

6. Use the Tab key to scroll until other columns on the right come into view.

Note how the row headings in column A remain displayed as you scroll.

7. Use the Page Down key to scroll until other rows lower in the worksheet come into view.

Note how the column headings in row 2 as well as the table title in row 1 remain displayed onscreen as you scroll.

8. Repeat Step 4 in this exercise, select the cell range J20:M25, and set the magnification to fit the display of this selection.

Note that this time with the addition of the frozen panes that retain the associated row and column headings, you can tell right away that you're looking at the 3rd Qtr operating expenses for all the divisions.

9. Return the Zoom setting to 100% and then position the cell cursor in cell B3 that you used to freeze the row and column headings.

Now you're going to save this screen magnification and frozen pane display as a custom view that you can reuse.

10. Click the Custom Views button on the Ribbon's View tab or press Alt+WC to open the Custom Views dialog box.

The Custom Views dialog box enables you to create new custom views as well as to select the views that you've already created.

11. Click the Add button in the Custom Views dialog box to open the Add View dialog box. Then, type **100% w/Row & Col Headings** as the view title in the Name text box, leaving the Print Settings and Hidden Rows, Columns and Filter Settings check boxes selected. Click OK.

    Excel adds your 100% custom view and closes the Custom Views dialog box. Next, you create another custom view that hides columns so that only the four quarterly subtotals and yearly grand totals are displayed.

12. Hide the column ranges B:D, F:H, J:L, and N:P. Next, select cell E3 and then, following Steps 10 and 11, name this view 100% w/4 Qtrs Display.

HINT

To hide columns, you select their column headings (by dragging through them — use the Ctrl key to select nonadjacent column ranges) and then choose Home➪Format➪Hide & Unhide➪Hide Columns on the Ribbon (Alt+HOUC).

13. Open the Custom Views dialog box and click the 100% w/Row & Col Headings view before you select the Show button.

    Excel immediately unhides all the columns you hid in Step 12, while at the same time repositioning the cell cursor in cell B3.

14. Open the Custom Views dialog box again and this time double-click the 100% w/4 Qtrs Display view to apply it to the worksheet. Hide the following row ranges: 4:8, 12:16, 20:24, 28:32 and then select cell E3. Save this view under the name 100% w/4 Qtrs Total Display.

HINT

To hide rows, you select their row headings (by dragging through them — hold down the Ctrl key to select nonadjacent row ranges) and then choose Home➪Format➪Hide & Unhide➪Hide Rows on the Ribbon (Alt+HOUR).

15. Return the worksheet to the 100% w/Row & Col Headings view, and then choose Freeze Panes➪Unfreeze Panes on the Ribbon or press Alt+WFF to remove the panes.

    Excel immediately removes the lines indicating the frozen panes.

16. Position the cell cursor in cell A1. Save this version of the Income Analysis worksheet with the custom views under the filename Income Analysis - CustomViews.xlsx in the Excel Practice folder and close the workbook.

Selecting the Ranges to Edit

Selecting occupied cells in the worksheet for editing is very much the same process as selecting blank cells for pre-formatting or data entry with one important exception. Because the cells already contain data, in addition to dragging through the ranges and clicking the first and last cell while holding down the Shift key, you can use a technique known as AutoSelect to quickly select an entire block of occupied cells in a couple of mouse clicks.

Moreover, you can use Excel's Go To and range name features to combine locating a cell range that needs editing and selecting its cells all at the same time!

Exercise 5-2: Selecting Cell Ranges for Editing

In Exercise 5-2, you practice using various techniques for selecting the cell ranges in a worksheet that require editing. These techniques include using AutoSelect, the Go To dialog box, and naming a cell range and then selecting its cells by selecting its range name in the Name box on the Formula bar.

1. Open the Exercise5-2.xlsx workbook file in the Chap5 folder inside the Excel Workbook folder.

   You can use the Schedule worksheet in this workbook to practice selecting cell ranges for editing.

2. Click cell A2 and then position the mouse pointer on the bottom edge of the cell cursor in cell A2. When the white cross changes to an arrowhead mouse pointer, click the bottom edge.

   AutoSelect extends the selection down to row 7, the last row in this range formatted as a table.

3. Hold down the Shift key as you double-click anywhere on the right edge of the extended selection.

   AutoSelect extends the cell selection to column N, the last occupied column in the data table, therefore selecting all cells in the range A2:N7.

4. Click cell A10 in the worksheet to position the cell cursor in this cell while at the same time deselecting the cell range A2:N7.

   Now you will practice selecting the cells in the data table using Excel's Go To feature, which is normally used to position the cell cursor in a different cell in the worksheet.

5. Press F5 or Ctrl+G to open the Go To dialog box and then type **A2** (it's okay to enter the reference as **a2**) and press Enter.

   The Go To dialog box disappears and the cell cursor jumps to cell A2, making it current.

6. Press F5 or Ctrl+G to open the Go To dialog box again and then type **N7** (or **n7**). This time, however, hold down the Shift key as you press Enter.

   Because you held down the Shift key, Excel selects the range A2:N7 (if you hadn't held down the Shift key, Excel would have just moved the cursor from A2 to N7).

   Next, use AutoSelect to select all the Table data including the column headings from the middle of the table.

7. Click cell G10 to deselect the previously selected range. Then, position the mouse pointer near the top of cell G2 until it changes to the black downward-pointing arrow, and single-click to select the column data G3:G7. Then position the mouse pointer on the top border of cell G2, and when you see the mouse pointer change to the white arrowhead, single click the mouse again, this time to select the entire table including headings.

This technique only works for a cell range previously formatted as a table, which can be done with the Format As Table button in the Styles group of the Home tab.

Next, you're going to name this cell selection.

8. Click the Name Box on the Formula bar that currently displays A2 and type **Target_data** (with an underscore and no space) and press Enter.

Excel assigns the range name Target_data to the cell selection, A2:N7.

Now you see how this named range is useful.

9. Use the Go To feature to move the cell cursor to cell IV4000 in the worksheet.

Next, select the target production schedule cell range by selecting its range name on the Formula bar.

10. Click the drop-down button attached to the Name Box on the Formula bar and then click Target_data on its drop-down list.

When you click Target_data, Excel responds by selecting the range A2:N7 and repositioning the worksheet so that this range is in view and displaying this range name in the Name box on the Formula bar.

Note that this worksheet already contains two other range names: Print_Titles given to column A and rows 1 and 2 when it was defined as the print title for this worksheet (see Chapter 4) and Table1 that was defined as the range with the table data when the cell range A2: N7 was formatted as a table (see Chapter 3).

Now, save your Schedule worksheet with your Target_data range name.

11. Click cell A1 to deselect the range A2:N7, and then save this workbook with the filename Target Schedule - named.xlsx in your Excel Practice folder and close the workbook file.

Editing Data Entries

In the previous exercises in this book, the sole technique you used to modify the entry in a cell is to replace it completely by entering the new value into that cell as though it were still blank. This method is fine as long as the replacement entry is short and easy to type. It's not, however, the preferred method when you only need to make slight corrections to a long text entry or a complex formula. Rather than replace the original entry, you need to put Excel into Edit mode so that you can edit its contents as you would a word or phrase in a word-processing program, such as Microsoft Word.

Excel gives you a choice of techniques for putting the program into Edit mode:

>> Click the I-beam cursor at the place in the current cell entry that needs editing on the Formula bar and then edit its contents on the Formula bar.

>> Double-click the white-cross mouse pointer at the place in the cell entry in the worksheet that needs editing and then edit its contents in the cell.

>> Press F2 to place the insertion point at the end of the current cell entry in the worksheet and edit its contents in its cell.

After you've placed Excel in Edit mode and positioned the insertion point somewhere in the entry, you can then use ← and → to move the flashing pointer in front of or immediately after the characters to modify. Press the Delete key to remove characters to the right of the insertion point or the Backspace key to remove characters to its left. To insert new characters at the insertion point and move existing characters out of the way and to the right, just type them.

After you finish modifying the contents of the entry, you still need to complete the edit as you do a new entry. Only, in this case, you need to rely on the Enter button on the Formula bar, Enter key, Tab, or clicking another cell as you can't use any of the arrow keys (↑, ↓,←, or →). In Edit mode, these cursor keys only move the insertion point within the characters of the entry.

TIP

If you need to abandon an edit without entering the changes you've made in the cell or on the Formula bar, press the Esc key or the Formula bar's Cancel button. If you complete a mistaken editing change, choose Home ⇨ Undo or press Ctrl+Z to undo the change (and keep in mind that Excel supports multiple levels of undo).

Try It

Exercise 5-3: Making Simple Edits to Cell Entries

In Exercise 5-3, you practice manually editing the contents of existing cell entries without replacing them.

1. Open the Exercise5-3.xlsx workbook file in the Chap5 folder in your Excel Workbook folder.

   You can use the Sales sheet in this workbook file to practice making simple editing changes to the contents of particular cells in the worksheet.

2. Increase the screen magnification to 150% using the Zoom slider and its Zoom In and Zoom Out buttons.

   Now, insert new text in the title of the worksheet table.

3. Click the I-beam pointer in front of the C in Category on the Formula bar, and then type **Media and** followed by a space to insert this text into the title. Click the Enter box to complete this edit in cell A1.

   The edited title in cell A1 now reads, CG Media – Sales by Media and Category.

4. Position the white-cross mouse pointer after the s in Discs in the row heading in cell A3 and then double-click to set the insertion point in this cell. Then, remove this extraneous s and the extra space between Compact and Disc.

HINT

Use ← and → to position the insertion point immediately after the extra s in Discs and, later, immediately in front of the D and, then in each instance, press the Backspace key to first remove the extra letter and then the extra space.

The edited row heading in cell A3 now reads, Compact Disc Sales.

5. Position the cell cursor in cell A14, press F2, and then replace Cassette in the row heading with Tape and press Tab to complete the edit.

HINT

Use ← to position the insertion point immediately after the final e in Cassette and then press the Backspace key until you have deleted its letters. Then, type **Tape** before you press Tab.

The row heading in cell A14 now reads, Total Tape Sales.

6. Select cell A1 again and save your editing changes in a new file named CG Media - edits.xlsx in your Excel Practice folder and then close the workbook file.

Deleting and Inserting Data and Cells

Deletions in a worksheet are a little more complicated than in other software programs. This is because Excel gives you a choice between deleting only the cell entry, leaving intact the cell structure and all assigned formatting attributes; clearing the cell of all its contents without disturbing its structure; and removing the cell structure along with everything it contains, causing the remaining cell entries in the neighboring cells to adjust to fill in the gap:

>> Press the Delete key to remove only the entry in the current cell.

>> Choose Home ⇨ Delete to remove the entry in the current cell plus all formatting attributes and notes (Excel automatically shifts up any cell entries in rows below).

>> Choose Home ⇨ Clear and then select what you want to remove from the cell: Clear All, Clear Formats, Clear Contents, Clear Comments and Notes, or Clear Hyperlinks.

>> Choose Delete ⇨ Delete Cells in the Cells group of the Home tab (Alt+HDD) to open the Delete dialog box. Choose between the Shift Cells Up or the Shift Cells Left options to remove the cell along with all its contents, formatting, and notes, and to adjust remaining cells in rows below or in columns on the right.

Choosing Insert ⇨ Insert Cells (Alt+HII) in the Cells group of the Home tab is the opposite of Delete ⇨ Delete Cells. You use it to open the Insert dialog box, where you can Shift Cells Right or Shift Cells Down to insert blank cells in regions where you need to squeeze in data entries that were somehow left out. In the process of squeezing in these blank cells, you also shift existing entries down to rows below or to columns to the right. Note that if you click the Insert button in the Cells group of the Home tab, Excel automatically shifts existing cell entries in the same column down to rows below.

You can delete entire rows and columns containing the cell cursor from the worksheet by choosing Delete ⇨ Delete Sheet Rows (Alt+HDR) or Delete ⇨ Delete Sheet Columns (Alt+HDC) in the Cells group of the Home tab. Likewise, you can insert an entire row or column by choosing Insert ⇨ Insert Sheet Rows (Alt+HIR) or Insert ⇨ Insert Sheet Columns (Alt+HIC). To delete or insert multiple rows or columns in the worksheet, select their row or column headings before you choose these commands.

WARNING

Be very cautious about deleting or inserting entire rows or columns in any worksheet, especially ones that you didn't create or are not that familiar with. You can easily take out vital data from tables and lists located in unseen regions of the worksheet when deleting something. Inserting new columns and rows can be almost as dangerous; however, as your insertions can just as well corrupt the accuracy or even disrupt the functionality of the formulas in these unseen tables and lists. To stay on the safe side, constrain your cell deletions and insertions to just the cell ranges in the region you're working in.

Try It

Exercise 5-4: Deleting and Inserting Cells in the Worksheet

In Exercise 5-4, you practice inserting and deleting cells in an existing worksheet without disturbing existing entries and by adjusting them as needed to accommodate the editing changes.

1. Open the Exercise5-4.xls workbook file in the Chap5 folder of the Excel Workbook folder.

   The Home Sales worksheet in this workbook file contains a copy of a House Sales table that you can use to practice deleting and inserting cells and cell entries.

2. Select cell C4 with the selling price of the first house on Elm Street and delete just this entry by pressing the Delete key.

   Excel deletes the contents of this cell.

3. Enter **1250000** in now-blank cell C4.

   Because you only deleted the contents in cell C4, Excel applies the remaining Currency style number format with no decimal places to the new entry you made, so it immediately appears as $1,250,000 in the cell.

4. Delete everything in cell C4 by choosing Clear⇨Clear All in the Editing group of the Ribbon's Home tab or press Alt+HEA.

   This time, Excel deletes the cell's number formatting as well as its contents.

5. Enter **735000** in the now-blank cell C4.

   This time, Excel does no number formatting to the 735000 value because you cleared the cell of formatting plus contents.

6. Use Format Painter (see Chapter 3) to restore the Currency style number format with no decimal places to cell C4.

HINT

   Position the cell cursor in cell C5 that still contains this Currency number formatting. Click the Format Painter button in the Clipboard group of the Home tab and then click cell C4 to copy just the formatting from cell C5.

7. Select the cell range A5:C5 listing a house sale on Apple Drive. Then click the Delete button in the Cells group of the Ribbon's Home tab. (Be sure you don't click the drop-down button that appears either to the side or beneath the Delete button's icon.)

   Excel removes the cells in the selected cell range A5:C5 while at the same time pulling up the data in the rows below so that there are no gaps in the table.

8. Choose Home⇨Undo (or press Ctrl+Z) to restore the deleted cell range.

   Now you'll insert blank cells in the table for a new home sale listing.

9. Leave the cell range A5:C5 selected and then click the Insert button in the Cells group of the Home tab.

   Excel inserts three blank cells above the Apple Drive sales information, shifting the remaining entries in this table down. Note the appearance of the Insert Options button at the fill handle in the lower-right corner of the extended cell cursor: You display its drop-down button by positioning the mouse pointer over the button and then use its options to copy cell formatting from the cells in the row below (it automatically uses the formatting in the cells in the row above) or to clear all formatting from the newly inserted cells.

10. Make the following entries in the new, empty cell selection, A5:C5:

    - The address, 500 King Street, in cell A5

    - The selling date, 4/1/2021, in cell B5

    - The selling price, 820000, in cell C5

11. Select cell A1 and then save your editing changes to the Home Sales worksheet in a new workbook named Home Sales - rev.xlsx in your Chap5 folder inside the Excel Practice folder.

Moving and Copying Data and Cells

Excel provides two methods for moving and copying a cell selection (along with its contents and formatting) to a new place in the same worksheet. You can either use

» Drag-and-drop to manually take the selection or a copy of it with the mouse pointer and drop it into its new place in the sheet

» Cut and paste to cut or copy the selection to the Windows clipboard and then paste it into its new position after moving the cell cursor to the first cell of that range

When using the cut-and-paste method, you can select what part of the cut or copied data is transferred when pasting data into their new position in the worksheet or workbook. You do this by selecting one of the icon options on the Paste button's drop-down menu (such as Formulas, Paste Values, No Borders, Transpose, or Paste Link) on the Home tab or by selecting Paste Special option on this button's drop-down menu and then selecting the appropriate Paste option in the Paste Special dialog box (see Table 5-1).

TIP

Use the Transpose option on the Paste button's drop-down menu or the Transpose check box in the Paste Special dialog box to transpose the data in the table so that data that used to run across the columns now run down the rows and vice versa.

Table 5-1   The Paste Options in the Paste Special Dialog Box

Paste Option	What It Does
All	Pastes all types of entries (numbers, formulas, and text), their formats, and notes from the selection in the paste area
Formulas	Pastes only the entries (numbers, formulas, and text) from the selection in the paste area
Values	Pastes only numbers and text from the selection in the paste area, converting all formulas to their current calculated values so they're pasted into the worksheet as numbers
Formats	Pastes only the formats from the selection into the paste area
Notes	Pastes only the notes from the selection into the paste area
Validation	Pastes only the entries in cells that use data validation into the paste area
All Using Source Theme	Pastes all types of entries with their formats using whatever theme is assigned to the cut or copied cells (from the pop-up gallery attached to the Themes button on the Ribbon's Page Layout tab)
All Except Borders	Pastes everything but the borders assigned to the cell selection into the paste area
Column Widths	Pastes everything into the paste area and adjusts the column widths in this area to match those of the original cell selection
Formulas and Number Formats	Pastes only the formulas and number formatting (omitting all text and numeric entries) from the cell selection into the paste area
Values and Number Formats	Pastes only the numbers and number formatting (omitting all text and converting all formulas to their calculated values) from the cell selection into the paste area

Try It

Exercise 5-5: Moving and Copying Cells in a Workbook

In Exercise 5-5, you practice moving and copying cells in a workbook using both the drag-and-drop method as well as copy-and-paste.

1. Open the Exercise5-5.xlsx workbook file in the Chap5 folder inside your Excel Workbook folder.

   You use the Target Production Schedule table in its Schedule sheet to practice moving and copying cells and their data entries. Note that this worksheet contains the range name Target_sched assigned to the cell range A1:N7 that you can use to select its cells.

2. With the table's cells (A1:N7) selected, use drag-and-drop to move it so that it now occupies the range B5:O11.

HINT

   Position the white-cross mouse pointer somewhere on the bottom edge of the selected cell range and when the pointer changes to an arrowhead, drag the selected range of cells to its new position. When the ScreenTip at the bottom of the outline representing the cell selection you're moving reads B5:O11, release the mouse button to drop it in place.

3. Use drag-and-drop to copy the table you've just moved to the cell range B5:O11 to the cell range B13:O19.

HINT

   Hold down the Ctrl key as you drag the outline of the copy of the selected cell range to its new position in the worksheet.

4. Cut the copy of the original Target Production Schedule table you moved to the cell range B5:O11 to the Clipboard by selecting this range and then choosing Home⇨Cut (or by pressing Ctrl+X).

Excel puts a marquee (marching ants) around the cell selection B5:O11 and displays the message "Select Destination and Press ENTER or choose Paste" on the Status bar.

5. Click the Sheet2 tab to make this worksheet active, move the cell cursor to cell B2, and then press Enter.

The moment you press the Enter key, Excel moves the table to the cell range B2:O8 on Sheet2 of the workbook.

6. Switch back to the Schedule sheet and select cell A1.

Excel deselects the cell range B5:O11 on the Schedule worksheet that used to contain the table you just moved to the cell range B2:O8 on Sheet2.

7. Click the drop-down button on the Name Box on the Formula bar and then click Target_sched on its drop-down menu.

Excel selects the cell range B2:O8 on Sheet2 of the Exercise5-5.xlsx workbook file. When you move a cell range that you've named to a new sheet in the same workbook, Excel can still identify and select the range using that name.

8. While the cell range B2:O8 is still selected on Sheet2, choose Home⇨Copy (or press Ctrl+C) to copy the cell selection to the Clipboard.

Again, Excel places a marquee around the cell selection and displays the message, "Select Destination and Press ENTER or choose Paste" on the Status bar.

9. Select cell B2 in the Schedule worksheet, and then choose Home⇨Paste⇨ Paste Values (or press Alt+HVV).

Excel makes a copy of the table without the formulas. Note also that this copy of the table contains none of the formatting assigned to the original; thus the decimal numbers appear in the cells in this table that were calculated by formulas.

10. Click cell D4 in the Schedule sheet to verify that the formulas are missing from this copy of the table.

In place of the formula =C4+(C4*0.055) on the Formula bar, the value 527.5 appears showing that the formula has been replaced by its calculated result.

11. Select the range B2:O8 and use drag-and-drop to move this table down until the ScreenTip reads B8:O14. Then, release the mouse button.

Excel displays an alert dialog box asking you if you want to replace the contents of the destination cells.

12. Click the Cancel button to close this alert dialog box.

As soon as you click Cancel, Excel undoes the move after closing the alert dialog box.

13. Use drag-and-drop to move this cell range selection with the copy of the table containing only values so that this table is temporarily located in the cell range B21:O27 beneath your original copy of the table that still contains formulas.

Next, you'll move the original copy of the table up near the top of the worksheet and then the copy with values only up so that it's right underneath.

14. Select the cell range B13:O19 and then move this original copy of the table up to the cell range B2:O8. Then, select the cell range B21:O27 with the values-only table and move it up to the cell range B10:O16 so that it is now directly beneath the original copy of the table in the worksheet.

Next, you use the Transpose option with the original table you moved to Sheet2 to see how you can use this Paste command to change the orientation of your data.

15. Switch to Sheet2 by clicking its sheet tab. Select the cell range B3:N7 that contains the headings and data in the original table and then choose Home⇨Copy (or press Ctrl+C).

Excel places a marquee around the selected cell range B3:N7, indicating that it's copied to the Clipboard and ready to paste.

16. Select cell B10 in Sheet2 and then choose Home⇨Paste⇨Transpose (or press Alt+HVT).

Excel copies the selected table data to the cell range B10:F22 so that part numbers are now the column headings and the months of the year form the row headings (see Figure 5-1).

17. Rename Sheet2 to Trans Schedule. Press the Esc key and then click cell A1 in the Trans Schedule worksheet.

Pressing the Escape key always removes a marquee from a cell selection. It does not, however, remove the cut or copied data from the Clipboard.

18. Select cell A1 in the Schedule worksheet and then save your work in a new workbook file named Target Schedule - cutncopy.xlsx in your Excel Practice folder. Then, close this workbook.

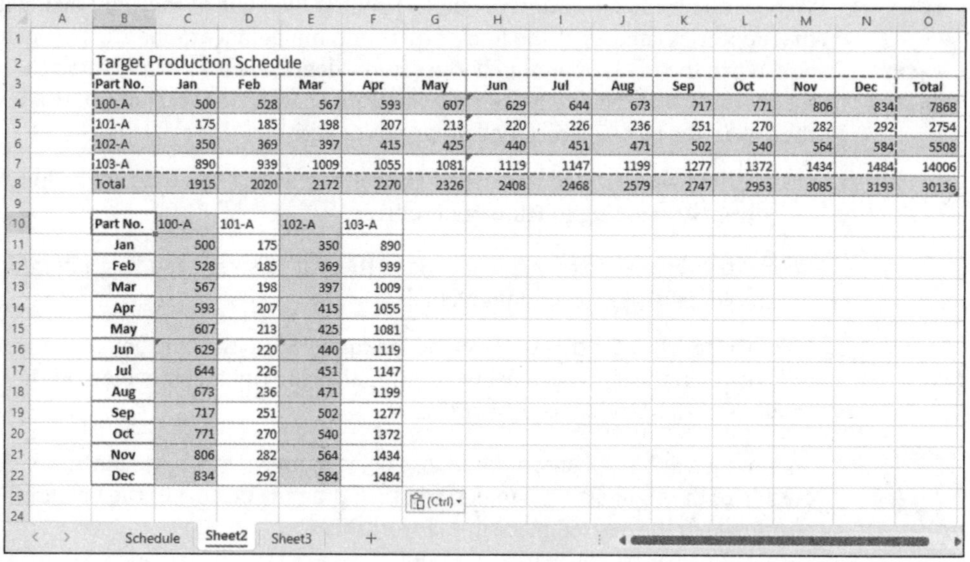

FIGURE 5-1:
Sheet2 after transposing the pasted table into the cell range B10:F22.

Adding Notes to the Worksheet

Excel enables you to attach notes to the cells of a worksheet. You can use these notes to remind yourself or your coworkers of changes that need to be made in the worksheet or data that needs to be reviewed and verified.

The key to adding and managing notes in a worksheet is the Notes group in the Review tab on the Ribbon. This group contains all the command buttons you need to add, edit, delete, display, hide, and navigate notes in the worksheet.

Try It

Exercise 5-6: Adding and Using Notes in a Worksheet

In Exercise 5-6, you practice annotating a worksheet by adding notes to it. In addition, you also get experience with hiding notes until you select them and finding all the notes you've added to a worksheet.

1. Open the Exercise5-6.xlsx workbook file in the Chap5 folder inside your Excel Workbook folder.

    This file contains an Employee List worksheet with a table of employees that you can use in practicing how to use notes in a worksheet.

2. Select cell J2 and then choose Review ⇨ Notes ⇨ New Note on the Ribbon or press Alt+RTN.

    Excel inserts a new text box with an arrow pointing to cell J2 containing your name.

3. Type **Verify this employee's status** as the text of this note and then resize the text box, making it wide enough for all the note text to appear on a single line of the box and short enough that there are no longer lines of empty space below the text.

HINT

    To resize a text box, position the mouse pointer over one of the eight sizing handles that appear as squares at the four corners and midpoints around the perimeter of the box. When the mouse pointer changes into a double-header arrow, drag the sides of the box until it is the size and shape you want (note that Excel automatically reflows the text in the box to accommodate these changes).

4. Select cell E6 and then add a note to this cell reminding you to change Cindy's department from Accounting to Human Resources.

    Notice that the text box for this note is in the way of salary and location information in the employee list for several individuals.

5. Move the text box for this note you added to cell E6 so that the box no longer obscures cell entries in the employee list by locating it to the right, somewhere in the blank columns of K, L, and M in the worksheet.

HINT

    To move a text box, position the mouse pointer anywhere on the outline of the box outside of the eight sizing handles and then drag the outline of the box until it is positioned in the desired place in the worksheet.

6. Select cell F20 and then add a note to this cell reminding you to verify Miriam's salary and then resize to remove its unused space and reposition the note's text box outside of the list in the empty columns K, L, and M.

7. Position the cell cursor in cell A1, and then position the mouse pointer over each of the three cells, J2, E6, and F20, that now contain notes.

   Note that positioning the mouse pointer over a cell with a note causes that note's text box to be displayed. Also note that each of these three cells now contains a tiny red triangle in the upper-right corner, indicating that the cell has a note attached to it.

8. Choose Review ⇨ Notes ⇨ Show All Notes or press Alt+RTS.

   Note this command button is a toggle switch that shows or hides all the notes in a worksheet.

9. Hide all three notes and then choose Review ⇨ Notes ⇨ Next Note (or press Alt+RTT) to display each of the three notes in succession.

   Note that the Review ⇨ Notes ⇨ Edit Note command button becomes active as you use Next Note to move to each of the three notes in succession. You use the Edit Note button to position the insertion point at the end of the note text in its box. You can also choose Review ⇨ Delete in the Comments group to remove a note.

10. When you reach the last note attached to cell F20, select the text of the note and then right-click the border of the text box and click Format Comment on the shortcut menu to open the Format Comment dialog box.

    The Format Comment dialog box enables you to modify all sorts of format settings for the selected text box, including the font and fill color it uses.

11. Change the note text to 10-point Calibri bold italic and the fill color of the text box to Gray. Then, change the formatting of the other two notes in cells J2 and E6 to match.

HINT

To change the fill color for a note's text box, click the Colors and Lines tab in the Format Comment dialog box. Then, click the Color option to display its drop-down color palette and click the color square you want to use.

12. Click cell A1 and then save this version of the Employee List worksheet with your notes with the filename Employee List - notes.xlsx in your Excel Practice folder. Close the workbook.

Using Find and Replace and Spell Checking

Just like Microsoft Word, Excel is equipped with a Find, Find and Replace, and Spelling feature that you can use in editing your worksheets:

>> Find (Find & Select ⇨ Find on the Home tab or Ctrl+F) enables you to search for and locate text or values in the worksheet or workbook that potentially need changing.

>> Find and Replace (Find & Select ⇨ Replace on the Home tab or Ctrl+H) enables you to select whether Excel replaces one set of text or values it locates in the worksheet or workbook with another set that you specify.

>> Spelling (Spelling command button on the Review tab or F7) enables you to catch and correct spelling errors using either the built-in dictionary or a custom dictionary you build.

When using Find and Find and Replace to locate entries in the worksheet or workbook, you can change any of the following search options to refine the search. You can use the

>> Within drop-down list box to choose between Sheet (the default) to look for the search text only in the cells of the current worksheet or Workbook to search the cells on all the sheets in the workbook.

>> Search drop-down list box to choose between By Rows (the default) to conduct the search across the rows and then down the columns of the worksheet or By Columns to conduct the search down each column and then across each row.

>> Look In drop-down list box to choose among Formulas (the default) to look for matches to the search text in the entries as they appear on the Formula bar, Values to look for matches in the entries as they appear in the cells of the worksheet, Notes to look for matches in the notes added to the cells of the worksheet, or Comments to look for matches in the worksheet or workbook comments.

>> Match Case check box to match the upper- and lowercase spelling in the cell entries with the search text.

>> Match Entire Cell Contents check box to match the entire contents of a cell with the search text.

>> Format button to specify formatting that the cell or cell entries must match.

Try It

Exercise 5-7: Editing with Find and Replace

In Exercise 5-7, you practice using Find and Replace and some of its many options to locate and modify cell entries that need updating.

1. Open the Exercise5-7.xlsx workbook file in the Chap5 folder inside your Excel Workbook folder. Make sure the Find, Replace & Spell worksheet is active.

   This workbook file contains a number of numeric and text cell entries that you can use to practice using the Find, Find and Replace, and Spelling features in Excel.

2. Choose Find & Select⇨Find on the Ribbon's Home tab or press Ctrl+F to open the Find and Replace dialog box with the Find tab selected. Then, enter **25?** in the Find What text box and click the Find Next button or press Enter.

   You can use the wildcard characters, ? (question mark) or * (asterisk), to stand for missing characters in the search text. The first time you select Find Next, Excel moves the cell cursor to cell A2 in the worksheet.

3. Continue to click the Find Next button to locate all the matches in the Find, Replace & Spell worksheet, and Excel returns the cell cursor to the cell with the first match.

Note that Excel considers the 2500 entered in cells A2, D2, and D5 as matches, but not the 2500 that's displayed in cell A7. This is because the 2500 in cell A7 is the calculated result of the formula =A5+A6 and not a static value entered on the Formula bar. The program also considers the date, May 25, 2022, entered in cell A17 as a match because of the 25 in the date.

4. Click the Options button in the Find and Replace dialog box to display the search options and select Values on the Look In drop-down list, and then click the Find All button to display the locations of all the cells with matching entries.

   This time, Excel considers the 2500 calculated in A7 as well as those entered into cells A2 and D5 as matches along with the May 25, 2022 date in cell A17. However, when Values is set as the Look In search option, the program no longer considers the $2,500.00 in D2 with its Currency Style number formatting as a match.

5. Select Notes in the Look In drop-down list in the Find and Replace dialog box and then click the Find Next button.

   Excel jumps the cell cursor to cell C12 in the worksheet.

6. Position the mouse pointer over cell C12 and verify that the note attached to this cell contains the value 25.

   Excel considers this a match because the message, "We need 25 lbs." in the note contains the value 25.

7. Modify the search text in the Find What box slightly by adding a comma between the 2 and the 5 so that 2,5? now appears in this text box. Then, select Values again in the Look In drop-down list before you click the Find All button.

   Now, Excel considers $2,500.00 in D2 as the only match because none of the other 25s or 2500s have a comma between the 2 and 5 as these entries appear in the cells of the Find, Replace & Spell worksheet.

8. Modify the search text in the Find What box again by prefacing 500 with a question mark wildcard character so that ?500 appears in this text box. Then, click the Find All button.

   This time, Excel includes all the cells containing 2500 (including the $2,500.00 in cell D2) as matches as well as the 1500 entered into cell A6.

9. Select the Match Entire Cell Contents check box in the Find and Replace dialog box before you click the Find All button.

   When the Match Entire Cell Contents check box is selected, the $2,500.00 in cell D2 is no longer considered to be a match because of the decimal point and two zeros that trail the 500 (the question mark wildcard only pertains to characters that precede 500).

10. Click the Replace tab in the Find and Replace dialog box and then set up the following conditions:

    - Position the cell cursor in cell A1 of the Find, Replace & Spell worksheet.
    - Enter **25** in the Find What text box on the Replace tab.
    - Enter **27** in the Replace With text box on the Replace tab.
    - Deselect the Match Entire Cell Contents check box on the Replace tab.

11. Click the Find Next button in the Find and Replace dialog box to locate the first instance to be replaced.

Excel positions the cell cursor in cell A2, the first cell containing an occurrence of the search text (25 in 2500).

12. Click the Replace button in the Find and Replace dialog box.

As soon as you click Replace, Excel changes 2500 in cell A2 to 2700 and immediately moves the cell cursor to the next instance of the search text in the worksheet (cell D2).

13. Continue to search for the remaining cells containing values of 2500 and replace them with 2700. Do not, however, replace the date, May 25, 2022 with May 27, 2022 in cell A17.

After Excel finds the final occurrence of your search text in the worksheet, the program no longer moves the cell cursor from the cell containing the last occurrence (cell A17 with May 25, 2022 in this case).

14. Select the 2021 Prod Sch worksheet by clicking its sheet tab and then use the Find and Replace feature to globally update the years in all the dates in the worksheet from 2021 to 2022.

HINT

Enter **2021** in the Find What text box and **2022** in the Replace With text box and then select the Replace All button. Excel then displays an alert dialog box indicating the number of replacements made (9 in this case).

WARNING

Be extra careful with performing global replacements in your own worksheets as you can all too easily wreak havoc in the worksheet at the click of the Replace All button. Should you make a major boo-boo with this feature, remember to press the Undo button with all due haste.

15. Click OK to close the Excel Alert dialog box. Close the Find and Replace dialog box.

16. Rename the 2021 Prod Sch worksheet to 2022 Prod Sch by editing its sheet tab. Click the Find, Replace & Spell sheet tab to select this worksheet and leave the Exercise5-7.xlsx workbook open for the following exercise.

Try It

Exercise 5-8: Spell Checking the Worksheet

In Exercise 5-8, you practice spell checking your worksheet to eliminate typos in your cell entries. You also find out how to add new words to the spelling dictionary.

1. Click cell A1 in the Find, Replace & Spell worksheet of the Exercise5-7.xlsx workbook and then click the Spelling command button on the Ribbon's Review tab or press F7 to spell check the entries in this worksheet.

Excel displays the Spelling: English dialog box and positions the cell cursor in E10 containing the unknown word Fetticine. This is a misspelling, so you must change it.

2. Accept the Spelling Checker's suggestion of Fettuccine by clicking the Change button.

    Excel moves the cell cursor to the cell with the second unknown spelling, Maccaroni, in cell E12. This is also a misspelling, so you must change it.

3. Accept the Spelling Checker's suggestion of Macaroni by selecting the Change button.

    The third unknown spelling occurs with Tagliolini in cell C14. This is a correct spelling so you can either ignore it once, ignore all occurrences, or add it to the dictionary.

4. Add the word to the dictionary by selecting the Add to Dictionary button.

REMEMBER

    When you click the Add to Dictionary button, Excel adds the unknown word to the main dictionary. If you wish to add the word to a custom dictionary, click the Options button in the Spelling dialog box to open the Excel Options dialog box with the Proofing tab selected. There, click the Custom Dictionaries button to open the Custom Dictionaries dialog box, where you can add a new custom dictionary or select one for spell checking your worksheet.

5. Close the alert dialog box indicating that the spelling check is complete by clicking OK, and then select cell A1. Save this edited version of the workbook under the filename FindReplaceSpell.xlsx in your Excel Practice folder. Then, close the workbook.

Editing Multiple Worksheets

Group editing enables you to save time by making the same editing changes to multiple sheets in the workbook at the same time. To put Excel in Group Edit mode, all you have to do is select all the sheets in the current workbook that you want to edit together. Excel indicates that a workbook is in Group Edit mode by appending [Group] to its filename on the Excel program window's title bar.

EXAMPLE

Q. How do I select individual, non-adjacent worksheets to be included for group editing?

A. Ctrl+click the sheet tab of each worksheet you want to include in the group.

Q. How can I quickly select all the sheets in a workbook for group editing?

A. Right-click one of the sheet tabs and then select the Select All Sheets item on the short-cut menu.

Q. How can I easily take the workbook out of group editing mode?

A. Click any single visible sheet tab other than the one for the active worksheet (indicated by the sheet tab name in bold lettering).

Exercise 5-9: Editing Multiple Worksheets Selected as a Group

In Exercise 5-9, you practice making simultaneous editing changes to three worksheets in a practice workbook that you select as a group. As long as these sheets are grouped together, any changes that you make to the active worksheet are reflected in all the others as well.

1. Open the Exercise5-9.xls workbook file in the Chap5 folder inside your Excel Workbook folder.

   This version of the CG Media Sales workbook file contains three worksheets, 2020 Sales, 2021 Sales, and 2022 Sales, that you can use to practice group editing.

2. Examine each of the three worksheets by clicking their sheet tabs in succession and then return to the first sheet, 2020 Sales.

   As you can see, all three of these sales tables are laid out in a similar manner and all contain the same level of detail.

3. Select all three worksheets for group editing.

HINT

   To select a group of adjacent worksheets, hold down the Shift key as you click the tab of the last sheet in the group (2022 Sales in this case). Note the appearance of Group after the workbook's filename on the Excel program window's title bar as in Exercise5-9.xlsx Group.

4. Select cell A1, and then choose Home⇨Cell Styles (or press Alt+HJ) to open the Cell Styles palette. Then, click the Title sample in the Titles and Headings section of this palette to apply this cell style to the worksheet title in cell A1.

   As soon as you click Title in the Cell Styles palette, Excel applies all this style's formatting to the worksheet title in cell A1 of the 2020 Sales worksheet.

5. Verify that this Title style has been applied to cell A1 in the 2021 Sales sheet and then the 2022 Sales sheet by clicking their sheet tabs in succession.

   Note that the moment you click the sheet tab of the 2021 Sales worksheet, Excel automatically takes the workbook out of Group mode.

6. Click the 2020 Sales sheet tab again and then regroup the three worksheets, 2020 Sales, 2021 Sales, and 2022 Sales. Select the cell ranges A3:A15 and B2:R2 and then select the Heading 4 sample in the Cell Styles palette.

   Excel formats all the row and column headings in these two ranges in the Heading 4 style.

7. Select the cell ranges B4:R8 and B10:R15 and then click the Comma [0] cell style in the Number Format section of the Cell Styles palette.

   Excel formats all the values in these two selected ranges in Comma style number format with no decimal places.

8. Select the cell range A15:R15 and then click the Total sample in the Titles and Headings section of the Cell Styles palette.

    Excel formats all the cells in this range with the formatting included in the Total cell style (bold text and a single line along the top and a double-underline along the bottom of the cells).

9. Edit the heading in cell A14 so that instead of Total Cassette Sales, this row heading now reads Total Tape Sales.

    Now it's time to verify that all the editing changes that you've made to the sales table in the 2020 Sales worksheet have been picked up and applied in the 2021 and 2022 worksheets.

10. Click the 2021 Sales sheet tab and the 2022 Sales sheet tab in succession to verify that all of the editing changes you made to the first worksheet are made as well on the other two worksheets.

    Note how much time you saved by making these changes in a group rather than to the individual worksheets.

11. Select cell A1 on the 2020 Sales sheet and then save your edited workbook under the filename CGMedia 20-22 - groupedit.xlsx in your Excel Practice folder before you close the workbook.

2
Using Formulas and Functions

Chapter **6**

Building Formulas

No one disputes that formulas are the center of almost every worksheet you create. Building formulas — both those that perform simple arithmetic calculations as well as those that perform more sophisticated computations using Excel's built-in functions — is a critical Excel skill. The exercises in this chapter give you a chance to practice building both types of formulas as well as modifying how and when the formulas in the worksheet are recalculated.

Building Formulas

All the formulas you build in an Excel worksheet, regardless of their function and degree of complexity, have one thing in common: They all begin with one simple character, = (the equal sign). Typing an equal sign activates the Enter and Cancel buttons on the Formula bar. It also changes the nature of the Name drop-down box so that its list displays commonly used functions rather than the range names assigned to the workbook.

If you forget to type the equal sign as your initial character when creating formulas by hand (Excel is always sure to put one in for you when you build formulas with the Insert Function button), the program inserts the string of operands — such as numbers or worksheet functions — and operators — such as addition (+) and multiplication (*) — you enter as a text reference.

If you build a legitimate formula, Excel either computes the answer and displays it in the current cell in the worksheet or, if unable to successfully calculate the answer, the program displays one of the following error values in the cell:

» #CALC! appears when Excel has come across a formula or expression that it doesn't support, such as an array nested inside an array.

» #DIV/0! appears when your formula attempts to divide by zero.

» #NULL! appears when your formula specifies an intersection of two ranges that do not, in fact, intersect.

» #FIELD! appears when your formula refers to a linked data type that doesn't exist or is in some other way invalid.

» #N/A appears when your formula refers to a value that is not available to it.

» #NAME? appears when your formula contains a text reference that Excel doesn't recognize (such as a reference to a range name that no longer exists in the workbook).

» #NUM! appears when your formula contains invalid numeric values (such as a text entry where a number is required).

» #REF! appears when your formula contains an improper cell reference.

» #SPILL! appears when your dynamic array formula can't spill the array results because the spill range contains one or more cells that aren't empty.

» #UNKNOWN! appears when your formula references a data type that isn't supported by your Excel version.

» #VALUE! appears when your formula contains some sort of improper argument type or operand (such as a text entry when the operator requires a value).

Building formulas by hand

To build a formula by hand, type = (an equal sign) and then designate the string of operands and operators that the formula should use in making its calculation(s). Operands can be constants that you type into the formula (such as 5.5 or 100), or they can be cell references (such as B5 or A10:J17) that you point directly to or type in the worksheet.

Table 6-1 shows you a list of all the operators, including their type, character, and operation.

Table 6-1   The Different Types of Operators in Excel Formulas

Type	Character	Operation	Example
Arithmetic			
	+ (plus sign)	Addition	=A2+B3
	- (minus sign)	Subtraction or negation	=A3-A2 or =-C4
	* (asterisk)	Multiplication	=A2*B3
	/	Division	=B3/A2
	%	Percent (dividing by 100)	=B3%
	^	Exponentiation	=A2^3
Comparison			
	=	Equal to	=A2=B3
	>	Greater than	=B3>A2
	<	Less than	=A2<B3
	>=	Greater than or equal to	=B3>=A2
	<=	Less than or equal to	=A2<=B3
	<>	Not equal to	=A2<>B3
Text			
	&	Concatenates (connects) entries to produce one continuous entry	=A2&" "&B3
Reference			
	: (colon)	Range operator that includes all cells between the colon	=SUM(C4:D17)
	, (comma)	Union operator that combines multiple references into one reference	=SUM(A2,C4:D17,B3)
	(space)	Intersection operator that produces one reference to cells in common with two references	=SUM(C3:C6 C3:E6)

Try It

Exercise 6-1: Building Simple Arithmetic Formulas

In Exercise 6-1, you practice building various types of simple arithmetic formulas by hand. In creating these formulas, you get experience building a formula by pointing to its cell references. You also get experience with using a range name as a cell reference and referring to a cell reference in your formulas (the so-called external reference).

1. If Excel is not already running, launch the program.

   Use the first two blank worksheets of the Book1 workbook as practice worksheets for building your formulas.

2. Change the name of Sheet1 of the workbook to Formulas. Click New Sheet (+) and then change the name of Sheet2 to Ext Ref.

To change the name of a worksheet, double-click its sheet tab, and then type the new name and press the Enter key.

Next, group the two sheets together (by Shift+clicking the second sheet's tab) so that you can increase the magnification setting for both sheets in a single operation.

3. Click the Formulas tab, then group the Formulas and Ext Ref sheets together by Shift+clicking the Ext Ref tab.

4. Right-click the Formulas sheet tab and then click the Ungroup Sheets option on its shortcut menu. Enter the value **42** in cell A2 of the Formulas worksheet and then name this cell Source.

To give a range name to the current cell, click the Name box on the Formula bar, type the range name (with no spaces between letters or words), and then press the Enter key.

5. Select cell A4 in the Formulas worksheet and then type = (equal sign) to start a new formula and click cell A2.

The formula you're in the process of entering into cell A4 now reads =Source, both in the cell and on the Formula bar. A marquee showing the cell named Source is displayed in cell A2.

6. Click the Enter button (the one with the check mark) on the Formula bar to complete the formula entry in cell A4.

The formula in cell A4 now returns 42 as its answer. This formula consists solely of an external reference to cell A2, the cell you named Source, so whatever value you enter into the source cell is immediately brought forward and dynamically copied to cell A4.

7. Update the value in the source cell, A2, from 42 to 128.

Because the link between cell A4 and A2 was created by your formula with the external reference, cell A4 of the worksheet now contains 128 as well.

8. Enter the following values into the designated cells of the Formulas worksheet:

- 34 in cell B4
- 47.5 in cell B5
- 2.2 in cell B6
- 10% in cell B7
- 3 in cell B8

9. Create an addition formula in cell C4 that adds the value in cell A4 to that in cell B4 by pointing to these cells:

   - Position the cell cursor in cell C4.
   - Type =.
   - Press ← twice to select cell A4 (the first operand).
   - Type + (the addition operator).
   - Press ← once to select B4 (the second operand).
   - When the formula reads =A4+B4, click the Enter button on the Formula bar.

10. Use this same pointing technique to create an addition formula in cell A5 that adds 5 to the value in cell A4.

    The addition formula in cell A5 should read =A4+5 on the Formula bar and the answer should appear as 133 in the cell.

11. With the cell cursor in cell A5, drag the fill handle to the cell range A6:A8.

    Excel copies the original formula you entered into cell A5 to cells A6, A7, and A8, which now contain the calculated values, 138, 143, and 148, respectively.

12. Build the following arithmetic formulas in the designated cells:

    - Subtraction formula in cell C5 that subtracts the value in cell B5 from that in cell A5. Remember that - (hyphen or dash) is the subtraction operator in Excel.
    - Division formula in cell C6 that divides the value in cell A6 by that in B6. Remember that / (forward slash) is the division operator in Excel.
    - Multiplication formula in cell C7 that multiplies the value in cell A7 by that in B7. Remember that * (asterisk) is the multiplication operator in Excel.
    - Exponentiation formula in cell C8 that raises the value in cell A8 by that in cell B8. Remember that ^ (caret) is the exponentiation operator in Excel.

13. Use the Side by Side feature to check your formulas against those in the Formulas worksheet in the Solved6-1.xlsx workbook in the Chap6 folder of the Excel Workbook folder.

    Make sure that not only your answers in the cells of this worksheet agree, but the contents of the formulas agree, as well.

14. When everything checks out, save the new workbook with the arithmetic formulas you built with the filename Practice Formulas.xlsx in your Excel Practice folder after closing the Solved6-1.xlsx file. Leave the Practice Formulas.xlsx workbook open with the Formulas worksheet active for the next exercise.

Exercise 6-2: Building Comparative Formulas

Arithmetic formulas in the worksheet (when properly formed) always return numeric results. Excel supports another type of formula, known as a comparative formula, which returns only one of two possible results, TRUE or FALSE. In Exercise 6-2, you practice in creating these types of formulas:

1. Use the Formulas worksheet of the Practice Formulas.xlsx workbook that you created in Exercise 6-1 to get some experience with building comparative formulas.

   Now you will add comparative formulas to this worksheet that indicate whether different comparisons in the worksheet are true or false.

2. Build a comparative formula in cell D4 that weighs the value in cell A4 against that in B4 and indicates whether they are equal to each other:

   - Type = in cell D4 to begin the formula.
   - Press the ← key three times to select cell A4.
   - Type = again, this time as the comparative operator.
   - Press the ← key twice to select cell B4 so that the formula now reads =A4=B4.
   - Click the Enter button on the Formula bar to complete the formula and compute the result (which is FALSE because the values in these two cells are not currently equal to one another).

   When you complete this formula, Excel enters the logical value FALSE into cell D4 because the values currently in cells A4 (128) and B4 (34) are not equal to one another.

3. Build the following comparative formulas in the designated cells:

   - In cell D5, a formula that compares the value in cell A5 to that in cell B5 and indicates whether the one in A5 is larger than the one in B5. Use the > (greater than) symbol as the operator.
   - In cell D6, a formula that compares the value in cell A6 to that in cell B6 and indicates whether the one in A6 is smaller than the one in B6. Use the < (less than) symbol as the operator.
   - In cell D8, a formula that compares the value in cell A8 to that in cell B8 and indicates whether the one in A8 is unequal to the one in B8. Use the <> (less than and greater than back-to-back) symbols as the operator.

     Note that Excel returns TRUE in cell D5 because the value currently in cell A5 (133) is larger than that in cell B5 (47.5). And Excel returns FALSE in cell D6 because the value currently in cell A6 (138) is not less than that in cell B6 (2.2). Finally, Excel returns TRUE in cell D8 because the current values in cells A8 (148) and B8 (3) certainly are unequal to one another.

4. Change the value in the Source cell, A2, from 128 to 34.

Check the contents of your formulas against those shown in Figure 6-1.

Note how Excel immediately updates all the formulas in columns A, C, and D whose computations depend in some way on this value. The answers change from FALSE to TRUE in cell D4 and TRUE to FALSE in cell D5 and remain unchanged in cells D6 and D8.

5. Save your changes to your Practice Formulas.xlsx workbook before proceeding on to Exercise 6-3.

FIGURE 6-1:
The Formulas sheet with the results of the updated arithmetic and comparative formulas displayed.

	A	B	C	D	E
1					
2	34				
3					
4	34	34	68	TRUE	
5	39	47.5	-8.5	FALSE	
6	44	2.2	20	FALSE	
7	49	10%	4.9		
8	54	3	157464	TRUE	
9					

D4 — fx =A4=B4

Try It

Exercise 6-3: Working with Error Values in Formulas

Well-designed worksheets contain many dependent formulas like your Practice Formulas.xls workbook. The problem comes when any of the formulas on which they depend return one of those dreaded error values covered earlier in this chapter. When that happens, the error values spread like wildfire to all the dependent formulas, making it very difficult, if not impossible, to identify the source of the problem. In Exercise 6-3, you use the formulas in your Formulas sheet of the Practice Formulas.xlsx workbook to get some experience with the error values that formulas can return and how they infect all dependent formulas in a worksheet:

1. Click the Name Manager button in the Defined Names group on the Ribbon's Formulas tab or press Alt+MN to open the Name Manager dialog box. Click Source to select it in the list box and then click the Delete button at the top of the Name Manager. Click OK in the alert dialog box and then click the Close button.

As soon as you click Close to close the Name Manager dialog box, most of the cells in this worksheet display the #NAME? error value. Every formula you created in this worksheet is dependent in some way upon the Source range name, inheriting this error value from the original formula in cell B4 with the external reference the moment you delete its name.

2. Choose Home⇨Undo (or press Ctrl+Z) to restore the Source range name to the workbook.

   You can tell that Excel restored the range name because those awful #NAME? error values all disappear from the Formulas worksheet.

3. Now click cell B6 and press the Delete key to delete the value (2.2) in cell B6.

   As soon as you empty cell B6, a #DIV/0! error value is returned by the division formula in cell C6. This is because all empty cells in any Excel worksheet carry the value of zero, and this is why #DIV/0! is the most common type of error value to plague worksheets. Often, a template or new worksheet you create contains division formulas referring to empty cells for which you do not have or have not yet entered values. These all naturally return #DIV/0! error values. (In Chapter 13, you find out how to create formulas that prevent this type of error value by using the IF function.)

4. Choose Home⇨Undo (or press Ctrl+Z) to restore the original 2.2 value to cell B6.

   The moment you restore the value to cell B6, the #DIV/0! error value disappears from cell C6.

5. In cell B7, replace 10% with **ten percent** to see what effect this has on the multiplication formula entered in cell C7.

   Although you can build formulas that deal with text, the one in cell C7 is not such a formula. When you enter ten percent as a text entry in cell B7, its formula essentially chokes, returning the #VALUE! error value to the cell.

6. Choose Home⇨Undo (or press Ctrl+Z) to restore the original 10% value to the cell.

   As soon as you restore the original numerical value of 10% to cell B7, Excel removes the #VALUE! error value from cell C7.

7. Leave your Practice Formulas.xlsx workbook open for the next exercise on building formulas using a few of Excel's built-in functions.

Building formulas with built-in functions

Excel offers a wide assortment of built-in functions that can save valuable time in creating the formulas needed in your worksheet. In place of the operands and operators of your hand-made formulas, built-in functions use function names and arguments. All the Excel functions follow the general syntax of the SUM function, the most widely used worksheet function:

```
=SUM(number1,number2, ...)
```

Note the following about this syntax in this example:

>> The function name is always shown in all caps because Excel automatically displays it that way on the Formula bar regardless of how you enter its name. (This means that there are no case restrictions when typing the function name. You just have to be careful to spell its name correctly.)

>> The argument(s) used by the function immediately follow the function name and they are enclosed in a balanced pair of parentheses. For every open parenthesis [(], you need a close parenthesis [)].

>> The functions that require or can take more than a single argument separate the individual arguments within the parentheses with commas.

REMEMBER

Even functions such as NOW that take no arguments require the use of a pair of parentheses to finish them; for example, =NOW(). If you omit the empty pair of parentheses, Excel fails to recognize the function and returns the #NAME? error value to its cell.

Excel classifies each of its built-in functions into one of thirteen categories (with a fourteenth being custom functions that you define yourself). Six of these function categories are available from dedicated command buttons on the Formulas tab, another six available via the Formulas tab's More Functions button, and all of them are available from the Insert Function dialog box, which you open by clicking the Insert Function button at the very beginning of the Formulas tab or on the Formula bar (both use the fx marking).

TIP

Building a formula from the Insert Function dialog box carries many benefits. Besides starting your formula by automatically entering the requisite = (equal sign) on the Formula bar for you, this dialog box, shown in Figure 6-2, contains the following features that aid you in locating and using any function:

>> Search for a Function enables you to look for a function by entering a brief description of the kind of calculation you want to do.

>> Select a Category enables you to find a function by selecting a category (Financial, Date & Time, and so on) other than the default Most Recently Used that keeps a record of the most commonly used functions, including the ones you've used most recently.

>> Select a Function enables you to display syntax information showing you the arguments plus a short description on any function you select in this list box.

>> Help on This Function displays online help (that you can also print) about the usage and arguments required by the function currently selected in the Select a Function list box.

As soon as you select your function and click OK in the Insert Function dialog box, Excel not only inserts the skeleton of the function on the Formula bar, but also displays a Function Arguments dialog box for the function, which you can use in selecting the cell references and values to be used in the computation.

EXAMPLE

Q. Can I mix built-in functions with hand-made formulas?

A. Yes, most definitely: Excel functions can serve as operands in any formula that you construct manually, as in =SUM(A5:J10)^2 to square the total of the range of values in the cell range A5:J10 of the worksheet returned by the SUM function.

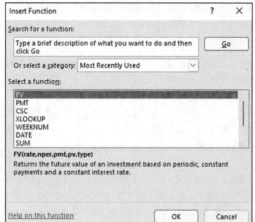

FIGURE 6-2:
The Insert
Function dialog
box helps you
locate and add
any Excel
function to a
worksheet
formula.

Try It

Exercise 6-4: Building Formulas with the AutoSum Command Button

In Exercise 6-4, use the Formulas worksheet of your Practice Formulas.xls workbook to get some experience using the SUM, AVERAGE, and COUNT functions in the worksheet. These functions are so frequently used that Excel doesn't even require you to access them from the Insert Function dialog box, making them readily available from the AutoSum command button on the Ribbon's Home tab.

1. Drag through the cell range A4:A8 to select all their values in the Formulas worksheet of your Practice Formulas.xlsx workbook.

    Note that the Average, Count, and Sum indicators on the Status bar immediately show you that the average of the values selected is 44, the count 5, and the total 220.

2. Click cell A9 in the Formulas worksheet and then choose Home ⇨ AutoSum (the one with Σ on it — be sure not to click its drop-down button to open its menu).

    Excel immediately responds by entering the SUM formula, =SUM(A4:A8), in cell A9. Note that the program also places a marquee bounding box around the cell range A4:A8 in the worksheet as well as selects the argument A4:A8 in the SUM function itself. This enables you to modify the range or ranges of cells to be totaled by the SUM function either by editing its argument in the function or dragging the boundaries of its marquee.

3. Click the Enter button on the Formula bar to complete this formula in cell A9.

    Excel enters the formula =SUM(A4:A8) in this cell as shown on the Formula bar and displays the total of the range, 220, in the cell.

4. This time, choose Home ⇨ AutoSum ⇨ Average.

    Excel now enters the formula =AVERAGE(A4:A8) for your editing or approval in cell A9.

5. Click the Enter button on the Formula bar to enter this formula in the cell.

   Excel enters the formula =AVERAGE(A4:A8) in this cell as shown on the Formula bar, and displays the average of the range, 44, in the cell.

6. Choose Home⇨Undo (or press Ctrl+Z) to restore the SUM formula in cell A9. Click cell B9 and then select the Count Numbers option on the AutoSum button's drop-down menu before you click the Enter button on the Formula bar to create a formula in cell B9 that returns the number of values in the range B4:B8.

   The formula you construct in cell B9 reads =COUNT(B4:B8) and this formula returns 5 as its result.

7. Replace the value 10% in cell B7 with the text entry **ten**.

   Ignoring the appearance of the #VALUE! error in cell C7 for the moment, note that the result returned to cell B9 changes from 5 to 4, indicating that the COUNT function counts only the numeric entries in the cells you include in its argument.

8. Restore 10% to cell B7 with Undo, position the cell cursor in cell C9, and click the Insert Function button on the Formula bar.

   Excel opens the Insert Function dialog box, where you can select any function built into or added to the program.

9. Move the Insert Function dialog box to the right out of the way of the values in your worksheet. Select Math & Trig as the category, select SUM in the Select a Function list box, and click OK.

   Excel opens the Function Arguments dialog box and supplies what the program finds as the most logical cell range address (C4:C8) in its Number1 Argument text box.

10. Drag through the cell range A4:A8 to replace the default Number1 argument of C4:C8 with this range.

   Note how Excel automatically condenses the Function Arguments dialog box to just the text box for the Number1 argument as you drag through the cell range and then immediately restores the dialog box the moment you release the mouse button.

11. Press Tab or click the Number2 argument text box and then drag through the cell range B4:B8 to select this range as the second to be included in the total.

   Note that as soon as you select the Number2 argument text box, Excel adds a Number3 text box to the Function Arguments dialog box.

12. Press Tab and designate the cell range C4:C8 as the third argument in the Number3 argument text box.

   Note that the Function Arguments dialog box shows the subtotals of each of the three ranges you've selected immediately following their respective argument text boxes and that the Formula bar now contains the whole SUM formula ready for insertion into cell C9:

   ```
   =SUM(A4:A8,B4:B8,C4:C8)
   ```

13. Click OK to close the Function Arguments dialog box and enter the SUM formula into cell C9.

    Excel enters the SUM function into cell C9. The formula with this function appears on the Formula bar and the result of totaling these three cell ranges (157855) appears in cell C9.

14. Save your changes to a workbook named Practice Formulas – Ex6-4.xlsx in your Excel Practice folder and leave the workbook open for the next exercise.

Editing formulas

Editing a formula, especially one that uses a function with multiple arguments, can take a little getting used to. Fortunately, Excel helps your formula editing chores by isolating the ranges and displaying them in different color bounding boxes when you put the program in Edit mode.

The only problem comes when you're dealing with a formula so complex and long that its contents can't be displayed within the worksheet display. Fortunately, on the rare occasion when this occurs, you can still edit the formula on the Formula bar as it automatically expands its rows to accommodate the extra length.

Try It

Exercise 6-5: Editing Formulas in a Worksheet

In Exercise 6-5, use the formulas you created in the Formulas worksheet of your Practice Formulas – Ex6-4.xlsx workbook to get some experience with formula editing. In this exercise, make changes to the SUM formula you previously constructed in cell C9 that totals the three ranges A4:A8, B4:B8, and C4:C8:

1. If the cell cursor is not already in cell C9, click this cell before you press F2 to put Excel into Edit mode.

   Excel responds by displaying the contents of the SUM formula in cell C9 of the worksheet. The addresses of each of the cell ranges in the three arguments of this SUM function appear in a different color and each of these colors corresponds to that of the bounding box that encloses its cell range in the worksheet.

2. Use ← to move the insertion point through the arguments in the SUM function until the insertion point is flashing between the 8 in the A8 and the comma that follows the first A4:A8 argument.

   Note as you move the insertion point to the left through the SUM function how the syntax for the SUM function appears right below it. Excel displays the number3, number2, and finally the number1 argument in bold as the insertion point travels through the cell range in the equivalent argument in the function above.

3. Hold down the Shift key as you press the ← key to select and highlight the range A4:A8 (from right to left).

4. Redefine the number1 argument by dragging through the cell range A2:A8 in the worksheet.

    A moving marquee appears in the cells you select as you redefine the cell range for the number1 argument in the SUM function.

5. Check the formula on the Formula bar in cell C9 to make sure that the cell range for the number1 argument of the SUM function is now A2:A8. Next click the Enter button on the Formula bar to complete the editing of the formula in cell C9.

    The result in cell C9 changes from 157855 to 157889 and the edited SUM formula appears on the Formula bar as

    ```
    =SUM(A2:A8,B4:B8,C4:C8)
    ```

6. Click the Comma Style button on the Home tab to format the result in cell C9 with this number format.

    Excel displays the result as 157,889.20 in cell C9 and automatically widens column C to display the value in the Comma Style format with two decimal places.

7. Save your editing changes to the formula in cell C9 in a workbook file named Practice Formulas – Ex6-5.xlsx in your Excel Practice folder. Leave this file open for the next exercise.

Altering the natural order of operations

When you build a formula that combines different operators, Excel follows the order of precedence shown in Table 6-2. When you use operators that share the same precedence level, the program performs the calculations on the operands in a strictly left-to-right order.

Sometimes, you need to override the natural order of precedence to get your formula to return the desired result. To override the natural order, you enclose the operand and operator of the operation you want performed first in parentheses.

For more complicated formulas, you may end up nesting sets of parentheses one within the other to obtain the desired computation order. When this is the case, Excel always performs the calculation within the innermost set of parentheses working its way out according to the sequence shown in Table 6-2.

Table 6-2   Natural Order of Operator Precedence in Formulas

Precedence	Operator	Type/Function
1	–	Negation
2	%	Percent
3	^	Exponentiation
4	* and /	Multiplication and division
5	+ and –	Addition and subtraction
6	&	Concatenation
7	=, <, >, <=, >=, <>	All comparative operators

Exercise 6-6: Changing the Order in Which Formulas Are Calculated

In Exercise 6-6, use the Formulas sheet of your Practice Formulas – Ex6-5.xlsx workbook to construct several new formulas and then experiment with adding parentheses to see what effect they have on the computed results.

1. Enter the following values in designated cells in the Formulas worksheet in your Practice Formulas - Ex6-5.xlsx workbook:

   - **100** in cell B11
   - **50** in cell C11
   - **2** in cell D11

2. Position the cell cursor in cell E11 and construct and enter the following formula:

   `=B11+C11/D11`

   Excel returns 125 because it performs the division between cell C11 and D11 (50/2=25) with its higher level of precedence of 4 before doing the addition between cell B11 and C11 (100+25) with its lower precedence level of 5.

3. With the cell cursor in cell E11, press F2 to put Excel in Edit mode.

4. Press the ← key until the insertion point is located between the = and the B in B11, and then type an open parenthesis, **(**. Then, press the → key until the insertion point is between the second 1 in C11 and the / and then type a closed parenthesis, **)**.

   The edited formula should appear as follows in cell C11:

   `=(B11+C11)/D11`

5. Click the Enter button on the Formula bar to complete the edit of the formula in cell E11.

   After the addition of the parentheses, the formula returns the result of 75, showing that it now performed the addition between cell B11 and C11 first (100+50) and then divided that result by the value in D11 (150/2).

6. Enter the following values in designated cells:

   - **300** in cell A13
   - **200** in cell B13
   - **100** in cell C13
   - **2** in cell D13

7. Position the cell cursor in cell E13 and enter the following formula:

```
=A13+B13–C13/D13
```

Note that Excel returns a result of 450 when you enter this formula because, following the natural order of precedence, it performs the computations as follows:

- C13/D13 or 100/2 = 50 to cell C13
- A13+B13 or 300 + 200 = 500 to cell B13
- B13–C13 or 500 − 50 = 450 to cell E13

8. Use pairs of parentheses to alter the computation order in the formula in E13 so that Excel performs the subtraction between cells B13 and C13 first, adds this result to the value in cell A13, and then, finally, divides the result of that addition by the value in D13, giving you a final result of 200.

When editing this formula, begin by enclosing the first operation to be performed inside a pair of parentheses (B13-C13), and then enclose the second operation in a second pair of parentheses, (A13+(B13-C13)) so that the edited formula appears as

```
=(A13+(B13–C13))/D13
```

9. With the cell cursor in cell E13, display all the formulas in the cells of the worksheet, widening column E and reducing the display magnification percentage as needed so that you can see all the formulas on your screen. (Check your results against those shown in Figure 6-3.)

Note that in this display mode, when the cell cursor is in a cell that contains a formula, Excel employs the same type of color coding as it does when you edit a formula in its cell. The colors assigned to the cell references within the formula correspond to that of the bounding box surrounding the actual cell or cell range in the worksheet.

10. Use the arrow keys to move the cell cursor to other cells in this worksheet that contain formulas, including cell C9.

11. Turn off the display of the formulas in the worksheet, select cell C9, and then save your changes in a workbook named Practice Formulas – Ex6-6.xlsx in your Excel Practice folder. Leave this version of the workbook file open for the next exercise.

FIGURE 6-3: The Formulas sheet with the added formulas displayed in their cells of the worksheet.

	A	B	C	D	E
1					
2	34				
3					
4	=Source	34	=A4+B4	=A4=B4	
5	=A4+5	47.5	=A5-B5	=A5>B5	
6	=A5+5	2.2	=A6/B6	=A6<B6	
7	=A6+5	0.1	=A7*B7		
8	=A7+5	3	=A8^B8	=A8<>B8	
9	=SUM(A4:A8)	=COUNT(B4:B8)	=SUM(A4:A8, B4:B8, C4:C8)		
10					
11		100	50	2	=(B11 + C11) / D11
12					
13	300	200	100	2	=(A13 + (B13 - C13)) / D13
14					
15					

Using External Reference Links

External references in a formula are those that refer to cells outside of the current worksheet, either on other sheets of the same workbook file or in sheets in other workbook files. Because their cells reside outside of the current worksheet, it isn't sufficient to specify the cell reference only, as you do with purely local cell references.

When you refer to a cell that resides in another worksheet of the same workbook, you preface the cell address with the sheet name separated by an exclamation point (!), following this syntax:

```
Sheet1!A1
```

When you refer to a cell that resides in a sheet in another workbook file, you need to include the filename (enclosed in square brackets) as well as the sheet name (enclosed in a pair of single quotation marks) and cell reference, following this syntax:

```
'[file.xlsx]Sheet1'!A1
```

Many times, you use external references to create links to values in another sheet that need to be brought forward to the new worksheet. When you set up a link rather than just pasting in a static value, any changes made to the value in the original cell are automatically updated in the linked cell.

TIP

The easiest way to create an external reference link is to click the Home tab's Copy button (or press Ctrl+C) to copy the cell to the Clipboard. Switch to the cell where you want to set up the link and then paste it with the Home tab's Paste ⇨ Paste Link command (or press Alt+HVN).

Try It

Exercise 6-7: Building Formulas with External Links

In Exercise 6-7, use your Practice Formulas – Ex6-6.xlsx workbook to get experience with constructing links using external references.

1. With the cell cursor in cell C9 of the Formulas worksheet that contains the SUM formula totaling the values in the cell ranges A2:A8, B4:B8, and C4:C8, copy the contents of this cell to the Clipboard (Ctrl+C).

   Now, paste a link to this formula in a cell in the second worksheet in your workbook named Ext Ref.

2. Click the Ext Ref sheet tab in the workbook to select this worksheet and then position the cell cursor in cell B3.

   Next, you paste a link to the formula in cell C9 of the initial Formulas worksheet.

3. Choose Paste⇨Paste Link in the Clipboard group of the Ribbon's Home tab or press Alt+HVN. Then, use AutoFit to widen column B.

   The value 157889.20 appears in cell B3 of the Ext Ref sheet and the following link formula with the external reference appears on the Formula bar:

   ```
   =Formulas!$C$9
   ```

4. Enter the heading Formulas Sheet Total in cell A3 and then widen column A of the Ext Ref sheet sufficiently to display the entire heading.

   Next, you change a value in a cell of the Formulas worksheet that is referenced in the SUM function in the original formula.

5. Switch back to the Formulas worksheet by clicking its sheet tab and then change the value in the source cell A2 of this sheet from 34 to 56.

   Note the effect that increasing this source value has on the total in cell C9 of this Formulas worksheet.

6. Click the Ext Ref sheet tab and verify that cell B3 in this worksheet now contains the same value as C9 in the Formulas worksheet, thanks to the linking formula you created there.

   Linking formulas are automatically updated whenever values in the cell they refer to change.

7. Click the New button on the customized Quick Access toolbar or press Ctrl+N to open a new blank workbook.

   Excel opens a blank Book2 workbook file.

8. Enter the heading Practice Formulas Workbook Total in cell A2, widen column A to fit the entire heading, and then save the Book2 workbook file with the filename External WrkBk Link.xlsx in your Excel Practice folder.

   Now you copy a link to the original SUM formula in cell C9 of the Formulas sheet in your Practice Formulas – Ex6-6.xlsx workbook file.

9. Click the Practice Formulas button on the Windows taskbar to activate this Excel file and then click the Formulas sheet tab to select this worksheet and copy the original formula in cell C9 to the Clipboard (Ctrl+C).

   Next, you need to switch over to your External Wrkbk Link.xlsx workbook file where you paste the link.

10. Click the External WrkBk Link button on the Windows taskbar to activate this new Excel file. Select cell B2 of its Sheet1 before you click the Paste Link option on the Paste button's drop-down list or press Alt+HVN. Then, use AutoFit to widen column B to display the contents of cell B2.

    The value 439,589.40 appears in cell B2 of the Sheet1 worksheet and the following link formula with the external reference appears on the Formula bar:

    ```
    ='[Practice Formulas – Ex6-6.xlsx]Formulas'!$C$9
    ```

11. Save your changes to the External WrkBk Link.xlsx workbook and then close this workbook file.

    As soon as you close the External WrkBk Link.xlsx file, Excel returns you to the Formulas sheet of your Practice Formulas – Ex6-6.xlsx workbook.

12. Select cell A2 in the Formulas sheet and then update the value in this cell from 56 to 72.

    As soon as you enter this new value, Excel automatically updates all the formulas on this worksheet that refer to this cell.

13. Check that the contents in cell B3 of the Ext Ref sheet has been updated to 779,438.27 to reflect the change to the value in cell C9 of the Formulas sheet. Then, switch back to the Formulas sheet, save your changes to this workbook with the same filename, Practice Formulas – Ex6-6.xlsx, in your Excel Practice folder, and close this file.

    Now, open the External WrkBk Link.xlsx file to see what happens when you open an external workbook file containing a link to a formula or value in another workbook whose result has changed.

14. Open the External WrkBk Link.xlsx workbook by selecting it from the Recent Workbooks list on the File menu (Alt+F).

    Note the Security Warning banner that appears at the top of the worksheet display when this workbook opens. This warning indicates that Excel has automatically disabled the updating of the links in this file.

15. Click the Enable Contents button in the Security Warning banner.

    Excel updates the value in cell B2 of Sheet1 to 779,438.27. Note that the external reference displayed on the Formula bar now contains the entire path name for the workbook file along with its sheet and cell reference.

16. Save this change to the External WrkBk Link.xlsx workbook and then close the file.

Controlling When Formulas Are Recalculated

Excel immediately and automatically recalculates all the formulas in a worksheet the moment you make a change to any cell referred to in its formulas. This automatic recalculation mode is fine as long as your worksheet is relatively small and your edits to it are few.

Working in this mode can, however, be a real drag (both literally and figuratively) when the worksheet is large and contains lots and lots of formulas: You may be forced to wait quite a few seconds while Excel recalculates every loving formula before you can do anything more after each and every editing change you make.

To avoid this hassle, change the recalculation mode from automatic to manual on the Calculation Options drop-down menu on the Formulas tab (Alt+MXM) so that Excel recalculates the formulas in the worksheet only when you specifically tell it to by clicking the Calculate Now or Calculate Sheet command button on the Formulas tab, pressing F9, or saving changes to the workbook.

Exercise 6-8: Controlling When Formulas Are Recalculated

In Exercise 6-8, you practice in switching to manual recalculation in a workbook and then using the Calculate Now option to update formulas whose input values have changed.

1. Open the Exercise6-8.xlsx workbook in the Chap6 subfolder inside the Excel Workbook folder.

   This workbook contains an earlier version of the now familiar Practice Formulas workbook with its Formulas and Ext Ref sheets.

2. Update the value in cell A2 of the Formulas sheet from 34 to 102. Then, use AutoFit to widen column C in the Formulas worksheet and column B in the Ext Ref worksheet to display the contents of cells C9 and B3, respectively.

   Verify that Excel has automatically recalculated the formulas in both your Formulas and Ext Ref worksheets and that cell C9 on the Formulas sheet and B3 on the Ext Ref sheet now both contain the same value: 1,816,854.91.

3. On the Formulas tab, choose Calculation Options ⇨ Manual (or press Alt+MXM).

   Excel switches the workbook to manual recalculation.

4. Update the value in cell A2 of the Formulas sheet from 102 to 144.

   Note that none of the calculated values in the Formulas sheet have been updated (C9 still contains 1,816,854.91) and that the Calculate indicator now appears on the Status bar.

5. Click the Formulas tab's Calculate Sheet command button (or press Alt+MJ).

   Note that Excel recalculates the formulas on the Formulas worksheet and that cell C9 now contains the value 4,412,310.20, but that the Calculate indicator has not disappeared from the Status bar. Then, switch to the Ext Ref sheet and note that the linked formula in cell B3 has not been updated and still contains the value 1,816,854.91.

6. Press F9 to have Excel recalculate all the formulas in the entire workbook.

   Note that not only does cell B3 of the Ext Ref worksheet now contain the updated value 4,412,310.20, but that the Calculate indicator has now disappeared from the Status bar.

7. Switch back to the Formulas worksheet, and then update cell A2 to 165.88. Then click the Calculate Now command button on the Ribbon's Formulas tab or press F9.

   Check to make sure that all the formulas on both sheets of the workbook have now been updated by verifying that both cells C9 in the Formulas sheet and B3 in the Ext Ref sheet contain 6,423,962.85.

8. Update cell A2 in the Formulas worksheet to 188 and then save this change to the Practice Formulas – manrecalc.xlsx workbook.

Note that Excel not only saves your change to cell A2 in the Practice Formulas –manrecalc.xlsx workbook file, but also recalculates the formulas using this new value and then saves these updated values as well.

9. Close the Practice Formulas – manrecalc.xlsx workbook file by exiting Excel.

Note that any changes you make to the recalculation mode are saved as part of the workbook file, so that they are in effect the next time anyone opens the file for editing.

Chapter **7**

Copying and Correcting Formulas

Copying an original formula to all the cells in a worksheet that perform the same type of computation is one of the more common tasks you perform as part of creating a new worksheet. Despite this fact, understanding just how Excel goes about adjusting the cell references when you copy a formula is not widespread among new users. The exercises in this chapter give you a chance to practice copying formulas using all the different types of cell references. In addition, you practice assigning range names to the cells that are referenced in worksheet formulas, creating array formulas that do away with the need for making formula copies, as well as tracing and eliminating the source of errors that have spread across the workbook.

Copying Formulas with Relative References

When your original formula uses cell references rather than constant values (as most should), Excel makes copying that formula to every place that requires the same type of computation a complete no-brainer. The program does this by automatically adjusting the cell references in the original formula to suit the position of the copies you make. It does this through a system known as *relative cell addresses*, whereby the column references in the cell address in the formula change to suit their new column position, and the row references change to suit their new row position.

REMEMBER

Excel indicates that a cell reference is relative by stating its column letter and row number without preceding either part of the reference with a $ (dollar sign), the symbol denoting an absolute reference, as in A1 or BC457.

Try It

Exercise 7-1: Copying Formulas in the R1C1 Reference Style

In Exercise 7-1, you practice copying an original formula with relative cell references. To help you understand how Excel adjusts cell references in copied formulas, you change the program from the familiar default cell reference system with column letters and row numbers to the R1C1 system, where both the cell's row and column are numbered:

1. If Excel isn't running, launch the program. Open the Exercise7-1.xlsx workbook file in your Chap7 folder in the Excel Workbook folder.

    This file contains a copy of the Production Schedule table without any formulas.

2. Position the cell cursor in cell K3 and click the AutoSum button on the Ribbon's Home tab to create a SUM formula that totals the Part 100s scheduled to be produced over the nine-month period from April to December in row 3. Then, click the Enter button on the Formula bar.

    AutoSum enters the following master formula in cell K3:

    ```
    =SUM(B3:J3)
    ```

3. Use the fill handle on the cell cursor to copy this formula down column K to the cell range K4:K7.

    Excel copies the original formula plus its formatting to the empty cells down the column, automatically adjusting the row reference in each formula copy.

4. Position the white-cross mouse pointer on the fill handle of the cell cursor and then, when the AutoFill Options drop-down button appears, click it. Select the Fill without Formatting item at the bottom of the drop-down list that appears.

    Selecting the Fill without Formatting option restores the border along the top edge of cell K7 that Excel took out when copying the formatting from cell K3 to this range. Now, take a moment to examine the copies you made of the original SUM formula in cell K3 by using the arrow keys to move the cell cursor through each cell: K4, K5, K6, and K7. Note how the row number changes in each copy made down the cells in column K.

To help you understand what Excel is really doing when you make copies of a formula containing relative cell references down the rows of a column, turn on the R1C1 Reference system. In this system, both the rows and columns of the worksheet are given numbers so that the cell reference A1, for example, becomes R1C1 (because column A is the first column from the left edge of the worksheet) and cell D6 becomes R6C4 (because column D is the fourth column from the left edge of the worksheet).

5. Choose File ⇨ Options or press Alt+FT, and then click the Formulas tab in the left pane. Select the R1C1 Reference Style check box and then click OK.

   You can tell you are "not in Kansas anymore" using the familiar row number, column letter reference type system. All the columns are now numbered from left to right just as the rows are from top down.

6. Position the cell cursor in cell K3 (now called R3C11, as indicated in the Name Box) and examine the contents of the original SUM formula on the Formula bar.

   In R1C1 notation, the formula entered in this cell now reads

   ```
   =SUM(RC[-9]:RC[-1])
   ```

   The first thing to note about cell references in formulas in R1C1 notation is that they are completely egocentric, always referring to the cell that contains the formula. (They couldn't care less about the worksheet at large.) This formula says, in essence, "Use the SUM function to total the range that starts at RC[-9], which means the same row as the formula cell, but nine columns to the left, and ends at RC[-1], which means the same row as the formula cell, but one column to the left." The minus sign in front of the number following the column reference denotes columns to the left of the current one just as the minus in front of a number following a row reference denotes rows above. (Positive integers in these references denote columns to the right and rows below the current one.)

7. Press the ↓ key to move the cell cursor down column K through all the cells, K4, K5, K6, and K7, that contain copies of the formula you constructed in cell K3, noting the contents of each copy on the Formula bar as you move the cursor down a row.

   Note that every cell in this column contains the exact same formula:

   ```
   =SUM(RC[-9]:RC[-1])
   ```

   Excel hasn't really adjusted anything in any of the formula copies you made! It's all a convenient fiction (that's fancy talk for a big lie) to say that Excel adjusts the relative row and column references in formula copies because that's the way it appears to work when the program is in its normal column letter, row number reference system. (Now that I've let you in on this little secret, just keep it under your hat.)

8. Position the cell cursor in cell R7C2 (erstwhile B7) and use AutoSum to construct a SUM formula that totals the part numbers scheduled to be produced in April.

   This formula in R1C1 notation appears on the Formula bar as follows:

   ```
   =SUM(R[-4]C:R[-1]C)
   ```

9. Use the fill handle to copy this formula across the rest of the columns of the table to the range R7C3:R7C10 (C7:J7).

   Verify that each of the copies in all these cells contains the identical formula in R1C1 notation as you constructed in cell B7, that is, R7C2.

10. Restore the old tried-and-true row number and column letter notation system by removing the check mark from the R1C1 Reference Style check box on the Formulas tab of the Excel Options dialog box.

    The Prod Sched worksheet once again identifies its cell references in the standard column letter and row number notation (as B7).

11. Move the cell cursor across the cell range B7:J7, noting how Excel adjusts the cell reference (in standard notation).

    When you make copies of a formula across the columns of a single row using relative references, Excel adjusts only the column letter.

12. Save this workbook with the filename Production Schedule – relref.xlsx in your Excel Practice folder and then close the workbook file.

Copying Formulas with Absolute References

Absolute cell references, as their name implies, do not change for nobody or nothing. An absolute reference firmly roots both the column and row reference (as opposed to a mixed reference that just plants either the row number or the column letter, but not both). This type of reference comes in handy when you need to refer to a cell that contains a value that acts like a constant that must remain unchanged in all formula copies.

REMEMBER Excel indicates that a cell reference is absolute by preceding both its column letter and row number with a $ (dollar sign), the symbol denoting an absolute reference, as in $A$1 or $BC$457. When building or editing a formula, you can convert a relative cell reference that contains the insertion point to an absolute cell reference by pressing F4.

Try It

Exercise 7-2: Copying a Formula with Absolute Cell References

In Exercise 7-2, you practice creating an original formula that contains an absolute cell reference to prevent Excel from adjusting any part of its cell reference in the formula copies that you make.

1. Open the Exercise7-2.xls workbook file in your Chap7 folder in the Excel Workbook folder.

   This file contains a copy of the Production Schedule table with all the formulas you created and copied in Exercise 7-1 for totaling the units to be produced by month across the columns and by part down the rows. In this exercise, you add a row of formulas that compute what percentage each monthly production quota represents of the projected nine-month total.

2. Enter the heading Percent of Total in cell A9 of the Prod Sched worksheet. Then, click the Wrap Text button in the Alignment group of the Ribbon's Home tab to wrap the row heading on two lines in cell A9.

Next, you construct a formula that calculates what percentage each monthly total is of the nine-month grand total in cell K7.

3. Construct a formula in cell B9 that divides the April quota in cell B7 by the grand total in cell K7 and then format the cell with the Percent Style number format with two decimal places.

The formula in cell B9 should read

```
=B7/K7
```

To format the result in cell B9 in the Percent Style with two decimal places, click the Percent Style command button in the Number group of the Ribbon's Home tab and then click the Increase Decimal command button (located in the same row of the Number group) twice.

4. Use the fill handle to copy the original formula you constructed in cell B9 to the cell range C9:J9.

Something is clearly wrong with the copies as they all contain those dreaded #DIV/0! error values rather than the desired percentages.

5. Position the cell cursor in cell C9 to examine the formula that Excel copied there.

The formula in this cell reads

```
=C7/L7
```

When Excel made the first copy, the program not only adjusted the column reference for the monthly quota (from B7 to C7) but for the projected total as well (K7 to L7). Because L7 is empty, the copy is, in essence, trying to divide by zero (all empty cells carry a zero value); thus the division error value.

To prevent this problem with the copies (and to correct it), in the original division formula, the divisor, K7, with the projected total must be an absolute cell reference (as in $K$7), so that it remains constant in all the copies in which Excel naturally adjusts the dividend (that is, the amount to be divided) containing the various monthly production quotas.

6. Position the cell cursor back in cell B9 with the original formula and then press F2 to put Excel in Edit mode.

7. With the insertion point positioned after the cell reference K7 (so that you don't have to move the insertion point to convert this cell reference), press F4 to convert the relative K7 cell reference to absolute $K$7 and then click the Enter button on the Formula bar.

Excel enters the formula =B7/$K$7. Note that this revised formula gives you the same result (11.35%). The question, however, is will it give you the same error value when you make your copies of this formula set?

8. Use the fill handle to copy this edited version of the original formula in cell B9 to the cell range C9:J9.

   That's more like it! This time all the formula copies return realistic percentages in place of those awful division errors.

9. Position the cell cursor in cell A1 of the Prod Sched worksheet and then save the workbook with the filename Production Schedule – absref.xlsx in your Excel Practice folder before you close the workbook.

Copying Formulas with Mixed References

Just as you'd expect, mixed cell references are those that mix relative and absolute references in a cell. A mixed cell reference can either have the row reference absolute and column relative (as in A$3) or the column reference absolute and the row relative (as in $A3).

REMEMBER

You can convert a cell reference you're entering or editing in a formula to either type of mixed reference by pressing F4 as follows:

>> First time to convert the cell reference from completely relative to completely absolute (C5 to $C$5)

>> Second time to convert from completely absolute to a mixed reference with the row absolute and the column relative ($C$5 to C$5)

>> Third time to convert from a mixed reference with the row absolute and the column relative to one with the column absolute and row relative (C$5 to $C5)

>> Fourth time to convert from a mixed reference with the column absolute and row relative back to a completely relative reference ($C5 to C5)

You only need to resort to mixed cell references in an original formula when you intend to copy this formula to empty cells in two directions — that is, both down the rows and then over the columns to the right or over to columns on the right and then down the rows — and you need to prevent Excel from adjusting either the column letter or the row number reference in all the copies.

Try It

Exercise 7-3: Creating a Loan Table with Mixed Cell References

Exercise 7-3 gives you practice in constructing a loan payment table that requires the use of mixed and absolute cell references in the original formula as well as two-dimensional formula copying. To create this original formula for the payment table, you use the PMT function, the arguments of which require all the different types of cell references (including both types of mixed cell references) for all the copies to refer to the correct cells.

1. Open a new workbook in Excel and use its blank Sheet1 worksheet to create this loan payment table.

   This table uses the PMT function to compute the monthly mortgage payments for a sequence of different loan amounts (principals) and interest rates. The PMT function is a Financial function that requires three arguments: Rate, which is the interest rate per payment period; Nper, which is the number or payment periods for the loan; and Pv, which is the present value or loan amount. (The function also accepts two other optional arguments that you won't need to use in this exercise.)

   You begin by entering the table headings and the three initial values (loan amount, term of the loan, and interest rate) to be used to generate the sequence of the different loan amounts and interest rates as well as in the construction of the original PMT formula that you then copy in two dimensions to the rest of table.

2. Enter the following headings in the designated cells and then widen column A to suit with AutoFit:

   - Loan Payment Table in cell A1
   - Principal in cell A2
   - Interest in cell A3
   - Period in cell A4

3. Enter the following values in the designated cells and format them as indicated:

   - 235000 in cell B2 formatted with the Accounting number format with zero decimal places
   - 4% in cell B3 formatted with two decimal places
   - 30 in cell B4

4. Create a formula in cell A7 that dynamically copies the initial principal value entered in cell B2 to this cell.

HINT

   To create a dynamic link between the value in one cell and another cell in the same worksheet, type = to start the formula, followed by the reference of the cell with which you want the value linked.

   Cell A7 contains the formula =B2 and displays the initial principal amount $235,000 brought forward from cell B2.

5. Create a formula in cell A8 that adds 500 to the value in cell A7 and then use the fill handle to copy this formula down the rows to the cell range A9:A17.

   Cell A8 contains the formula =A7+500 and displays the result $235,500.

6. Create a formula in cell B6 that dynamically copies the initial interest rate entered in cell B3 to this cell.

   Cell B6 contains the formula =B3 and displays the initial interest rate amount 4.00%.

7. Create a formula in cell C6 that adds 0.25% to the value in cell B6 and reduce the number of decimal places to two.

Cell C6 contains the formula =B6+0.25% and displays the result 4.25%.

8. Use the fill handle to copy this formula across the columns to the cell range D6:J6.

Now that your range of principals and interest rates are created, you're ready to construct the initial formula using the PMT function that you will copy down to row 17 in column B of the table and then over to column J.

9. Position the cell cursor in cell B7 and then choose Formulas ⇨ Financial ⇨ PMT.

Excel inserts =PMT() into cell B7 and immediately opens its Function Arguments dialog box.

10. Drag the PMT Function Arguments dialog box to the right so that it's out of the way and no longer hides cell B7 in the worksheet.

The first argument to specify is the Rate argument, for which you will select cell B6 that is linked to the starting interest rate in cell B3. Note that you must consider what part of this cell reference, if any, should be adjusted when you copy this formula down the rows of this table (from 7 through 17) and then across the columns (from B through J) and adjust its reference accordingly.

Note that when you copy the PMT formula down the rows of the table, you don't want Excel to adjust the row number because all of the interest rates are in row 6, meaning that this part of the cell reference must be absolute. When you then copy the PMT formula to columns on the right, you do, however, need the column letter to be adjusted to pick up the quarter percentage point entered into the succeeding columns in row 6, so you do need to keep this part of the cell reference relative. Therefore, for this argument, you need to convert B6 from its completely relative reference to the mixed cell reference, B$6 (column adjusted but not the row).

Moreover, because the starting interest rate you entered into cell B3 and bring forward to cell B6 is a yearly rate and the PMT function calculates the monthly payment, you need to divide this yearly interest amount by twelve so that the Rate argument represents a monthly portion.

11. With the insertion point in the Rate text box, click cell B6 to select and enter its reference, and then press F4 twice to convert it to the mixed reference, B$6, before you type **/12**, and then press Tab.

B$6/12 now appears in the Rate argument text box and the calculated result 0.003333333 appears to its right.

The Nper argument picks up the single loan period value entered in cell B4. Because this value acts like a constant in the table, all the loan payments calculated by the PMT function refer to it. Therefore, this reference has to be completely absolute, $B$4, so that Excel adjusts neither its column letter nor its row number in any of the copies. In addition, because this period is in years (30 years to begin with), you need to multiply it by twelve so that the PMT function is dealing with the total number of months.

12. With the insertion point in the Nper text box, click cell B4, and then press F4 once to convert its reference to $B$4 and type ***12** before you press Tab.

$B$4*12 now appears in the Nper argument text box and the calculated result 360 appears to its right.

The last required argument is the present value or loan amount for which you will select cell A7 that is linked to the initial principal entered into cell B2. When you copy the PMT formula down the rows of column B, you want Excel to adjust the row number so that it picks and uses the increased principals (that increment by $500 in each subsequent row). You do not, however, want Excel to adjust the column letter in this argument when you copy the formula to the columns to the right because all the principals are entered in only one column. Therefore, for this last PMT argument, you need a mixed cell reference of $A7 (with column reference absolute and row reference relative).

13. With the insertion point in the Pv text box, click cell A7, and then press F4 three times to convert it to the mixed reference, $A7.

   Check the arguments in your Function Arguments dialog box against those shown in Figure 7-1 and note the Formula result of -1121.925944 near the bottom. When each argument checks out, proceed to Step 14. If you discover that you need to change the type of cell reference in any argument, edit the formula (F2) and then position the blinking cursor in that reference. Press F4 until the correct mixed or absolute reference appears.

14. Click OK to close the Function Arguments dialog box and to complete the formula with the PMT function in cell B7, and then use the fill handle to copy this formula down the rows of column B to cell B17.

   Now that you've copied the original formula down column B, you're ready to copy it to the right to column J.

15. While the range B7:B17 is still selected by the cell cursor, use its fill handle to copy the original PMT formula across the columns of the table to and including column J. (The entire cell range B7:J17 is selected when you finish copying the formulas in the second direction across the columns.)

   Now you need to widen columns C through J to display all the calculated results.

16. Use AutoFit to widen columns C:J sufficiently to display their contents.

   The results in your loan table should match those shown in Figure 7-2.

17. Change the period from 30 to 15 in cell B4 and note the increase to the monthly payments in the table, and then choose Home⇨Undo (or press Ctrl+Z) to return the loan term to its original 30 years.

   Note as soon as you change the period Excel immediately recalculates all the PMT formulas in your loan table.

18. Put Excel into manual recalculation mode and then experiment with changing the initial principal in cell B2 to 125000 and a starting interest rate in B3 of 3.00%. Click the Calculate Now button or press F9 to update the loan table by recalculating the monthly payments using the new principal amounts and interest rates.

HINT

To put the workbook into manual recalculation mode, click the Manual option on the Calculation Options button's drop-down menu on the Formulas tab of the Ribbon or press Alt+MXM.

As soon as you change the initial principal amount in cell B2, the Calculate indicator appears on the Status bar, letting you know that the formulas in the loan table are no longer up to date. As soon as you finish entering the new initial interest rate and choose Calculate Now, Excel updates all the formulas and the Calculate indicator disappears.

19. Use Undo to restore the original 235000 and 4% values in cells B2 and B3, respectively, and position the cell cursor in cell B7. Save your Loan Payment Table with the filename Loan Table – manrecalc.xlsx in your Excel Practice folder. Then, close the workbook.

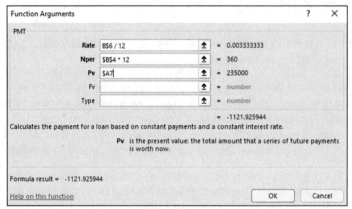

FIGURE 7-1: The Function Arguments dialog box showing the final arguments for the PMT function.

B7 =PMT(B$6 / 12,$B$4 * 12,$A7)

	A		B	C	D	E	F	G	H	I	J
1	Loan Payment Table										
2	Principal		$235,000.00								
3	Interest		4.00%								
4	Period		30								
5											
6			4.00%	4.25%	4.50%	4.75%	5.00%	5.25%	5.50%	5.75%	6.00%
7	$	235,000.00	($1,121.93)	($1,156.06)	($1,190.71)	($1,225.87)	($1,261.53)	($1,297.68)	($1,334.30)	($1,371.40)	($1,408.94)
8	$	235,500.00	($1,124.31)	($1,158.52)	($1,193.24)	($1,228.48)	($1,264.21)	($1,300.44)	($1,337.14)	($1,374.31)	($1,411.94)
9	$	236,000.00	($1,126.70)	($1,160.98)	($1,195.78)	($1,231.09)	($1,266.90)	($1,303.20)	($1,339.98)	($1,377.23)	($1,414.94)
10	$	236,500.00	($1,129.09)	($1,163.44)	($1,198.31)	($1,233.70)	($1,269.58)	($1,305.96)	($1,342.82)	($1,380.15)	($1,417.94)
11	$	237,000.00	($1,131.47)	($1,165.90)	($1,200.84)	($1,236.30)	($1,272.27)	($1,308.72)	($1,345.66)	($1,383.07)	($1,420.93)
12	$	237,500.00	($1,133.86)	($1,168.36)	($1,203.38)	($1,238.91)	($1,274.95)	($1,311.48)	($1,348.50)	($1,385.99)	($1,423.93)
13	$	238,000.00	($1,136.25)	($1,170.82)	($1,205.91)	($1,241.52)	($1,277.64)	($1,314.24)	($1,351.34)	($1,388.90)	($1,426.93)
14	$	238,500.00	($1,138.64)	($1,173.28)	($1,208.44)	($1,244.13)	($1,280.32)	($1,317.01)	($1,354.18)	($1,391.82)	($1,429.93)
15	$	239,000.00	($1,141.02)	($1,175.74)	($1,210.98)	($1,246.74)	($1,283.00)	($1,319.77)	($1,357.02)	($1,394.74)	($1,432.93)
16	$	239,500.00	($1,143.41)	($1,178.20)	($1,213.51)	($1,249.35)	($1,285.69)	($1,322.53)	($1,359.85)	($1,397.66)	($1,435.92)
17	$	240,000.00	($1,145.80)	($1,180.66)	($1,216.04)	($1,251.95)	($1,288.37)	($1,325.29)	($1,362.69)	($1,400.57)	($1,438.92)
18											

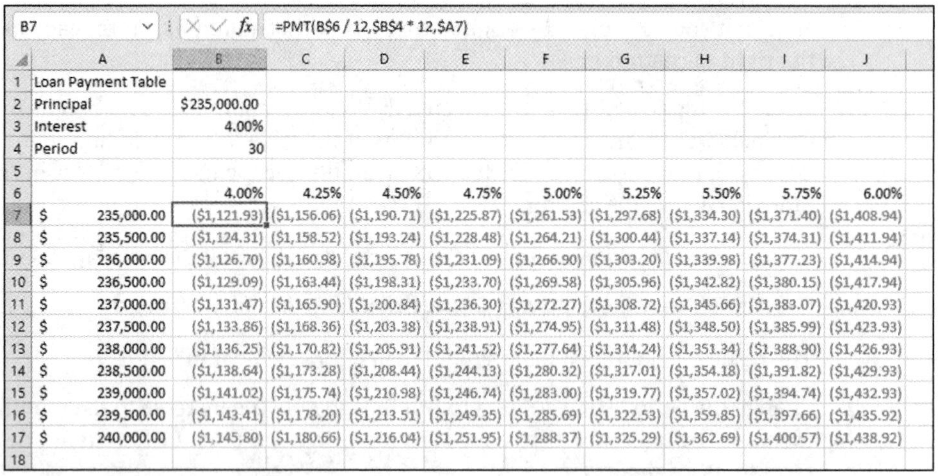

FIGURE 7-2: The completed Loan Payment Table after copying the PMT function and widening the columns to suit.

Using Range Names in Formulas

In completing the exercises in Chapter 6, you got experience with assigning a range name to a cell that held a constant (named Source) and then using that name in a linking formula. This linking formula supplied the basic value used in most of the hand-made formulas you then constructed on the worksheet.

Instead of assigning range names to constants that you enter into particular cells of the worksheet, you can create range names that store constant values not tied to entries in any cell. You can then paste the constant's range name into any formula that needs its value to successfully perform its calculations.

Another important use for range names is as identifiers of the cell references used in the operands and arguments of the formulas constructed for a typical data table. In this situation, you have Excel assign the table's row and column headings as the range names for data cells in the corresponding rows and columns. You then have Excel substitute these range names for the cell references in all the formulas in the table that refer to these data cells.

Try It

Exercise 7-4: Creating Ranges Names for Formulas

In Exercise 7-4, you practice defining range names from the headings in a table and then assigning the names to formulas in a worksheet table.

1. Open the Exercise7-4.xlsx file in your Chap7 folder inside your Excel Workbook folder.

   This file contains a variation on the Spring Sale table that you can use to practice assigning a range name to a constant as well as creating range names from a table's row and column headings.

2. Choose Formulas ⇨ Define Name (or press Alt+MMD) to open the New Name dialog box, and then type Discount_rate (don't forget the underscore) as the range name in the Name text box. (This name replaces the title of the table that automatically appears as the suggested range name because its cell, A1, is selected in the worksheet.)

   Note that by default the scope of a range name is the entire workbook. You can, if you want, restrict the scope of the range name you're defining to the current worksheet or another particular sheet in the workbook.

3. Press Tab three times to select ='Spring Sale'!$A$1 in the Refers To text box, replace this reference by typing **=15%**, and then click OK.

   Excel now adds a range name called Discount_rate to the workbook that sets the discount percentage equal to a constant 15%. Note, however, that this range name does not refer to any particular cell in the worksheet.

4. Position the cell cursor in cell D3 and construct a formula that multiplies the retail price of the table item with the code number 12–305 in cell C3 by the 15% discount rate. Type =, click cell C3, type *****, and then click the Use in Formula button on the Formulas tab and click Discount_rate on its drop-down menu.

   The formula in cell D3 now reads

```
=C3*Discount_rate
```

5. Click the Enter button on the Formula bar and then copy this formula down to the cell range D4:D7.

   Note in each of the copies of the formula that although Excel adjusts the row number of each reference to the cell in the Retail Price column, it treats the range name, Discount_rate, as an absolute reference.

6. Create a formula in cell E3 that computes the sale price of the table item code numbered 12-305 by subtracting its discount amount from its retail price, as in =C3-D3, and then copy this formula down the cell range E4:E7.

   Next, you're going to have Excel assign range names to the table cells in the range C3:E7 from the row and column headings in row 2 and column B of the Sale Table.

7. Select the cell range B2:E7 that includes the column and row headings and then choose Formulas⇨Create from Selection (or press Alt+MC).

   Excel opens the Create Names from Selection dialog box. This dialog box contains four check boxes, Top Row, Left Column, Bottom Row, and Right Column, that you can select to indicate which row and column headings to use in assigning the new range names.

8. Make sure that only the Top Row and Left Column check boxes are selected, and then click OK.

   Next, you create a list of the range names that you defined for this sales table on Sheet2 of the workbook.

9. Double-click Sheet2 and then rename its tab Range Names. Increase the magnification to 150%, enter the heading, Range Name List, in cell A1 of the Range Names sheet, and position the cell cursor in cell A2.

   To create a list of the current range names in the workbook, you need to open the Paste Name dialog box and use its Paste List command.

10. Open the Paste Name dialog box by choosing Formulas⇨Use in Formulas⇨ Paste Names. Then, click the Paste List command button in Paste Name dialog box.

    Excel pastes an alphabetical list of range names in the cell range A2:B11. Note that this alphabetical listing of the range names in the workbook is static, so you'd have to generate it again with the Paste List button if you edit the names in this workbook and then want an up-to-date list.

11. Use AutoFit to widen columns A and B of the Range Names sheet so that all the entries in the first and second columns of this list are completely displayed in the worksheet. Right-align the range names in the cell range A2:A11 and then click cell A1.

    Next, you create a new window in the Exercise7-4.xlsx workbook that enables you to compare the Sale Table in the Spring Sale sheet and the Range Name List in the Range Names sheet side by side on your screen.

12. Choose View⇨New Window on the Ribbon or press Alt+WN to create a new window in the workbook named Exercise7-4.xlsx:2. Then, click the Switch Windows button and click the Exercise7-4.xlsx:1 option on its drop-down menu (or press Alt+WW1) to make the first window active. Finally, click the View Side by Side command button followed

by the Reset Window Position button to display both the Exercise7-4.xlsx:1 and the Exercise7-4.xlsx:2 windows together on the screen, one on top of the other.

After you open new windows on the same workbook, you can display a range of cells on any of its worksheets in the different window panes.

TIP

13. Click the Spring Sale sheet tab in the Exercise7-4.xlsx:1 window on the top to make the sheet with the Spring Sale sheet active in the top window. Use the Zoom slider to reduce the magnification display percentage to 100% in the workbook. Then, check your screen against the one shown in Figure 7-3.

    Note that both the Spring Sale worksheet in the top window (Exercise7-4.xlsx:1) and the Range Names sheet in the lower window (Exercise7-4.xlsx:2) are affected equally by the zoom command.

14. Click the View Side by Side button to display only the Spring Sale worksheet and then increase the screen magnification percentage to 150%.

    Now, you're ready to apply the range names listed in the Range Name Listing on the Range Names sheet to the formulas you constructed and copied in the Sale Table in the Spring Sale worksheet.

15. Select the formulas in column D (cell range D3:D7) in the sales table. Then, choose Formulas ⇨ Define Name ⇨ Apply Names (or press Alt+MMA) to open the Apply Names dialog box.

    The Apply Names dialog box contains a list with all the range names you've defined in the workbook selected.

16. Select the Options button to expand the Apply Names dialog box and then deselect the Omit Column Name If Same Column and the Omit Row Name If Same Row check boxes and click OK.

    When these check boxes are selected, Excel does not bother to repeat row and column range names in the formulas. As a result, the formulas copied down the rows of this column of the table all end up with the same descriptions (which pretty much defeats the purpose of displaying them in the formulas in the first place).

17. Repeat Steps 15 and 16, this time selecting the formulas in column E (cell range E3:E7) before you open the Apply Names dialog box. Deselect the Omit Column Name If Same Column and the Omit Row Name If Same Row check boxes before you click OK.

18. Examine the use of the range names created from the row and column headings in all the individual formulas in the cell range D3:E7.

    Note that the operand of each formula now includes both the row and the column range name (separated by a space that represents the Intersection operator) created from the cell's row and column heading. For example, the subtraction formula in cell E6 now reads

    ```
    =Buffet Retail_Price-Buffet Discount
    ```

    This identifies the formula as subtracting the value in the cell at the intersection of the Buffet row and Discount column range names from the value in the cell at the intersection of the Buffet row and Retail_Price column range names.

19. Select cell A1 in the Spring Sale worksheet and then save your changes to this workbook with the filename Spring Furniture Sale – namedfrmls.xlsx in your Excel Practice folder, and then close the workbook.

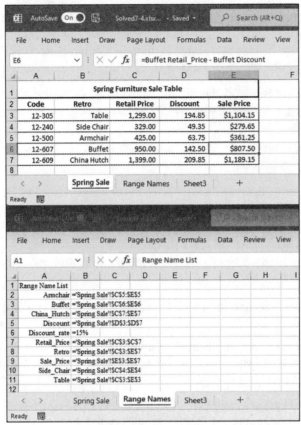

FIGURE 7-3: The workbook with the Spring Sale worksheet displayed in the top window and Range Names displayed in the bottom one.

Building Array Formulas

Instead of copying a formula to all the cells that perform the same type of calculation, you can build an array formula that performs the desired calculation not only in the active cell but in all the other cells to which you would normally copy the formula. An array formula is a special formula that operates on a range of values. If this range is supplied by a cell range (as is often the case), it is referred to as an *array range*. If this range is supplied by a list of numerical values, they are known as an *array constant*.

Note that in Excel 2019 and later, Excel creates array formulas automatically when one or more formula operands refer to a range or an array constant. These are known as *dynamic* arrays. In earlier versions of Excel, you need to enter your formulas in a special way (specifically, by pressing Ctrl+Shift+Enter instead of just Enter) to tell Excel you're creating an array formula. You practice creating both types of array formulas in Exercise 7-5.

You are already quite familiar with arrays even though you may not realize it. This is because the Excel worksheet grid with its column-and-row structure naturally organizes your data ranges into one-dimensional and two-dimensional arrays. (One-dimensional arrays take up a single row or column, whereas two-dimensional arrays take up multiple rows and columns.)

Figure 7-4 illustrates a couple of two-dimensional arrays with numerical entries of two different sizes. The first array is a 3-by-2 array in the cell range B2:C4. This array is a 3-by-2 array because it occupies three rows and two columns. The second array is a 2-by-3 array in the cell range B6:D7. This array is a 2-by-3 array because it uses 2 rows in three columns. If you were to list the values in the first 3-by-2 array as an array constant in a formula, they would appear as follows:

```
{1,4;2,5;3,6}
```

Here are several things to note in this expression:

» The array constant is enclosed in a pair of braces ({}).

» Columns within each row are separated by commas (,) and rows within the array are separated by semicolons (;).

» Constants in the array are listed across each row and then down each column, not down each column and across each row.

The second 2-by-3 array expressed as an array constant appears as follows:

```
{7,8,9;10,11,12}
```

Note again that you list the values across each row and then down each column, separating the values in different columns with commas and the values in different rows with a semicolon.

FIGURE 7-4:
Worksheet containing a 3-by-2 array in cell range B2:C4 and a 2-by-3 array in range B6:D7.

Try It

Exercise 7-5: Constructing Dynamic and Old-Fashioned Array Formulas

In Exercise 7-5, you practice creating old-fashioned (that is, prior to Excel 2019) array formulas for a worksheet in cell ranges that need to perform the same type of calculation. This gives you a chance to compare the technique of entering a single array formula into an entire cell range with that of entering an original formula in a single cell that you then copy to the entire range.

1. Open the Exercise7-5.xlsx file in your Chap7 folder inside your Excel Workbook folder.

   This file contains a copy of the February Hourly Wage worksheet (named Old-Fashioned Array Formulas) that you can use to practice constructing array formulas. This worksheet is designed to compute the bi-weekly wages for each employee by multiplying the hourly rate by the number of hours worked. Rather than create an original formula for each period that computes the wages for the first employee and then copying it down rows for all the others, array formula can accomplish the same thing.

2. Position the cell cursor in cell R10 and then select the cell range R10:R13.

   You are going to construct the following array formula that you then enter as a single entry into the cell range R10:R13 you just selected:

   ```
   ={A4:A7 * R4:R7}
   ```

   The range A4:A7 contains the hourly rates for all four employees, whereas the range R4:R7 contains the total hours each one worked in the first period.

3. Type = to start the array formula and then select the cell range A4:A7. Type * (asterisk), the multiplication operator, and then select the cell range R4:R7.

   To complete an array formula, you must press a special key combination, Ctrl+Shift+Enter. This key combination lets Excel know you're constructing an array formula as well as informs it to enter this array formula into all the cells in the selected range.

4. Press Ctrl+Shift+Enter to complete the array formula and enter it into the selected range R10:R13.

   Excel enters the array formula ={A4:A7 * R4:R7} in all the cells in the selected range R10:R13.

5. Construct an array formula in the cell range AI10:AI13 that multiplies the hourly rates in the cell range A4:A7 by the second-period hour totals in the cell range AI4:AI7.

   The array formula you enter into the cell range AI10:AI13 appears on the Formula bar as follows:

   ```
   ={A4:A7 * AI4:AI7}
   ```

6. Construct an array formula in the cell range AJ10:AJ13 that totals the two pay periods for each employee.

   The array formula you enter into the cell range AJ10:AJ13 appears as follows on the Formula bar:

   ```
   ={R10:R13 + AI10:AI13}
   ```

7. Select cell AJ10 to deselect the cell range and then press the Delete key to remove the addition formula from this cell.

   Excel responds by displaying an alert dialog box informing you that you cannot change part of an array. When editing array formulas, you must work entirely with the ranges specified as the operands.

8. Click OK to close the alert dialog box and now select the range AJ10:AJ13 before you press Delete.

   This time, Excel deletes the array formula from the entire range.

9. Choose Home⇨Undo (or press Ctrl+Z) to restore the deleted array formula to the range AJ10:AJ13.

10. Switch to the Dynamic Array Formulas worksheet and position the cell cursor in cell R10.

    You are going to construct the following dynamic array formula that Excel will automatically enter — or *spill* —into the cell range R10:R13:

    ```
    =A4:A7 * R4:R7
    ```

    The range A4:A7 contains the hourly rates for all four employees, whereas the range R4:R7 contains the total hours each one worked in the first period.

11. Type = to start the dynamic array formula and then select the cell range A4:A7. Type * (asterisk), the multiplication operator, and then select the cell range R4:R7.

12. Press Enter to complete the dynamic array formula.

    Note that, with a dynamic array, you don't press the special Ctrl+Shift+Enter key combination as you did for the older type of array.

    Excel spills the array formula =A4:A7 * R4:R7 into the range R10:R13.

13. Construct a dynamic array formula in cell AI10 that multiplies the hourly rates in the cell range A4:A7 by the second-period hour totals in the cell range AI4:AI7, and then press Enter.

    The dynamic array formula you enter into cell AI10 appears on the Formula bar as follows:

    ```
    =A4:A7 * AI4:AI7
    ```

14. Construct a dynamic array formula in cell AJ10 that totals the two pay periods for each employee, and then press Enter.

    The dynamic array formula you enter into cell AJ10 appears as follows on the Formula bar:

    ```
    =R10:R13 + AI10:AI13
    ```

15. Select cell A1 and save this workbook with the filename Feb Wages – arrayformulas.xlsx in your Excel Practice folder before you close the workbook.

Tracing and Eliminating Formula Errors

As you found out firsthand when performing Exercise 6-3 in Chapter 6, an error value returned by a single faulty formula can spread like wildfire to all the cells that refer to its value throughout the entire worksheet, making it very difficult to determine its source. Fortunately, Excel offers some very effective Formula Auditing tools that you can use to track down the cell that's causing your error woes by tracing the relationships between the formulas in the cells of your worksheet.

By tracing the relationships, you can test formulas to see which cells, called *direct precedents* in Excel jargon, directly feed the formulas and which cells, called *dependents* (nondeductible, of course), depend upon the results of the formulas. Excel even offers a way to visually backtrack the potential sources of an error value in the formula of a particular cell. To display the precedents and dependents of a formula as well as for tracing the source of errors, you can use the command buttons in the Formulas tab's Formula Auditing group.

When you click the Trace Precedents and Trace Dependents buttons on the Formulas tab, Excel shows the relationship between a formula and the cells that directly and indirectly feed it as well as those cells that directly and indirectly depend upon its calculation. The program establishes this relationship by drawing arrows from the precedent cells to the active cell and from the active cell to its dependent cells.

If these cells are on the same worksheet, Excel draws solid red or blue arrows extending from each of the precedent cells to the active cell and from the active cell to the dependent cells. If the cells are not located locally on the same worksheet (they may be on another sheet in the same workbook or even on a sheet in a different workbook), Excel draws a black dotted arrow. This arrow comes from or goes to an icon picturing a miniature worksheet that sits to one side, with the direction of the arrowheads indicating whether the cells on the other sheet feed the active formula or are fed by it.

Try It

Exercise 7-6: Finding the Source of Error Values in a Worksheet

In Exercise 7-6, you get some practice using Excel's formula auditing features to trace the precedents and dependents of a formula to find the source of error values in a worksheet.

1. Open the Exercise7-6.xlsx workbook in your Chap7 folder inside your Excel Workbook folder.

   This workbook contains a copy of the Practice Formulas workbook you created as part of the exercises in Chapter 6. You can use its Formulas and Ext Ref worksheets to practice tracing and eliminating errors.

2. Remove the range name, "Source", given to cell A2 in the Formulas worksheet by choosing Formulas ➪ Name Manager (or pressing Alt+MN) to open the Name Manager dialog box. Click the Source range name in the list box to select it and then click the

Delete button. Click OK in the alert dialog box asking you if you're sure you want to delete the range name and then click the Close button to close the Name Manager.

As soon as you remove the range name, the worksheet on the Formulas worksheet fills with #NAME? error values.

3. Click cell C9 with the SUM function that sums the three cell ranges A2:A8, B4:B8, C4:C8 to select it.

Now, trace the source of this error value.

4. Choose Formulas ⇨ Error Checking (or press Alt+MKK) to open the Error Checking dialog box.

Excel displays the Error Checking dialog box, which briefly explains that this error value means the formula now contains unrecognized text. This is not something that you can fix by editing the formula on the Formula bar, so, in this case, you need to trace the error.

5. Click the Trace Error button in the Error Checking dialog box.

Excel draws a diagonal arrow from cell A4 pointing to cell C9, indicating that this is the direct source of the error (if you select the Previous button in the Error Checking dialog box, Excel steps the cell cursor back through each of the cells with the #NAME? error value in the order in which they spread in this worksheet).

In this situation, you need to identify the cell or cells that feed the cells containing the #NAME? error values.

6. Click the Close button (the one with the X) in the Error Checking dialog box and then choose Formulas ⇨ Trace Precedents (or press Alt+MP).

Excel adds three arrows pointing directly to cell C9, showing the precedents of its error value, the most telling of which is the one drawn from cell A2. If you didn't already know that cell A2 was the culprit causing all these error values (having removed its range name yourself), this precedents diagram would have tipped you off immediately.

7. Choose Formulas ⇨ Trace Precedents (or press Alt+MP) a second time.

Clicking the Trace Precedents button a second time (or double-clicking it to begin with) displays all the indirect precedents and dependents of the formula in the current cell. In this case, Excel now shows the flow and direction of all the sum formulas both down the columns and across the rows that contribute both directly and indirectly to its computed value.

8. Choose Formulas ⇨ Remove Arrows (or press Alt+MAA).

Excel removes all arrows from the worksheet display.

9. Position the cell cursor in cell A4, the first one with a #NAME? error value, and then choose Formulas ⇨ Trace Dependents (or press Alt+MD).

The program draws arrows showing the direct dependents of the formula in this cell, which include the formulas down the column that use its value to compute their own and the formulas across the row in C4 and D4 and, of course, the formula in cell C9.

10. Choose Formulas ⇨ Trace Dependents (or press Alt+MD) a second time.

Excel draws arrows showing the indirect dependents of the formula in cell C9. Note that this includes a black dotted arrow line drawn from cell C9 to a graphic showing a tiny worksheet. This is Excel's way of alerting you to the fact that there are cells dependent on this one on other worksheets of the workbook to which its error value has naturally spread.

11. Click the Ext Ref sheet tab to make this worksheet active and note that cell B3, which contains the linking formula, also now contains a #NAME? error value. Click cell B3 and then choose Formulas ⇨ Trace Precedents (or press Alt+MP).

   Excel draws a black dotted line to cell B3 from a graphic showing a tiny worksheet, indicating that the source of this error value is on another worksheet.

12. Choose Formulas ⇨ Remove Arrows (or press Alt+MA) and then click the Formulas sheet tab to switch back to this worksheet. There, reassign the range name, Source, to cell A2 by selecting the cell and then typing this range name into the Name Box on the Formula bar before you press Enter.

   Note that the moment you rectify the source of the error (both literally and figuratively), all the nasty #NAME? error values in the worksheet immediately disappear along with all the arrows depicting the direct and indirect dependents.

13. Close the Exercise7-6.xlsx workbook file without saving your changes.

Dealing with Circular References

A *circular reference* in a formula is one that depends, directly or indirectly, upon its own value. The most common type of circular reference occurs when you mistakenly refer in the formula to the cell in which you're building the formula itself. For example, suppose that cell B10 is active when you build this formula:

```
=A10+B10
```

As soon as you complete this formula entry in cell B10, Excel displays an alert box that says that it cannot calculate the formula due to the circular reference. As soon as you press Enter or click OK to close this alert box, Excel inserts 0 in the cell with the circular reference and the indicator Circular References followed by the cell address with the circular reference appears on the Status bar.

Excel is not able to resolve this example of a circular reference in cell B10 because the formula's calculation depends directly upon the formula's result, creating an endless loop that continuously requires recalculating and can never be resolved.

Not all circular references are impossible for Excel to resolve. Some formulas contain a circular reference that can eventually be resolved after many recalculations of its formula (referred to as iterations) because the results get closer and closer to a resolution point with each go-round or iteration of the formula.

Exercise 7-7: Solving a Circular Reference in a Formula

In Exercise 7-7, you practice with a circular reference in a formula that Excel can eventually resolve by doing multiple iterations.

1. Open the Exercise7-7.xlsx workbook in your Chap7 folder in your Excel Workbook folder.

   This workbook contains an income statement worksheet with a circular reference in cell B13 that Excel catches the moment you open the file.

2. Read the text of the alert dialog box that appears the moment you open the Exercise7-7.xlsx workbook and then click the Help button.

   Excel switches to your default web browser and displays a Microsoft Support web page that gives you information either on locating and removing a circular reference or on making a circular reference work by changing the number of times that the program evaluates its formula.

3. Click the Learn About Iterative Calculation link to display its information in the web browser. Look over this information or print it before you close the Help window. Then click OK to close the alert box.

   Excel draws arrows that point to the cells involved in this circular reference, from the Total Other Income cell B15 to cell B13, which computes the bonuses; from the Income before Taxes cell B17 to cells B15 and B13; and to and from this Income Before Taxes cell B17 to cell B19, which computes the net income.

   These computations constitute a circular reference because the formula in cell B13 computes the amount of the bonuses as a percentage of the net income in cell B19 (=B19*20%), which, in turn, is dependent upon the amount of the bonus as it is included in the other income calculation in cell B15 that is then fed to the total income (loss) calculation in cell B17, which is itself used in calculating the net income in cell B19.

4. Choose File⇨Options (or press Alt+FT). Click Formulas in the left pane, select the Enable Iterative Calculation check box, and then click OK.

   Excel resolves the circular reference in cell B13 that calculates the bonuses based on the net income and all the arrows showing all the cells involved in this circular reference disappear from the worksheet.

5. Click cell A1 and then save this version of the Income Statement with the filename Income Statement −circref.xlsx in your Excel Practice folder before you close this file.

Chapter **8**

Creating Date and Time Formulas

ormulas that perform calculations between dates and between times are quite common in spreadsheets. The exercises in this chapter give you a chance to build formulas that calculate the difference between starting and ending dates and times as well as to use Excel Date and Time functions to perform a variety of tasks, including returning the current date and time in a spreadsheet, converting text entries to valid date and time numbers, and more.

Constructing Date and Time Formulas

You already have some experience entering dates and times in a worksheet and then changing how they appear by assigning different date and time number formats. Remember that all you need to do when you enter a date or time number in a worksheet is to follow one of these date or time number formats when making the entry.

The only thing the least little bit baffling about date and time entries in a worksheet is the way that Excel stores the date and time numbers. On the surface you see the date or time using the format you used, but behind the scenes lies a serial number. In the case of dates, this serial number represents the number of days that have elapsed between the date you enter and the beginning of the twentieth century (making January 1, 1900 serial date number 1). In the case of time, the serial number is a fraction representing the number of hours, minutes, and seconds that have elapsed since midnight (which is serial number 0.0, so that twelve noon is 0.5).

To build a basic date formula that calculates the number of days that have elapsed between two dates entered in the worksheet, subtract the cell containing the starting date from the one containing the ending date. Excel then displays the calculated result in a date format, which you then have to reformat with another number format (such as Number with no decimal points) to see the number of days that this "date" actually represents.

To build a basic time formula that calculates the fractional part of the day that has elapsed between two times entered in the worksheet, you subtract the cell containing the starting time from the one containing the ending time. Excel then displays the calculated result as a fraction that you can then convert into hours by multiplying by 24.

REMEMBER

When entering times in a spreadsheet that you intend to use in formulas to compute elapsed times, be sure to enter all times after twelve noon either using a twenty-four clock (as in 13:05 for 1:05 PM) or with the PM signifier after the time number. Otherwise, Excel interprets all the times you enter as occurring in the AM.

Try It

Exercise 8-1: Building Formulas that Calculate Elapsed Dates and Times

In Exercise 8-1, you practice building simple formulas that calculate the differences between different dates and different times entered into the cells of a worksheet.

1. If Excel isn't running, launch the program. Select Blank Workbook, and use Book1 to build some simple formulas that calculate elapsed times and dates. If the program is already running, click the New button on your customized Quick Access toolbar or press Ctrl+N to create a new workbook for this purpose.

   You start by entering some column headings in row 2 of the new worksheet.

2. Enter the following headings in the designated cells:

   - **Start** in cell A2
   - **End** in cell B2
   - **Elapsed** in cell C2

3. Enter the following dates in the designated cells:

   - 12-18-2021 in cell A3
   - 2-15-2022 in cell B3

4. Construct a formula in cell C3 that subtracts the starting date from the ending date, that is, =B3 – A3.

   Excel now displays 59 as the answer in cell C3.

5. Enter the following dates in the designated cells:

   - 4-26-2020 in cell A4
   - 7-21-2022 in cell B4
   - 11-30-2019 in cell A5
   - 5-19-2022 in cell B5

6. Use the fill handle to copy the formula in cell C3 down to the range C4:C5.

   Excel finds the difference between the dates in cells B4 and A4 to be 816 days and the difference between the dates in cells B5 and A5 to be 901 days.

7. Enter the following times in the designated cells:

   - 8:12 AM in cell A7
   - 2:15 PM in cell B7

   Be sure that you enter a space between the last number in the times and the AM and PM designation. Otherwise, Excel interprets the time entry as text.

8. Construct a formula in cell C7 that calculates the difference between the ending time and the starting time, that is, =B7 - A7.

   Excel calculates the difference between the two times and returns 6:03 AM to cell C7. You need to convert this time into a simple number by formatting it with the Number format.

9. Click the drop-down button attached to Number Format on the Ribbon's Home tab and then click the Number option on its drop-down menu to format cell C7 with the Number format with two decimal places.

   Excel now displays 0.25 as the answer in cell C7.

10. Convert the fraction of the day into hours by editing the formula in cell C7 so that the program multiplies the difference between the two cells by 24.

HINT

   When editing the formula, be sure to enclose the subtraction operation in parentheses so that Excel performs the subtraction first and then multiplies this difference by 24, as in

```
=(B7–A7) * 24
```

   After you edit the formula, Excel returns 6.05 as the number of hours in cell C7.

11. Enter the following times in the designated cells:

   - 7:35 AM in cell A8
   - 15:05 in cell B8
   - 9:45 in cell A9
   - 6 PM in cell B9

12. Use the fill handle to copy the formula in cell C7 down to the range C8:C9.

   Because you edited the basic formula in cell C7 so that it returns the number of hours elapsed (rather than the fractional part of the day) and formatted the result with the Number format with two decimal places before you copied the formula, the copies in cells C8 and C9 automatically return the number of hours expressed with two decimal places, 7.50 and 8.25, respectively.

13. Position the cell cursor in cell A1 and then save this new workbook with the filename Date & time frmls.xlsx in the Excel Practice folder and then close the workbook.

Working with Simple Date Functions

Excel contains a number of straightforward Date functions that help you work with dates in your spreadsheets. These functions run the gamut from those that return the current date to those that convert text to date serial numbers (so you can use them in formulas that compute the number of days that have elapsed).

Try It

Exercise 8-2: Using the TODAY, NOW, DATE, and DATEVALUE Date Functions

In Exercise 8-2, you practice using several of the simple date functions offered on the Date & Time button's drop-down menu on the Ribbon's Formulas tab:

1. Open the Exercise8-2.xlsx workbook file in your Chap8 folder in your Excel Workbook folder.

   This workbook contains a Date Formulas worksheet that you can use to practice building formulas with several of Excel's Date functions.

2. With the cell cursor in cell B1, click the Date & Time button on the Ribbon's Formulas tab or press Alt+ME and then click TODAY on its drop-down menu.

   Excel inserts the =TODAY() formula in cell B1 and displays its Function Arguments dialog box. This dialog box explains that this function takes no arguments.

3. Click OK in the Function Arguments dialog box or press Enter.

   Excel enters the current date into cell B1.

4. Click cell D1 in the Date Formulas worksheet, and then select the NOW function on the Date & Time button's drop-down menu and click OK in its Function Arguments dialog box.

   Excel inserts the current date and time in cell D1.

5. Press Ctrl+1 to open the Format Cells dialog box. Then, click Time in the Category pane and click the 1:30 PM sample in the Type list box before you click OK.

Excel formats the current date and time in cell D1 so that only the time is displayed, as in 12:22 PM.

6. Click cell D3, and then select the DATE function on the Date & Time button's drop-down menu. Next, designate the numeric entries in cells A3, B3, and C3 of the worksheet as the Date function's arguments in its Function Arguments dialog box in the following order:

   - Click cell C3 when the insertion point is in the Year argument text box
   - Press Tab and then click cell A3 for the Month argument
   - Press Tab and then click cell B3 for the Day argument and then click OK

   When you click OK to close the Function Arguments dialog box, Excel returns the date 2/15/1949 to cell D3.

7. Use the fill handle on cell D3 to copy its formula with the DATE function down to the cell range D4:D8.

   Note that contents of the cell range D3:D8 is composed of DATE function formulas rather than date serial numbers. To convert these formulas to their calculated date values, you copy them to the Clipboard and then paste their values in column E to the right, using the Paste Values option on the Paste button's drop-down menu.

8. Leave the cell range D3:D8 selected and then press Ctrl+C to copy this range to the Clipboard.

   Excel places a marquee around the cell range D3:D8.

9. Click cell E3 and then choose Home ⇨ Paste ⇨ Paste Values (or press Alt+HVV).

   Excel copies the date serial numbers into the range E3:E8. Note that the date serial numbers copied into this cell range are completely static: Unlike the DATE function formulas in the cell range D3:D8, revising the numeric entries made in the cells in the range A3:C8 would have no effect on them.

10. Use the Format Cells dialog box (Ctrl+1) to format these date serial numbers in cell range E3:E8 with the Date number format that uses the sample 14-Mar-12.

    Next, you use the DATEVALUE function to convert the date entries in the cell range A10:A14 of the Date Formulas worksheet that have been entered as text (prefaced with an apostrophe) to their corresponding date serial numbers.

11. Click cell B10 and then select the DATEVALUE function on the Date & Time button's drop-down menu. Click cell A10 to enter this cell address as the Date_Text argument in the Function Arguments dialog box and click OK.

    Excel displays the calculated date serial number 32546 in cell B10.

12. Use the fill handle to copy this DATEVALUE formula in cell B10 down to the cell range B11:B14 and then use Format Cells dialog box (Ctrl+1) to format these date serial numbers with the Date number format that uses the sample 14-Mar-12.

    Now, you're ready to save your work in the Date Formulas worksheet.

13. Position the cell cursor in cell F3 of the Date Formulas sheet and save a copy of the workbook with the filename Date Function Practice.xlsx in your Excel Practice folder, and leave the workbook open for Exercise 8-3.

Working with Excel's Fancier Date Functions

In addition to the straightforward Date functions such as TODAY, NOW, DATE, and DATE-VALUE, Excel includes a bunch of more sophisticated and powerful Date functions that you can use to calculate elapsed dates, future dates, days of the week, weeks of the year, and the like. These more sophisticated Date functions are all available on the Date & Time button's drop-down menu and take an array of different required and optional arguments. Among the most important of these Date functions on this drop-down menu are

- » EDATE(start_date,months) calculates the elapsed date so many months ahead (positive months argument) or behind (negative months argument) the start_date argument you specify.

- » EOMONTH(start_date,months) calculates the last day of the month so many months ahead (positive months argument) or behind (negative months argument) the start_date argument you specify.

- » NETWORKDAYS(start_date,end_date,[holidays]) calculates the number of work days between the start_date and end_date arguments. The optional holidays argument can specify a range of holiday dates to be excluded from the workday total.

- » WEEKDAY(serial_number,[return_type]) calculates a number indicating the day of the week specified by the serial_number argument. The optional return_type argument can be the number 1, 2, or 3 where 1 (or no return_type argument specified) starts the week on Sunday (1) and ends it on Saturday (7), 2 starts the week on Monday (1) and ends it on Sunday (7), and 3 starts the week on Monday (0) and ends it on Sunday (6).

- » WEEKNUM(serial_number,[return_type]) calculates a number indicating where the week in the date specified by the serial_number argument falls within the year — the optional return_type argument can be the number 1 or 2, where 1 (or no return_type argument specified) starts the week on Sunday (1) and ends it on Saturday (7) and 2 starts the week on Monday (1) and ends it on Sunday (7).

- » WORKDAY(start_date,days,[holidays]) calculates the work date that is so many days ahead (positive days argument) or behind (negative days argument) the start_date argument you specify. The optional holidays argument can specify a range of holiday dates to be excluded from the calculation.

- » YEARFRAC(start_date,end_date,[basis]) calculates the fraction of the year between the start_date and end_date arguments you specify. The optional basis argument can be a number between 0 and 4 that signifies the following:

  - 0 (or no basis argument) bases the year fraction on the U.S. (NASD) method of 30/360 (whereby if the starting date is equal to the 31st of the month, it becomes equal to the 30th; if the ending date is equal to the 31st of the month, the ending date becomes the 1st of the following month).

  - 1 bases the year fraction on the actual days divided by the actual days.

  - 2 bases the year fraction on the actual days divided by 360.

  - 3 bases the year fraction on the actual days divided by 365.

- 4 bases the year fraction on the European method of 30/360 (whereby starting and ending dates that fall on the 31st of the month are made equal to the 30th of the same month).

Exercise 8-3: Using the WEEKDAY, WEEKNUM, and YEARFRAC Date Functions

In Exercise 8-3, you practice using a few of Excel's more sophisticated Date functions, WEEK-DAY, WEEKNUM, and YEARFRAC on the Date & Time button's drop-down menu.

1. Use the Date Formulas worksheet in the Date Function Practice.xlsx workbook file you modified when doing the previous exercise.

   You start by creating a formula in cell F3 that uses the WEEKDAY function to return the day of week of the date entered in cell E3.

2. With the cell cursor in cell F3, select the WEEKDAY function on the Date & Time button's drop-down menu. Then, click cell E3 to enter this cell address in the Serial_ number argument text box and press Tab to select the Return_type text box. Then, type 2 in this text box and click OK.

   Excel returns 2 to cell F3, indicating that this date in 1949 fell on a Tuesday (when you select 2 as the return_type, 1 is Monday, 2 is Tuesday, 3 is Wednesday, 4 is Thursday, 5 is Friday, 6 is Saturday, and 7 is Sunday).

3. Use the fill handle to copy this formula with the WEEKDAY function down to the cell range F4:F8.

   Next, you use the WEEKNUM Date function to determine the number of the week of each date entered in the range B10:B14.

4. Click cell C10 and then select the WEEKNUM function on the Date & Time button's drop-down menu. Click cell B10 to enter this address in the Serial_number text box and press Tab and type 2 in the Return_type text box and click OK.

   Excel returns 7 to cell C10, indicating that February 7th fell in the 7th week of 1989 when you designate Monday as the first day of the week.

5. Copy the WEEKNUM formula in cell C10 down to the cell range C11:C14.

   Next, you use the YEARFRAC Date function to determine what fractional part of a year the number of days elapsed between two dates represents.

6. Click C17 and select the YEARFRAC function at the very bottom of the Date & Time button's drop-down menu. Click cell A17 to enter this address in the Start_date text box. Then, press Tab and click cell B17 to enter its address in the End_date text box. Finally, press Tab and then type 3 in the Basis text box and click OK.

   Excel returns 0.19726 to cell C17.

7. Format the result in cell C17 with the Number format on the drop-down menu attached to the Number Format command button on the Ribbon's Home tab. Use the fill handle to copy this formula down to the cell range C18:C19.

   Now you're ready to check your formulas and their answers before you save your work.

8. Check your answers against those shown in the Date Formulas sheet in the Solved8-3.xlsx workbook file in your Chap8 subfolder in the Excel Workbook folder. When everything checks out, save your changes to the Date Function Practice.xlsx workbook (Ctrl+S) and then close the workbook.

Working with the Time Functions

Excel's Time functions are a smaller subset of the Date functions. They include the NOW function, which returns the current date and time; TIME, which creates a time fraction from values representing the hour, minutes, and seconds; and TIMEVALUE, which converts a time entered or imported into the worksheet as text so that you can use it in formulas that calculate elapsed times.

Try It

Exercise 8-4: Building Formulas with Common Time Functions

In Exercise 8-4, you practice using a few of Excel's Time functions. These Time functions, such as the Date functions you used in Exercises 8-2 and 8-3, are available on the Date & Time button's drop-down menu on the Ribbon's Formulas tab.

1. Open the Exercise8-4.xlsx file located in your Chap8 folder in the Excel Workbook folder on your hard disk.

   The file contains a Time Formulas worksheet that you can use to practice using some of the Time functions.

2. Display the current time in cell B1 using the NOW function and format the result with the 1:30 PM Time format.

   Next, use the TIME function to create various times using the hour, minutes, and seconds entered into the cell range A3:C8.

3. Click cell D3 and then select the TIME function on the Date & Time button's drop-down menu. Then, click A3 to enter its address in the Hour text box; press Tab and click cell B3 to enter its address in the Minute text box; and press Tab and click C3 to enter its address in the Second text box. Finally, click OK to close the TIME Function Arguments dialog box.

   Excel enters the time formatted as 1:10 AM in cell D3.

4. Open the Format Cells dialog box (Ctrl+1) and then format this cell with the Time type 1:30:55 PM sample. Then, use the fill handle to copy the formula down to the cell range D4:D7.

Excel displays the times with hours, minutes, and seconds displayed in this cell range.

5. Widen column D to display all the times. Then, copy the times calculated in the cell range D3:D7 and then paste their fractional values in the range E3:E7.

To paste only the values from a cell range, choose Home⇨Paste⇨Paste Values (or press Alt+HVV).

6. In cell B10, select the TIMEVALUE function on the Date & Time button's drop-down menu to convert the text entry in cell A10 to a bona fide time.

Excel returns the fractional time value 0.52083 to cell B10.

7. Open the Format Cells dialog box (Ctrl+1) and format the result in this cell with the 13:30:55 type time format and then copy this formula down to the cell range B11:B14.

Now you're ready to check your time formulas and their answers before you save your work.

8. Use the Side by Side feature to check your answers against those shown in the Time Formulas sheet in the Solved8-4.xlsx workbook file in your Chap8 folder inside your Excel Workbook folder. When everything checks out, click cell B1 in your Time Formulas worksheet and save it in a new workbook named Time Function Practice.xlsx inside your Excel Practice folder. Then exit Excel.

» Using the basic investment
   accumulation, discounting, and
   amortization functions

» Using the program's depreciation
   functions

Chapter 9

Financial Formulas and Functions

As the old song says, "Money makes the world go round." To that end, Excel supplies you with plenty of built-in functions for getting the latest spin on how much you're making and spending. In this chapter, you get the chance to practice using some of the basic investment, depreciation, and currency conversion functions that make up a part of the program's financial group.

Working with Financial Functions

Excel offers a fair number of sophisticated financial functions for determining such things as the present, future, or net present value of an investment; the payment, number of periods, or the principal or interest part of a payment on an amortized loan; the rate of return on an investment; and the depreciation of your favorite assets.

The key to using many of Excel's financial functions is in understanding the terminology used by their arguments. Many of the most common financial functions such as PV (Present Value), NPV (Net Present Value), FV (Future Value), and PMT (Payment) take similar arguments:

» Pv is the present value that is the principal amount of the annuity.

» Fv is the future value that represents the principal plus interest on the annuity.

>> Pmt is the payment made each period in the annuity. Normally, the payment is set over the life of the annuity and includes principal plus interest without any other fees.

>> Rate is the interest rate per period. Normally, the rate is expressed as an annual percentage.

>> Nper is the total number of payment periods in the life of the annuity. It is calculated by taking the Term (the amount of time that interest is paid) and multiplying it by the Period (the point in time when interest is paid or earned) so that a loan with a three-year term with 12 monthly interest payments has 3 x 12, or 36, payment periods.

REMEMBER

When using financial functions,the fv, pv, or pmt arguments can be positive or negative, depending on whether you're receiving the money (as in the case of an investment) or paying out the money (as in the case of a loan). You also need to express the rate argument in the same units as the nper argument. For example, if you make monthly payments on a loan and you express the nper as the total number of monthly payments (as in 360 (30 x 12) for a 30-year mortgage), you need to express the annual interest rate in monthly terms as well. So if, for example, you pay an annual interest rate of 7.5% on the loan, you express the rate argument as 0.075/12 so that it's monthly as well.

Using the Basic Investment Functions

The following six functions form the core Excel financial functions for determining whether a particular investment is worthwhile:

>> FV(rate,nper,pmt,[pv],[type]) — Future Value — calculates the future value of an investment, assuming a constant interest rate and constant payments on a periodic basis.

>> PV(rate,nper,pmt,[fv],[type]) — Present Value — calculates the present value of an investment; that is, the total amount that a series of future payments is worth now.

>> PMT(rate,nper,pv,[fv],[type]) — Payment — calculates the payment for a loan, assuming a constant interest rate and stream of payments.

>> RATE(nper,pmt,pv,[fv],[type],[guess]) calculates the interest rate for any type of annuity.

>> NPER(rate,pmt,pv,[fv],[type]) — Number of Periods — calculates how many periods are required for an investment, assuming a constant interest rate and constant payments on a periodic basis.

>> NPV(rate,value1,[value2],[. . .]) — Net Present Value — calculates the present value of an investment by using a discount rate and a series of future payments (negative values) and income (positive values).

As you can see in this list, the syntax of these functions is similar, requiring, with the exception of NPV, their own particular combination of the standard rate, nper, pmt, and pv arguments discussed in the previous section. The functions that use these combinations also take the following optional arguments (indicated in the square brackets):

>> [Pv] optional argument in the FV function is the present value or lump-sum amount for which you wish to calculate the future value: If you omit the pv argument, Excel assumes a present value of zero (0).

>> [Fv] optional argument in the PV, PMT, RATE, and NPER functions represents the future value or cash balance you want to have after making your last payment: If you omit the fv argument, Excel assumes a future value of zero (0).

>> [Type] optional argument in the FV, PV, PMT, RATE, and NPER functions indicates whether the payment is made at the beginning or the end of the period: Enter 0 (or omit the type argument) when the payment is made at the end of the period and use 1 when it is made at the beginning of the period.

>> [Guess] optional argument for the RATE function indicates the estimated rate percentage (assumed to be 10 percent if this optional argument is omitted). Note that this optional argument does not appear in the Function Arguments dialog box for the RATE function; therefore, you can only add this optional argument to the RATE function when you manually enter it into a cell's formula.

Try It

Exercise 9-1: Building Formulas with the FV, PV, PMT, RATE, and NPER Functions

In Exercise 9-1, you get a chance to practice using the FV, PV, PMT, RATE, and NPER financial functions to solve a series of seven real-world problems found on the four worksheets (FV, PV, PMT, and NPER) in the Exercise9-1.xlsx workbook file.

1. If Excel is not currently running, launch the program. Then open the Exercise9-1.xlsx workbook file inside your Chap9 folder in the Excel Workbook folder.

   Use the problems found on the FV, PV, PMT, and NPER worksheets in this workbook to practice creating financial formulas using the FV, PV, PMT, RATE, and NPER functions.

2. Position the cell cursor in cell C4 of the FV worksheet, the answer cell for Question 1, and then click the FV option on the Financial button's drop-down menu on the Ribbon's Formulas tab. Then, use the Hint cells in the range C7:C11 to construct the appropriate arguments for the FV function.

HINT

   When defining the arguments for your FV function in its Function Arguments dialog box, move the dialog box out of the way of the cell range B7:C11 and then click the appropriate cell in this range to define the three required (Rate, Nper, and Pmt) and two optional arguments (PV and Type) when the insertion point is located in its argument text box.

   Excel returns a future value of $5,938.43 in the answer cell C4 of the FV worksheet.

3. Position the cell cursor in cell C15 of the FV worksheet, the answer cell for Question 2, and select the FV option on the Financial button's drop-down menu to construct a formula using the FV financial function (with the appropriate cells in the range B18:C22 as its arguments) that calculates the total amount of money that you pay on the loan.

   Excel returns a future value of -$14,519.23 in the answer cell C15 of the FV worksheet.

   Now, switch to the PV worksheet and get some practice creating formulas that use the Present Value financial function.

4. Click cell C4 of the PV worksheet, the answer cell for Question 3, and then select the PV option on the Financial button's drop-down menu to construct a formula using the PV financial function (with the appropriate cells in the range B7:C11 as its arguments) that calculates the amount of money you should pay for the property.

   Excel returns a present value of -$718,227.17 in the answer cell C4 of the PV worksheet.

5. Position the cell cursor in cell C15 of the PV worksheet, the answer cell for Question 4, and select the RATE option on the Financial button's drop-down menu to construct a formula using the RATE financial function (with the appropriate cells in the range B7:C11 as its arguments) and your answer to Question 3 in cell C4 to check the interest rate.

   Excel returns an interest rate of 6.50% in the answer cell C15 of the PV worksheet (same as the rate entered into cell C7 of this worksheet).

6. Click cell C4 of the PMT worksheet, the answer cell for Question 5, and then select the PMT function on the Financial button's drop-down menu to construct a formula using the PMT financial function (with the appropriate cells in the range B7:C11 as its arguments) that calculates your monthly loan payment.

HINT

   Be sure that you convert the rate argument and the nper argument for the PMT function you construct to the equivalent months by entering the appropriate calculations to their cell references in the Rate and Nper argument text boxes of the Function Arguments dialog box for the PMT function. In that way, the annual interest rate in C7 is divided by 12 and the number of years in C8 is multiplied by 12.

   Excel returns a payment of -$3,987.02 to the answer cell C4 of the PMT worksheet.

7. Click cell C15 of the PMT worksheet, the answer cell for Question 6, and construct a formula using the PV financial function with the appropriate cells in the range B7:C11 as its arguments to check the loan amount you used in Question 5.

   The formula with the PV in cell C15 should compute the same $465,000 amount entered in cell C9 that you used as the PV argument of the PMT function in cell C4.

8. Click C4 of the NPER worksheet, the answer cell for Question 7, and then select the NPER function on the Financial button's drop-down menu to construct a formula using the NPER financial function (with the appropriate cells in the range B7:C11 as its arguments) that calculates how long it will take you to pay off your loan.

REMEMBER

   Be sure that you convert the answer returned by the NPER function in months to the equivalent years.

   Excel returns -13.64 years to the answer cell C4 of the NPER worksheet (after you divide the -163.71 months returned by the NPER function by 12).

9. Check your answers against those in the equivalent worksheets in the Solved9-1.xlsx workbook located in your Chap9 folder in the Excel Workbook folder.

   After you check your financial formulas and answers, you're ready to save your work in a new practice workbook.

10. Click cell A1 of the FV worksheet and save your work in a new workbook file named Financial Function Practice.xlsx in your Excel Practice folder. Close this new workbook.

Exercise 9-2: Building Formulas with the IRR and NPV Functions

The NPV function returns the sum of any series of cash flows, discounted to the present day, using a particular discount rate. The cash flows tracked by the NPV function are either income (money you make) indicated by positive numbers in the function's values argument, or payments (money you pay out) indicated by specifying negative numbers.

REMEMBER

When using the NPV function to determine the wisdom of an investment, this function assumes that the cash flows (be they income or payments) specified by the values argument(s) are all made at the end of the first period. As this assumption does not conform to the understanding of net present value in standard accounting, when using this function, you always need to include a Time 0 (even if its value is $0) for your answer to be in accord with the accepted definition of NPV.

In Exercise 9-2, you practice using both the NPV and IRR (Internal Rate of Return) functions to determine the advisability of making certain capital expenditures in the form of equipment purchases. The IRR function returns the interest rate received for an investment consisting of cash flows (income and payments) made at regular intervals. Note that unlike when using the RATE function, the cash flows do not have to be equal, although they must be made regularly on a periodic basis (monthly, quarterly, annually, and the like).

The IRR function computes its result using an iterative process (similar to that used to resolve certain circular references like the one you encountered in Chapter 7). For this reason, the function takes an optional guess argument, where you may specify your best guess or target percentage. If you don't specify a guess argument for an IRR function, Excel automatically uses 10% as its target.

1. Open the Exercise9-2.xlsx workbook file inside your Chap9 folder in the Excel Workbook folder.

   In this exercise, you finish the model constructed on its NPV & IRR worksheet. In doing so, you practice using the NPV and IRR functions to determine the financial wisdom of making capital expenditures in the form of purchased equipment, given the level of anticipated income resulting from the asset acquisition, the anticipated taxes on that extra income, and the depreciation of those assets over their three year life.

2. Select the cell range B3:C7 and then click the Create from Selection button on the Formulas tab or press Alt+MC to open Create Names from Selection dialog box. Make sure that only the Left Column check box is selected in this dialog box before you click OK.

   Excel assigns the row headings in B3:B7 to the cells in C3:C7.

3. Make the following entries in the designated cells:

   - **38000** in cell C3
   - **1500** in cell C4

- **15000** in cell C5
- **6%** in cell C6
- **27%** in cell C7

4. Click cell H10 and type =- (an equal sign followed by a minus sign with no spaces) and then click cell C3. Click the Enter button on the Formula bar.

   Cell H10 contains the formula =-Initial_Cost and returns the value -38,000 to the cell in the worksheet.

5. Click cell C11 and type = (an equal sign) and then click cell C5 before you click the Enter button on the Formula bar.

   Cell C11 contains the formula =Expected_Income and returns 15,000 to the cell in the worksheet.

6. Click cell D11 and then select the SLN (Straight LiNe depreciation) function on the Financial button's drop-down menu.

   The SLN function takes three arguments; cost, with the initial cost of your asset; salvage, with the value of the asset at the end of its useful life; and life, which indicates the number of years that the asset is expected to be in use.

7. While the insertion point is in the Cost argument text box, click cell C3 in the worksheet to insert the range name Initial_Cost in this box. Then, press Tab and click cell C4 to insert the range name Salvage_Value in the Salvage argument text box. Finally, press Tab again and type 3 in the Life argument text box and then click OK.

   Excel inserts an SLN function in cell D11 and returns the answer 12,167 to its cell in the worksheet.

8. Click cell E11 and construct a formula that subtracts the first-year depreciation amount in cell D11 from the pre-taxable income in cell C11.

   Excel returns 2,833 to cell E11.

9. Click cell F11 and construct a formula that deducts the estimated taxes using the tax rate percentage in cell C7 from the taxable income in cell E11.

   The standard way to construct this type of formula is to multiply the taxable income by 1 minus the tax rate. In this particular case, this formula in F11 would appear as

   ```
   =E11 * (1 - Tax_Rate)
   ```

   Excel returns an after-tax amount of 2,068 to cell F11.

10. Click cell H11 and there construct a SUM formula that adds the depreciation value in cell D11 to the after-tax income in cell F11 to the salvage value in cell G11. (I explain more about depreciation and salvage values in the next section of this chapter.)

    Excel inserts the formula =SUM(D11,F11,G11) in cell H11 and returns a sum of 14,235 to the cell in the worksheet.

11. Use the fill handle to copy the entries in the cell range C11:H11 down to the range C12:H13.

    Now, you're ready to build the formula that brings the salvage value in cell C4 to cell G13 in the table.

12. Click cell G13 and construct a formula with a reference to the Salvage_Value cell C4.

    This formula in cell G13 appears as

    ```
    =Salvage_Value
    ```

13. Click cell F2 and type = (equal sign), click cell H10 in the worksheet to select it, and type a space and then + (plus sign).

    The formula in the cell and on the Formula bar in F2 now reads

    ```
    =H10 +
    ```

14. Type another space, click the Financial button on the Formulas tab; click the NPV option on its drop-down menu to insert NPV() into the formula and open the Function Arguments dialog box. Click cell C6 to insert the Interest_Rate range name in the Rate argument text box. Press Tab and then select the cell range H11:H13 in the worksheet to insert this range address in the Value1 text box and then click OK.

    Excel inserts the following formula in cell F2 that computes the net present value of the investment in cell F2 as $1,310:

    ```
    =H10 + NPV(Interest_Rate, H11:H13)
    ```

15. Click cell H2 and then select the IRR option on the Financial button's drop-down menu to insert the function and open the Function Arguments dialog box. Select the cell range H10:H13 in the worksheet to insert this range address in the Values argument text box and then click OK.

    Excel computes an 8% internal rate of return on this investment, which is certainly acceptable.

16. Check your model against the one in the NPV & IRR worksheet in the Solved9-2.xlsx workbook in your Chap9 folder of your Excel Workbook folder.

    If everything checks out, proceed to the next step, where you change some of the basic assumptions of your model.

17. Enter the following values in the designated cells:

    • **1000** in the Salvage_Value cell C4

    • **12000** in the Expected_Income cell C5

    Note that at this salvage value and anticipated income amount, the net present value is a loss of $4,884, and the internal rate of return has now sunk to a dismal =-1%. With these figures, the capital investment is decidedly not a wise one.

18. Choose Home⇨Undo (or press Ctrl+Z) until you have restored the original salvage value and expected income figures to the spreadsheet.

Now you're ready to save your work.

19. Click cell A1 and then save your work in a new workbook named NPV & IRR Function Practice.xlsx in your Excel Practice folder and then close this new workbook.

Figuring the Depreciation of an Asset

The moment you put an asset you purchase into service, it begins to depreciate (lose value). Excel lets you choose between four different Depreciation functions, each of which uses a slightly different method for depreciating an asset over time. These built-in Depreciation functions include

» SLN to calculate straight-line depreciation

» SYD to calculate sum-of-years-digits depreciation

» DB to calculate declining balance depreciation

» DDB to calculate double-declining balance depreciation

All four depreciation functions require the following cost, salvage, and life arguments, and in addition, all except the SLN function require the period argument:

» *Cost*, indicating the initial cost of the asset that you're depreciating.

» *Salvage*, indicating the value of the asset at the end of the depreciation (also known as the salvage value of the asset).

» *Life*, indicating the number of periods over which the asset is depreciated (also known as the useful life of the asset).

» *Period*, indicating the period over which the asset is being depreciated. Note that the units you use in the period argument must be the same as those used in the life argument of the Depreciation function. For example, if you express the life argument in years, you must also express the period argument in years.

HINT

Note that DB function accepts an optional month argument. This argument is the number of months the asset is in use in the first year. If you omit this optional argument from your DB function, Excel assumes the number of months of service to be 12. Also, when using the DDB function, you can add an optional factor argument. This argument is the rate at which the balance declines in the depreciation schedule. If you omit this optional argument, Excel assumes the rate to be 2 (thus, the name *double-declining balance*).

Exercise 9-3 gives you an opportunity to practice using all four types of depreciation in a partially completed Depreciation Table that then enables you to compare the amount of depreciation each year in the useful life of an asset.

Exercise 9-3: Building Formulas with the SLN, SYD, DB, and DDB Depreciation Functions

In Exercise 9-3, you practice creating a depreciation table that uses all four types of depreciation functions: SLN, SYD, DB, and DDB.

1. Open the Exercise9-3.xlsx workbook file inside your Chap9 folder in the Excel Workbook folder.

    This workbook contains a Depreciation worksheet with a Depreciation Table comparing the four depreciation methods side by side that you will complete.

2. Select the cell range B3:C6 and then click the Create from Selection button on the Ribbon's Formulas tab or press Alt+MC to open the Create Names from Selection dialog box. Make sure that only the Left Column check box is selected in this dialog box and then click OK.

    Excel assigns the row headings in the range B3:B6 to the cells C3:C6 in the Depreciation worksheet.

3. Make the following entries in the designated cells:

    - **Office Furniture** in the Type_of_Asset cell, C3
    - **50000** in the Cost cell, C4
    - **10** in the Life_in_years cell, C5
    - **1000** in the Salvage cell, C6

4. Click cell C9 and construct a formula that references the Cost cell, C4, and then use the fill handle to copy this formula across the row to the cell range D9:F9.

    Now you're ready to build a formula that deducts the straight-line depreciation for the first year in cell C10.

5. Click cell C10 and type = (an equal sign). Then click cell C9 and type − (minus sign).

    The formula in the cell and on the Formula bar now reads

    `=C9−`

6. Click the SLN option on the Financial button's drop-down menu. Then, click C4 to insert the Cost range name in the Function Arguments Cost text box. Press Tab and then click C6 to insert the Salvage range name in the Salvage text box. Finally, press Tab and click cell C5 to insert the range name Life___in_years cell (C5) in the Life text box before you click OK.

    Excel inserts the formula =C9−SLN(Cost,Salvage,Life___in_years) and returns $45,100 in cell C10 in the worksheet.

7. Copy the formula in cell C10 down to the cell range C11:C19.

   Next, you need to construct a formula that calculates the first-year depreciation using the sum-of-years-digits method.

8. Click cell D10 and construct a formula that takes the cost amount in D9 and subtracts from the first-year depreciation returned by the SYD function using the following arguments:

   - Cost cell in the Cost text box
   - Salvage cell in the Salvage text box
   - Life___in_years cell in the Life text box
   - Cell B10 in the Per text box

9. Copy the formula in cell D10 down the cell range D11:D19.

   Now, you're ready to construct a formula that calculates the first-year depreciation using the declining balance method.

10. Click cell E10 and construct a formula that takes the cost amount in E9 and subtracts the first-year depreciation returned by the DB function using the following arguments:

    - Cost cell in the Cost text box
    - Salvage cell in the Salvage text box
    - Life___in_years cell in the Life text box
    - Cell B10 in the Period text box

11. Copy the formula in cell E10 down the cell range E11:E19.

    Next, you construct the formula that calculates the first-year depreciation using the double-declining balance method.

12. Click cell F10 and construct a formula that takes the cost amount in F9 and subtracts the first-year depreciation returned by the DDB function using the following arguments:

    - Cost cell in the Cost text box
    - Salvage cell in the Salvage text box
    - Life___in_years cell in the Life text box
    - Cell B10 in the Period text box

13. Copy the formula in cell F10 down the cell range F11:F19.

    Now your depreciation table is complete. All you have to do is check your table against the one in the Depreciation worksheet in the Solved9-3.xlsx workbook.

14. Check the formulas in your Depreciation worksheet against those in the Solved9-3.xlsx workbook file in your Chap9 folder in your Excel Workbook folder.

    When everything checks out, proceed to Step 15.

15. Make the following updates in the designated cells:

    - 25000 in the Cost Cell (C4)

    - 5 in the Life___in_years cell (C5)

    - 500 in the Salvage cell (C6)

    Note that when Excel finishes recalculating the Depreciation Table using your new inputs, the depreciation formulas in the Straight Line column (C) return negative values to all the rows below Year 5 and #NUM! error values to the SYD, Declining Balance, and Double-declining Balance columns.

16. Choose Home⇨Undo (or press Ctrl+Z) until you have restored the original Cost, Life___in_years, and Salvage values to cells C4, C5, and C6 in the table. Next, save your work in a workbook file named Depreciation Function Practice.xlsx in your Excel Practice folder before you close the file.

Chapter **10**

Using Math Functions

The Math & Trig group of functions includes a wide variety of mathematical functions for computing new values as well as for controlling the results of calculations. This group also includes a large assortment of trigonometric functions most often needed in engineering and scientific endeavors. In this chapter, you get a chance to practice using some of the math functions more commonly needed in spreadsheets for business applications.

Rounding Off Values

Rounding off numbers that have fractions is one of the more frequent tasks you may undertake in Excel. Excel includes three functions in the Math & Trig category that you can use for rounding off the numbers in a worksheet:

» ROUND(number,num_digits) to round the value specified by the number argument to the number of digits specified by the num_digits argument

» ROUNDUP(number,num_digits) to round up the value away from 0 (zero) that is specified by the number argument to the number of digits specified by the num_digits argument

» ROUNDDOWN(number,num_digits) to round down the value toward 0 (zero) that is specified by the number argument to the number of digits specified by the num_digits argument

What's the difference between using one of Excel's rounding functions to round off values to a particular decimal place and using a number format to control how many decimal places are displayed?

Formatting a number only changes the way the value appears in the cell, whereas rounding off a number with one of the Excel functions actually changes the number of digits in the value entered in that cell.

Try It

Exercise 10-1: Building Formulas with the ROUND, ROUNDUP, and ROUNDDOWN Functions

In Exercise 10-1, you practice using the ROUND, ROUNDUP, and ROUNDDOWN Math functions to change the precision of various values in a worksheet.

1. If Excel isn't running, launch the program. Then open the Exercise10-1.xlsx workbook file in your Chap10 folder in the Excel Workbook folder.

   This file contains a Rounding Functions worksheet, where you can practice using the ROUND, ROUNDUP, and ROUNDDOWN functions on the value of the mathematical constant pi (π), accurate to nine decimal places, returned by the PI function to cell A3.

2. Click cell B3 and then choose Formulas⇨Math & Trig⇨ROUND. Then, click cell A3 to insert its address in the Number text box of the Function Arguments dialog box. Press Tab, type 0 in the Num_digits text box, and click OK.

   B3 contains the formula =ROUND(A3,0) and displays 3 in its cell.

3. In cell B4, construct a formula with the ROUND function that rounds off the value of pi in cell A3 to one decimal place.

   Because all the rounding formulas you're going to create for this exercise use the same value in cell A3, you can save time by making copies of the original ROUND formula and then editing the function name and/or the num_digits argument in the copies as needed. To do this, however, you must remember to convert the reference to cell A3 from relative to absolute when constructing the formula with the Insert Function feature.

   B4 contains the formula =ROUND(A3,1) and displays 3.1 in its cell.

4. In cell B5, construct a formula with the ROUND function that rounds off the value of pi in cell A3 to two decimal places.

   B5 contains the formula =ROUND(A3,2) and displays 3.14 in its cell.

5. In cell B6, construct a formula with the ROUND function that rounds off the value of pi in cell A3 to three decimal places.

   B6 contains the formula =ROUND(A3,3) and displays 3.142 in its cell.

6. Click cell B7 and then choose Formulas⇨Math & Trig⇨ROUNDUP. Click cell A3 to insert its address into the Number text box of the Function Arguments dialog box. Then, press Tab, type **2** in the Num_digits text box, and click OK.

   B7 contains the formula =ROUNDUP(A3,2) and displays 3.15 in its cell.

7. In cell B8, construct a formula with the ROUNDUP function that rounds up the value of pi in cell A3 to four decimal places.

   B8 contains the formula =ROUNDUP(A3,4) and displays 3.1416 in its cell.

8. Click cell B9 and then choose Formulas⇨Math & Trig⇨ROUNDDOWN. Click cell A3 to insert its address into the Number text box of the Function Arguments dialog box. Then, press Tab, type **2** in the Num_digits text box, and click OK.

   B9 contains the formula =ROUNDDOWN(A3,2) and displays 3.14 in its cell.

9. In cell B10, construct a formula with the ROUNDDOWN function that rounds down the value of pi in cell A3 to four decimal places.

   B10 contains the formula =ROUNDDOWN(A3,4) and displays 3.1415 in its cell display. Compare your spreadsheet to the one shown in Figure 10-1. If everything checks out, proceed to Step 10.

10. Save your workbook file in your Excel Practice folder with the filename Round Off Practice.xlsx and then close the workbook.

FIGURE 10-1: A practice worksheet with ROUND, ROUNDUP, and ROUND-DOWN formulas.

	A	B	C	D
1	**Rounding Off Numbers**			
2	**Value of π**	**Rounding Off π**		**Rounding Function Used**
3	3.141592654	3		Round to zero digits
4		3.1		Round to one digit
5		3.14		Round to two digits
6		3.142		Round to three digits
7		3.15		Round up to two digits
8		3.1416		Round up to four digits
9		3.14		Round down to two digits
10		3.1415		Round down to four digits
11				

B10 — fx =ROUNDDOWN($A$3, 4)

Finding Products, Powers, and Square Roots

Although you can create formulas that multiply values using the asterisk (*) operator as well as those that raise a number to a particular power by using the caret (^), Excel also includes PRODUCT and POWER functions that perform these types of calculations for you. And for those times when you need to find the square root of a value, the program includes a SQRT function. These three Math functions work with the following arguments:

- » PRODUCT(number1,number2, . . .) where the number1 and number2 arguments are the values you want to multiply with one another

- » POWER(number,power) where the number argument is the value you want to raise to the power specified by the power argument

- » SQRT(number) where the number argument is the value for which you want the square root

Try It

Exercise 10-2: Building Formulas with PRODUCT, POWER, and SQRT

In Exercise 10-2, you practice using the Math & Trig PRODUCT function to calculate the product of a range of values, the POWER function to square and cube values, and the SQRT function to find the square root of values.

1. Open the Exercise10-2.xlsx workbook file in your Chap10 folder in the Excel Workbook folder.

   This file contains a Misc. Math Functions worksheet where you can practice using the PRODUCT, POWER, and SQRT functions in a couple of tables.

2. Click cell D3 and then choose Formulas⇨Math & Trig⇨PRODUCT. Drag through cells B3 and C3 to insert the range B3:C3 in the Number1 text box of the PRODUCT Function Arguments dialog box and click OK.

   D3 contains the formulas =PRODUCT(B3:C3) and displays 46 in its cell.

3. Format the computed amount in cell D3 with the Accounting Number Format button in the Number group of the Ribbon's Home tab and then copy this formula down to the cell range D4:D5.

   Next, you use the POWER function to square and cube values in the worksheet.

4. Click cell B9 and then choose Formulas⇨Math & Trig⇨POWER. Then, click A9 to insert its address in the Number text box of the Function Arguments dialog box. Press Tab, type **2** in the Power text box, and click OK. Then, copy this POWER formula down to the cell range B10:B11.

   Next, create a formula using the POWER function that cubes a value by raising the number to the power of 3.

5. In cell C9, construct a formula with the POWER function that cubes the value in cell A9 and then copy this POWER formula down to the cell range C10:C11.

   Now you use the SQRT function to find the square roots of values in the worksheet.

170 PART 2 **Using Formulas and Functions**

6. Click cell D9 and then choose Formulas⇨Math & Trig⇨SQRT to insert the function and open the Function Arguments dialog box. Then click cell A9 to insert its address into the Number text box of the SQRT Function Arguments dialog box and click OK. Then, copy this SQRT formula down to the cell range D10:D11.

Cell D11 returns a #NUM! error value in the cell because the SQRT function cannot compute square roots for negative numbers (multiplying one negative number by another always results in a positive product).

To avoid the #NUM! error in this formula, you can nest the ABS function that returns the absolute value of cell A11 (which is always positive) inside the SQRT function as follows:

```
=SQRT(ABS(A11))
```

7. Edit the original formula in cell D9 by positioning the insertion point between the T in SQRT and the open parenthesis. Type **(ABS** and then position the insertion point between 9 in A9 and the close parenthesis, and then type **)** (another close parenthesis). When you're done, click the Enter button on the Formula bar.

The edited formula should appear on the Formula bar as follows:

```
=SQRT(ABS(A9))
```

8. Copy this edited version of the SQRT formula with the nested ABS function over the original formula copies in the cell range D10:D11.

Check your results against those shown in Figure 10-2. If everything checks out, proceed to Step 9.

9. Save your workbook file in the Excel Practice folder with the filename Prod Power Sqrt Practice.xlsx and then close the workbook.

FIGURE 10-2:
A practice worksheet with PRODUCT, POWER, and SQRT formulas.

D11		fx	=SQRT(ABS(A11))	
	A	B	C	D
1				
2	Code	Price	Qty	Total Price
3	908978	$ 23.00	2	$ 46.00
4	456078	$ 45.00	3	$ 135.00
5	234478	$ 67.00	4	$ 268.00
6				
7				
8	Value	Squared	Cubed	Square Root
9	24	576	13824	4.898979486
10	35	1225	42875	5.916079783
11	-9	81	-729	3
12				

Doing Fancier Sums

Without any doubt, SUM is the preeminent function in the Math & Trig category. This function is so central to spreadsheet formula making that the Home tab of the Ribbon contains its own AutoSum button to facilitate the construction of all your SUM formulas.

The SUM function is not the only function in the Math & Trig category capable of computing totals. In addition, the program offers more specialized summing functions for use when you need to total the products or squares of the values in a range or total values only when a particular condition is met.

Summing products, squares, and their differences

You can use the SUMPRODUCT function to have Excel total the products returned by multiplying the values in corresponding arrays. For one array to correspond to another, each must consist of the same number of rows and columns.

For example, suppose you have a spreadsheet with a 2-x-1 array in the cell range B2:B3 that contains the values 4 and 5 (expressed as {4;5}), and another 2-x-1 array in the cell range D2:D3 that contains the values 6 and 3 (expressed {6;3}). (See Chapter 7 for a quick refresher on arrays.) Because both of these arrays have the same number of rows (2) and columns (1), they correspond and can be used as arguments in the SUMPRODUCT function.

The SUMPRODUCT function uses the following syntax:

```
SUMPRODUCT(array1,array2, ...)
```

Note that the SUMPRODUCT function accepts up to a maximum of 30 array arguments. The SUMPRODUCT function is not the only summing function to use these arguments. The following summing functions also follow the same syntax as SUMPRODUCT:

>> SUMX2MY2 (SUM X squared minus Y squared) to sum the difference between the squares of two corresponding arrays

>> SUMX2PY2 (SUM X squared plus Y squared) to return the grand total of the sums of the squares in two corresponding arrays

>> SUMXMY2 (SUM X minus Y squared) to sum the squares of the differences in two corresponding arrays

The SUMSQ function that totals the squares of the arguments is similar to these summing functions except that you can use individual numbers as well arrays for its arguments.

Exercise 10-3: Building Formulas with the SUMPRODUCT, SUMSQ, and SUMX2MY2 Functions

In Exercise 10-3, you practice using the Math functions SUMPRODUCT, SUMSQ, and SUMX2MY2 to calculate products and square roots in arrays that you've entered into a worksheet.

1. Open the Exercise10-3.xlsx workbook file in your Chap10 folder in the Excel Workbook folder.

   This file contains a SUM Formulas worksheet with two 2-x-1 arrays, the first in light yellow in the cell range B2:B3 and the second in light green in the cell range D2:D3. You use these arrays to practice using the SUMPRODUCT, SUMSQ, and SUMX2MY2 functions.

2. Click cell F6 and then choose Formulas⇨Math & Trig⇨SUMPRODUCT to insert the function and open the Function Arguments dialog box. Drag through cells B2 and B3 to enter the range address B2:B3 in the Array1 text box of the Function Arguments dialog box. Then, press Tab, drag through cells D2 and D3 to insert the range address D2:D3 in the Array2 text box, and click OK.

   Excel inserts the formula =SUMPRODUCT(B2:B3,D2:D3) into cell F6 and returns a result of 39 as the sum of the products of the two arrays.

3. Verify the calculated result returned by the SUMPRODUCT formula in cell F6 by constructing the following simple formulas in the designated cells that replicate the computation made by the SUMPRODUCT function:

   - Formula in cell C6 that multiplies the value in B2 by that in D2
   - Formula in cell D6 that multiplies the value in B3 by that in D3
   - Formula in cell E6 that adds the value in C6 to that in D6

   The calculated total returned to cell E6 should be 39, just like the one in cell F6 next door.

4. Click cell G8 and then choose Formulas⇨Math & Trig⇨SUMSQ to insert the function and open the Function Arguments dialog box. Then, select cell B2 in the worksheet as the Number1 argument and cell D2 as the Number2 argument in the SUMSQ Function Arguments dialog box and click OK.

   Excel returns a total of 52 to cell G8.

5. Verify the calculated result returned by the SUMSQ formula in cell G8 by constructing the following simple formulas in the designated cells that replicate its computation:

   - Formula in cell D8 that squares the value in B2
   - Formula in cell E8 that squares the value in D2
   - Formula in cell F8 that adds the value in D8 to that in E8

HINT

To square a value in a cell with a simple formula, insert the cell reference followed by the caret (^) operator and **2** (for example, =B2^2 to square the value in B2). To square a value with a function, select the POWER option on the Math & Trig button's drop-down menu and then select B2 as the Number argument and type **2** as the Power argument.

The calculated total returned to cell F8 should also be 52, matching the one in cell G8 next door.

6. Click cell G10 and then choose Formulas⇨Math & Trig⇨SUMSQ to insert the function and open the Function Arguments dialog box. Then, select the cell range B2:B3 as the Number1 argument and cell range D2:D3 as the Number2 argument and click OK.

   Excel inserts the formula =SUMSQ(B2:B3,D2:D3) in cell G10 and returns a sum of 86.

7. Verify the calculated result returned by the SUMSQ formula in cell G10 by constructing the following simple formulas in the designated cells that replicate its computation:

   - Formula in cell B10 that squares the value in B2
   - Formula in cell C10 that squares the value in B3
   - Formula in cell D10 that squares the value in D2
   - Formula in cell E10 that squares the value in D3
   - Formula in cell F10 that sums the values in cell range B10:E10

   The calculated total returned to cell F10 should now be 86, matching the one in cell G10.

8. Click cell G12 and then choose Formulas⇨Math & Trig⇨SUMX2MY2 to insert the function and open the Function Arguments dialog box. Then, select the cell range B2:B3 as the Array_x argument and cell range D2:D3 as the Array_y argument and click OK.

   Excel inserts the formula =SUMX2MY2(B2:B3,D2:D3) in cell G12 and returns a sum of –4.

9. Verify the calculated result returned by the SUMX2MY2 formula in cell G10 by constructing the following simple formulas in the designated cells that replicate its computation:

   - Formula in cell B12 that squares the value in B2
   - Formula in cell C12 that squares the value in B3
   - Formula in cell D12 that squares the value in D2
   - Formula in cell E12 that squares the value in D3
   - Formula in cell F12 that subtracts the sum of D12 plus E12 from the sum of B12 plus C12

   When constructing the formula in cell F12 that subtracts the sum of D12 plus E12 from that of B12 plus C12, be sure to enclose the values to be summed (B12+C12) and (D12+E12) in parentheses.

   The calculated total –4 returned to cell F12 should now match the one in cell G12.

10. Open the Solved10-3.xlsx workbook in the Chap10 folder in the Excel Workbook folder and check the results in your SUM Formulas sheet against its formulas. If everything checks out, save your work in a workbook in your Excel Practice folder with the file-name SumProd-Sq-Diff Practice.xlsx and then close this workbook.

Conditional totals

All the variations of the SUM function you've used up to now calculate their totals come rain or shine. The SUMIF function, however, is a little different: It only sums its designated values when a particular condition is true. The SUMIF function, although located in the Math & Trig category, could have just as easily been classified as one of the Logical functions (see Chapter 13) because it basically works only when its comparative condition returns the logical value TRUE. (Refer to Chapter 6 for a refresher on creating comparative formulas that return TRUE or FALSE as their answers.)

The syntax of the SUMIF function includes the following arguments:

```
SUMIF(range,criteria,[sum_range])
```

The range argument specifies the cells that you want Excel to evaluate using the condition or conditions specified by the criteria argument. The optional sum_range argument specifies the cells you want Excel to sum when the condition in the criteria argument is found TRUE. You only need to specify a sum_range argument when the cell range to be summed is not the same as the one whose values are evaluated as to whether they meet the condition set up by the criteria argument.

To get some practice using the SUMIF function, you work with the January Sales worksheet in the workbook containing the data list of the January sales for the fictitious company, Chris's Cookies. This data list tracks the sales by store location, the type of baked item sold (lemon tarts, blueberry muffins, Lots of Chips cookies, and strawberry pie), the date of sale, the number of dozens sold, the price per dozen, and the daily sales total. Most of these fields tracked in the data list have range names assigned to their data (Store_name to the data in the Store field, Date_sold to the data in the Date field, Item_sold to data in the Item field, and Daily_sales to the data in the Daily Sales field) that you can refer to in place of cell ranges in the formulas you construct using the SUMIF function.

Try It

Exercise 10-4: Using the SUMIF Function

In Exercise 10-4, you practice using the SUMIF function to calculate different totals depending upon conditions you specify.

1. Open the Exercise10-4.xlsx workbook file in your Chap10 folder in the Excel Workbook folder.

   Use its January Sales worksheet to practice using the SUMIF function by constructing a formula that uses this function to total the daily sales for all lemon tarts sold in the month of January.

2. Click cell I3 to select it, type **=sum** into the cell, and then double-click SUMIF on the drop-down menu that appears to select this function.

Excel inserts =SUMIF(in cell I3 and displays the arguments used by this function as a ScreenTip beneath the cell. This SUMIF function uses the Item_sold range as its range argument and the Daily_sales range as its sum_range argument. The condition for the criteria argument is where the item sold is equal to lemon tarts, which is expressed as follows:

```
"=lemon tarts"
```

Note that because you are evaluating a text string in this comparative expression that contains a space, you must enclose the entire criteria argument inside double quotation marks.

3. With the insertion point just inside the open parenthesis of the SUMIF function, click the Use in Formula button on the Formulas tab and then click Item_sold on its drop-down menu.

Excel inserts this range name as the range argument so that the formula in cell I3 now reads

```
=SUMIF(Item_sold
```

4. With the insertion point at the end of the Item_sold range name, type a comma (,) and then type **"=lemon tarts"** followed by another comma (,).

The formula in cell I3 now reads

```
=SUMIF(Item_sold,"=lemon tarts",
```

5. With the insertion point after the comma following the criteria argument in the SUMIF function, click the Use in Formula button on the Formulas tab and then click Daily_sales on its drop-down menu. Then, type **)** (a close parenthesis) to finish the formula and click the Enter button on the Formula bar to insert into cell I3.

The completed formula in cell I3 now reads

```
=SUMIF(Item_sold,"=lemon tarts",Daily_sales)
```

and the formula returns $815.00 to the cell.

6. Use the same technique to construct on your own a SUMIF function in cell I4 that totals the daily sales for just blueberry muffins.

Be sure the criteria argument for this SUMIF function includes the quotation marks:

```
"=blueberry muffins"
```

Cell I4 contains the formula =SUMIF(Item_sold,"=blueberry muffins",Daily_sales) and the formula returns $1,305.00 to the cell.

7. Construct a SUMIF function in cell I5 that totals the daily sales for just Lots of Chips cookies.

   Cell I5 contains the formula =SUMIF(Item_sold,"=lots of chips cookies",Daily_sales) and the formula returns $771.12 to the cell.

8. Construct a SUMIF function in cell I6 that totals the daily sales for just strawberry pie.

   Cell I6 contains the formula =SUMIF(Item_sold,"=strawberry pie",Daily_sales) and the formula returns $2,256.49 to the cell.

9. Construct a SUMIF function in cell I8 that totals the daily sales for all items except for strawberry pie.

   Use the <> operator with strawberry pie to have Excel exclude it from the total, while at the same time summing the daily sales for all the other baked items:

   ```
   "<>Strawberry pie"
   ```

   Cell I8 contains the formula =SUMIF(Item_sold,"<>strawberry pie",Daily_sales) and the formula returns $2,891.12 to the cell.

10. Click cell I10 and then save your work in your Excel Practice folder with the filename SumIf Function Practice.xlsx before closing the file.

» Finding the maximum and minimum values

» Counting the cells in a range of data

» Using the Statistical functions offered by the Analysis ToolPak add-in

Chapter **11**

Using Common Statistical Functions

Excel includes one of the most complete sets of statistical functions available outside of a dedicated statistics software program. These functions run the gamut from the garden-variety AVERAGE, MAX, and MIN functions to the more exotic CHITEST, POISSON, and PERCENTILE statistical functions. The program also offers an assortment of counting functions that enable you to count the number of cells that contain values, are nonblank (and thus contain entries of some kind), or count only the cells in a cell range that meet the criteria you specify. In this chapter, you get a chance to practice working with the most commonly used statistical functions, AVERAGE, MAX, and MIN, as well as the different counting functions.

Computing Averages

The average is the arithmetic mean computed by summing all the values to be averaged and then dividing this total by the number of values. Excel's AVERAGE function, which calculates the average of a range or series of values, uses the following syntax:

```
AVERAGE(number1,[number2],[...])
```

One way to understand the workings of the AVERAGE function is to display the corresponding SUM and COUNT formulas that return the exact same result. For example, suppose you want to find the average of the values in the cell range D4:D8 in your spreadsheet by entering the following formula in a cell:

```
=AVERAGE(D4:D8)
```

In place of this AVERAGE function, you could obtain the same result by entering the following formula:

```
=SUM(D4:D8)/COUNT(D4:D8)
```

Note that the COUNT function shown as the divisor in this equivalent formula returns the number of cells in the specified range that contain numeric entries. (See Exercise 11-3 for practice in using COUNT.)

REMEMBER

If the values in the number arguments of the AVERAGE function contain cells with text entries, logical values (TRUE or FALSE), or that are blank, Excel ignores them in the counting calculation (they are naturally ignored in the summing). However, if the cells in the number arguments contain 0 (zero) values, they are used in the counting calculation (even though they add nothing to the sum).

In addition to the AVERAGE function used to calculate the arithmetic mean in a range or series of values, Excel also includes a MEDIAN function, which takes the same kind of arguments. Instead of the arithmetic mean, the MEDIAN function returns the value that lies precisely in the middle of those in the range or series specified as its arguments, with half greater and half less.

Try It

Exercise 11-1: Building Formulas with the AVERAGE and MEDIAN Functions

In Exercise 11-1, you practice using the AVERAGE function to calculate the statistical average value in a range of values and the MEDIAN function to calculate the middle value in a range.

1. If Excel is not currently running, launch the program. Then, open the Exercise11-1.xlsx workbook file in your Chap11 folder inside the Excel Workbook folder.

   This workbook contains a Home Sales worksheet with a concise data table showing the recent house sales in a small subdivision during April and May. You can use the sampling in this sales table to practice using the AVERAGE and MEDIAN functions.

2. Select the cell range D4:D8 in the Home Sales worksheet. Click the Name box, type the range name, **Selling_price**, and press Enter.

   You use the range name Selling_price as the argument of the AVERAGE and MEDIAN functions in the formulas you now add to the Home Sales worksheet.

3. Click cell D10, type **=av**, and then double-click AVERAGE on the Function drop-down menu. Then, click the Selling_price on the Use in Formula button's drop-down menu

on the Formulas tab. Finally, type **)** — the close parenthesis — to complete the formula and then click the Enter button on the Formula bar to insert it in cell D10.

Cell D10 contains the formula =AVERAGE(Selling_price) and returns $743,500 to the cell.

4. Enter the following formula in cell E10:

```
=SUM(Selling_price)/COUNT(Selling_price)
```

As you can see, this division formula using the SUM and COUNT functions in cell E10 returns the same value as the AVERAGE function in D10.

5. Delete the formula in cell E10. Click cell D12 and then click the More Functions button on the Ribbon's Formulas tab. Then, highlight Statistical on its drop-down menu and click the MEDIAN option on the continuation menu. Then drag through the cell range D4:D8 in the worksheet to insert the range name Selling_price in the Number1 text box of the MEDIAN Function Arguments dialog box before you click OK.

D12 contains the formula =MEDIAN(Selling_price) and returns $645,000 to the cell. Note the difference between the average and the median sales price as computed by Excel in cells D10 and D12. The average selling price for a home in the sample shown in this table is nearly $100,000 more than the median.

6. Save your work in a new workbook file in your Excel Practice folder. Name the file Stat Function Practice.xlsx and leave this file open in Excel for the next exercise.

Finding the Highest and Lowest Values

The MAX and MIN functions compute the highest and lowest values in a cell range or series, respectively. They take the same type of arguments as the AVERAGE and MEDIAN statistical functions. Although they may not seem very powerful when using them on very small samples (such as the selling prices in the Home Sales worksheet you used in Exercise 11-1), where you can visually pick out the highest and lowest selling prices in an instant, they come in quite handy when dealing with large data sets, where it would take a long time to locate these key values.

Try It

Exercise 11-2: Building Formulas with the MAX and MIN Functions

In Exercise 11-2, you practice using the MAX Statistical function to return the highest value in a range and the MIN function to return the lowest value.

1. Use the Stat Function Practice.xlsx workbook you saved in your Excel Practice folder at the end of Exercise 11-1 to practice adding MAX and MIN functions to the spreadsheet table located on the Home Sales worksheet.

Begin by creating a formula in cell D14 that calculates the highest selling price in the Selling_price range (D4:D8).

2. Click in cell D14 in the Home Sales worksheet and construct a formula using the MAX function with the range name Selling_price (assigned in Exercise 11-1) as its argument to find the largest selling price in the range.

Cell D14 contains the formula =MAX(Selling_price) and Excel returns $1,085,000 to the cell as the highest selling price in this range.

3. Construct a formula in cell D16 using the MIN function with Selling_price as its argument to find the lowest selling price in the range.

Cell D16 contains the formula =MIN(Selling_price) and Excel returns $550,000 as the lowest selling price in the range.

4. Insert two new rows into the sales table immediately above the row containing the sales data for 566 Elm Street in the cell range B7:D7.

To insert two rows of blank cells in this table, select the cell range B7:D8 and then click the Insert command button in Cells group of the Ribbon's Home tab.

5. Update the sales table by making the following data entries into the newly inserted blank rows of cells:

- 211 River Road in cell B7, 5/15/2021 in cell C7, and 495000 in cell D7

- 8989 King Place in cell B8, 5/23/2021 in cell C8, and 1,500,000 in cell D8

Note the effect that your table edits have on the average price, high price, and low price cells in the spreadsheet as calculated by the AVERAGE, MAX, and MIN functions, respectively. The median price remains the same.

6. Save your changes and then close this workbook file.

Counting Cells

Excel includes three counting functions, COUNTA, COUNT, and COUNTBLANK. You can use these functions to build formulas that compute the number of cells in a particular region or worksheet that are occupied, contain numeric entries, or are blank. The syntax of these functions is as follows:

>> COUNTA(value1, [value2], [. . .]) to return the number of nonblank cells in the number argument(s)

>> COUNT(value1, [value2],[. . .]) to return the number of cells containing numeric entries in the number argument(s)

>> COUNTBLANK(range) to return the number of blank cells in the range argument

In addition to these standard counting functions, the program includes a COUNTIF function that works much like the SUMIF function you encountered in Chapter 10. You can use this function to return the count in a cell range of only those cells whose entries meet the condition you set up in its criteria argument. This function uses the following syntax:

```
COUNTIF(range, criteria)
```

HINT

When specifying a number for the criteria argument of the COUNTIF function, you enter the number or the reference to the cell that contains the number. When specifying a comparative expression or text for the criteria argument, you must remember to enclose the argument in a set of double quotation marks. For example, to use COUNTIF to find the number of cells in the range E15:E45 that contain the number 50, you would enter the following formula:

```
=COUNTIF(E15:E45, 50)
```

If, however, you want to know the number of cells in this range that contain values greater than or equal to 50, you would enter this formula:

```
=COUNTIF(E15:E45, ">=50")
```

Further, suppose that cell D10 contains the numeric entry 50 and you want to construct the COUNTIF formula using this cell reference in the criteria argument rather than the number itself. You would have to enter this version of the formula as

```
=COUNTIF(E15:E45, ">="&D10)
```

REMEMBER

The & (ampersand) acts as the concatenation text operator that connects text to another entry (in this case, it connects the text ">=" to the cell reference, D10) to produce one continuous entry. See Chapter 6 to brush up on all the operators that you can use with Excel.

WARNING

If you enclose a cell reference (such as D10 in the previous example) inside quotation marks in the COUNTIF criteria argument, Excel interprets the cell address as a text string to locate in the entries in the function's range argument.

Try It

Exercise 11-3: Building Formulas with the COUNT, COUNTBLANK, COUNTA, and COUNTIF Functions

In Exercise 11-3, you practice using the various COUNT Statistical functions to calculate the number of entries in a range of cells.

1. Open the Exercise11-3.xlsx workbook file in your Chap11 folder in the Excel Workbook folder.

   This workbook contains a version of the Home Sales worksheet that you can use to practice using the counting functions.

2. Select the cell range B1:D8 in the Home Sales worksheet. Click the Name box on the Formula bar, type **Sales_table**, and then press Enter.

   Excel assigns the range name Sales_table to the cell range B1:D8 so that you can use this range name as the argument of your formulas using the COUNT functions.

3. Click D12 and construct a formula using the COUNTA statistical function with Sales_ table as its argument that returns the number of cells with entries of any kind in this range.

   Cell D12 contains the formula =COUNTA(Sales_table) and returns 19 to the cell.

4. Position the cell cursor in D14 and construct a formula using the COUNT function with Sales_table as its argument that returns the number of cells with numeric entries in this range.

Cell D14 contains the formula =COUNT(Sales_table) and returns 10 to the cell.

5. Position the cell cursor in D16 and construct a formula using the COUNTBLANK function with Sales_table as its argument that returns the number of empty cells in this range.

Cell D16 contains the formula =COUNTBLANK(Sales_table) and returns 5 to the cell.

6. Position the cell cursor in cell D10 and construct a formula that computes the total number of cells in the Sales_table range.

HINT

The total number of cells in the Sales_table range is equal to the number of occupied cells returned by the COUNTA function in cell D12 plus the number of empty cells returned by the COUNTBLANK function in cell D16.

Cell D10 contains the formula =D12+D16 and returns 24 to the cell.

7. Position the cell cursor in cell D18 and create a formula with the COUNTIF function that returns the number of addresses within the cell range B4:B8 in the Sales table that have the word *Street* in them.

REMEMBER

When specifying text in the criteria argument of the COUNTIF function, you can use the * (asterisk) as the wildcard character to stand in for multiple, unnamed characters or the ? (question mark) to stand in for individual characters. For example, use "*Street" to find addresses of any length that end with the word Street.

Cell D18 contains the formula =COUNTIF(Sales_table,"*Street") and returns 2 to the cell.

8. Position the cell cursor in cell D20 and create a formula with the COUNTIF function that returns the number of selling prices just within the cell range D4:D8 of the Sales table that are above $600,000.

HINT

Don't forget to enclose the criteria argument with the > (greater than) operator in a set of double quotation marks.

Cell D20 contains the formula =COUNTIF(Sales_table,">600000") and returns 3 to the cell.

9. Enter the value **400000** in cell F3 and then format it with Accounting Number format with no decimal places.

You can now edit the formula with the COUNTIF function in cell D20 so that it refers to the contents of cell F3 rather than the static amount 600000.

10. Edit the formula in cell D20 so that the criteria argument immediately following the ">" (greater than) operator refers to contents in cell F3 rather than the static value of 600000.

HINT

When referring to a cell reference in the criteria argument of the COUNTIF function, don't omit the & (ampersand) text operator immediately following the ">" (greater than) operator and immediately preceding the reference to cell F3.

Cell D20 now contains the edited formula =COUNTIF(Sales_table,">"&F3) that returns 5 to the cell.

11. Replace the $400,000 entered into cell F3 with **$700,000**.

Note that the COUNTIF function immediately updates the result in cell D20 from 5 to 2 (only two entries in the range D4:D8, cells D4 and D8, have selling prices over $700,000).

Next, convert the label in cell C20 into a text formula (see Chapter 14 for details) that will reflect whatever value you happen to enter into cell F3.

12. Edit the contents of cell C20, Number of Selling Prices over $600,000, as follows:

```
="Number of Selling Prices over $"&F3
```

Start by pressing F2 and then the Home key to put the insertion point at the beginning of the text entry. Then, type = (equal sign) followed by " (double quote). Next, delete 600,000 at the end of the cell entry and then type a second " (double quote) followed by & (ampersand). Finally, click cell F3 and then click the Enter button on the Formula bar.

After you click the Enter button, the label, Number of Selling Prices over $700000, appears at the bottom of the Home Sales worksheet to the left of the value 2 in cell D20.

13. Change the value in F3 from 700000 to **500000**.

Cell D20 now contains 5 again and the label in C20 to the left reads Number of Selling Prices over $500000.

14. Use Excel's Side by Side feature to check your Home Sales worksheet against the one shown in the Solved11-3.xlsx workbook in the Chap11 subfolder of your Excel Workbook folder. When everything checks out, save your workbook as a new file named Count Function Practice.xlsx in your Excel Practice folder on your hard disk and then close the file.

Using the Statistical Functions in Analysis ToolPak Add-in

For you serious statisticians out there, the Analysis ToolPak add-in contains a whole bunch of extra statistical functions that may come in handy in your work. These supplementary statistical functions are automatically activated when you install Excel on your computer.

To use any of the functions included in the Analysis ToolPak add-in, select them from the Statistical category located in the Insert Function dialog box and on the drop-down menu that appears when you choose More Functions ⇨ Statistical on the Ribbon's Formulas tab.

Chapter **12**

Using Lookup Functions

The Lookup functions in the Lookup & Reference category of Excel functions are designed to automate the process of matching values in two separate lists or tables in a workbook and then returning a related value. For example, you can set up a price lookup table in a worksheet where you store and update the prices for all the items your company sells. After that, you construct formulas in a sales table using the appropriate lookup function that match an item number entered into a field in the sales table with an item number entered into the price lookup table. When the function finds a match between these item numbers, Excel then takes the price associated with that item number in the price lookup table and enters it into the appropriate field in the sales table.

The Reference functions are primarily designed to return specific types of information about particular cells or regions of a worksheet. This part of the Lookup & Reference category also includes functions that create hyperlinks to different worksheets and documents and that transpose the data in a table so that data that originally ran across the rows now runs down the columns, and vice versa.

In this chapter, you get a chance to practice creating formulas that automate table lookup, including looking up a single value, either across a row of a lookup data table or down one of its columns, as well as using the Lookup Wizard to perform a lookup that uses two values to find the matching data in a lookup data table.

Looking Up Stuff with XLOOKUP

In early February 2020, Microsoft released an Excel update for Microsoft 365 subscribers on Windows and Mac. That update included support for an XLOOKUP function, which Microsoft touted as a simpler and more versatile replacement for the very popular (yet oft maligned) lookup function VLOOKUP (and its horizontal cousin, HLOOKUP).

For those of you not yet familiar with VLOOKUP (deemed the third most-used function right after SUM and AVERAGE), this function searches the leftmost column of a specified range until it finds a value that matches or exceeds the target value, skips across to the column specified by an offset value, and then returns the data from that cell. Although tremendously useful for locating particular items in a long list or column of a range in your worksheet, the VLOOKUP function has several limitations. Here's how XLOOKUP improves upon those limitations:

>> XLOOKUP defaults to finding exact matches for your lookup value in the lookup range.

>> XLOOKUP can search both vertically (by row) and horizontally (by column) in a table, thereby replacing the need for using the HLOOKUP function when searching horizontally by column.

>> XLOOKUP can search left or right so that the lookup range in your lookup table doesn't have to be in a column to the left of the one designated as the return range for the function to work.

>> When the exact match default is used, XLOOKUP works even when values in the lookup range are not sorted in a particular order.

>> XLOOKUP can search from the bottom row to the top in the lookup array range, using an optional *search_mode* argument.

The XLOOKUP function has six arguments, the first three of which are required and the last three optional, using the following syntax:

```
XLOOKUP(lookup_value,lookup_array,return_array,[if_not_found],
    [match_mode],[search_mode])
```

The *lookup_value* argument designates the value for which you're searching; the *look_up* array argument designates the range of cells to be searched for this lookup value; and the *return_array* argument designates the range of cells containing the value you want returned when Excel finds an exact match.

REMEMBER

When designating the *lookup_array* and *return_array* arguments in your XLOOKUP function, both ranges must be of equal length; otherwise Excel returns the #VALUE! error to your formula. This is all more the reason for you to use range names or table column names when defining these arguments rather than pointing to them or typing their cell references.

The optional *if_not_found* argument specifies a text string to return to the formula if XLOOKUP fails to locate a matching value in the *lookup_array*.

The optional *match_mode* argument can contain any of the following four values:

- » 0 for an exact match (the default, same as when no *match_mode* argument is designated)
- » -1 for exact match or next lesser value
- » 1 for exact match or next greater value
- » 2 for partial match using wildcard characters: ? to match a single character and * to match any number of characters. To search for either a question mark or asterisk, precede the character with a tilde: ~? or ~*.

The optional *search_mode* argument can contain any of the following four values:

- » 1 to search first-to-last, that is, from top to bottom (the default, same as when no *search_ mode* argument is designated)
- » -1 to search last-to-first, that is, bottom to top
- » 2 for a binary search in ascending order
- » -2 for binary search in descending order

WARNING

Unfortunately, the XLOOKUP function is not backward compatible with earlier versions of Microsoft Excel that only support the VLOOKUP and HLOOKUP functions. This means that if you share a workbook containing XLOOKUP formulas with co-workers or clients who are using a version of Excel that doesn't support this new lookup function, all these formulas return #NAME? error values when they open its worksheet.

Try It

Exercise 12-1: Building Formulas that Use XLOOKUP to Perform Lookups in a Table

The best way to understand the power and versatility of the XLOOKUP function is to see it in action in an Excel worksheet. In Figure 12-1, I have a worksheet with sales data arranged by country.

FIGURE 12-1: A sample worksheet showing customer sales by country.

	A	B	C	D	E	F
1	Customer Sales by Country					
2					Lookup #1	
3	Country	Total Sales	Strength		Country	Total Sales
4	U.S.A.	$ 25,000.00	Strong		Costa Rica	
5	Canada	$ 18,500.00	Strong			
6	Mexico	$ 10,000.00	Moderate			
7	Costa Rica	$ 4,900.00	Weak			
8	Panama	$ 5,700.00	Moderate			
9						

In Exercise 12-1, you use XLOOKUP to return the total sales from this range in cell F4 based on the country you enter in cell E4 of the worksheet:

1. If Excel is not currently running, launch the program. Then, open the Exercise12-1.xlsx workbook file in your Chap12 folder in the Excel Workbook folder.

   This workbook contains the Customer Sales worksheet with the Customer Sales by Country table you need to practice using the XLOOKUP function.

2. Position the cell cursor in cell F4 of the worksheet.

3. On the Formulas tab, click Lookup & Reference and then click XLOOKUP.

   Excel displays the Function Arguments dialog box.

4. Click in the *Lookup_value* argument text box and then click cell E4.

5. Click in the *Lookup_array* argument text box, and then select the range A4:A8.

   A4:A8 is the range that XLOOKUP searches for whatever value you enter into cell E4.

6. Click in the *Return_array* argument text box, and then select the range B4:B8.

   B4:B8 is the range that XLOOKUP uses to select the return value based on the results of the search.

7. Click OK to enter the following XLOOKUP formula in cell F4:

   ```
   =XLOOKUP(E4,A4:A8,B4:B8)
   ```

8. Save your work in a new workbook named XLookup Function Practice.xlsx in your Excel Practice folder and then close this workbook file.

With Costa Rica entered into the lookup cell E4, your XLOOKUP function returns 4900 as the result because, as you can see in the sales table, this is indeed the total sales made for that country.

Returning Single Values from a Lookup Table

Before XLOOKUP came along, the most popular of the Lookup & Reference functions were the HLOOKUP (for Horizontal Lookup) and VLOOKUP (for Vertical Lookup) functions. The VLOOKUP function searches vertically (top to bottom) the leftmost column of a lookup table until the program locates a value that matches or exceeds the one you are looking up. The HLOOKUP function searches horizontally (left to right) the topmost row of a lookup table until it locates a value that matches or exceeds the one you're looking up.

The VLOOKUP function uses the following syntax:

```
VLOOKUP(lookup_value,table_array,col_index_num,[range_lookup])
```

The HLOOKUP function follows nearly identical syntax:

```
HLOOKUP(lookup_value,table_array,row_index_num,[range_lookup])
```

The arguments of these two lookup functions can be explained as follows:

>> The *lookup_value* argument designates the range that contains the values or text to be looked up in the table.

>> The *table_array* argument designates the range with the data table you want looked up in the lookup table as well as the data you want returned from the lookup table.

>> The *col_index_num* argument in the VLOOKUP function designates the number of the column in the lookup table (starting with 1 for the leftmost column and increasing by one with each column to the right) that contains the data you want returned to the data table.

>> The *row_index_num* argument in the HLOOKUP function designates the number of the row in the lookup table (starting with 1 for the topmost row and increasing by one down each row) that contains the data you want returned to the data table.

>> The optional *range_lookup* argument is a TRUE or FALSE value that indicates whether you want Excel to find an approximate match (TRUE or argument omitted) or exact match (FALSE) to numerical entries in the range designated by the function's lookup_value argument.

REMEMBER

When using the VLOOKUP and HLOOKUP functions, the text or numeric entries in the lookup column or row (that is, the leftmost column of a vertical lookup table or the top row of a horizontal lookup table) must all be unique (no duplicates allowed). These entries must also be arranged or sorted in ascending order; that is, alphabetical order for text entries, lowest-to-highest order for numeric entries. (See Chapter 17 for exercises on sorting data in a list or table.)

Performing a horizontal lookup

You use the HLOOKUP function when you're dealing with a lookup table where the data to look up is entered in the first (top) row, arranged sequentially (that is, alphabetically for text entries and from smallest to largest in the case of numeric entries) by columns from left to right. Figure 12-2 shows just such a lookup table at the top of the January Sales worksheet — the Price Lookup table in the cell range C3:F4.

First off, note that pastries listed in the top, lookup row of this Price Lookup table are text values arranged in alphabetical order from left to right as follows:

>> Blueberry muffins in cell C3

>> Lemon tarts in cell D3

>> Lots of Chips cookies in cell E3

>> Strawberry pie in cell F3

	A	B	C	D	E	F	G
1		Chris' Cookies - Daily Sales by Store for January					
2			Price Lookup Table				
3		Pastry	Blueberry muffins	Lemon tarts	Lots of chips cookies	Strawberry pie	
4		Price/Doz	3.75	2.50	1.89	8.99	
5							
6	No.	Store	Item	Date	Dozens	Price/Doz	Daily Sales
7	1	Mission Street	Lemon tarts	January 1	35		-
8	2	Mission Street	Blueberry muffins	January 1	28		-
9	3	Mission Street	Strawberry pie	January 1	42		-
10	4	Mission Street	Lots of chips cookies	January 1	18		-
11	5	Mission Street	Lemon tarts	January 2	19		-
12	6	Mission Street	Blueberry muffins	January 2	25		-
13	7	Mission Street	Strawberry pie	January 2	35		-
14	8	Mission Street	Lots of chips cookies	January 2	47		-
15	9	Mission Street	Lemon tarts	January 3	28		-
16	10	Mission Street	Blueberry muffins	January 3	36		-
17	11	Mission Street	Strawberry pie	January 3	18		-
18	12	Mission Street	Lots of chips cookies	January 3	23		-
19	13	Mission Street	Lemon tarts	January 4	14		-
20	14	Mission Street	Blueberry muffins	January 4	24		-
21	15	Mission Street	Strawberry pie	January 4	16		-
22	16	Mission Street	Lots of chips cookies	January 4	45		-
23	17	Mission Street	Lemon tarts	January 5	32		-

January Sales Sheet2 Sheet3 +

FIGURE 12-2: A sample worksheet with Price Lookup table immediately above the Daily Sales spreadsheet.

Second, note that the price per dozen for each pastry is listed in a corresponding column immediately below in the second row of the table (cell range, C4:F4). The order of the values in the cells in this row is dictated entirely by the order of their associated pastries in the row above.

Try It

Exercise 12-2: Building Formulas that Perform Horizontal Lookups in a Table

In Exercise 12-2, you use the information kept in this Price Lookup table to supply the missing information to the Price/Doz column in the Daily Sales data list below it. To do this, you construct a formula using the HLOOKUP function that matches the pastry listed as sold in the Item column of the data list (C7:C66) against the items shown in the top row of the Price Lookup table. It then returns the price per dozen for the matched item to the appropriate cell in the Price/Doz column in the data list (F7:F66).

1. Open the Exercise12-2.xlsx workbook file in your Chap12 folder in the Excel Workbook folder.

   This workbook contains the January Sales worksheet with the Price Lookup table and the Daily Sales data list you need to practice using the HLOOKUP function.

2. Using the Name box on the Formula bar, assign the following range names to the designated cell ranges:

   • Item_match to cell range C7:C66

   • Price_info to cell range C3:F4

3. Click cell F7 and then click the HLOOKUP option on the Lookup & Reference button's drop-down menu to insert the function and open the Function Arguments dialog box. Then, click and drag through the cell range C7:C66 to insert the range name Item_ match into the Lookup_value text box. Press Tab, and then drag through the cell range C3:F4 to insert the Price_info range name into the Table_array text box. Press Tab and then type **2** into the Row_index_num argument text box. Finally, press Tab, enter FALSE in the Range_lookup argument text box, and click OK.

Note that you enter 2 as the Row_index_num argument because you want Excel to return the appropriate prices from the second row (as you count down) of the Price_ info range. You enter FALSE into the Range_lookup argument text box because you only want exact matches between the pastries entered into the Item_match range (C7:C66) and the pastries entered into the top row of the Price_info range.

Cell F7 now contains the following formula:

```
=HLOOKUP(Item_match,Price_info,2,FALSE)
```

Excel returns 2.50 to the cell and also fills the formula down into the cell range F8:F66.

Check the prices returned by the copies of the original HLOOKUP formula in the top rows of the Daily Sales data list against those shown for the various pastries in the Price Lookup table. The price per dozen for the blueberry muffins is 3.75, strawberry pie is 8.99, and Lots of Chips cookies is 1.89.

4. Increase the price per dozen for Lots of Chips cookies in cell E4 of the Price Lookup table from 1.89 to 3.89.

Note that this change to the basic price is immediately updated in all the sales of Lots of Chips cookies in the Daily Sales data list. By using a lookup table to supply the basic price per dozen data to this list, you only need to make a single change to a price in the Price Lookup table to update every single sale of that item in the entire data list.

5. Save your work in a new workbook named HLookup Function Practice.xlsx in your Excel Practice folder and then close this workbook file.

Performing a vertical lookup

You use the VLOOKUP function when the data to look up is entered in the first (leftmost) column, arranged sequentially (that is, alphabetically for text entries and from smallest to largest in the case of numeric entries) by rows from top to bottom. Figure 12-3 shows you just such a vertical lookup table in the form of its Tip Schedule in the cell range B4:C103 (of which only the first twenty-some rows are visible in the figure).

The Tip Schedule in the Tip Lookup worksheet is arranged in two columns: Pretax Total and Tip Amount. Because the Pretax Total column is the first or leftmost column in this table, it contains the data to look up and match against the Food Total entered in cell F2 of this spreadsheet. As B is the lookup column, you note that its values are arranged in numerical order from smallest to largest.

	A	B	C	D	E	F	G
1							
2		**Tip Schedule**			Food Total	$9.33	
3		Pretax Total	Tip Amount		Tip		
4		0.00	0.15		Tax	0.70	
5		1.00	0.15		Total with Tip and Tax	$10.03	
6		2.00	0.30				
7		3.00	0.45				
8		4.00	0.60				
9		5.00	0.75				
10		6.00	0.90				
11		7.00	1.05				
12		8.00	1.20				
13		9.00	1.35				
14		10.00	1.50				
15		11.00	1.65				
16		12.00	1.80				
17		13.00	1.95				
18		14.00	2.10				
19		15.00	2.25				
20		16.00	2.40				
21		17.00	2.55				
22		18.00	2.70				
23		19.00	2.85				
24		20.00	3.00				
25		21.00	3.15				
26		22.00	3.30				

Tip Lookup Sheet2 Sheet3 +

FIGURE 12-3: A practice worksheet with Tip Schedule for looking up the tip amount based on the pretax food total.

Try It

Exercise 12-3: Building Formulas that Perform Vertical Lookups in a Table

In Exercise 12-3, you construct a formula using the VLOOKUP function that returns the tip amount to cell F3 from the Tip Amount column of the Tip Schedule table based on the Food Total entered into cell F2 and matched against the amounts listed in the Pretax Total column. Note that this represents a situation where you do not want Excel to use exact matching because the amount entered into the Food Total cell can often fall between the whole dollar amounts listed in the Pretax Total column of the Tip Schedule. When this happens (and you don't specify FALSE as the optional range_lookup argument in the VLOOKUP function), Excel returns the amount from the row above.

1. Open the Exercise12-3.xlsx workbook file in your Chap12 folder in the Excel Workbook folder.

   This workbook contains the Tip Lookup worksheet with the Tip Schedule that you need to practice using the VLOOKUP function.

2. Assign the following range names to the designated cells and cell ranges:

   • Food_total to cell F2

   • Tip_table to the cell range B4:C103

   When naming the Tip_table range, use the AutoSelect feature to select the cell range B4:C103 in a couple of clicks.

HINT

194   PART 2 **Using Formulas and Functions**

3. Click cell F3 and then click the VLOOKUP option on the Lookup & Reference button's drop-down menu to insert the function and open the Function Arguments dialog box. Then, click cell F2 in the worksheet to insert the range name Food_total into the Lookup_value argument text box. Press Tab and type **Tip_table** in the Table_array argument text box. Finally, press Tab and then type **2** into the Col_index_num argument text box. Click OK to close the VLOOKUP Function Arguments dialog box.

Cell F3 contains the formula =VLOOKUP(Food_total,Tip_table,2) and returns $1.35 to the cell.

Note that you enter **2** into the Col_index_num argument text box because you want Excel to return the appropriate tip amounts from the second column (as you count from left to right) of the Tip_table range. Note that you omit the optional Range_lookup argument for this particular VLOOKUP function because you want Excel to return a tip amount even when the program doesn't find an exact match between the amount in the Food_total cell and the whole dollar amounts listed in the Pretax Total column.

The Formula result shown at the bottom of the Function Arguments dialog box is a perfect example of this situation. Currently, the Food_total cell F2 contains $9.33. When Excel matches this in the Pretax Total column of the Tip Schedule, it does not find an exact match. In this case, it returns 1.35 as the formula result, the tip amount for a pretax total of 9.00 in row 13 of the Tip Schedule.

REMEMBER

When you don't use exact matching for numerical values Excel always selects the value from the row in the table_array argument in a VLOOKUP function or the column in an HLOOKUP function whose value is closest but doesn't exceed the value specified by the lookup_value argument.

4. Change the Food Total value in cell F2 from $9.33 to $87.20.

The moment you complete the edit in this cell, Excel returns a new tip amount of $13.05 to cell F3 (this tip amount is 15% of 87.00, the nearest value in the Tip Schedule that does not exceed the Food Total value).

5. Save your changes to the Tip Lookup worksheet in a new workbook in your Excel Practice folder. Name the workbook VLookup Function Practice.xlsx and then close the workbook file.

Chapter **13**

Using Logical Functions

The Logical function category is a small but powerful group of functions (including TRUE, FALSE, IF, AND, OR, and NOT) that you can use in decision-making formulas. (A decision-making formula is one where one set of values should be used or action taken when a particular condition is met and another when it is not.) You can also combine them with certain Information functions (such as ISBLANK, ISNUMBER, ISTEXT, and ISERROR) to create error-trapping formulas that prevent Excel error values (especially #DIV/0!, #NUM!, and #VALUE! errors) from spreading to other dependent formulas in the worksheet.

In this chapter, you get a chance to practice using the Logical functions in worksheets to create both decision-making and error-trapping formulas.

Working with the Logical Functions

The logical functions, as their name implies, deal exclusively with the logical values of TRUE and FALSE. With the exception of the TRUE and FALSE functions (the only purpose of which is to return the logical values TRUE and FALSE, respectively), the Logical functions IF, AND, OR, and NOT evaluate expressions entered as their arguments and return either TRUE or FALSE.

The granddaddy of all the logical functions is the IF function, which follows this syntax:

```
IF(logical_test,value_if_true,value_if_false)
```

The IF function works by evaluating a comparative expression that you enter as its logical_test argument as being either TRUE or FALSE. If the expression is found to be TRUE, Excel then uses the value or text or executes the expression you enter as the value_if_true argument of the function. If the expression is found to be FALSE, the program uses the value or text or executes the expression you enter as the value_if_false argument.

When entering a number or reference to a cell that contains a number or formula that returns a number for the value_if_true and value_if_false arguments, you simply enter the value or cell address. When entering text for these arguments, you need to enclose the text in a set of double quotation marks. And when entering an expression, you enter the operands and operator or function name and arguments as you would in any formula.

Constructing Decision-Making Formulas

The biggest use for the IF function is performing conditional operations in a formula: one set of operations when the IF condition expressed by its logical_test argument is found to be TRUE and another when it is not. These decision-making formulas can be one of two types: those formulas that perform their computations using alternate values depending upon the outcome of the condition, or those that perform alternate calculations based on the outcome.

Choosing between alternate values

Figure 13-1 shows an example where alternate values can be put to good use. The worksheet shown in this figure contains a variation of the Tip Lookup worksheet you encountered in Chapter 12. In this version, the Tip Schedule contains tip amounts for alternate tip percentages (15% in column C and 20% in column D), and the input section of the worksheet contains a Tip Percentage cell (G2), where the user can specify either 15 or 20 percent as the tip percentage.

A	B	C	D	E	F	G
1						
2		Tip Schedule			Tip Percentage	
3	Pretax Total	15% Tip	20% Tip		Food Total	$9.33
4	0.00	0.15	0.20		Tip	
5	1.00	0.15	0.20		Tax	0.70
6	2.00	0.30	0.40		Total with Tip and Tax	$10.03
7	3.00	0.45	0.60			
8	4.00	0.60	0.80			
9	5.00	0.75	1.00			
10	6.00	0.90	1.20			
11	7.00	1.05	1.40			
12	8.00	1.20	1.60			
13	9.00	1.35	1.80			
14	10.00	1.50	2.00			
15	11.00	1.65	2.20			
16	12.00	1.80	2.40			

FIGURE 13-1: The Tip Schedule with alternate 15% and 20% tip percentages.

To take advantage of the alternate percentages in this revised Tip Schedule in the following exercise, you need to nest an IF function inside the VLOOKUP function as its col_index_num argument. This IF function then selects the appropriate column of the Tip Schedule to use (2 for the 15% Tip amount in column C or 3 for the 20% Tip amount in column D), depending upon whether the Tip Percentage cell, G2, contains 15% or 20% as its data entry.

Exercise 13-1: Using the IF Function to Build Formulas that Select Alternate Values

In Exercise 13-1, you practice using the IF function with a VLOOKUP function to decide whether to give a 15% or 20% tip based on the amount of the food total.

1. If Excel is not currently running, open the program. Then, open the Exercise13-1.xlsx workbook file in your Chap13 folder in the Excel Workbook folder.

   You use this expanded version of the Tip Lookup worksheet to practice adding the IF function to a VLOOKUP function that selects between the 15% or 20% column of the Tip Schedule, depending upon which percentage is entered into the Tip Percentage cell, G2.

2. Click cell G2 to select it.

   This Tip Percentage cell can contain only one of two entries: 15% or 20%. Use Excel's Data Validation feature in this cell to ensure that it can contain no other data entry.

3. Choose Data ⇨ Data Validation on the Ribbon or press Alt+AVV to open the Data Validation dialog box.

   The Data Validation dialog box contains three tabs: Settings enables you to define what data is allowed in a cell; Input Message enables you to define a ScreenTip message indicating what type of data is allowed; and Error Alert enables you to define an error message that appears when a user tries to make an entry that is not allowed.

4. Click the List option in the Allow drop-down button on the Settings tab. Then, enter 15% and 20% in the Source text box separated by a comma (with no spaces, as in 15%, 20%) before you click OK.

   When you select the List as the Data Validation option, you can either select the cell range that contains the allowable data entries in the Source text box or type the allowable entries.

   Note when you close the Data Validation dialog box, Excel adds a drop-down button to cell G2. When you click this button, the drop-down list contains the only two allowed values for this cell: 15% or 20%.

5. Click the drop-down button that now appears on the right side of the Tip Percentage cell, G2, and then select 20% on its drop-down menu.

   Next, you need to assign some range names that you need to define the arguments for the formula with your VLOOKUP function.

6. Assign the following range names to the designated cells or cell ranges:

   - Tip_percent to cell G2

   - Food_total to cell G3

   - Tip_table to the cell range B4:D103

7. Click cell G4 and then type **=vl**. Next, double-click VLOOKUP that appears in the drop-down menu beneath cell G4 to display =VLOOKUP(in the cell with a list of VLOOKUP arguments appearing beneath it.

   As you may remember from Chapter 12, the VLOOKUP function takes the following arguments:

   - Lookup_value: Specifies the cell containing the value you want looked up in the first column of the vertical lookup table (the cell named Food_total, in this case).

   - Table_array: Specifies the cell range containing the values in the lookup table (the cell range named Tip_table, in this case).

   - Col_index_num: Specifies the number of the column, counting from left to right, that contains the values you want returned from the lookup table (in this case, that number is 2 when the Tip Percentage is 15% or 3 when the Tip Percentage is 20%).

8. Choose Formulas ⇨ Use in Formula and then click Food_total to paste the range named Food_total in the formula as the lookup_value argument. Then type a comma (,), choose Formulas ⇨ Use in Formula, and then click Tip_table to paste Tip_table into the formulas as the table_array argument. Finally, type a second comma (,) in preparation for entering the col_index_num argument.

   Now you need to construct a formula using the IF function for the col_index_num text argument. The IF function inserts 2 as the column index number when the cell named Tip_percent contains 15% as its entry; otherwise, it inserts 3. This is how this function should appear in the col_index_num argument text box:

   ```
   IF(Tip_percent=15%,2,3)
   ```

9. With the insertion point immediately following the second comma (separating the table_array and col_index_num arguments), choose Formulas ⇨ Logical ⇨ IF option to insert the function and open the Function Arguments dialog box. Click cell G2 to insert the Tip_percent range name in the Logical_test argument text box and then type **=15%**. Then, press Tab and then type **2** in the Value_if_true argument text box. Finally, press Tab again and then type **3** in the Value_if_false argument text box before you click OK.

   Excel displays an alert dialog box indicating that the formula that you're trying to enter in cell G4 contains an error (the formula needs a second close parenthesis to close off the arguments for the VLOOKUP function). This dialog box also suggests fixing this error by adding the second close parenthesis so that both the parentheses enclosing the arguments for both IF and VLOOKUP functions are balanced.

10. Click the Yes button or press Enter to have Excel correct the formula by adding a second close parenthesis **)** to close off the IF function nested as the col_index_num argument of the VLOOKUP function.

Cell G4 contains the formula

```
=VLOOKUP(Food_total,Tip_table,IF(Tip_percent=15%,2,3))
```

and this formula returns the value $1.80 (the tip amount for a food total of $9.33 at 20%). If this checks out, proceed to Step 11.

11. Change the Tip Percentage from 20% to 15% by positioning the cell cursor in cell G2 and then selecting 15% on its drop-down list.

Excel immediately decreases the tip amount in cell G4 from $1.80 to $1.35.

12. Increase the food total in cell G3 to 75.50.

Excel increases the tip amount in cell G4 from $1.35 to $11.25.

13. Type **17** in the Tip Percentage cell and then click the Enter button on the Formula bar.

Excel beeps at you and displays an error dialog box with the message, "This value doesn't match the data validation restrictions defined for this cell."

14. Click the Cancel button and then open the Data Validation dialog box again (choose Data ⇨ Data Validation on the Ribbon or press Alt+AVV).

Now, you create an input message that the user sees whenever he selects the cell.

15. Click the Input Message tab and then, in the Input Message text box, type **Click this drop-down button and then select 15% or 20% on its drop-down list.**

Next, create an error message that is displayed whenever a user tries to enter a value that is no longer allowed.

16. Click the Error Alert tab and then, in the Error Message text box, type **The entry in this cell is limited to 15% or 20% only! Click Cancel and then select 15% or 20% on the cell's drop-down list.** Then, click OK to close Data Validation dialog box.

A text box with your input message now appears next to the lower-right of cell G2.

17. Click the text box with your input message and drag it up until the top of the message box is even with the top of the Tip Percentage cell, G2, and position its left edge so that it's now touching the cell's drop-down button without obscuring any part of it.

18. Type **12** in the Tip Percentage cell, G2, and then press Enter.

This time, Excel displays your custom error message in its error alert dialog box.

19. Select the Cancel button in the error alert dialog box to close it and restore the current 15% entry to the cell.

20. Click cell A1 and then save your work in a new workbook called Alt VLookup Practice. xlsx in your Excel Practice folder and then close the workbook file.

Selecting between alternate calculations

In addition to selecting alternate values, you can use IF functions to perform alternate calculations depending upon the outcome of the condition stated by its logical_test argument. A common situation is to have Excel perform the calculation only when the IF condition is TRUE and perform no computation when it is FALSE.

Figure 13-2 shows you an example of this situation. Here, you see a slightly different version of the Spring Sale worksheet that you use in earlier exercises. This table contains a Discounted column, which determines whether a furniture item is to be discounted based on its suggested retail price listed in the Retail Price column. It also contains a Discount Amount column, which computes the amount of the discount only if the Discounted column indicates that the furniture item is eligible for a discount.

FIGURE 13-2:
The Spring Sale
table with
Discounted
and Discount
Amount
columns.

	A	B	C	D	E	F
1						
2			Spring Sale Furniture Prices			
3	Code	Description	Retail Price	Discounted	Discount Amount	Sales Price
4	02-305	36-inch round table	1,250.00			$1,250.00
5	02-240	72-inch dining table	1,400.00			$1,400.00
6	04-356	Hutch	2,500.00			$2,500.00
7	01-234	Side chair	350.00			$ 350.00
8	03-003	Armchair	500.00			$ 500.00
9	01-240	Armoire	1,750.00			$1,750.00

Try It

Exercise 13-2: Using the IF Function to Build Formulas that Perform Alternate Calculations

In Exercise 13-2, you construct the necessary formulas with IF functions for this version of the Spring Sale worksheet. One set to determine whether the furniture item should be discounted and another set to compute the discount amount only when the item is eligible for the discount.

1. Open the Exercise13-2.xlsx workbook file in your Chap13 folder in the Excel Workbook folder.

   You use this expanded version of the Spring Sale worksheet to practice constructing the formulas with IF functions needed to determine whether a furniture item is eligible for a discount. If it is, you create formulas to compute the discount amount and sale price.

2. Position the cell cursor in cell D4, where you build the formula that determines whether the 36-inch round table is to be discounted.

   The determinant for eligibility for a discount is whether the suggested retail price is greater than or equal to $1,000. In terms of the Logical_test argument text box, you need to create this type of comparative expression using cell C4, as in

   ```
   C4>=1000
   ```

3. Choose Formulas⇨Logical⇨IF to insert the function and open the Function Arguments dialog box. Then, click cell C4 in the worksheet to insert its address in the Logical_test argument text box and type **>=1000** before pressing Tab. Then, type **Yes** in the Value_if_true argument text box and press Tab again. Type **No** in the Value_if_false argument text box. Press Tab and note that Excel has automatically surrounded these last two argument values with double quotation marks. Click OK.

   Cell D4 contains the formula =IF(C4>=1000,"Yes","No") and the formula returns Yes to the cell because the value currently entered into cell C4 is indeed greater than 1000.

4. Use the fill handle to copy this formula in D4 down to the cell range D5:D9.

   Now, you need to create a formula using the IF function that checks whether the cell in the Discounted column contains "Yes" or "No" and then calculates the discounted amount accordingly.

5. Click cell E4 and then choose Formulas⇨Logical⇨IF to insert the function and open its Function Arguments dialog box. Then, fill in the three argument text boxes in this dialog box with the following values:

   - **D4="Yes"** in the Logical_test argument text box
   - **C4*20%** in the Value_if_true argument text box
   - **0** in the Value_if_false argument text box

   Click OK in the Function Arguments dialog box. Cell E4 now contains the formula

   ```
   =IF(D4="Yes",C4*20%,0)
   ```

   and the formula returns 250.00 to the cell because cell D4 contains Yes (the value in C4 is greater than 1,000). Therefore, the formula calculates a discount of 20% (1250*0.20=250).

6. Use the fill handle to copy this formula in cell E4 down to the cell range E5:E9.

   In the final table, all the furniture items except for the Side chair and Armchair should be discounted and have discounted amounts computed in column E.

7. Use Excel's Side by Side feature to check your results against those shown in the Solved13-2.xlsx workbook file in your Chap13 folder. If everything checks out, click cell A1 and then save your changes to a new workbook named If Function Practice.xlsx in your Excel Practice folder. Leave this file open for Exercise 13-3.

Nesting IF functions

IF functions in decision-making formulas are great when you're dealing with situations that only require two alternatives — one that comes into play when a certain condition exists, and the other that comes into play when it does not. But what about a situation where you have more than two alternatives?

For example, in the Spring Sale worksheet you used in the previous IF function exercise, suppose you still only want to discount furniture that retails over $1,000, but want to use two different discount amounts as well: 15% for suggested retail prices that are lower than $1,500, and 20% for suggested retail prices that are greater than or equal to $1,500.

To accommodate such a case, you would have to nest a second IF function within the original one, making the second nested IF function either the value_if_true or value_if_false argument of the original. Specifically, in the Spring Sale worksheet example, you would nest the second IF function as the value_if_true argument of the original IF function. The first IF condition then tests if the furniture item is to be discounted (indicated by a Yes in the Discounted column, meaning that the item's retail is above $1,000). If this item is found to be eligible for a discount, the second value_if_true argument IF function determines whether it receives a 20% or 15% discount.

TIP

Although I don't discuss it in detail in this chapter, you should know that if you have a scenario where you need to make three or more logical decisions, forget about nesting IF functions and turn instead to the powerful IFS function:

```
IFS(logical_test1, value_if_true1, [logical_test2, value_if_true2,...])
```

IFS consists of a series of logical tests, each of which has an associated return value. The function performs each logical test in order and, when IFS comes upon the first logical test to return TRUE, it returns that logical test's associated value. You can include up to 127 test/value pairs.

Try It

Exercise 13-3: Building Formulas with Nested IF Functions

In Exercise 13-3, you practice nesting IF functions in a single formula so that you can add more conditions that automatically determine what calculations are performed.

1. Use the If Function Practice.xlsx workbook file you created in Exercise 13-2. (If you don't have access to this file, open the Solved13-2.xlsx workbook in your Chap13 folder in the Excel Workbook folder.)

    You use this version of the Spring Sale worksheet with the completed formulas in the Discounted and Discount Amount columns to practice using one IF function as an argument of another.

2. Select cell E4. On the Formula bar, place the insertion point immediately in front of the C in C4 in the value_if_true argument of the IF function in this cell.

    You now edit the formula by inserting another, nested IF function.

3. Type **IF(** — open parenthesis — and then click cell C4 in the worksheet.

    The edited formula on the Formula bar should now read:

    ```
    =IF(D4="Yes",IF(C4C4*20%,0)
    ```

4. Type **>=1500,** — a greater than and equal sign, 1500, and a comma — to complete the value_if_true argument for the new nested IF function.

    The edited formula on the Formula bar should now read:

    ```
    =IF(D4="Yes",IF(C4>=1500,C4*20%,0)
    ```

5. Click the I-beam mouse pointer to position the insertion point between the % (percent sign) and the comma (,) immediately preceding 0 in this formula. Be sure not to press the → key.

6. Type a comma (,) and then click cell C4 in the worksheet.

   The edited formula on the Formula bar should now read:

   ```
   =IF(D4="Yes",IF(C4>=1500,C4*20%,C4,0)
   ```

7. Type ***15%)** — that is, an asterisk, 15%, and a close parenthesis — to complete the value_if_false argument for the nested IF function.

   The final edited formula on the Formula bar should now read:

   ```
   =IF(D4="Yes",IF(C4>=1500,C4*20%,C4*15%),0)
   ```

   In essence, this edited form of the formula with nested IF function in the value_if_true argument of the original IF function is saying

   - Evaluate the contents of cell D4 and, if Excel finds that this cell contains Yes as its entry, the program evaluates the contents of cell C4; otherwise, it just enters 0 (zero) in the current cell.

   - If Excel does end up evaluating the contents of cell C4, the program checks to see if this cell contains a value greater than or equal to 1,500. If the cell does, it then multiplies this value by 20%; otherwise, the program multiplies the value in C4 by 15%.

8. Click the Enter button on the Formula bar and then copy this edited formula down to the cell range E5:E9.

   In this version of the Spring Sale table, the Hutch and Armoire are now discounted 20%, the 36-inch round table and 72-inch dining table are both discounted 15%, and the Side and Armchairs still receive no discount at all.

9. Use Excel's Side by Side feature to check your results against those shown in the Solved13-3.xlsx workbook file in your Chap13 folder inside your Excel Workbook folder. If everything checks out, click cell A1 and then save your changes in the If Function Practice.xlsx workbook and then close this file.

Constructing Error-Trapping Formulas

Sometimes, you know ahead of time that certain error values are unavoidable in a worksheet as long as certain data entries are missing. The most common error value that gets you into this kind of trouble is the #DIV/0! error value. This error value appears not only when the divisor in a division formula is actually 0 (zero) but also when the divisor refers to an empty cell (which carries the numerical equivalent) in which you haven't yet had an opportunity to make any data entry (as when generating a new workbook from an Excel template file).

Fortunately, you can use the IF function to suppress the appearance of such error values in formulas. When you do this, you not only get the benefit of not having to look at them (there is, after all, nothing subtle about them), but you also ensure that they don't spread to any other parts of the worksheet containing dependent formulas. This means that in suppressing the display of error values in their original formulas, you also end up trapping them in their original cells.

When using IF functions in the construction of error-trapping formulas, you often use them in combination with some of the functions in the Information category, the most versatile of which is the ISERROR function. This nifty little function evaluates the cell reference you specify as its value argument and returns TRUE if the cell contains any of those pesky error values (#N/A, #VALUE!, #REF!, #DIV/0!, #NUM!, #NAME?, and #NULL!) and FALSE if it contains any other kind of entry. You can use its little brother function, ISERR, to test for all error values in a cell, excluding #N/A, for Not Available, which some users do not consider an error value per se.

Figure 13-3 shows a situation where you need to construct an error-trapping formula. Here, you see an empty version of the Production Schedule worksheet that is on its way to being saved as an Excel template file. Before that can happen, however, you would need to suppress all those #DIV/0! error values in the cell range B9:J9 until you begin entering the production quota figures for the corresponding months. (The error values appear because cell K7 with the grand total that it used as the divisor in their formulas contains a zero, 0.) The way you do this is to create a formula that traps this error in the original formula and all its copies.

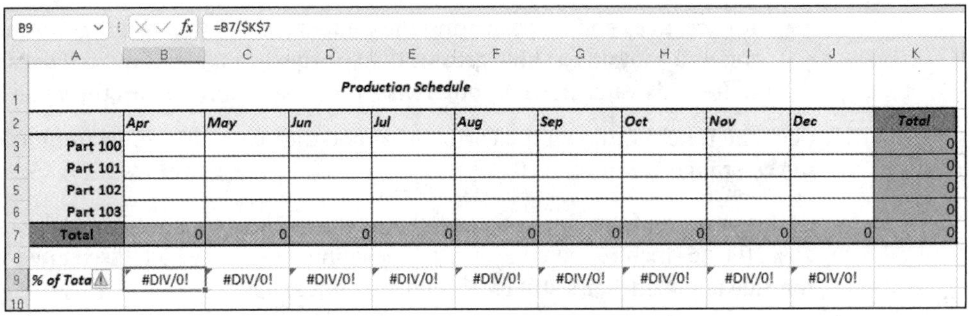

FIGURE 13-3: An empty Production Schedule worksheet with #DIV/0! Error values.

Exercise 13-4: Building Formulas that Trap Errors

In Exercise 13-4, you practice creating formulas with IF functions that trap #DIV/0! error values in the worksheet by replacing them with zeros so that they don't spread throughout the worksheet.

1. Open the Exercise13-4.xlsx workbook in your Chap13 folder in the Excel Workbook folder.

   You use this empty version of the Production Schedule worksheet to practice constructing error-trapping formulas using the IF function.

2. Click cell B9 that contains the original division formula.

   You need to edit this formula by adding an IF function that inserts 0 (zero) rather than the #DIV/0! error value in the cell if cell K7 is empty or contains 0 (zero) as is currently the case.

3. Press F2 to place Excel in Edit mode and then press the ← key to position the insertion point between = (equal to sign) and the B in B7. Then, type **IF(** — open parenthesis — and then select cell K7.

   The edited formula in the cell and on the Formula bar should now read:

   ```
   =IF(K7B7/$K$7
   ```

4. Press F4 one time to convert the relative cell reference, K7, to the absolute reference, $K$7. Then, type **=0,0,** (that is, the equal to sign followed by zero, a comma, and then another zero and comma). Finally, click the I-beam mouse pointer at the very end of the formula, after the 7 in the final $K$7 cell reference to position the insertion point there and then type **)** — close parenthesis.

   The final, edited formula in the cell and on the Formula bar should now read:

   ```
   =IF($K$7=0,0,B7/$K$7)
   ```

5. Click the Enter button on the Formula bar to complete this edit and enter the edited formula with the IF function into cell B9.

   In place of that ugly #DIV/0! error value in cell B9, the benevolent 0.00% should now appear.

6. Copy the edited formula in cell B9 to the right of the cell range C9:J9.

   Now all the #DIV/0! error values are gone from the Production Schedule worksheet, replaced by 0.00% entries.

7. Position the cell cursor in cell B3 and enter the #N/A value using the NA function in the Information function category from the More Functions drop-down menu on the Formulas tab.

   The NA function is one of those few Excel functions that doesn't require any arguments; therefore, you can use this function to enter the #N/A error value into the current cell simply by entering **=NA()** and clicking the Enter button.

   Note that the moment you enter the #N/A value into B3, this error value spreads to the subtotal cells, K3 and B7, and from there to the grand total in cell K7, and from there to all the division formulas that use its value as their divisor.

   To trap this in cell K7 and prevent its spread to the cell range B9:J9, you need to edit the original formula in cell B9 by adding the ISERROR function and then copy this version across the columns of this row.

8. Position the cell cursor in cell B9 and then edit the IF function in this cell's formula by replacing the logical_test argument, $K$7=0, with **ISERROR($K$7)**.

   Don't forget to enclose the $K$7 as the value argument of the ISERROR function in its own pair of open and close parentheses nested within the IF function's pair of open and close parentheses.

   The final, edited formula in the cell and on the Formula bar should now read:

   ```
   =IF(ISERROR($K$7),0,B7/$K$7)
   ```

9. Copy this new version of the error-trapping formula to the cell range C9:J9.

   As soon as you finish copying this revised error-trapping formula, Excel replaces all the #N/A values in this % of Total cell range with 0.00%, restricting the #N/A values to the production table itself without enabling these values to spread beyond it.

10. Position the cell cursor in the Home cell, A1, and then save your work in a new workbook file named Error Trap Practice.xlsx in your Excel Practice folder. Close this file.

» Creating formulas that combine
text entries stored in different
cells

» Changing the case of text entries
using the Text functions

Chapter **14**

Text Formulas and Functions

At first, thinking about text formulas and functions in spreadsheets may seem strange, accustomed as we all are to thinking of spreadsheets as number crunchers. Nevertheless, not only can you construct formulas that use text as operands with the special concatenation or linking operator, but you can also build formulas using a number of functions in Excel's Text category that require text exclusively in their arguments.

In this chapter, you practice building text formulas that link together separate text cell entries whose text should be entered together in the same cell. You also use text functions to convert text entries to the proper upper- and lowercase letters.

Constructing Text Formulas

Basic text formulas (that is, those that don't rely on any text functions) merely join pieces of text — often called *strings* — together using the & (ampersand) operator. It's the so-called concatenation operator. (In Excel, *concatenation* means to join one or more strings.) Here are a couple of caveats to keep in mind about text formulas:

>> The text operands must be enclosed in sets of quotation marks.

>> Spaces and/or punctuation must be included in the operands (and within the quotes) if you don't want the text to glom together as a single hard-to-read clump of letters.

For example, if you want to create a text formula in cell B2 that joins the word Summary to the text entry Order, entered in cell A2, and you enter the following formula in this cell:

```
=A2 & Summary
```

Excel returns the #NAME? error value because you didn't enclose the text Summary in quotation marks. Note that this is necessary even when the text you're entering is just a single word with no spaces.

Also, suppose you have the first name Keith entered in cell A3, and the last name Smith entered next door in cell B3, and you enter the following text formula in cell C3:

```
=A3 & B3
```

Excel returns to cell C3 the following glommed-together text:

```
KeithSmith
```

To have the text formula return the first and last name separated by the customary space, you need to enter this version of the text formula in cell C3:

```
=A3 & " " & B3
```

Note that in this version, the space (entered by pressing the spacebar) is enclosed in quotation marks.

EXAMPLE

Q. When would I typically need to create text formulas in a worksheet?

A. You may often work with tables where pieces of information such as the first, middle, and last name as well as the person's title along with his street, city, state, and zip code are all stored in separate cells (for purposes of sorting). Text formulas that join these separate pieces of information can save hours of retyping when you need to reassemble this disparate information in mailing lists.

Try It

Exercise 14-1: Building Simple Text Formulas that Join Data Entries

In Exercise 14-1, you practice building text formulas that join pieces of text entered into different cells of a worksheet together as a long string in other cells.

1. If Excel is not currently running, launch the program. Then open the Exercise14-1.xlsx workbook file in the Chap14 folder in the Excel Workbook folder.

   You use the entries in the Client Addresses list in its Text Formulas worksheet to practice creating simple text formulas.

2. Position the cell cursor in cell G1 and construct a text formula that joins the text entry Client in cell B1 with the text entry Addresses in cell C1.

Add a space enclosed inside quotation marks and sandwiched between & (ampersand) operators in the middle of the cell references to prevent the two text entries from being joined into ClientAddresses in the cell.

Cell G1 contains the formula

```
=B1&" "&C1
```

and the formula returns Client Addresses to the cell.

3. Choose Home ⇨ Copy (or press Ctrl+C) to copy the formula in cell G1 to the Clipboard. Click cell B1 and then choose Home ⇨ Paste ⇨ Paste Values.

Excel pastes the text and not the formula on top of the Client entry in cell B1.

Note the repetition of Addresses in G1, which still contains the formula that combines the text in B1 (Client Addresses) with the text entry in C1 (Addresses) so that it now reads Client Addresses Addresses.

4. Delete the Addresses entry in cell C1.

Although both B1 and G1 now show Client Addresses, in cell B1, this is the result of a text entry created from a copy of the original text formula; whereas in G1, it's the result of the original text formula you constructed.

5. Position the cell cursor in cell G3 and construct a new text formula that joins the house number in cell A3 with the street name in B3.

The text formula you enter in cell G3 should appear on the Formula bar as

```
=A3&" "&B3
```

Although the entry in cell A3 is the number 123 (not entered as a text with a preceding quotation mark nor formatted with the Text format), Excel has no problem joining this value to the obvious text entry in cell B3 using the concatenation operator.

6. Copy the text formula in cell G3 down to the cell range G4:G17 and then use AutoFit to widen column G as needed to display all the concatenated street addresses.

7. Position the cell cursor in cell H3 and construct a text formula that combines the city name in cell C3 with the state abbreviation in cell D3 and the zip code in cell E3, making sure that there is a comma and a space immediately following the city and a space between the state and zip code.

Be sure that you enclose the comma and the trailing space after the reference to cell C3 with the city in quotation marks, as in

```
=C3&", "&
```

Cell H3 contains the formula

```
=C3&", "&D3&" "&E3
```

and the formula returns Centerville, IL 60789 to the cell.

8. Copy the text formula in cell H3 down to the cell range H4:H17 and then use AutoFit to widen column H as needed.

Now you're ready to construct a text formula that combines the concatenated text in cell G3 with that in H3 to make one long text entry.

9. Position the cell cursor in cell I3 and construct a formula that joins the text in cell G3 with that in cell H3. Make sure that this formula inserts a comma and a trailing space between the street address in cell G3 and the city, state, and zip in cell H3.

Cell I3 contains the formula

```
=G3&", "&H3
```

and the formula returns 123 Niles Avenue, Centerville, IL 60789 to the cell.

10. Copy the text formula in cell I3 down to the cell range I4:I17 and then use AutoFit to widen column I to suit (you may also have to scroll the screen to the right to display all the data).

Finally, you need to sort these addresses.

11. With the cell range I3:I17 still selected, choose Data⇨Sort A to Z (or press Alt+ASA). When the Sort Warning dialog box appears, select the Continue with the Current Selection option button, and then click Sort. (Excel is concerned that you forgot to include data that needs sorting in the cell range G3:H17.)

Note that nothing changes in the order of the addresses in the selected range when you finish the Sort operation. This is because the cells contain text formulas rather than the actual text entries you see displayed. If you want to be able to find and sort text entries that you create in a worksheet with text formulas, you need to replace the formulas with their values. In this particular case, you copy the value on top of the formulas, thereby replacing them.

12. With the cell range I3:I17 still selected, choose Home⇨Copy (or press Ctrl+C). Next, without doing a thing to the cell selection, choose Home⇨Paste⇨Paste Values (or press Alt+HVV).

Excel replaces the formulas with their calculated values in the same range. (You can verify this because the contents of the Formula bar now reads 123 Niles Avenue, Centerville, IL 60789, instead of =G3&", "&H3.)

13. Choose Data⇨Sort A to Z (or press Alt+ASA) again, select the Continue with the Current Selection option button, and then click Sort.

Note how, at the time you use the Sort A to Z option, Excel rearranges the text in the cell selection.

14. Choose Data⇨Sort Z to A option (or press Alt+ASD). In the Sort Warning dialog box, select the Continue with the Current Selection option button, and then click Sort.

This time, Excel arranges the addresses in descending order (following the street number.) For more on how Excel sorts values, see Chapter 17.

15. Position the cell cursor in cell A1 and then save your work with the filename Text Frmls Practice.xlsx in your Excel Practice folder and leave the workbook open to complete Exercise 14-2.

Using Text Functions

Excel's Text functions offer a wide variety of methods for searching and manipulating text entries in a worksheet. These functions include the CONCAT function for joining together strings of text (specified as its text arguments) — just like the & (ampersand) operator in the handmade formulas you constructed in Exercise 14-1 — and, perhaps even more useful to most, the UPPER, LOWER, and PROPER functions for changing the capitalization of text entries in the worksheet. (Most of the other Text functions are seldom required outside of macros and specialized VBA programming applications.)

Figure 14-1 shows you an example of a worksheet that is in desperate need of the PROPER function, which changes the case of the text specified as its sole argument to Title case, where only the first letter in each word is uppercase.

	A	B
1	**Client List**	
2	*Last Name*	*First Name*
3	AIKEN	CHRISTOPHER
4	AIKEN	CLAY
5	AIKEN	SEAN
6	BRYANT	MICHAEL
7	DUONG	JOANNA
8	SMITH	CANDACE
9	GOODMAN	STEPHEN
10	HENDON	KATE
11	MCAVOY	MARCIA
12	MCCLINTON	INGRID
13	MUNDELL	BETH
14	PETERSON	KATIE
15	SHAFER	JO ANN
16	SPEH	JOHN
17	SPEH	SUZANNE
18		

FIGURE 14-1: The Client List worksheet with the names in all capital letters.

As you can see in this figure, both the first and last names of each of the clients in the list are all uppercase letters and need to be converted to Title case. This is a situation that you sometimes encounter when using tables stored in text files that you import with the Text Import Wizard into an Excel worksheet. (This wizard opens automatically when you try to open a text file.)

Exercise 14-2: Building Formulas with Text Functions that Join Data Entries and Change Their Case

Exercise 14-2 shows you how to take care of problems in a worksheet using the PROPER function. Knowing how to convert text entries to the desired case in a worksheet is very important because it can literally save you from hours of text editing, not to mention retyping, both of which are a colossal waste of your time.

1. Open the Exercise14-2.xlsx workbook file in your Chap14 folder in the Excel Workbook folder.

   Use the uppercase first and last name text entries in the Client List in its Text Functions worksheet to practice using a couple of Excel's Text functions.

2. Click cell C3 and then choose Formulas⇨Text⇨PROPER to insert the function and open its Function Arguments dialog box. Click cell A3 in the worksheet to enter its cell reference into the Text Argument text box in the Function Arguments dialog box and then click OK.

   Cell C3 contains the formula =PROPER(A3) and this formula returns Aiken to the cell.

3. Use the fill handle to copy this formula with the PROPER function down to the cell range C4:C17 and then over to the cell range D3:D17.

   Note that all the first and last name entries are now correct with the exception of Mcavoy (which should be McAvoy) in cell C11 and Mcclinton in cell C12 (which should be McClinton). You have to manually edit these entries later as the PROPER function is only able to deal with the first letters in words.

4. Click cell E3 and then choose Formulas⇨Text⇨CONCAT to insert the function and open its Function Arguments dialog box. Then, click cell D3 in the worksheet to enter its cell reference in the Text1 Argument text box and then press Tab. Type " (a double quotation mark), press the spacebar, and then type " (a double quotation mark) to insert a blank space in the Text2 Function Argument text box before you press Tab. Finally, click cell C3 in the worksheet to enter its cell reference in the Text3 Argument text box and click OK.

   Cell E3 contains the formula = CONCAT(D3," ",C3) and this formula returns the text Christopher Aiken to the cell.

5. Copy the formula in cell E3 down to the cell range E4:E17 and then use AutoFit to widen column E.

   Now, you need to replace the text formulas with the CONCAT functions with their text so that you can edit and sort the names in this list.

6. Replace the CONCAT formulas in the selected cell range E3:E17 by choosing Home⇨Copy and then Home⇨Paste⇨Paste Values.

7. Edit the entries in E11 and E12, changing Mcavoy in cell E11 to McAvoy and Mcclinton in cell E12 to McClinton.

8. Choose View⇨Arrange All (or press Alt+WA) to open the Arrange Windows dialog box and then click the Vertical option button before you click OK.

   Excel now displays windows with parts of the Exercise14-2.xlsx workbook and Text Frmls Practice.xlsx workbook side by side.

9. Scroll the Text Functions worksheet in the Exercise14-2.xlsx workbook so that column F is visible in the window.

   Now, you're ready to copy the addresses from the Text Formulas sheet of the Text Frmls Practice.xlsx workbook to the Text Functions sheet of the Exercise14-2.xlsx workbook.

10. Click a cell in the Text Formulas worksheet in the Text Frmls Practice.xlsx workbook to make it active and then scroll until column I comes into view and select the cell range I3:I17 (containing the concatenated addresses).

11. Choose Home⇨Copy, switch to the Text Functions worksheet in the Exercise14-2.xlsx workbook, click cell F3, and then choose Home⇨Paste⇨Paste Values.

   Excel copies the addresses into the cell range F3:F17 in the Text Functions worksheet.

12. Click the Close button in the upper-right corner of the Text Frmls Practice.xlsx workbook window followed by the Don't Save button in the alert dialog box.

   Now, maximize the Text Functions worksheet of the Exercise14-2.xlsx workbook so that it fills the Worksheet area.

13. Click the Maximize button in the upper-right corner of the Exercise14-2.xlsx workbook window.

   Next, widen column F in the Text Functions worksheet so that all the copied addresses fit within it.

14. Use the AutoFit feature to widen column F in the Text Functions worksheet.

15. In cell G3, create a formula using the CONCAT text function that joins the first and last name in cell E3 with the address information in cell F3, making sure to add a comma and trailing space after the last name.

   Cell G3 contains the formula

   ```
   =CONCAT(E3,", ",F3)
   ```

   and the formula returns Christopher Aiken, 788 Rincon Road, Bend, OR 97700 to the cell.

16. Copy the formula in cell G3 down to the cell range G4:G17 and then widen column G and scroll the worksheet as needed to completely display the names and addresses in this range on your screen.

   Next, you want to replace the Text formulas with their text so that you can sort them in alphabetical order.

17. Replace the formulas in the cell range G3:G17 with their text values. Choose Data ⇨ Sort A to Z, select the Continue With the Current Selection option, and then click Sort.

Check your results against those shown in Figure 14-2. If they match, proceed to the final step.

18. Select cell A1 and then save your work in a new workbook named Text Func Practice. xlsx in your Excel Practice folder. Then, close the workbook file as you exit Excel.

	E	F	G
1			
2			
3	Christopher Aiken	788 Rincon Road, Bend, OR 97700	Beth Mundell, 2091 Elm View Drive, Casa, CA 90345
4	Clay Aiken	78 Main Street, Hillsdale, CO 30405	Candace Smith, 3412 15th Street, Merry, RI 2903
5	Sean Aiken	775 St. George St., Nestor, MT 59800	Christopher Aiken, 788 Rincon Road, Bend, OR 97700
6	Michael Bryant	665 Peach Tree Ln., Statesburg, VA 23405	Clay Aiken, 78 Main Street, Hillsdale, CO 30405
7	Joanna Duong	450 East 72nd St., Middleton, IA 50456	Ingrid McClinton, 228 Anderson Ave., Covina, CA 90210
8	Candace Smith	3412 15th Street, Merry, RI 2903	Jo Ann Shafer, 1345 Baker Street, Littleton, NY 14200
9	Stephen Goodman	25 Walnut Circle, Myrtle, TX 75700	Joanna Duong, 450 East 72nd St., Middleton, IA 50456
10	Kate Hendon	2341 Tulip Drive, Redford, WA 98030	John Speh, 123 Niles Avenue, Centerville, IL 60789
11	Marcia McAvoy	234 James Blvd., Crabtree, NH 3304	Kate Hendon, 2341 Tulip Drive, Redford, WA 98030
12	Ingrid McClinton	228 Anderson Ave., Covina, CA 90210	Katie Peterson, 1400 S. Center St., Meteor, NV 89420
13	Beth Mundell	2091 Elm View Drive, Casa, CA 90345	Marcia McAvoy, 234 James Blvd., Crabtree, NH 3304
14	Katie Peterson	1400 S. Center St., Meteor, NV 89420	Michael Bryant, 665 Peach Tree Ln., Statesburg, VA 23405
15	Jo Ann Shafer	1345 Baker Street, Littleton, NY 14200	Sean Aiken, 775 St. George St., Nestor, MT 59800
16	John Speh	123 Niles Avenue, Centerville, IL 60789	Stephen Goodman, 25 Walnut Circle, Myrtle, TX 75700
17	Suzanne Speh	1045 Vincent Street, Yarrow, PA 15120	Suzanne Speh, 1045 Vincent Street, Yarrow, PA 15120
18			

FIGURE 14-2: The concatenated worksheet after sorting the names and addresses in column G alphabetically by first name.

3

Working with Graphics

Chapter **15**

Charting Worksheet Data

Besides the actual data entry and building the formulas for a worksheet, charting the data may well be one of the most essential tasks you perform in Excel. When you present worksheet data in a visual form, relationships between the data that were not apparent in numerical form often become quite obvious. Fortunately, Excel offers you a wealth of different types of charts with which to depict these relationships. Half the fun of charting is selecting the most appropriate chart type and customizing it to your needs.

In this chapter, you get a chance to practice charting worksheet data, both in the worksheet and on separate chart sheets. You also get practice with customizing the various parts of the basic chart so that they present the data in the clearest possible way.

Understanding Excel Charts

Excel charts are directly tied to the worksheet data they represent in the worksheet. As a result, the editing changes you make to the underlying data have a direct and immediate effect on their contents (somewhat analogous to the way that changes you make to data entries referred to in a formula immediately affect the calculated result when Automatic Recalculation is in effect).

Figure 15-1 shows you a typical clustered column chart created as part of a worksheet from the data in a worksheet table (not currently visible). As you see in this figure, a typical Excel chart contains a variety of distinct elements (explained in Table 15-1). It's important that you become familiar with these elements: Each is an editable part of the chart that you're often required to modify after construction of the basic chart.

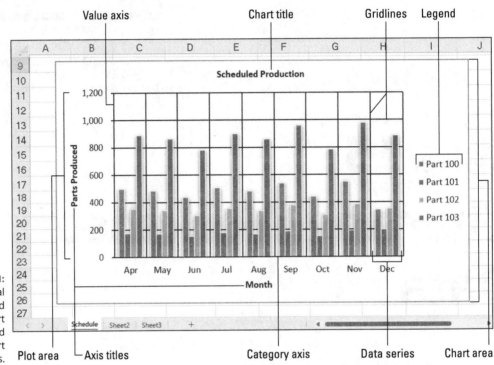

Excel not only offers you a wide array of basic chart types from which to choose, but it also enables you to decide where you want to place the chart — either in the worksheet along with the data it represents graphically or on a separate chart sheet in the workbook.

A chart like the one shown in Figure 15-1 that is placed on the worksheet is referred to as an embedded chart (although it's not so embedded that you can't still move and resize it on the worksheet as needed). Figure 15-2, on the other hand, shows you this same clustered column chart now on its own chart sheet.

TIP

You select and manipulate a chart sheet in the Excel workbook via its sheet tab, just the same as you do with a regular worksheet.

EXAMPLE

Q. What benefits do I get from placing a chart on its own chart sheet rather than embedding it in the worksheet?

A. Charts that you place on their own chart sheets generally print larger and are easier to print. All you have to do is select the chart sheet before you open the Print panel in Backstage View (File ⇨ Print). In addition, you may find it somewhat easier to edit a chart that you place in its own sheet because you don't have to worry about inadvertently selecting the chart area when you intend to select the chart title or legend for editing.

Table 15-1   Typical Chart Elements

Element	Description
Chart	Everything inside the chart window including all parts of the chart (labels, axes, data markers, tick marks, and other elements in this table).
Data marker	A symbol on the chart, such as a bar in a bar chart, a pie in a pie chart, or a column in a column chart, that represents a single value in the worksheet. Data markers with the same shape, pattern, or color represent a single data series in the chart.
Chart data series	A group of related values, such as all the values in a single row in the worksheet — all the production numbers for Part 100 in the sample chart, for example. A chart can have just one data series (shown in a single bar or line), but it usually has several.
Series formula	A formula describing a given data series. The formula includes a reference to the cell that contains the data series name, references to worksheet cells containing the categories and values plotted in the chart, and the plot order of the series. The series formula can also have the actual data used to plot the chart. You can edit a series formula and control the plot order.
Axis	A line that serves as a major reference for plotting data in a chart. Two-dimensional charts have two axes — the x (horizontal) axis and the y (vertical) axis. In most two-dimensional charts (except, notably, bar charts), Excel plots categories (labels) along the x-axis and values (numbers) along the y-axis. Bar charts reverse the scheme, plotting values along the x-axis. Pie charts have no axes. Three-dimensional charts have an x-axis, a y-axis, and a z-axis. The x- and y-axes delineate the horizontal surface of the chart. The z axis is the depth axis, showing the depth of the third dimension in the chart.
Tick mark	A small line intersecting an axis. A tick mark indicates a category, scale, or chart data series. A tick mark can have a label attached.
Plot area	The area where Excel plots your data, including the axes and all markers that represent data points.
Gridlines	Any optional lines extending from the tick marks across the plot area, making it easier to view the data values represented by the tick marks.
Titles	The labels you add to identify the chart. You can add a chart title to identify the entire chart, a horizontal axis title to identify the data on the x- or category axis, and a vertical axis title to identify the data (and units) on the y- or value axis.
Legend	A key that identifies patterns, colors, or symbols associated with the markers of a chart data series. The legend shows the data series name corresponding to each data marker (such as the name of the red columns in a column chart).

Try It

Exercise 15-1: Modifying an Existing Embedded Chart

In Exercise 15-1, you practice working with an embedded clustered bar chart that has already been added to a worksheet to visually represent the number of parts produced each month for a year.

1. If Excel is not currently running, launch the program. Then open the Exercise15-1.xlsx workbook file in your Chap15 folder in the Excel Workbook folder.

    You use the embedded clustered column chart in the Schedule worksheet to practice selecting different parts of the chart and switching the chart placement between embedding in the worksheet and placing it on a separate chart sheet.

2. Click anywhere on the embedded clustered column chart right below the Production Schedule table to select this chart.

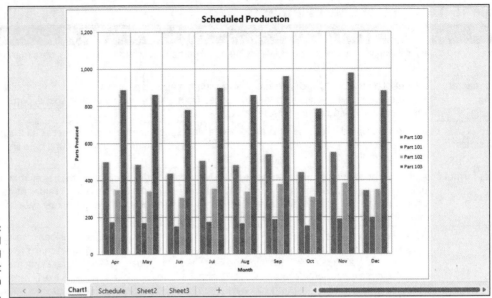

FIGURE 15-2:
Typical
clustered
column chart
on its own
chart sheet.

Eight sizing handles appear around the perimeter of the embedded Clustered Column chart indicating that it is now selected. In addition, the Chart Design and Format contextual tabs appear at the end of the Ribbon and the worksheet data used in creating the chart is indicated by different colored bounding boxes surrounding the row and column heads as well as the data entries.

3. Position the mouse pointer on the sizing handle that's located in the middle on the right edge. When the mouse pointer changes to a double-headed arrow, drag the thin black outline of the chart area until its right edge is flush with the right edge of column J in the worksheet. Release the mouse button.

Note that Excel redraws the clustered column chart to fit in the new width.

4. Click the Chart Design contextual tab to display its tools.

The Chart Design contextual tab contains buttons that enable you to change the chart type, layout, and style.

5. Click the More button in the lower-right corner of the Chart Styles group to display all the style thumbnails in this palette. Then, click the Style 12 thumbnail.

Excel assigns this style (with its multi-colored data series outlined against a black background) to the clustered column chart and displays the other colors that use this same type of outlining on the Chart Styles group of the Chart Design contextual tab.

6. Click the chart title, Scheduled Production.

Four round sizing handles appear on the perimeter of a box drawn around the text in the Chart Title, indicating that you can now move or resize the title in the chart area.

7. Click the chart title a second time to open the title for editing. Edit the title so that it reads, **Production Scheduled**. Click outside the Chart Title text box in an empty place in the chart area to deselect the chart title and set your edit.

Now, try making some changes to a few of the worksheet values represented in the chart.

8. Make the following editing changes to entries in the designated cells, noting the change in the column of the chart representing the data point you're changing:

   - 353 in cell D4 containing the scheduled production of Part 101 for June

   - 660 in cell E3 containing the scheduled production of Part 100 for July

   - 475 in cell H5 containing the scheduled production of Part 102 for October

   Each time you change a value that's represented graphically in the chart, its data marker changes.

9. Click anywhere on the embedded clustered column chart to select it and then choose Chart Design ⇨ Move Chart (or press Alt+JCV) to open the Move Chart dialog box.

   The Move Chart dialog box contains two options: New Sheet and Object In (currently selected).

10. Select the New Sheet option button, replace the generic Chart1 name in the associated text box with Schedule Chart, and click OK.

    Excel inserts a new chart sheet named Schedule Chart as the first sheet in your Exercise15-1.xlsx workbook in front of the Schedule sheet. This new chart sheet contains the erstwhile clustered column chart.

11. Reposition the Schedule Chart sheet so that it's located immediately after the Schedule worksheet in the workbook by dragging its sheet tab.

    Next, see how the chart on its own sheet prints.

12. With the Schedule Chart sheet selected, press Ctrl+P to open the Print panel with the Print Preview area in the Backstage View.

    Note that Excel automatically selects the landscape orientation for the chart in the print preview to print it full size on the page.

13. Press Esc to exit the Excel Backstage View and return to the Normal view of the Schedule Chart sheet.

    Now, move the clustered column chart back to the Schedule worksheet as an embedded object.

14. Move the clustered column chart back to the Schedule sheet and then move the chart object so that the top edge of the chart area is flush with the bottom edge of row 9 and the left edge is flush with the left edge of column B. Then, resize the chart so that the bottom edge of the chart is flush with the top edge of row 27 and the right edge of the chart is flush with the right edge of column I.

    Now you're ready to save your changes in a new Excel workbook.

15. Position the cell cursor in cell A1 and then save your work in a new workbook named Production Sch – embedchrt.xlsx in your Excel Practice folder. Close the workbook file.

Creating Charts

Creating a new embedded chart in Excel involves three general steps:

1. Select the data and headings in the worksheet that you want represented in the new chart.

2. Use the Ribbon's Insert tab to select the type of chart to create by clicking the button for the general type of chart (Column, Line, Pie, Bar, and so on) and then clicking the thumbnail of the subtype you want to use on the button's drop-down gallery.

3. Refine the new chart as needed using the command buttons on the Chart Design and Format contextual tabs.

EXAMPLE

Q. Do I have to select the data I want to graph before I select the type of chart on the Ribbon's Insert tab?

A. No, as long as the cell cursor is located in one of the cells of the table of data you want to chart, you can have Excel make a guess as to the data range to be graphed (which you can refine, if the program leaves out necessary data or includes extraneous data).

Try It

Exercise 15-2: Creating a New Embedded Chart

In Exercise 15-2, you practice creating and formatting a new embedded chart that represents only the quarterly sales data in two sales categories that are contained in a much larger, more detailed sales table.

1. Open the Exercise15-2.xlsx workbook file in your Chap15 folder in the Excel Workbook folder.

   This workbook contains a Sales worksheet with the CG Media – Sales by Category and Date table showing only the quarterly subtotals and the annual total (the columns with the supporting monthly data are currently hidden). Use this quarterly sales data to practice creating a new embedded chart.

2. Without moving the cell cursor out of cell A1, choose Insert⇨Column (or press Alt+NC1) to display the Column chart drop-down gallery. Then, click the Clustered Column thumbnail at the beginning in the first column of the first row of this gallery.

   Excel inserts a new embedded clustered column chart in the Sales worksheet, as shown in Figure 15-3. Note that this initial chart contains more data than you want represented. (You don't need the annual totals or the total sales for both the CDs and tapes to be represented in this chart.)

3. Move the new chart so that its top edge is flush with the top edge of row 17 and its left edge is flush with the left edge of column E. Then, scroll down, if necessary, and resize the embedded chart so that its bottom edge is flush with the top edge of row 36 and its right edge is flush with the right edge of column S.

Next, you need to remove the annual total and total sales for CDs and tapes from the clustered column chart. Begin by removing the Annual Total data markers from the chart.

4. Choose Chart Design ⇨ Select Data (or press Alt+JCE) to open the Select Data Source dialog box.

    If the Chart Design and Format contextual tabs don't appear on your Ribbon, this means that the new clustered column chart you created is not currently selected. To make the Chart Design and Format contextual tabs appear on your Ribbon, click an empty space in the clustered column chart area to select it.

    The Select Data Source dialog box contains two columns: Legend Entries (Series) on the left side and Horizontal (Category) Axis Labels on the right. Each column currently contains the names of the entries that appear in the legend and on the x-axis of the chart.

    To remove the Annual Total from the chart, you need to temporarily switch the rows and columns of this chart so that the annual sales appear on the legend.

5. Click the Switch Row/Column button in the Select Data Source dialog box.

    Excel switches the chart so that there are data series for each of four quarters plus the annual total in the clustered bars arranged by type of sales.

6. Click CG Media – Sales by Category and Date Annual Total at the bottom of the Legend Entries (Series) column and then click the Remove button at the top of the column.

    Excel removes the data series for the Annual Total from the body of the chart and from the legend.

7. Click the Switch Row/Column button again to return the four quarters to the category x-axis of the chart and the types to the legend.

    Now, you need to delete the empty Compact Discs and Cassettes series from the chart and legend along with the Total Sales data series.

8. Click Compact Discs at the top of the Legend Entries (Series) column and then click the Remove button.

    Excel removes this empty heading that did not represent any charted data from the legend.

9. Repeat this procedure to remove Cassettes (another empty label) and Total Sales from the legend. Then, click OK to close the Select Data Source dialog box.

    Now, the chart represents only two data series, Total CD Sales and Total Tape Sales, listed in the legend.

10. Save your work in a new workbook file named CG Media – embedchrt.xlsx in your Excel Practice folder and then leave the workbook file open for Exercise 15-3.

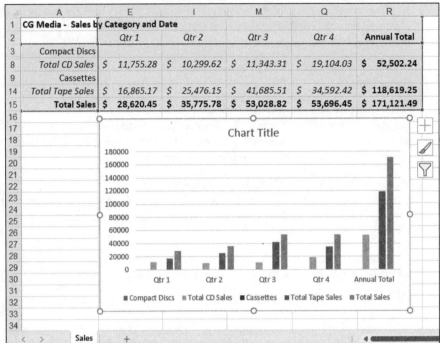

FIGURE 15-3:
The new
embedded
clustered
column chart
immediately
after creation.

Formatting Charts

Often you find that you have to finesse the formatting of elements in the particular chart that Excel initially produces for you. You can make short work of making large and small formatting changes using the command buttons found on the two contextual tabs:

» **Chart Design:** Change the basic type, layout, or style of the chart.

» **Format:** Change the font, line, or fill of a particular chart element.

Try It

Exercise 15-3: Making Formatting Changes to a Chart

In Exercise 15-3, you practice making formatting changes to the clustered column chart you created in the previous exercise. This exercise gives you practice selecting a new chart style as well as making formatting changes to selected elements of the chart, including the chart area, titles, and axes.

1. Use the clustered column chart in your CG Media – embedchrt.xlsx workbook that you created in the previous exercise to practice making formatting changes to a fin-ished chart.

    This chart represents the correct data in the Sales worksheet but still lacks any titles.

2. If your clustered column chart is not already selected, click somewhere on a blank space in the chart area to select this object. Then, scroll up the rows of the worksheet, if necessary, so that the entire clustered column chart is visible on your computer screen.

Clicking somewhere on the embedded chart not only selects this graphic object, but also adds the Chart Design and Format contextual tabs to the end of the Ribbon.

REMEMBER

3. On the Chart Design contextual tab, click the More button in the Chart Styles group (or press Alt+JCS) to open the Chart Styles drop-down gallery. Then, click the Style 14 thumbnail in this drop-down gallery.

Excel applies the 3-D multicolor style to the clustered columns in your chart.

4. Choose Chart Design ⇨ Quick Layout (or press Alt+JCL) to open the Chart Layouts drop-down gallery. Then, click the Layout 1 thumbnail (first row, first column) in this drop-down gallery.

Excel adds a legend beside the Plot Area.

5. Choose Chart Design ⇨ Add Chart Element ⇨ Gridlines ⇨ Primary Major Vertical (or press Alt+JCAGV).

Excel adds major vertical gridlines to your clustered column chart.

6. Click the Format tab and then in the Shape Styles gallery, click Colored Outline – Black, Dark 1 thumbnail (first row, first column).

Note that the moment you highlight this thumbnail in the Shape Styles group, Live Preview displays this outline around the entire chart (because Chart Area is currently selected in the Chart Elements combo box in the Current Selection group on the Format tab) even before you set it by clicking this thumbnail.

7. In the Format contextual tab's Current Selection group, click the drop-down button attached to the Chart Elements combo box and then click the Chart Title option on its drop-down menu.

Excel selects the Chart Title in your clustered column chart (indicated in the chart area by the appearance of its text box with sizing handles).

8. On the Format contextual tab, click More in the WordArt Styles group to open this gallery and then click the Gradient Fill: Aqua, Accent Color 5, Reflection thumbnail (the blue A with a reflection).

9. Edit the chart title to read CG Media Quarterly Sales. Click somewhere in a blank space in the chart area to deselect the Chart Title.

Next, assign a gradient fill to the interior of the chart area using the Shape Fill button.

10. On the Format tab, click the Shape Fill button in the Shape Styles group and then highlight Gradient on its drop-down menu or press Alt+JOSFG. Then, click the From Center thumbnail on its gallery (second row, second column in the Variations section).

Now, assign a glow shape effect to the border of the chart area using the Shape Effects button.

11. On the Format tab, click the Shape Effects button in the Shape Styles group and then highlight Glow on its drop-down menu or press Alt+JOSEG. Then, click the Glow: 18 pt, Aqua, Accent Color 5 thumbnail on its gallery (fourth row, fifth column of the Glow Variations section).

   Excel displays a glow effect around the black border of the selected clustered column chart.

12. On the Format tab, click the Vertical (Value) Axis option on the Chart Elements drop-down button's menu.

   Excel selects the vertical axis of your clustered column chart (indicated by the text box with sizing handles around the vertical axis and values on the left side of the chart).

13. Choose Format⇨ Format Selection to open the Format Axis task pane, click Axis Options, and then click Number to expand the Number section. Select Currency in the Category drop-down list, and then click the Decimal Places text box and replace 2 with **0** before you click Close. Then, click somewhere in a cell in the worksheet to deselect the chart.

14. On the Format tab, click the Plot Area option on the Chart Elements drop-down button's menu.

15. Drop down the Shape Fill gallery and select White, Background 1.

16. Choose Chart Design⇨ Select Data to open the Select Data Source dialog box. In the Chart Data Range box, adjust the range to =Sales!$A$2:$Q$15, and then click OK.

   Check your formatted chart against the one shown in Figure 15-4. When everything checks out, go on to Step 17.

17. Use the Zoom slider to reduce the magnification percentage until the entire worksheet table and chart are displayed on your screen, and then click cell A1 and save your work in a new file named CG Media – fmtclscolchrt.xlsx in your Excel Practice folder. Leave the workbook open for Exercise 15-4.

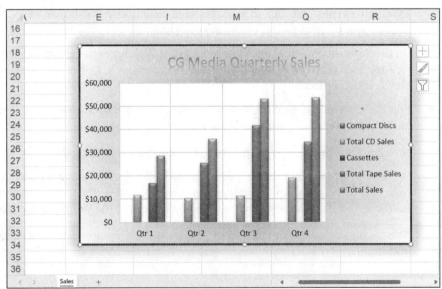

FIGURE 15-4: The embedded clustered column chart after formatting.

Editing Charts

Excel makes it easy to edit any chart you create. All you have to do is click somewhere in a blank area of the chart in the worksheet if the chart's embedded or its chart sheet if it's not. Excel then selects the chart area and activates the Chart Tools contextual tab. You can then use the command buttons on its Design, Layout, and Format tabs to make all the necessary changes.

Try It

Exercise 15-4: Editing the Chart Type, Layout, and Style

In Exercise 15-4, you practice changing the type of an existing chart, its layout, and its basic style.

1. Use the CG Media – fmtclscolchrt.xlsx workbook file with the embedded clustered column chart you formatted on its Sales worksheet in the previous exercise to practice making editing changes to a finished chart.

   Begin by changing the type of chart from clustered column to a 3-D stacked bar chart.

2. Click somewhere on a blank space in the chart area of your clustered column chart to select the object and then choose Chart Design ⇨ Change Chart Type (or press Alt+JCC) to open the Change Chart Type dialog box.

   The Change Chart Type dialog box is divided into two columns: The name of chart types from Column to Radar appear beneath the Templates option in the left column and thumbnails of the subtypes available for each type appear in rows and columns on the right.

3. Click Bar in the left column of the Change Chart Type dialog box and then click the thumbnail of the 3-D Stacked Bar subtype on the right side (the fourth one in the first row of the Bar section) before you click OK.

   Excel redraws your embedded chart as a 3-D stacked bar chart.

4. Choose Chart Design ⇨ Quick Layout and then click the Layout 2 thumbnail (first row, second column) in the Quick Layout gallery.

   In this new layout, Excel displays the chart's legend at the top of the clustered bar chart right below the chart's title. This new layout also displays the quarterly totals for each type of sale (CD or tape) on the appropriate section of the bars in the chart.

5. Choose Chart Design ⇨ Add Chart Elements ⇨ Gridlines ⇨ Primary Major Vertical (or press Alt+JCAGV). Choose Chart Design ⇨ Add Chart Elements ⇨ Gridlines ⇨ Primary Minor Vertical (or press Alt+JCAGM).

   Excel redraws the 3-D chart with major and minor vertical gridlines down its back and bottom walls.

6. Choose Chart Design ⇨ Add Chart Elements ⇨ Gridlines ⇨ Primary Major Horizontal (or press Alt+JCAGH). Choose Chart Design ⇨ Add Chart Elements ⇨ Gridlines ⇨ Primary Minor Horizontal (or press Alt+JCAGZ).

Excel now adds major and minor horizontal gridlines to the back and side walls of the chart.

7. Choose Format⇨Shape Fill (or press Alt+JASF) to open its drop-down menu. Click the White, Background 1 square (first row, first column of the Theme Colors palette).

   Excel removes the gradient from the background of your 3-D stacked bar chart.

8. Choose Format⇨Shape Effects (or press Alt+JASE) to open its drop-down menu. Highlight the Glow option and then click the No Glow thumbnail in its submenu.

   Excel removes the glow effect from the borders of your 3-D stacked bar chart.

9. Choose Format⇨Chart Elements and then click the Vertical (Category) Axis option on its drop-down menu.

   Excel selects the category labels Qtr 4 through Qtr 1 on the left side of the 3-D stacked bar chart (indicated by the text box with its sizing handles).

10. Use the command buttons in the Font group of the Ribbon's Home tab to select 12 points as the font size for the quarterly category labels and make their text bold.

    The category titles along the vertical axis at the left end of the stacked bar chart are now much easier to read.

    Now check your final 3-D stacked bar chart against the one shown in Figure 15-5. If everything checks out, move on to Step 11.

11. Save your 3-D stacked bar chart in a new workbook file named CG Media −3dstckbrchrt.xlsx in your Excel Practice folder and then close it by exiting Excel.

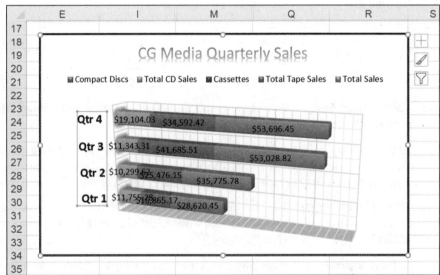

FIGURE 15-5: The final 3-D stacked bar chart created from the original clustered column chart.

Chapter **16**

Adding Graphics to Worksheets

As you discover in Chapter 15, the embedded charts you add to a worksheet are actually graphic objects that you can move and resize as needed. Embedded charts are by no means the only graphic objects you can have in your worksheet. Excel also enables you to add graphic objects you create yourself as well as those you import from Clip Art and other kinds of graphics files.

In this chapter, you get a chance to practice using all these different types of graphic objects to improve the overall look of your worksheets and make their data and charts even more interesting and legible to the user.

Understanding Graphic Objects

The most important thing to remember about graphic objects is that they are distinct elements: that is, they're separate from the cells of the worksheet and they float "above" the worksheet on their own layers. Because they are distinct objects, you can select them for moving and resizing as you can for embedded charts. (See Chapter 15.) Because graphic objects remain on separate layers, you can move them one on top of the other, with the object on the topmost layer obscuring some or all the objects on layers below.

To select a graphic object, you click some part of it (which can sometimes be a bit tricky when different objects overlap each other). As Figure 16-1 demonstrates, when you select a graphic object, Excel displays the name of the object in the Name box on the Formula bar (Right Arrow 1, in this case) while at the same time displaying white circular sizing handles around the perimeter of its shape, orange circular shaping handles (for adjusting the proportions of the object), and a circular rotation handle at the top. (You use the rotation handle to change the orientation of the object by rotating it to any desired angle.) Some graphic objects, such as the block arrow shown in Figure 16-1, also display one or more shaping handles that you can use to modify the basic shape (in this case, the thickness of the body of the arrow in relation to its arrowhead).

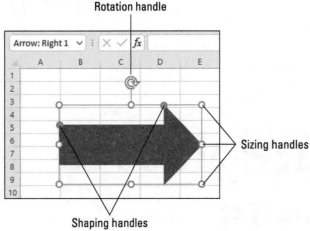

FIGURE 16-1: When you select a graphic object, Excel displays various handles for manipulating the object and its name appears in the Formula bar's Name box.

To move the selected graphic object, position the mouse pointer somewhere inside the object's perimeter. Then, when the pointer becomes an arrowhead with a double cross at its point, drag the object to its new position within the worksheet. To copy the selected object, hold down the Ctrl key as you drag the graphic. When you hold down the Ctrl key, a plus sign, indicating that the object is being copied, appears above the arrowhead pointer.

You can "nudge" a selected graphic object into its desired position by pressing the arrow keys: ↑ for Up, ↓ for Down, ← for Left, or → for Right. When you press an arrow key, Excel moves the object just a very little bit in that direction. Nudging is very useful when you have an object that's almost in place and requires very little handling to get it into just the right position.

TIP

When graphic objects overlay each other, you can move an object that is on higher levels to lower levels by clicking the object to select it and choosing Shape Format ⇨ Send Backward (or by pressing Alt+JDAEB). To move an object that's on a lower level up towards the top, click the object and then choose Shape Format ⇨ Bring Forward (or press Alt+JDAFF).

Excel also makes it possible to group different graphic objects together to create a single composite graphic object by selecting the individual objects (by Ctrl+clicking them) and then choosing Shape Format ⇨ Group ⇨ Group (or press Alt+JDAGG). Excel indicates that the selected graphics are now grouped (and for all intents and purposes, a single graphic object) by placing a single set of sizing handles around the perimeter formed by all the former separate graphics. You can then manipulate the grouped graphic as a single entity, moving, sizing, rotating, and so on as you would any other object.

REMEMBER

When grouping a bunch of different objects Excel never forgets that they were once separate objects that you could independently manipulate. That means that you can always turn them back into separate graphics by ungrouping them. To do this, click the composite graphic object and then choose Shape Format ⇨ Group ⇨ Ungroup (or press Alt+JDAGU).

Try It

Exercise 16-1: Manipulating the Graphic Objects in a Worksheet

In Exercise 16-1, you practice working with graphic objects by repositioning two existing objects so they overlap one another. You then get practice grouping them together as a single object and using the controls in the Selection task pane to hide and redisplay them in the worksheet.

1. If Excel is not currently running, launch the program. Then open the Exercise16-1.xlsx workbook file in the Ch16 folder in your Excel Workbook folder.

   The Graphic Objects worksheet in this workbook contains a block arrow and a "This way to success!" WordArt graphic object. You use these two shapes to practice manipulating graphic objects, including moving and resizing them, sending them to different layers, and finally grouping them together as one composite graphic.

2. Click the blue right arrow to select its shape.

   Excel displays the sizing, shaping, and rotation handles in the object's bounding box and the Drawing Tools contextual tab with its single Format tab appears at the end of the Ribbon. In addition, the name of the graphic shape, Right Arrow 1, appears in the Name box on the Formula bar.

   Note that the right arrow graphic object contains two shaping handles: one on the shaft or body of the arrow that you can drag up and down to widen and narrow the arrow shaft, and one on the arrowhead that you can drag to the left and right to widen and flatten the head of the arrow.

3. Drag the shape handle attached to the shaft of the arrow downward to narrow the body of the arrowhead until it's just slightly wider than the text, "This way to" in the WordArt graphic object. Then, drag the sizing handle attached to the very tip of the arrowhead to the right to widen the arrow so that it's about twice as long as before.

   Note that Excel shows you the outline of the shaft and arrowhead as you drag the respective shaping and sizing handle so that you can visualize the new arrow shape before you release the mouse button.

4. Drag the right arrow's rotation handle downward to the left until its arrowhead is rotated counterclockwise so that it is pointed up approximately at a forty-five degree angle.

   Note that Excel shows you the outline of the entire right arrow shape as you drag the rotation handle so that you can visualize its new angle when you release the mouse button.

5. With the right arrow graphic still selected, choose Shape Format ⇨ Selection Pane (or press Alt+JDAP).

Excel opens the Selection pane on the right side of the worksheet area.

6. Click Rectangle 2 in the Selection pane to select the WordArt graphic object in the worksheet.

Note that selecting this object causes Excel to display its name, Rectangle 2, in the Name box on the Formula bar.

7. Position the mouse pointer somewhere on the border of the shape's outline and then, when the four-headed arrow appears at the tip of the arrowhead, drag the WordArt graphic object until the left end of its outline overlays the end of the shaft of the right arrow.

Now you need to rotate the WordArt object counterclockwise to match the angle of the right arrow.

8. Use the rotation handle on the WordArt object to rotate its text counterclockwise to match the basic angle of the right arrow object. Then reposition the WordArt object and continue to adjust its angle so that the text overlays the right arrow below.

At this point, your overlaid arrow and WordArt graphic objects should basically match those shown in Figure 16-2.

FIGURE 16-2: The right arrow and WordArt graphic objects after overlaying and rotating.

9. Click a cell in the worksheet to deselect the WordArt object. Then, position the four-headed arrow mouse pointer somewhere on the right arrow shape and click to select the object. Then choose Shape Format ⇨ Bring Forward ⇨ Bring to Front (or press Alt+JDAFR).

Excel positions the right arrow shape on top of the WordArt graphic object, obscuring most of its text.

10. Choose Shape Format ⇨ Send Backward ⇨ Send to Back (or press Alt+JDAEK).

Excel returns the right arrow to its original position beneath the WordArt object.

11. Ctrl-click the WordArt graphic object in the Selection pane so that both the right arrow shape and the WordArt object are selected. Then, choose Shape Format➪Group➪Group (or press Alt+JDAGG).

Excel replaces the two bounding boxes with a single rectangular bounding box that encompasses all of the right arrow and most of the WordArt text. In the Selection task pane, Excel displays the names of the three objects in the Graphic Objects worksheet: Group 3, the name given to the grouped object, Rectangle 2, and Right Arrow 1. Note that Excel shows that the Rectangle 2 and Right Arrow 1 graphic objects are grouped together to make up the Group 3 object by indenting their names under Group 3 in this pane.

12. Click the eye icon that appears to the right of the Right Arrow 1 object in the Selection task pane.

Excel temporarily hides the Right Arrow 1 graphic object in the worksheet (although its name continues to appear in the Selection task pane).

13. Click the Right Arrow 1 object's eye icon again in the Selection task pane to redisplay the image in the worksheet. Then, choose Shape Format➪Group➪Ungroup (or press Alt+JDAGU).

Excel removes the Group 3 name from the Selection pane and bounding boxes appear around both the Right Arrow 1 and Rectangle 2 objects in the worksheet.

14. Click cell A1 in the worksheet.

Excel deselects both the graphic objects in the sheet and the Shape Format contextual tab disappears from the Ribbon.

15. Click the Rectangle 2 name in the Selection task pane.

Excel selects the WordArt object in the worksheet.

HINT

If you have difficulty selecting individual graphic objects that overlay each other in the worksheet, select them by clicking their names in the Selection task pane. To select multiple objects, hold down the Ctrl key as you click the individual object names.

16. Regroup the Rectangle 2 and Right Arrow 1 objects and then close the Selection task pane.

Now all you have to do is to save your changes in a new workbook file.

17. Click cell A1 and then save your work as a new workbook with the filename Graphic Objects Practice.xlsx in your Excel Practice folder. Close the workbook.

Adding Various Types of Graphic Objects

The Illustrations and Text groups of Excel's Insert tab are packed with great tools for creating and adding all types of graphic objects. These graphics include icons, illustrations, art, and images from other graphics files (including digital photos) that you import into Excel, as well as graphic shapes and SmartArt graphics that you create yourself.

Inserting prefab art

Microsoft includes a wide variety of ready-to-use images that you can insert in your worksheets. These image types include photos, icons, cutout people (that is photos of people with transparent backgrounds), stickers, and illustrations. For each type of art, Excel provides a search box and several categories for browsing.

Exercise 16-2: Adding Prefab Art to a Worksheet

In Exercise 16-2, you practice finding the appropriate image to add to an invoice worksheet that you will convert into a template file (for generating the real invoices you fill out). You also get practice correctly sizing and positioning the selected image in the invoice header.

1. Open the Exercise16-2.xlsx workbook file in the Chap16 folder in your Excel Workbook folder.

   This workbook contains the ITB Invoice worksheet with a copy of an invoice template for a store called Into the Blue that sells kites and accessories. In this exercise, you get to practice finding and adding prefab art by sprucing up the otherwise dull invoice heading with an image of a kite.

2. Choose Insert⇨Icons (or press Alt+NNS).

   Excel displays a dialog box with five tabs: Images, Icons, Cutout People, Stickers, and Illustrations. Because you chose the Icons command, the Icons tab is selected by default. Each tab comes with a search box (each of which includes a sample search keyword) and, below the search box, you see several buttons with category names, where clicking a category displays the prefab images associated with that category.

3. Enter **kite** as the search text in the Icon tab's Search text box.

   Excel returns a couple of kite image thumbnails.

4. Click the first kite thumbnail and then click Insert to insert the image into the ITB Invoice worksheet.

   Excel inserts the kite image and adds the Graphics Format contextual tab to the end of the Ribbon.

5. Use the sizing handles to resize the kite graphic so that the height of its outline is essentially the same as that of the invoice header.

   Note that prefab images have only sizing handles. These images do not offer a rotation handle for changing the orientation or a shaping handle for manipulating the shape. Be sure to drag one of the corner sizing handles diagonally to resize the image without distorting it.

6. Drag the resized kite clip art image so that the image is positioned within the invoice header and its left edge is roughly flush with column E's left edge. Use Figure 16-3 as a guide.

7. Choose Graphics Format⇨Graphics Fill and then click the Dark Blue, Text 2, Lighter 80% color swatch (second row, fourth column in the Theme Colors section).

Now, all that remains is to save your worksheet as a template file.

8. Select cell A1. Save your work as a new template with the filename ITB Invoice.xltx in your Excel Practice folder and then close the workbook.

Remember that you must change the file type by selecting Excel Template (*.xltx) in the Save As Type drop-down menu of the Save As dialog box as well as change the filename before clicking the Save button.

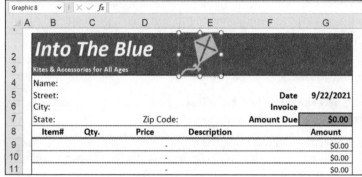

FIGURE 16-3:
An ITB Invoice
with resized
kite clip art
image added
to the header.

Importing graphics files

Besides the prefab images discussed in Chapter 15, you can also insert graphic files that you keep in any folder containing your artwork and digital photographs, such as your Windows user account's Pictures folder.

To insert a picture into the worksheet, choose Insert⇨Pictures⇨This Device (or press Alt+NPD) to open the Insert Picture dialog box. This dialog box works just like the Open dialog box except that it's set to display only the graphics files that Excel can import.

After you locate the graphics file you want to insert in the worksheet, click its thumbnail in the Insert Picture dialog box and then click the Insert button to import it into the current worksheet. Excel then displays the image from the file you selected with sizing handles around the perimeter and a rotation handle connected to the sizing handle in the middle at the top of the image. You can then reposition, resize, or rotate the image as needed.

Excel also adds the Picture Format contextual tab to the end of the Ribbon. You can use the Picture Format tab's command buttons in the Adjust and Size groups to edit the selected photo. Among other things, these tools make it possible to increase or decrease the brightness or contrast of the image, crop unwanted areas around the edges, and compress the image so that it doesn't bulk up the size of your workbook (as high-resolution images can).

Exercise 16-3: Adding Images from Graphic Files to a Worksheet

In Exercise 16-3, you practice adding digital photos to a worksheet that you then resize and reposition.

1. Open the Exercise16-3.xlsx workbook file in your Chap16 folder in the Excel Workbook folder.

   This workbook contains a copy of the Home Sales Apr/May worksheet that you worked with earlier. You add a new worksheet to this workbook for the 905 Hudson Lane listing in which you add a couple of digital photos.

2. Insert a new worksheet into the Exercise16-3.xlsx workbook after the Home Sales worksheet that you name 905 Hudson Ln.

HINT

   To insert the new worksheet, click the Insert Worksheet button that appears immediately following the Home Sales sheet tab.

3. Copy the street address in cell A8 of the Home Sales worksheet to cell A1 of the 905 Hudson Ln worksheet. Make its font bold, increase its font size to 14 points, and then use AutoFit to resize column A.

REMEMBER

   The easiest way to copy entries between worksheets is to press Ctrl+C (copy) and Enter or Ctrl+V (paste).

4. Make the following entries in the designated cells of the 905 Hudson Ln worksheet:

   - Sold On in cell A2

   - Sold For in cell A3

   Then, use the appropriate buttons in the Font and Alignment groups of the Home tab to format the entries in cells A2 and A3 so that they are bold and right-aligned in their cells.

   Next, you need to copy the date value in cell B8 of the Home Sales sheet to cell B2 of the 905 Hudson Ln worksheet.

5. Use the copy and paste method to copy the date in cell B8 in the Home Sales worksheet to cell B2 in the 905 Hudson Ln worksheet.

   Next, copy a link to the sales prices in cell C8 of the Home Sales worksheet to cell B3 of the 905 Hudson Ln sheet.

6. Use the Copy and Paste Link method to paste an external link to the sales prices in C8 in the Home Sales worksheet into cell B3 in the 905 Hudson Ln sheet. Then, widen columns A and B as needed to display their entire contents in the worksheet.

HINT

   The easiest way to do this is to position the cell cursor in cell C8 of the Home Sales sheet and then choose Home ⇨ Copy before you switch to the 905 Hudson Ln worksheet. Click cell B3 and then choose Home ⇨ Paste ⇨ Paste Link (or press Alt+HVN). Use AutoFit to widen column A and B as needed.

Cell B3 now contains the formula = 'Home Sales' !$C$8 and returns $1,085,000 to the cell.

7. Position the cell cursor in cell A5 of the 905 Hudson Ln worksheet and then choose Insert ⇨ Pictures ⇨ This Device (or press Alt+NPD).

   Excel opens the Insert Picture dialog box. The photos you want to insert are located in the Graphics subfolder inside the Chap16 subfolder in your Excel Workbook folder.

8. Select Documents in the left pane, and then double-click the Excel Workbook folder icon, followed by the Chap16 folder icon, followed by the Graphics folder icon.

   This folder contains three graphics files: two digital photos saved in the JPEG graphics format and one company logo graphic saved in the GIF graphics format. Note that the Files of Type drop-down list box is automatically set to display all the graphic file formats that Excel supports. Also note that Excel automatically displays thumbnails of each of these graphics files along with their filenames.

9. Click the Hudson Lane Front.jpg thumbnail to select it and then select the Insert button to bring it into the 905 Hudson Ln worksheet.

   Excel inserts the selected photo complete with sizing and rotation handles, while at the same time displaying the Picture Format contextual tab on the Ribbon.

10. Move the photo so that its left edge is flush with the left edge of column B and its top edge is flush with the top of row 6; resize the graphic so that its bottom edge is flush with the bottom of row 22 (and its right edge nearly extends to the right edge of column D).

    Next, increase the contrast in this photo and decrease its brightness.

11. Choose Picture Format ⇨ Corrections and then click the Sharpen 25% thumbnail in the Sharpen and Soften section at the top of its drop-down gallery.

    Now put a border around the imported photo.

12. On the Picture Format tab, click More in the Picture Styles gallery and then click the Simple Frame, White thumbnail (first row, first column) in the Quick Styles drop-down gallery.

    Excel draws a border around the selected home photo.

13. Click cell F6 to position the cell cursor in this cell, and then import the Hudson Lane Rear.jpg file into the worksheet, resizing it so that its left edge is flush with the left edge of column F and its bottom edge is flush with the bottom of row 22. Then format this interior photo with the same Simple Frame, White border and select the Brightness: 0% (Normal) Contrast: -40% thumbnail on the Corrections drop-down gallery.

    Next, you're going to get the new worksheet ready for printing.

14. Click cell A1 in the 905 Hudson Ln worksheet and then click the Page Layout button on the Status bar. Choose Page Layout ⇨ Orientation ⇨ Landscape.

    Now add a custom header to the page.

15. Click the Add Header text at the top of the page in Page Layout mode and then choose Header & Footer ⇨ Picture.

    Excel opens the Insert Pictures dialog box.

16. Click From a File to open the Insert Picture dialog box, click the thumbnail of the Mind Over Media Trademark.gif file with the Mind Over Media, Inc. logo in the Graphics subfolder, and then click Insert.

    Excel closes the Insert Picture dialog box and then inserts an &[Picture] code in the Center section.

17. Click the Format Picture button on the Design tab, enter 75% in the Height text box in the Scale section of the Size tab in the Format Picture dialog box, and click OK.

    Next, you add a footer to the bottom of the printed page.

18. Scroll down the page and then click the Add Footer text at the bottom of the page. Then, click the 905 Hudson Ln, Page 1 option on the Footer button's drop-down menu on the Header & Footer Tools' Design tab.

    905 Hudson Ln appears centered in the middle section of the footer and Page 1 appears flush right in the right section of the footer.

19. Open Print Preview on the Print panel by pressing Ctrl+F2.

    The Print Preview area now displays Page 1 of the report in landscape mode with both the entire exterior and interior photos together on the page, the Mind Over Media, Inc. logo centered in the top margin, and the sheet name centered and the page number right-aligned in the bottom margin as shown in Figure 16-4.

20. Click the File Menu button to exit the Backstage View, click the Normal button on the Status bar, and then select cell A1 of the Home Sales worksheet. Save the workbook in a new file named Home Sales – photos.xlsx in your Excel Practice folder and close the file.

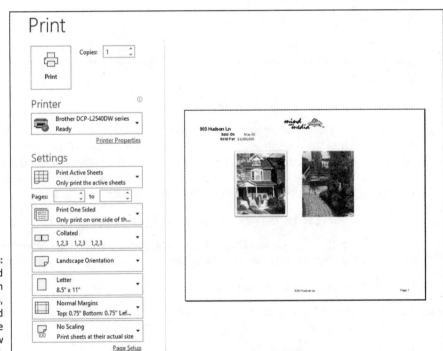

FIGURE 16-4: Completed worksheet with photos, header, and footer in the Backstage View Print panel.

Adding graphic shapes and text boxes

The Shapes button (located in the Insert tab's Illustrations group) enables you to manually construct a wide variety of graphic shapes: straight lines, arrows, rectangles and squares, ovals and circles, to name but a few. To draw these shapes, you click the appropriate thumbnail that appears on the Shapes button's drop-down gallery and then drag the thin, black cross pointer to draw the shape's outline. When drawing a line or arrow, Excel draws the line from the place where you originally click the mouse button to the place where you release it.

TIP

When drawing a rectangle or an oval, you can constrain the tool to draw a square or circle (respectively) by holding down the Shift key as you drag the mouse. Note that when drawing a two-dimensional shape such as a rectangle, square, oval, or circle, Excel automatically draws the shape with a blue color fill that obscures any data or graphic objects that are beneath the shape on layers below.

A text box is a special type of graphic object that combines text with a rectangular graphic shape. It's great for calling attention to significant trends or special features in the charts that you create. To create a text box, choose Insert ➪ Text Box (or press Alt+NX) and then drag the mouse pointer to draw the outline of the box. When you release the mouse button, Excel places the insertion point in the upper-left corner of the box.

You can then start typing the text you want displayed in the text box. When the text you type reaches the right edge of the text box, Excel automatically starts a new line. If you reach the end of the text box and keep typing, Excel enters the text outside the bottom dotted line that indicates the bottom border of the box. You then have to resize the text box to display all the text you've entered within its borders. If you want to break the line before it reaches the right edge of the text box, press the Enter key. When you finish entering the text, click anywhere on the screen outside of the text box to deselect.

When you select text boxes, like other graphic objects in Excel, they display sizing handles along with a rotation handle. Text boxes also display two different border patterns when you select them:

>> Dotted line outline when you click inside the text box, enabling you to format and edit the text (including deleting individual text characters)

>> Solid line outline when you click the border of the text box, indicating that you can reposition and resize the box itself

REMEMBER

Text boxes are similar to the notes you can create (see Chapter 5) in the sense that they also display the text that you enter in a rectangular box. Text boxes differ from notes, however, in that they are not attached to particular cells and are always displayed in the worksheet so long as you don't click their eye icons in the Selection task pane (Alt+JDAP) to temporarily hide them in the sheet.

Exercise 16-4: Adding Graphic Shapes and Text Boxes to Annotate a Chart

In Exercise 16-4, you practice annotating an existing embedded chart through the addition of graphic shapes and text boxes.

1. Open the Exercise16-4.xlsx workbook file in your Chap16 folder in the Excel Workbook folder.

    This workbook contains a 3-D Clustered Column chart on its own chart sheet called 3-D Clstrd Col immediately following the initial Sales worksheet with the table showing the CG Media quarterly subtotals. Use this 3-D chart to practice drawing graphic shapes and text boxes.

2. Click the 3-D Clstrd Col sheet to make this chart sheet active and then click somewhere on the Chart Area to make the chart active. Next, choose Insert⇨Shapes and then click the Oval thumbnail (first row, second column in the Basic Shapes section).

    The mouse pointer becomes a thin black cross. Use this pointer to draw an oval shape around the third-quarter column in the chart representing that quarter's total tape sales (the tallest purple column in the chart) that will call attention to this chart column.

3. Position the black-cross mouse pointer slightly above and to the left of this tallest purple column representing the total third quarter tape sales and then drag this pointer down and to the right until the outline of the oval shape entirely encloses this chart column. Release the mouse button.

    Excel draws a long blue oval on top of the column that entirely obscures it. The program also displays the buttons on the Shape Format contextual tab on the Ribbon.

4. Choose Shape Format⇨Shape Fill⇨No Fill.

    Excel removes the blue fill color from the long oval so that you can now see the chart column under it.

5. Choose Shape Format⇨Shape Outline and then click the red color square in the Standard Colors section of its drop-down palette menu. Choose Shape Format⇨Shape Outline⇨Weight, and then click the 3 pt option on the continuation menu that appears to increase the thickness of the red outline.

    The oval surrounding the third-quarter tape sales column in the chart now calls attention to this column with its 3-point red line.

6. In the Shape Format tab's Insert Shapes group, click the Text Box button (it's the one in the top-left corner of the gallery). Position the mouse pointer in the blank area in the upper-right section of the chart area and drag the mouse pointer down and to the right diagonally to draw a rectangle (use Figure 16-5 as a guide) and then release the mouse button.

    Excel draws the text box outline with dotted lines with the insertion point positioned at the beginning of the first line in this box.

7. Type **Summer Blow-Out Sale** in the text box. Then, drag with the insertion point to select this text.

   Note that Excel automatically selects the Ribbon's Home tab as soon as you start typing.

8. Use the command buttons in the Font and Alignment groups of the Home tab to make the following changes to the selected text:

   - On the Font Color drop-down menu, change the text color to red.
   - On the Font Size drop-down menu, increase the point size of the text to 16 points.
   - Use the Bold and Italic buttons in the Font group to make the text bold and italic.
   - Click the Middle Align and Center buttons to center the text horizontally and vertically on two lines within the text box. Then, increase the width of the text box so that all the text fits on a single line.

   The Summer Blow-Out Sale text is now centered on one line in the text box.

9. Click somewhere on the dotted-line border of the text box to select it.

   The text box outline changes from a dotted to a solid line.

10. In the Shape Format tab's Shape Styles gallery, click the More button and then, click the Subtle Effect – Blue, Accent 1 thumbnail (the blue one in the fourth row, second column of the Theme Styles section).

    Excel fills the text box with the blue gradient used by this shape style.

    Next, you need to draw an arrow from the text box to the oval outline surrounding the purple column representing total third-quarter tape sales.

11. In the Shape Format tab's Insert Shapes group, click the Arrow thumbnail in the first row of the gallery. Position the thin black-cross mouse pointer on the sizing handle in the lower-left corner of the text box and drag it diagonally down and to the left until the arrowhead touches somewhere on the red oval outline. Release the mouse button.

    Excel draws an arrow with the arrow pointing to and touching the red oval outlining the tape sales third-quarter column.

12. Choose Shape Format ⇨ Shape Outline ⇨ Weight, and then click the 3 pt option on its continuation menu.

    Excel increases the line weight of the arrow to 3 points.

13. Click somewhere in a blank space in the Chart Area to deselect the arrow. Make sure that your chart annotation matches that shown in Figure 16-5. Then, save your work in a new workbook called CG Media – graphics.xlsx in your Excel Practice folder. Leave this workbook file open for Exercise 16-5.

Constructing WordArt

The WordArt button (it's in the Insert tab's Text group) enables you to insert fancy text in your worksheets. You can combine WordArt with other graphic shapes to produce some interesting effects.

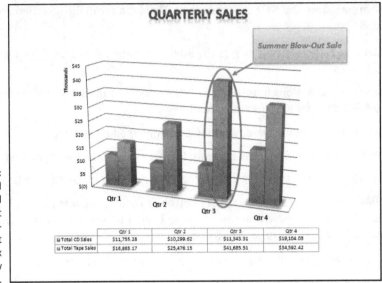

FIGURE 16-5:
Completed
3-D clustered
column chart
with oval-
shaped callout
and text box
with arrow
annotations.

To insert a WordArt graphic object in your worksheet, you first choose Insert ⇨ WordArt to open the drop-down WordArt gallery. This gallery contains a wide variety of different text styles illustrated by rows and columns of letter-A thumbnails.

After selecting a WordArt style by clicking its A-thumbnail in the WordArt drop-down gallery, Excel adds an outlined shape to the worksheet containing the dummy text Your Text Here that you then replace with the words or phrase that you want presented in the WordArt style you selected in the drop-down gallery. You can then use the buttons in the WordArt Styles group on the Shape Format tab to further enhance your WordArt graphic.

Try It

Exercise 16-5: Using WordArt to Annotate a Chart

In Exercise 16-5, you practice using WordArt to annotate your 3-D clustered column chart on its own chart sheet.

1. Make sure that the CG Media – graphics.xlsx workbook that you created in the last exercise is open and its 3-D Clstrd Col chart sheet is active.

   You now add a WordArt graphic with the name of the company in the upper-left corner of the 3-D clustered column chart showing the quarterly totals for CD and tape sales.

2. Click somewhere on the blank space in the 3-D clustered column's chart area and then choose Insert ⇨ WordArt (or press Alt+NW) to open the drop-down WordArt Gallery. Then, click the Fill: Red, Accent color 2; Outline: Red, Accent color 2 thumbnail.

   Excel inserts a text box using the chosen style with the text, Your Text Here, in the middle of the 3-D clustered column chart.

3. Replace the Your Text Here placeholder by typing CG Media and then move the text box containing your new text to the blank area in upper-left corner of the 3-D clustered column chart's area.

Next, change the shape of the WordArt text to make it curve down.

4. Choose Shape Format⇨Text Effects⇨Transform, and then click the Curve Down thumbnail (fourth row, second column of the Warp section).

Excel warps the CG Media WordArt text so that its text curves down and to the right.

5. Move the curved CG Media WordArt so that it fits better in the blank space in the upper-left of the Chart Area and does not obscure any part of the 3-D chart or its title. Then, click somewhere in the blank space of the chart to de-select the WordArt object.

Check your results against those shown in Figure 16-6.

6. Click the WordArt graphic, and then choose Shape Format⇨Selection Pane (or press Alt+JOAP) to open the Selection task pane on the right side of the Excel screen.

Note that the Selection task pane lists Chart 1 as the only graphic: The program does not recognize the oval and arrow shapes, text box, and WordArt as graphic objects separate from the 3-D clustered column chart and all its elements. This would not be the case if you added these shapes to an embedded chart in a worksheet.

7. Close the Selection task pane and then save your changes to the workbook file (Ctrl+S) before you close this workbook file by exiting Excel.

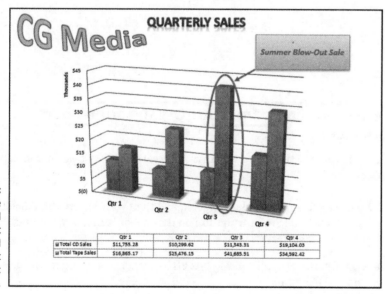

FIGURE 16-6:
The 3-D clustered column chart with final WordArt graphic added to it.

Constructing SmartArt

SmartArt is a graphic object in Excel that gives you the ability to quickly construct complex professional-looking graphical lists and diagrams in your worksheet. SmartArt lists and diagrams come in a wide array of configurations that includes a variety of organization charts and flow diagrams that enable you to add your own text to predefined graphic shapes.

To insert a SmartArt list or diagram into the worksheet, click the SmartArt button (it's in the Insert tab's Illustrations group) or press Alt+NM. Excel then opens the Choose a SmartArt Graphic dialog box (shown in Figure 16–7) where you select the category in the navigation pane on the left followed by the list's or diagram's thumbnail in the center section and click OK.

Excel then inserts the basic structure of the list or diagram into your worksheet along with a text pane (with "Type Your Text Here" on its title bar) containing a text outline to its immediate left. Here's where you enter the text for the various parts of the list or diagram. At the same time, the SmartArt Design tab contextual tab appears on the Ribbon with Layouts and SmartArt Styles galleries for the particular type of SmartArt list or diagram you originally selected.

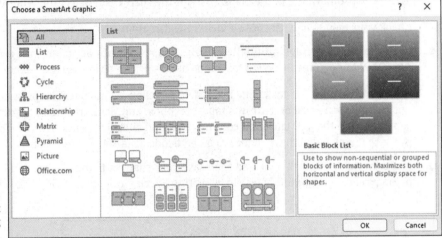

FIGURE 16-7:
The Choose a SmartArt Graphic dialog box.

Try It

Exercise 16-6: Adding a SmartArt Organization Chart to a Worksheet

In Exercise 16-6, you practice using SmartArt by creating a very basic organization chart in a new worksheet.

1. Launch Excel, create a new blank workbook, and then with Sheet1 of the Book1 workbook displayed, click the SmartArt button on the Ribbon's Insert tab or press Alt+NM to open the Choose a SmartArt Graphic dialog box.

   The Choose a SmartArt Graphic dialog box offers a choice between many different types of lists and diagrams.

2. Click the Hierarchy category in the left pane, click the Organization Chart thumbnail (first row, first column), and click OK.

   Excel inserts a blank organization chart into the Sheet1 worksheet: This chart is divided into a Type Your Text Here section that you can use to enter the text for the new organization chart and the chart section itself that contains the various boxes (all of which contain the placeholder "[Text]") with lines connecting them.

Note that if the Type Your Text Here section doesn't appear in the blank Organization Chart graphic, you can display this section by clicking the button that appears on the left edge of the new organization chart containing a left pointing arrow.

3. In the first line of the outline displayed in the Type Your Text Here section, type **Michael Scott**, press Shift+Enter to start a new line, and then type **Regional Manager**. Then, click the bulleted and indented [Text] item on the second line in the outline displayed in the Type Your Text Here section.

Excel displays this name and title both in the outline and the organization chart itself. Note that when you click the second [Text] item in the outline in the section on the left, Excel selects the box in the chart in the section on the right where the text you type next will go.

4. Type **Dwight K. Schulte**, press Shift+Enter to start a new line, type **Assistant Regional Manager**, and then click the bulleted and further indented [Text] item on the third line in the outline displayed in the Type Your Text Here section.

Excel inserts the name and title into the box in the second row of the organization chart.

5. Type **Angela Martin**, press Shift+Enter to start a new line, type **Senior Accountant,** and then click the bulleted [Text] item at the same level on the fourth line in the outline displayed in the Type Your Text Here section.

Excel inserts the name and title of this employee into the first box in the third row of the organization chart.

6. Type **Andy Bernard**, press Shift+Enter to start a new line, type **Regional Sales Director**, and then click the bulleted [Text] item at the previously indented level on the fifth line in the outline displayed in the Type Your Text Here section.

Excel inserts the name and title and name of this employee into the second box in the third row of the organization chart.

7. Type **Pam Beesly**, press Shift+Enter to start a new line, type **Receptionist**, and then press Enter.

Excel inserts the name and title of this employee into the third text box in the third row of the chart. Also, because you pressed Enter after making this text entry, Excel has added a new item (at the same outline level) to the Type Your Text Here section and the organization chart as well.

HINT

Complete the entry by pressing the Enter key whenever you need to insert an item at the same level into a diagram or list. Press the Tab key if you need to indent this new level or press Shift+Tab if you need to move the item to a previous level in the hierarchy.

8. Type **Meredith Palmer**, press Shift+Enter to start a new line, and type **Supplier Relations Manager** as the last entry in the sixth line of the Type Your Text Here section.

Now that you have the text entered for your new organization chart, you're ready to modify some of its formatting.

9. Click the Close box in the upper-right corner to hide the Type Your Text Here section of the diagram. Then, choose SmartArt Design⇨Change Colors. Click the Colorful – Accent Colors thumbnail (the one in the first column of the Colorful section) on its drop-down gallery.

   Excel assigns different colors to each level in this organization chart, while displaying all items on the same level in the same color.

10. On the SmartArt Design tab, open the SmartArt Styles gallery and click the Intense Effect thumbnail.

    Excel adds this 3-D effect to all the boxes in the organization chart.

    Now you're ready to move the SmartArt organization chart into its final position and resize it.

11. Move the organization chart so its top border is flush with the top of row 2 and its left edge is flush with the right edge of column A. Resize the chart so that its bottom edge is flush with the bottom of row 22 and its right edge with the right edge of column L. Then remove the gridlines from the worksheet by deselecting View⇨Gridlines. Finally, redisplay the chart's text box by clicking the left-pointing arrow on the left edge of the organization chart.

    Your finished organization chart should now look like the one shown in Figure 16-8.

12. Click cell A1 and then save your work in your Excel Practice folder under the name of SmartArt Practice.xlsx before you exit the program.

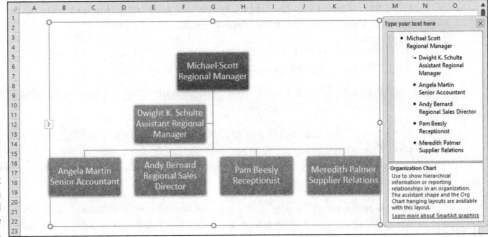

FIGURE 16-8:
The completed organization chart formatted with a colorful and intense 3-D effect.

4

Managing and Securing Data

IN THIS PART. . .

Create, sort, filter, and query tables.

Protect worksheet data from unwanted and unintended changes.

Chapter **17**

Building and Maintaining Tables

Besides its considerable computational abilities, Excel is also very accomplished at maintaining vast collections of related data in what are commonly referred to as *tables*. This chapter gives you a chance to practice all the basic aspects of creating and maintaining tables in Excel, including building the table, adding and editing its data, filtering the table to temporarily remove unwanted data, subtotaling values in a table, and creating tables from data external to the worksheet.

Creating a Table

In Excel, a table is a range of worksheet data with a special structure. Unlike the other types of ranges that you might create in Excel, a table uses only column headings (technically known as field names) to identify the different kinds of items the table tracks. Each column in the table contains information for each item you track in the database, such as the client's company name or telephone number (technically known as a field of the table). Each row in the table contains complete information about each entity that you track in the table, such as ABC Corporation or National Industries (technically known as a record of the table).

All you have to do to start a new table in a worksheet is to enter the names of the fields that you want to track in the first row of whatever range you want to use (usually the top row of the worksheet) and then enter the first record of data in the row beneath. When entering the field names (as column headings), be sure each field name in the table is unique and, whenever possible, keep the field name as short as possible while still clearly labeling the type of data the column contains. When naming fields, you can align the field name in the cell so that its text wraps to a new line (by pressing Alt+Enter). Also, you should not use numbers or formulas that return values as field names. (You can, however, use formulas that return text, such as a formula that concatenates labels entered in different cells.)

When deciding on what fields to create, you need to think of how you'll be using the data that you store in your table. For example, in a client table, you split the client's name into separate first name, middle initial, and last name fields if you intend to use this information in generating form letters and mailing labels with your word processor. That way, you can address the person by first name (as in Dear Jane) in the opening of the form letter you create, as well as by full name and title (as in Dr. Jane Smith) in the mailing label you generate.

Likewise, you split up the client's address into separate street address, city, state, and zip code fields when you intend to use the client table to generate form letters and you want to be able to sort the records in descending order by zip code, say, or to send letters only to clients located in certain states. By keeping discrete pieces of information in separate fields, you are assured that you can use that field in finding particular records and retrieving information from the table, such as finding all the records where the state is California, or the zip code is between 94105 and 95101.

When entering the row with the first data record, be sure to format all the cells the way you want the entries in that field to appear in all the subsequent data records in the table. For example, if you have a salary field in the table, and you want the salaries formatted with the Currency style number format without any decimal places, be sure to format the salary entry in the first record in this manner. That way, all subsequent records pick up that same formatting for the salary field.

Adding records to a new table

After entering the row of field names and the first record, you can then append additional records to the table using the data form that Excel generates for the table or directly in the worksheet cells of the table itself (after formatting the table as an Excel data table). Note, however, that the data form is only available when you add the Form button to a custom tab on the Ribbon, as outlined in Chapter 1.

Try It

Exercise 17-1: Constructing a New Table and Adding Records with the Data Form

In Exercise 17-1, you practice setting up a new table by entering its field names and the first record. You then practice adding a second record to the table using the data form that Excel generates. You also practice formatting your table as an Excel table and, after adding a third record directly in the table, filtering and sorting its records using the table's drop-down Filter buttons.

1. If Excel is not currently running, launch the program and create a new, blank workbook. Use the Sheet1 worksheet of the new Book1 workbook to practice creating a new table and then adding and editing its data with the data form by entering the following field names for your new Employee Table:

   - **ID No** in cell A1
   - **First Name** in cell B1
   - **Last Name** in cell C1
   - **Gender** in cell D1
   - **Dept** in cell E1
   - **Salary** in cell F1
   - **Location** in cell G1
   - **Date Hired** in cell H1
   - **Years of Service** in cell I1
   - **Profit Sharing** in cell J1

   Then, after entering these field names in row 1, widen their columns to 15, center their entries in their cells, and make these cells bold.

   Now that your new table has its field names in the top row, you're ready to add the first record in the table in row 2.

2. Make the following data entries in the designated cells in row 2 as the first record in your new table:

   - **'000928** in cell A2
   - **Joy** in cell B2
   - **Adamson** in cell C2
   - **F** in cell D2
   - **Accounting** in cell E2
   - **$34,400** in cell F2
   - **Boston** in cell G2
   - **10-21-87** in cell H2
   - **Yes** in cell J2

   You skipped the entry in the Years of Service field in cell I2 because this is a calculated field that requires a formula that you must now construct.

3. Create the following formula in cell I2 using the YEAR and TODAY functions, and then format the cell with the Number format using no decimal places:

   ```
   =YEAR(TODAY()) - YEAR(H2)
   ```

   This formula calculates the years of service by taking the current year as returned by the TODAY function and subtracting the year entered in the Date Hired field.

4. Rename Sheet1 Employee Table and then click the Form button on your customized Ribbon tab to open the data form for the Employee Table.

   Excel creates the data form for the Employee Table, which it displays in a dialog box containing a list of the table fields along with a number of command buttons that you can use to add to and maintain the table records.

5. Click the New button to start a new record and then enter the following entries into the designated fields (press Tab to move the insertion point to the next field and Shift+Tab to move it back to the previous field):

   - **'000634** in the ID No field
   - **Gene** in the First Name field
   - **Poole** in the Last Name field
   - **M** in the Gender field
   - **Engineering** in the Dept field
   - **75000** in the Salary field
   - **Chicago** in the Location field
   - **9-15-2000** in the Date Hired field
   - **No** in the Profit Sharing field

   After entering all the new information in the appropriate fields of the new record, you still have to enter this record into the table.

6. Press the Enter key to insert Gene Poole's record into the table.

   Excel responds by clearing the fields in the data form so you can enter the next (third) record, while at the same time entering the data entries you made in the Data Form into the appropriate columns in the second row of the table itself.

REMEMBER

You don't have to use the data form to enter records for your table. If you prefer, you can make entries in the appropriate cells in the table itself. Excel has a feature called Table AutoExpansion that automatically expands your table by one row when you enter a new record in the empty row immediately below your existing records. Table AutoExpansion also automatically formats each new entry to match the existing formatting in each field (column) as well as copies any formulas needed to produce the correct results in calculated fields (as in the Years of Service field in the Employee Table).

7. Select the Close button in the Employee Table data form, position the cell cursor in cell A1, and then choose Home ➪ Format As Table (or press Alt+HT). Click the Light Blue, Table Style Light 2 thumbnail in the drop-down gallery (first row, second column of the Light section at the top of the gallery). Excel displays the Format As Table dialog box asking you to confirm $A$1:$J$3 as the data for your table with the assumption that this table range has a header row at the top. Click OK to make it so.

   Excel formats your employee table with this light-blue banded formatting. The program also adds drop-down Filter buttons to each of the field names in row 1 of the table.

8. Click cell A4 and then enter the third record of your employee table right in the worksheet without the help of the data form. Use the → key to complete each field entry until you reach cell J4, where you can complete the entry by clicking the Enter button on the Formula bar:

- **'000262** in the ID No field in cell A4
- **Lance** in the First Name field in cell B4
- **Bird** in the Last Name field in cell C4
- **M** in the Gender field in cell D4
- **Human Resources** in the Dept field in cell E4 and then widen the column with AutoFit
- **21100** in the Salary field in cell F4
- **Boston** in the Location field in cell G4
- **8-13-97** in the Date Hired field in cell H4
- **Yes** in the Profit Sharing field in J4

Note how Excel automatically formats your field entries in Lance Bird's record as you make them using the table format you assigned to the Employee Table.

9. Click the drop-down Filter button on the Location field in cell G1 and then deselect the (Select All) check box. Then, select the Boston check box and click OK.

Excel filters your table by hiding Gene Poole's record because his location is Chicago rather than Boston. Note that Excel adds a filter cone icon to the Location field's drop-down button to indicate that the table is currently filtered (and therefore not showing all its records) using values in this particular field.

10. Click the Location field's Filter button again and then select the (Select All) check box and click OK.

Excel removes the filtering from this table by displaying all three of its records. The program also removes the filter cone icon from the Location field's drop-down button.

11. Click cell A1 and then save your new employee table in a new workbook named Table Practice.xlsx in your Excel Practice folder before you close the workbook file.

Editing records in the data form

The data form is not only useful for appending new records to a table but also for editing field entries in existing records or even deleting entire records from the table. You can use the Criteria button in the data form to quickly find the records that need editing (this is especially helpful in longer tables where it is no longer practical to search the records manually). When you click the Criteria button in the data form, Excel clears all the field text boxes so that you can enter the criteria to search for in the record that needs editing.

When entering the criteria for locating matching records in the data form, you can use the question mark (?) and the asterisk (*) wildcard characters just as you do when using the Excel Find feature to locate cells with particular entries (see Chapter 5).

When using the Criteria button in the data form to find records, you can use the following comparative operators when entering search criteria in fields that use numbers or dates:

>> Equal to (=) for finding records with the same text, value, or date you enter

>> Greater than (>) for finding records after the text characters (in the alphabet) or the date, or larger than the value you enter

>> Greater than or equal to (>=) for finding records the same as the text characters, date, or value you enter or after the characters (in the alphabet), after the date, or larger than or equal to the value you enter

>> Less than (<) for finding records before the text characters (in the alphabet) or date or smaller than the value you enter

>> Less than or equal to (<=) for finding records the same as the text characters, date, or value you enter or before the characters (in the alphabet) or the date, or larger than or equal to the value you enter

>> Unequal to (<>) to find records not the same as the text, value, or date you enter

For example, to find all the records where the employee's annual salary is $50,000, you can enter **=50000** or simply **50000** in the Salary field text box of the Criteria data form. However, to find all the records for employees whose annual salaries are less than or equal to $35,000, you enter **<=35000** in the Salary field text box. To find all the records for employees with salaries greater than $45,000, you would enter **>45000** in the Salary field text box instead. If you wanted to find all the records where the employees are female and make more than $35,000, you would enter **F** in the Gender field text box and **>35000** in the Salary field text box in the same Criteria data form.

Try It

Exercise 17-2: Finding and Editing Records with the Data Form

In Exercise 17-2, you practice using the data form generated for an Excel table to find and edit particular records in the table.

1. Open the Exercise17-2.xlsx file in the Chap17 folder in your Excel Workbook folder.

   This workbook contains a complete version of the Employee Table you created in the previous exercise. You can use this version of the Employee Table worksheet to practice using the data form to find records that need editing.

2. Click the Form button on your customized Misc tab on the Ribbon to open the data form for the Employee Table and then click the form's Criteria button.

   Excel displays a blank data form where you can enter the search criteria in the appropriate fields.

You need to find Sherry Caulfield's record in the table to edit it. Unfortunately, you don't remember how she spells her last name, only that it begins with a C (and not a K) and that she works in the Boston office.

3. Enter **C*** in the Last Name field and Boston in the Location field.

   The wildcard character (the asterisk) you entered after the C stands for all the other missing letters in her name.

4. Click the Find Next button in the data form.

   The first record that Excel finds where the last name begins with the letter C and the office location is Boston is that of William Cobb.

5. Click the Find Next button a second time.

   This time, Excel locates Sherry Caulfield's record, the 25th record of the 32 total.

6. Change Sherry's profit sharing status from no to yes by replacing No with **Yes** in the Profit Sharing field in the data form. Click the Criteria button.

   Next, find Charles Smith's record in the Employee Table, an employee in the Administration department.

7. Select the Clear button to clear the previous search criteria and then enter **Smith** in the Last Name field and **Administration** in the Dept field. Then, click the Find Next button.

   Excel finds the record for Steven Smith in Administration.

8. Click the Find Next button a second time.

   This time, Excel locates Charles Smith's record, the 29th record of the 32 total.

9. Change Charles Smith's location from San Francisco to **Chicago**. Click the Close button to make the change and, at the same time, close the data form.

10. Save your changes to the Employee Table worksheet in a new workbook named Employee Table - edited.xlsx in the Excel Practice folder. Leave the workbook file open for the next exercise.

Sorting Tables

Excel's Sorting feature enables you to rearrange the records or even the fields in your table. You sort the records in your table by sorting the rows, whereas you sort the fields in the table by sorting the columns.

In sorting, you can specify either ascending or descending sort order for your data. When you specify ascending order (which is the default), Excel arranges text in A-to-Z order and values from smallest to largest. When you specify descending order, Excel reverses this order and arranges text in Z-to-A order and values range from largest to smallest. When sorting on a date field, ascending order puts the records in least-recent-to-most-recent date order, whereas descending order gives you the records in most-recent-to-least-recent date order.

When you choose the ascending sort order for a field that contains multiple data types, Excel places numbers (from smallest to largest) first, then text (in alphabetical order), followed by Logical values (TRUE followed by FALSE), error values, and, finally, blank cells. When using the descending sort order, the program uses the same general arrangement for the different types of entries, but numbers go from largest to smallest, text runs from Z to A, and the FALSE logical value precedes the TRUE logical value.

Using sorting keys

To sort your data, Excel uses sorting keys to determine how the records or fields should be reordered in the table. When sorting records, you indicate by cell address which field (column) contains the first or primary sorting key. When sorting fields, you indicate which record (row) contains the primary sorting key. Excel then applies the selected sort (ascending or descending) to the data in the key field or record to determine how the program reorders the fields or records during sorting.

When a key field contains duplicate entries, Excel lists these records in the order in which they were entered in the table. To indicate how Excel should order records with duplicates in the primary key, you define a secondary key. For example, if, when organizing the table in alphabetical order by the Last Name field, you have several records where the last name is Smith, you can have Excel order the Smiths' records in alphabetical order by first name by defining the First Name field as the secondary key. If the secondary key contains duplicates (say you have two Jane Smiths in your company), you can define a third key field (the Middle Name field, if your table has one) that determines how the duplicate Jane Smith records are arranged when the table is sorted.

Although sorting is most often applied to rearranging and maintaining table records and fields, you can use the Sort command to reorder data in any worksheet range.

REMEMBER

Exercise 17-3: Sorting the Records in a Table

In Exercise 17-3, you practice sorting records in the employee table you edited in the previous exercise, using various fields as the sorting keys.

1. With the Employee Table worksheet active in the Employee Table - edited.xlsx file, click the Last Name field's drop-down Filter button in cell C1 and then click the Sort A to Z option on its drop-down menu.

    Excel sorts all the records in the Employee Table so that they are in alphabetical order by last name. Note that the program indicates that the table has been sorted in ascending order using the values in the Last Name field by displaying an arrow pointing upward on this field's Filter drop-down button.

2. Click the Salary field's Filter button in cell F1 and then click Sort Largest to Smallest on its drop-down menu.

    Excel sorts all the records in the Employee Table so that they are in numerical order from largest to smallest by salary. This time, the program indicates that the table has been sorted in descending order using the values in the Salary field by displaying an arrow pointing downward on this field's Filter button.

3. Choose Data ⇨ Sort (or press Alt+ASS).

The Sort dialog box appears and Excel selects all of the records in your table (omitting the field names in the first row with the field names). The Sort dialog box enables you to add multiple levels of sorting keys to be used in the sort operation.

Begin by sorting the records in the table so that they are in alphabetical order by department and then in descending order by salary.

4. Click the Sort By drop-down list button and then click Dept on its list field in the Sort By drop-down list box and then click the A to Z option in the Order column. Then, click the Add Level button and select the Salary field in the Then By drop-down list box. Select the Largest to Smallest option in its Order drop-down list and click OK.

Excel reorders the records in the Employee Table so that first they are in alphabetical order by department (Accounting, Administration, Engineering, and so on) and then within each department in order from highest to lowest salary ($38,000, $34,400, $29,000 and so on).

Next, sort the records in the table alphabetically by department, location, and then last name. To perform this sort operation, you need to define three keys all using the A to Z Order option.

5. Open the Sort dialog box and then define the Dept field as the Sort By key, the Location field as the first Then By key, and the Last Name field as the second Then By key (added by clicking the Add Level button), each with its A to Z Order option selected, and click OK.

Excel reorders the records in the Employee Table so that first they are in alphabetical order by department (Accounting, Administration, Engineering, and so on), and then within each department in order by location (Boston, Detroit, San Francisco, and so on), and finally in order by Last Name (Edwards, Percival, Savage, and so on).

6. Close the Employee Table - edited.xlsx workbook file without saving your changes to the file.

Sorting a table on multiple keys

Sometimes, you may need to sort on more than three fields as you practiced in the previous exercise. For example, suppose you are working with a personnel table and you want to organize the records in alphabetical order first by department, and then by supervisor, and finally by last name, first name, and middle name. To sort the records in this table by these five fields, you have to define the following five keys in the Sort dialog box:

➤➤ Sort by Department in A to Z order

➤➤ Then by Supervisor in A to Z order

➤➤ Then by Last Name in A to Z order

➤➤ Then by First Name in A to Z order

➤➤ Then by Middle Name in A to Z order

Exercise 17-4: Sorting a Table on Five Keys

In Exercise 17-4, you practice sorting the data in a sample personnel table on five sorting keys:

1. Open the Exercise17-4.xlsx file in the Chap17 folder in your Excel Workbook folder.

    This workbook contains a copy of the personnel table that you sort in alphabetical order first by the department name, and then by the supervisor's name, and finally by the employee's last, first, and middle name.

2. Choose Data⇨Sort (or press Alt+ASS), then define the five keys (Department, Supervisor, Last Name, First Name, and Middle Name) using the A to Z Order option, and click OK.

    Check the Department and Supervisor fields in the re-sorted table and verify that they are now in alphabetical order first by department name and then by supervisor name. Note in the case of supervisor Johnson in the Administration department that the name of his two William Smith employees are in order by their middle names (William Dennis Smith before William Mathew Smith).

3. Save your sorted personnel table worksheet in a new workbook file named Pers Table – 5keysort.xlsx in your Excel Practice folder and leave the workbook file open for the next exercise.

Sorting the fields (columns) in a table

You can use Excel's column sorting capability to change the order of the fields in a table without having to cut and paste columns. To sort the fields in a table, add a row at the top of the table containing numbers from 1 to the number of the last field in the table (these numbers indicate the desired order of the fields). You then sort the table by column using this row as the sole sorting key.

WARNING

When sorting the columns in a table, you must remember to click the Options button and select the Sort Left to Right option button in the Orientation section of the Sort Options dialog box. Otherwise, Excel sorts your records instead of your columns and, in the process, the row of field names become sorted in with the other data records in your table!

To see how to go about sorting the columns of a table, sort the columns of the Personnel Table you worked with in the previous exercise so that the fields appear in the following order: SSN, Department, Supervisor, First Name, Middle Name, Last Name, Title, Salary.

Exercise 17-5: Sorting the Fields in a Table

In Exercise 17-5, you practice sorting the fields to change the order of the fields in an existing table.

1. With the Personnel Table worksheet active in the Pers Table – 5keysort.xlsx workbook file whose records you sorted in the previous exercise, select row 1 in the worksheet and then click the Insert button on the Ribbon's Home tab.

   Excel inserts a blank row at the top of the Personnel Table worksheet.

2. Make the following numerical entries in the designated cells of the new, blank row 1:

   - **1** in cell A1
   - **6** in cell B1
   - **4** in cell C1
   - **5** in cell D1
   - **2** in cell E1
   - **3** in cell F1
   - **7** in cell G1
   - **8** in cell H1

   You now use the values you entered into the cells in row 1 to sort the columns of the table. However, Excel doesn't allow you to sort columns when a range is configured as a table. The only way to sort a table's columns is to first convert the table to a normal cell range, sort the columns, and then convert the range back to a table.

3. Click cell A2, choose Table Design➪Convert to Range, and then click Yes in the alert dialog box asking whether you want to convert the table into a normal cell range.

   Now you're ready to open the Sort dialog box so that you can sort the columns of the table.

4. Select the cell range A1:H20 and then choose Data➪ Sort (or press Alt+ASS) to open the Sort dialog box.

   The first thing to do is to change the options so that Excel sorts the columns from left to right rather than the rows from top to bottom.

5. Click the Options button to open the Sort Options dialog box, click the Sort Left to Right option button in the Orientation section, and click OK.

   This step is crucial because it's only by selecting the Sort Left to Right option that you sort by columns instead of the usual rows.

   Now you're ready to define row 1 as the sole sorting key.

6. Click Row 1 in the Sort By drop-down list, leave the default Smallest to Largest option selected, and click OK.

   The fields of the Personnel Table are now arranged in this order: SSN, Department, Supervisor, First Name, Middle Name, Last Name, Title, and Salary.

7. Delete the top row of the Personnel Table by clicking the row's header on the left edge of the worksheet and then clicking the Delete button on the Cells group of the Home tab.

   Excel removes the row with the column numbers used in sorting the fields of the table.

8. Click cell A1 and then choose Home⇨Format As Table. Then, click the White, Table Style Light 15 thumbnail in the drop-down gallery, and click OK in the Format As Table dialog box asking you to confirm $A$1:$H$19 as the table range with row 1 containing its headers.

   Excel reapplies the table formatting, adding the filter buttons to each of the field names in row 1.

9. Click cell A1 and then save the Personnel Table worksheet with the sorted fields and records in a new workbook named Pers Table – fieldsort.xlsx in your Excel Practice folder and then close the workbook file.

Subtotaling a Table

You can use Excel's Subtotals feature to subtotal data in a sorted table. To subtotal a table, you first sort the records in the table on the field you want subtotaled and then designate the field that contains the values you want totaled. (These don't necessarily have to be the same fields in the table.)

When you use the Subtotals feature, you aren't restricted to having the values in the designated field added together with the SUM function. You can instead have Excel return the number of entries with the COUNT function, the average of the entries with the AVERAGE function, the highest entry with the MAXIMUM function, the lowest entry with the MINIMUM function, or even the product of the entries with the PRODUCT function.

Try It

Exercise 17-6: Subtotaling the Records in a Table

In Exercise 17-6, you practice adding subtotals and grand totals to fields in a version of the employee table.

1. Open the Exercise17-6.xlsx file in your Chap17 folder in the Excel Workbook folder on your hard disk.

   This workbook contains a copy of the employee table that you can use to practice using Excel's Subtotal feature.

2. Sort the employee table, first alphabetically by department, and then numerically, from largest-to-smallest order by salary.

HINT

Be sure to select the Largest to Smallest Order option after selecting Salary as the Then By key in the Sort dialog box (Alt+ASS).

You sort the records in the table by the Dept field and then the Salary field because you want Excel to subtotal the salaries in each department. The Dept field provides what is referred to as the break in the subtotals report because each time the department entry changes, Excel computes a subtotal (in this case, a subtotal of the values entered in the Salary field).

However, before you can subtotal the table, you must convert its table into a normal range of cells.

3. Click cell A2, choose Table Design⇨Convert to Range, and then click Yes in the alert dialog box asking you to confirm converting the table into a normal cell range.

   Excel removes the filter buttons from the table.

4. Choose Data⇨Subtotal (or press Alt+AB) to open the Subtotal dialog box.

   You must supply at least three pieces of information in the Subtotal dialog box:

   - Field at which the subtotals break in the At Each Change In drop-down list box
   - Function to use in computing the subtotals (Sum is the default, but you can also select Count, Average, Max, Min, or Product) in the Use Function drop-down list box
   - Field(s) whose values are to be subtotaled by selecting the check box in front of the field name in the Add Subtotal To list box

5. Click the Dept option on the At Each Change In drop-down list box. Then, click Sum on the Use Function drop-down list box. Finally, select the Salary check box in the Add Subtotal To list box, deselect any other check boxes in this list, and click OK.

   Excel subtotals the salaries in Employee Table by department, while at the same time adding outline buttons to the rows. (Figure 17-1 shows how the first part of this table should now appear in your Employee Table in Excel.)

   You can use these outline buttons to collapse and expand the subtotals in the table.

6. Click the number 1 button at the top of the row header to collapse the subtotals down to the grand total of all the salaries for all departments in row 39 and then widen column F, if necessary, to display its grand total.

   The first level of the outlined rows shows only the grand total. Next, display the subtotals for each of the departments in the table.

7. Click the number 2 button at the top of the row header.

   Excel now displays the rows with the salary totals for Accounting in row 7, Administration in row 13, Engineering in row 26, Human Resources in row 33, and Information Services in row 38, along with the grand total of all salaries in row 39.

8. Click the number 3 button at the top of the row header to redisplay the rows with all the records in the table along with the Salaries Department subtotals and Salary grand total. Press Ctrl+8 to hide the outline buttons.

Use Ctrl+8 whenever you want to hide or display the buttons and other controls in any spreadsheet you've outlined.

TIP

9. Click cell A1 and then save the employee table with the subtotals in a new workbook file named Employee Table – subtotal.xlsx in your Excel Practice folder and then close the workbook file.

1 2 3		A	B	C	D	E	F	G
	1	ID No	First Name	Last Name	Gender	Dept	Salary	Location
	2	000222	Mary	King	F	Accounting	$38,000	Detroit
	3	000928	Joy	Adamson	F	Accounting	$34,400	Boston
	4	000226	Adam	Rosenzweig	M	Accounting	$29,000	Detroit
	5	000159	Sherry	Caulfield	F	Accounting	$24,100	Boston
	6	000174	Cindy	Edwards	F	Accounting	$21,500	San Francisco
	7					Accounting Total	$147,000	
	8	000199	Steven	Smith	M	Administration	$100,000	Seattle
	9	000339	Charles	Smith	M	Administration	$87,800	San Francisco
	10	000146	Edward	Krauss	M	Administration	$86,200	Chicago
	11	000101	Michael	Bryant	M	Administration	$30,440	Santa Rosa
	12	000192	Deborah	Mosley	F	Administration	$20,800	Detroit
	13					Administration Total	$325,240	
	14	000634	Gene	Poole	M	Engineering	$75,000	Chicago
	15	000211	Stuart	Johnson	M	Engineering	$62,000	Seattle
	16	000210	Victoria	Morin	F	Engineering	$40,700	Seattle
	17	000247	Elaine	Savage	F	Engineering	$38,900	Atlanta

FIGURE 17-1:
The first part of the Employee Table after subtotaling its salaries by department.

Filtering a Table

It's one thing to set up a table and load it with tons of data, but it's quite another to get just the information you need out of the table. The procedure for specifying what data you want displayed in an Excel table is called filtering the table. The procedure for extracting only the data you want from the table is called querying the table.

At the most basic level, Excel enables you to filter out all but the information you need with its AutoFilter feature, which temporarily hides the display of unwanted records. To filter a table, you must display the Filter drop-down buttons in the row of cells containing the fields for the table.

TIP

A table's filter buttons are displayed by default, but if for some reason you don't see them, click any cell in the table and select the Table Design tab's Filter Button check box.

Excel adds drop-down buttons to each of the field names in the top row of the table. When you click a field's Filter drop-down button, its drop-down menu contains a (Select All) check box item (selected by default) at the top of a list of check box items for all the individual items in that field. When you deselect the (Select All) check box, all the check boxes for all the individual entries are all automatically deselected. You can then filter the table to just those records containing particular entries by selecting the check box beside each of those entries.

The filter drop-down menu also contains one of the following three menu items, depending upon the type of entries in that field, each attached to its own continuation menu of criteria options:

» Text Filters for text fields to filter the records of the table using text criteria such as Begins With, Ends With, Contains, and Does Not Contain, and the like

» Date Filters for date fields to filter the records of the table using date criteria such as Today, Tomorrow, This Week, Last Week, This Month, Last Month, and so on

>> Number Filters for calculated fields or fields with numeric entries to filter the records of the table using numerical criteria such as Equals, Does Not Equal, Greater Than, Less Than, Top 10, Above Average, and so forth

The continuation menus attached to each of the three options — Text Filters, Date Filters, and Number Filters — contain a Custom Filter command that you can select to open the Custom AutoFilter dialog box. The Custom AutoFilter dialog box enables you to use more complex filtering criteria. You specify the values to be evaluated in the first and second condition in the associated combo boxes. You also specify the type of relationship between the two conditions with the And or Or option buttons: And means that both criteria must be true for the record to appear in the filter; Or means that at least one of the criteria must be true for the record to appear in the filter.

When selecting the operator for the first and second condition in the leftmost drop-down list boxes at the top and bottom of the Custom AutoFilter dialog box, you have the following choices:

>> Equals

>> Does not equal

>> Is greater than

>> Is greater than or equal to

>> Is less than

>> Is less than or equal to

>> Begins with

>> Does not begin with

>> Ends with

>> Does not end with

>> Contains

>> Does not contain

Note that you can use the Begins with, Ends with, and Contains operators and their negative counterparts when filtering a text field. You can also use the question mark (?) and asterisk (*) wildcard characters when entering the values for use with these operators. (The question mark wildcard stands for individual characters and the asterisk for one or more characters.) You use the other logical operators when dealing with numeric and date fields.

When specifying the values to evaluate in the associated combo boxes on the right side of the Custom AutoFilter dialog box, you can type the text, number, or date, or you can select an existing field entry by clicking the box's drop-down button and then selecting the entry on the drop-down list.

Exercise 17-7: Filtering Records in a Table

In Exercise 17-7, you practice filtering the records in the now-familiar employee table using a number of different criteria.

1. Open the Exercise17-7.xlsx file in your Chap17 folder in the Excel Workbook folder.

    This workbook contains a copy of the Employee Table that you can use to practice querying a table by filtering out all records except for those that contain the data with which you want to work.

2. Click any cell in the table, click the Table Design contextual tab, and then select the Filter Button check box.

    Excel responds by adding filter drop-down list boxes to each of the field names in row 1 of the Employee Table.

    Start by filtering the table to include just the records where the employee is part of the profit-sharing plan.

3. Click the filter drop-down list box in the Profit Sharing field name and then select No on the drop-down list to remove its check mark as well as the check mark in the (Select All) check box. Click OK.

    Excel hides all the records where the Profit Sharing is No, leaving displayed only those where the Profit Sharing entry is Yes.

4. Click the Clear Filter from Profit Sharing option on the Profit Sharing field's drop-down list to redisplay all the records in the table.

    When you filter the records in a table, Excel simply temporarily hides the records.

5. Click the Years of Service filter drop-down button, highlight the Number Filters option, and then click Top 10 on the continuation menu to open the Top 10 AutoFilter dialog box, and click OK.

    The Top 10 AutoFilter dialog box enables you to display only the records with the top or bottom 10 (more or less) values (by selecting Items in the rightmost drop-down list box) or percentage (by selecting Percent in this drop-down list box) in the selected field.

6. Click the Sort Largest to Smallest option on the Years of Service drop-down list to sort the filtered records so that they are displayed from the longest to shortest top ten years of service.

    Excel reorders the filtered records so that they are now in descending order according to the number of years of employment.

7. Redisplay all the records in the table and then click the Salary filter button. Highlight the Number Filters option and then click Custom Filter on the continuation menu to open the Custom AutoFilter dialog box.

    Use the Custom AutoFilter dialog box to filter out all the records except for those where the annual salary is between $40,000 and $75,000.

8. Select Is Greater Than or Equal To in the first drop-down list box and then click the second combo box to its immediate right and type **40000**. Select Is Less Than or Equal To in the second drop-down list box below the AND and OR option buttons (the AND should be selected). Type **75000** in the combo box to its immediate right and click OK.

    Excel filters out all the records in the table except for those where the annual salary is equal to $40,000 or more and $75,000 or less.

9. Sort the filtered records so that they are displayed in descending order by salary (largest to smallest).

    Because the AutoFilter only temporarily hides the display of the records in a table, you need to copy the filtered records to a new part of the worksheet or to a new worksheet when you want to retain the subset for future reference and use.

10. Copy the filtered and sorted records currently displayed in the cell range A1:J33 (including the field names in row 1) on the Employee Table worksheet to the same range on the Sheet2 worksheet. Widen Columns E and G of Sheet2 with AutoFit to display all the entries in this table. Rename the Sheet2 worksheet Salary Subset and then click the Employee Table worksheet to reselect it.

11. Redisplay all the records in the table on the Employee Table worksheet. Use the Custom AutoFilter dialog box to filter the table so that only the records where the department is either Engineering or Information Services are displayed and the records are sorted in ascending (A to Z) order by department name.

HINT

Be sure to select the OR option button in the Custom AutoFilter dialog box. Note that you can select the department names, Engineering and Information Services, from the two Combo boxes after selecting the Equals or Contains operator in the associated drop-down list boxes in this dialog box.

12. Copy the filtered and sorted records (including the field names) to the equivalent cell range in Sheet3 and then rename Sheet3 to Dept Subset.

    You now have filtered and sorted subsets of the larger Employee Table on separate worksheets where you can more easily work with their data.

13. Redisplay all the records in the table on the Employee Table worksheet, position the cell cursor in cell A1, and then save your work in a new workbook called Employee Table – fltrd.xlsx in your Excel Practice folder. Close the workbook file as you exit Excel. If Excel displays a dialog box saying "There is a large amount of information on the Clipboard. Do you want to be able to paste this information into another program later?", click No.

Querying External Database Tables

Excel makes it possible to query other external databases to which you have access and then extract the data that you're interested in into your worksheet for further manipulation and analysis. The external databases that you can query can be anything from those you maintain with a dedicated database management program such as Microsoft Access all the way up to and including the corporate database itself.

To create a query that acquires data from an external database, you must complete two basic procedures:

>> Define the data source; that is, the external database that contains the data you want to query

>> Specify the query itself, including all the columns of data that you want extracted along with the criteria for selecting them

Exercise 17-8: Importing a Data Table from an Access Database

In Exercise 17-8, you practice importing the Products data table from the Northwind database that accompanies Microsoft Access, and then sorting and filtering the records in this data table.

1. Open a new workbook (Ctrl+N), and then choose Data ⇨ Get Data ⇨ From Database ⇨ From Microsoft Access Database (or press Alt+APNDC).

   Excel opens the Import Data dialog box where you specify the Access database to query.

2. Select the Northwind.accdb file inside the Chap17 folder inside the Excel Workbook folder and click the Open button.

   Excel opens the Navigator dialog box listing all the data tables and queries defined for the Northwind database. Enlarge this dialog box as needed to see more of the many tables and queries created for this sample database.

3. Select Products and then choose Load ⇨ Load To.

   Excel opens the Import Data dialog box, where you specify whether to import the data as a regular table using the Table (default) option, a PivotTable (see Chapter 20) using the PivotTable Report option, or a PivotChart using the PivotChart option. You can also choose between importing the Access data to a particular cell range in the current worksheet or on a new worksheet added to a new workbook file.

4. Leave the Table option selected, select the Existing Worksheet option (with cell $A$1 designated as the first cell into which to import the data), and then click OK.

   Excel imports all the data in the Product data table into the Sheet1 worksheet of your new workbook. When the program imports this data into your worksheet, it automatically formats it as a table using Green, Table Style Medium 7 table style. Excel also displays the Queries & Connections pane, which you can close.

5. Assign the White, Table Style Light 8 style to the product table and then rename Sheet1 as **NW Product Table**.

   In this lighter table style, the data records are somewhat easier to read.

6. Sort this product table in Smallest to Largest order on the UnitsInStock field and then filter the records so that only those for products that have not been discontinued are displayed.

Sort the table by selecting the Sort Smallest to Largest option on the UnitsInStock field's filter button's drop-down menu and then filter the records by selecting only the FALSE option in the Discontinued field's filter button's drop-down menu.

7. Save the new workbook with the NW Product Table worksheet containing the Products data table in your Excel Practice folder under the filename NWdb Query Practice.xlsx and then leave the workbook open for the next exercise.

Try It

Exercise 17-9: Querying Data in a Data Table in an Access Database

Instead of importing all the fields and all the records in a data table in an external database into an Excel worksheet as you did in the previous exercise, you can create a query that brings in only the fields you want and the records that meet the criteria you set. In Exercise 17-9, you practice setting up such a query that imports just the fields in a sample Microsoft Access database table that meet the criteria you set up.

1. With the NWdb Query Practice.xlsx file that you created in Exercise 17-8 open in Excel, click New Sheet to add the Sheet2 tab, and then rename Sheet2 as NW Prd Qry. Then, choose Data ⇨ Get Data ⇨ From Other Sources ⇨ From Microsoft Query (or press Alt+APNOM).

   The Choose Data Source dialog box opens, where you indicate the source (database, query, or cube) that holds the data you want to import.

2. Click the MS Access Database option on the Databases tab in the Choose Data Source dialog box and then click OK.

   The Select Database dialog box opens where you select the Access .accdb file to use (Northwind.accdb in the Chap17 folder inside your Excel Workbook folder, in this case).

3. If necessary, double-click Documents in the Directories list box and then double-click the Excel Workbook folder followed by the Chap17 folder. Finally, click Northwind. accdb in the Database Name list box and click OK.

   The Query Wizard - Choose Columns dialog box opens where you select the tables and the fields (columns) from those tables that you want to include in the query.

4. Scroll down the Available Tables and Columns list box on the left until you locate Products. Then, click the Expand button (+) to display the names of its fields. Add the following five fields to the Columns in Your Query list box on the right side of the dialog box by clicking their field names in the Available Tables and Columns list box and then clicking the > button in succession:

   - ProductName
   - QuantityPerUnit
   - UnitPrice
   - UnitsInStock
   - Discontinued

The Columns in Your Query list box now displays the names of these five fields in the order in which you added them.

5. Click the Next button to display the Query Wizard – Filter Data dialog box. Then, click UnitPrice in the Column to Filter list box and set up a condition where only records in which the products cost between $10.00 and $25.00 are queried.

In the Only Include Rows Where list box, set up an AND condition where UnitPrice is greater than or equal to 10 and is less than or equal to 25.

HINT

6. Click Discontinued in the Column to Filter list box and then set up a condition where only records in which the items that have not been discontinued are queried.

In the Only Include Rows Where list box, set up the condition, Discontinued equals 0 (the equivalent of FALSE).

HINT

7. Click the Next button to open the Query Wizard – Sort Order dialog box. Then, click ProductName in the Sort By drop-down list, leave the Ascending option button selected, and then click Next.

The Query Wizard – Finish dialog box appears. Here, you choose between viewing the data and editing the query in Microsoft Query or returning the data to Excel. In addition, you can save the query for re-use at a later time.

8. Click the Save Query button to open the Save As dialog box. Then replace the default filename, Query from MS Access Database.dqy with **NWdb Products in Stock.dqy** and then click Save.

The Save As dialog box closes and you return to the Query Wizard – Finish dialog box, where the Return Data to Microsoft Excel option button is selected.

9. Click the Finish button to close the Query Wizard dialog box. Then, with cell $A$1 of the NW Prd Qry sheet in your NWdb Query Practice workbook selected, click OK in the Import Data dialog box to import the queried data from the Northwind Products data table into Excel.

Excel imports the records that meet your filtering criteria (unit price between $10 and $25 and not discontinued) sorted by product name. Note, however, that these filtered records only include entries for the ProductName, QuantityPerUnit, UnitPrice, UnitsInStock, and Discontinued fields of the Products data table.

10. Assign the White, Table Style Light 8 style to the queried Product table on the NW Prd Qry sheet of your workbook.

Now you can insert a new column in the queried Product table that calculates the extended price by multiplying the unit price in column C by the number of units in stock in column D.

11. Insert a new column between columns D and E in the queried Product table and then rename this column in cell E1 from Column1 to Extended Price. Then, create a formula in cell E2 that multiples the value in C2 by that in D2.

Note that as soon as you create the formula =C2*D2 in cell E2, Excel instantly copies it to all the other rows of the table in the Extended Priced column (the real benefit of formatting a range as an Excel table).

12. Save the changes you've made before you exit Excel.

Chapter **18**

Protecting Workbooks and Worksheet Data

E xcel enables you to secure your work on two levels:

» Use a password to protect the workbook file so that only the people you trust with the password can open the file to view, print, or edit the data.

» Use a password to protect the worksheets in a workbook from unwarranted changes so that only people with that password can modify the contents and design of the worksheet.

In this chapter, you practice securing your Excel workbooks and worksheets on both these levels. You also get to practice doing data entry in a protected worksheet where all your movements and edits are restricted to the unlocked cells where such changes are allowed.

Password-Protecting the Workbook

By password-protecting the workbook, you can prevent unauthorized users from opening the workbook and editing it. You set a password for opening the workbook file when it contains worksheets whose data are of a sufficiently sensitive nature that only a certain group of people in the company should have access to them (such as worksheets dealing with personnel information and salaries). Of course, after you set a password for opening a workbook, you must supply this password to those people who need access to it for them to be able to open the file.

You set a password for modifying the workbook when you're dealing with worksheets whose data needs to be viewed and printed by different users, none of whom are authorized to make changes to any of the entries. For example, after a workbook has been through a complete editing and review cycle and all the suggested changes have been merged, you might assign a password for modifying it to those who have the authority can do so before distributing the workbook company-wide.

When you're dealing with a worksheet that contains sensitive data that should not be modified even by users authorized to open the workbook, you need to set both a password for opening and a password for modifying the workbook file. You can assign either one or both of these types of passwords to a workbook file when you first save it by choosing File ⇨ Save (Ctrl+S) or File ⇨ Save As (F12) or click the Save button on the Excel title bar.

WARNING A password-protected workbook file for which you can't remember the correct password can be a big problem — especially if you're talking about an important workbook with loads of vital data. So, for heaven's sake, don't forget your password. If you think that you might forget the workbook's password, you may want to write it down somewhere and keep that piece of paper in a secure place (preferably under lock and key). It's often better to be safe than sorry when it comes to passwords for opening vital, but sensitive, workbook files.

Try It

Exercise 18-1: Assigning a Password for Opening and Editing a Workbook

In Exercise 18-1, you practice assigning passwords that are required to open and to edit the contents of an Excel workbook file.

1. If Excel is not currently running, launch the program. Then open Exercise18-1.xlsx in your Chap18 folder in the Excel Workbook folder.

    This workbook contains three worksheets: Employee Data List, Salary Subset, and Department Subset. Use this sample workbook file to practice assigning a password for opening the workbook and another for editing its worksheets.

2. Choose File ⇨ Save As (or press Alt+FA), and then click More Options to open the Save As dialog box. (You can also just press F12 to open the Save As dialog box.) Then, open the Excel Practice folder and replace the filename Exercise18-1.xlsx with **Employee List – protected.xlsx** in the File Name text box, but don't click the Save button quite yet.

To assign a password for opening and/or for editing the workbook, you need to open the General Options dialog box.

3. Click the Tools button to the left of the Save button at the bottom of the dialog box and then select General Options on its drop-down list to open the General Options dialog box.

The General Options dialog box contains a Password to Open and a Password to Modify text box where you can enter these passwords. This dialog box also contains an Always Create Backup check box that, when selected, tells Excel to automatically make a backup copy of the workbook you're saving. (You can use the backup if the original file is corrupted and becomes unusable.) The Read-Only Recommended check box, when checked, assigns read-only status to the workbook you're saving. However, a user can override the read-only status by opening the file and then clicking Edit Anyway in the information bar that appears.

4. Type **opensesame** (all lowercase letters) as the password in the Password to Open text box and then click the Password to Modify text box.

Note that Excel automatically masks each character as you type it by replacing it with a dot. Keep in mind that all passwords are case-sensitive; for example, the passwords opensesame, Opensesame, and OpenSesame are three different passwords.

5. Type **abracadabra** in the Password to Modify text box and then click OK.

Excel displays the Confirm Password dialog box, where you must reenter the opensesame password for opening the Employee List - protected.xlsx workbook file.

6. Type **opensesame** in the Reenter Password to Proceed text box and then click OK.

A second Confirm Password dialog box appears, where you must reenter the abracadabra password for modifying the Employee List - protected.xlsx workbook file.

7. Type **abracadabra** in the Reenter Password to Modify text box and then click OK.

Assuming that you were able to faithfully and exactly reproduce the opensesame password to open and abracadabra password to modify, Excel returns you to the Save As dialog box.

8. Click the Save button to save the Employee List - protected.xlsx file with the passwords to open and modify the workbook. Then close the workbook (Ctrl+W).

Now try reopening the password-protected workbook file.

9. Choose File ⇨ Recent and then click Employee List – protected.xlsx on at the top of the document list on the Recent Workbooks panel or press Alt+FR and type the number assigned to file.

Excel displays a Password dialog box, informing you that the Employee List – protected.xlsx file is protected.

10. Type the password to open the file, **opensesame**, in the Password text box and then click OK.

As soon as you click OK to close the first Password dialog box where you entered the password to open the workbook file, a second one appears prompting you to enter the password for write access to the file. Note that if you are unable to provide this password, Excel opens the workbook file in read-only mode (so that changes to the file can only be saved in a copy of the file).

11. Type the password to modify, **abracadabra**, in the second Password text box and then click OK.

    As soon as you correctly enter the second password, Excel opens the Employee List - protected.xlsx workbook for editing or printing just as it would a non-protected workbook.

    Go ahead and remove the password to modify the workbook as this kind of protection amounts to little more than saving the workbook file as a read-only file.

12. Choose File⇨Save As and then click More Options (or press F12) to get back to the Save As dialog box, and then open the General Options dialog box by choosing Tools⇨General Options.

    To remove a password from a file, delete it from the Password to Open or Password to Modify text box in the General Options dialog box.

13. Select all the masked characters in the Password to Modify text box, press the Delete key to remove them, and click OK.

14. Click the Save button in the Save As dialog box, and then click Yes in the confirmation alert dialog box to save the Employee List - protected.xlsx workbook without a write-access password.

15. Close the Employee List - protected.xlsx workbook and then try reopening it again.

    This time, you only need to reproduce the opensesame password to open the workbook file.

16. Close the Employee List - protected.xlsx workbook a last time without saving any further changes to it.

Protecting the Worksheet

After you've toiled to get your worksheet set up just so, you'll want to use Excel's Protection feature to prevent inadvertent and unauthorized changes to the worksheet. Few things are as unpleasant as having an inexperienced data entry operator doing major damage to the data and formulas that you've worked so hard to construct and validate. To keep the data and formulas in a worksheet safe from all unwarranted changes, you need to protect the worksheet.

All cells in the workbook have one of two different protection formats: locked or unlocked and hidden or unhidden. In a new workbook, all the cells are locked and unhidden. However, these formats mean nothing until you turn on protection in the worksheet. Once you activate worksheet protection, Excel prevents users from making any editing changes to all locked cells and from using the Formula bar to view the contents of all hidden cells when they contain the cell cursor.

However, you'll rarely want to lock every cell in the worksheet. Instead, you'll want to lock most cells, but unlock only those cells that users are allowed to edit. What this means in practice is that prior to turning on worksheet protection, you go through the worksheet removing the Locked protection format from all the cell ranges where you or your users still need to be able to do data entry and editing even when the worksheet is protected. You also assign the Hidden protection format to all cell ranges in the worksheet where you don't want the contents of the cell to be displayed when protection is turned on in the worksheet. Then, after activating protection, the user can make changes only to the unlocked cells and display on the Formula bar the contents of the unhidden cells in the sheet.

TIP

When setting up worksheet templates, unlock all the cells where users need to input new data and keep locked all the cells that contain headings and formulas that never change. You may also want to hide cells with formulas if you're concerned that their display might tempt the users to waste time trying to fiddle with or finesse them. Then, turn on worksheet protection prior to saving the file in the template file format. You are then assured that all worksheets generated from that template automatically inherit the same level and type of protection as you assigned in the original worksheet.

When you open the Protect Sheet dialog box (choose Review ➪ Protect Sheet or press Alt+RPS) to turn on protection, Excel gives you an opportunity to assign a password to unprotect the sheet. This is highly recommended because otherwise, a savvy user could remove the worksheet protection by choosing Review ➪ Unprotect Sheet. This dialog box also contains the following list of check boxes that enable you to specify the worksheet editing actions that users allowed to perform even after you turn on worksheet protection:

>> **Select Locked Cells:** Enables users to move the cell cursor into the locked cells of the worksheet even when they can't change their contents. Note that this check box is selected by default but you can deselect it when you want to restrict movement to just the cells containing the unlocked protection format that allow data entry.

>> **Select Unlocked Cells:** Enables users to move the cell cursor into the unlocked cells of the worksheet so that they can make changes to them. Note that deselecting this check box automatically deselects the Select Locked Cells check box as well, making it impossible to move the cell cursor to any cells in the worksheet and subsequently make any type of editing changes in the worksheet, which is very rarely your intention.

>> **Format Cells:** Enables the formatting of cells (with the exception of changing the locked and hidden status on the Protection tab of the Format Cells dialog box).

>> **Format Columns:** Enables formatting so that users can modify the column widths and hide and unhide columns.

>> **Format Rows:** Enables formatting so that users can modify the row heights and hide and unhide rows.

>> **Insert Columns:** Enables users to insert new columns in the worksheet.

>> **Insert Rows:** Enables users to insert new rows in the worksheet.

>> **Insert Hyperlinks:** Enables users to insert new hyperlinks to other documents, both local and on the Web.

>> **Delete Columns:** Enables users to delete columns in the worksheet.

>> **Delete Rows:** Enables users to delete rows in the worksheet.

>> **Sort:** Enables users to sort data in unlocked cells in the worksheet (see Chapter 17).

>> **Use AutoFilter:** Enables users to filter data in the worksheet (see Chapter 17).

>> **Use PivotTable and PivotChart:** Enables users to create and work with PivotTables and PivotCharts in the worksheet (see Chapter 20).

>> **Edit Objects:** Enables users to edit graphic objects such as text boxes, embedded images, and the like, in the worksheet (see Chapter 16).

>> **Edit Scenarios:** Enables users to edit what-if scenarios, including modifying and deleting them (see Chapter 19).

Try It

Exercise 18-2: Protecting a Worksheet

In Exercise 18-2, you practice password–protecting a worksheet so that further modifications are restricted to a single range of data–entry cells.

1. Open Exercise18-2.xlsx in your Chap18 folder in the Excel Workbook folder.

    This workbook contains a copy of the Depreciation worksheet that you worked with in Chapter 9. You use the Depreciation Table on this worksheet to practice unlocking cells before turning on protection in the worksheet.

2. Select the cell range C3:C6 in the Depreciation worksheet and then choose Home⇨Format⇨Lock Cell (or press Alt+HOL) to deactivate the Lock Cell command.

    These four cells constitute the input cells for the Depreciation Table where users can still be able to enter new values even after you turn on worksheet protection. By leaving the protection status of the other cells set to locked in the worksheet, you ensure that no one can make any changes to the formulas in the table itself, either intentionally or otherwise.

3. Choose Review⇨Protect Sheet (or press Alt+RPS) to open the Protect Sheet dialog box (see Figure 18-1).

FIGURE 18-1:
The Protect Sheet dialog box when it first opens.

When the Protect Sheet dialog box first opens, only the Protect Worksheet and Contents of Locked Cells check box and the Select Locked Cells and Select Unlocked Cells check boxes in the Allow All Users of This Worksheet To box are selected.

4. Type **stet** (the Latin command meaning "Let it stand") in all lowercase letters in the Password to Unprotect Sheet text box and then click OK without bothering to de-select any of the three check boxes that are automatically selected.

   Now you must re-enter the stet password exactly as you entered it the first time to set it in the worksheet.

5. Retype **stet** in the Reenter Password to Proceed text box in the Confirm Password dialog box before clicking OK.

   Now without the stet password, users of this worksheet can only make changes in the four cells you unlocked in Step 2, although they can still select any cell in the sheet.

6. Make the following changes to the designated cells in the Depreciation worksheet:

   - **35000** in the Cost cell, C4
   - **7** in the Life_in_years cell, C5
   - **5000** in the Salvage cell, C6

   Excel enables you to make these changes because you assigned the unlocked protection formatting to these cells before turning on worksheet protection. Because the worksheet still uses the default automatic recalculation setting, the program recalculates the depreciation values in the Depreciation Table (C9:F19) each time you update an input value.

7. Position the cell cursor in cell D17 containing the first of the #NUM! error values in the table and then press F2 to put Excel in Edit mode.

   Excel beeps at you and displays a warning dialog box indicating that the cell or chart you're trying to change is protected.

8. Click OK and then position the cell cursor in the merged cell B2 and then press the Delete key to remove its contents.

   Again, Excel beeps at you and displays the warning dialog box indicating that the cell or chart you're trying to change is protected.

9. Click OK and then open the Home tab's Insert and Format buttons' pull-down menus and notice how many of the commands are grayed out, indicating that they are currently unavailable.

   These commands are not available to users unless you specifically enable them when turning on worksheet protection.

10. Choose Review⇨Unprotect Sheet or press Alt+RPS to open the Unprotect Sheet dialog box. Then type **stet** in its Password text box and click OK.

    Excel turns off the worksheet protection, leaving all cell entries in the sheet at risk.

11. Press the Delete key again when the cell cursor is in cell B2.

    This time, Excel gets rid of the heading at the top of this table.

12. Choose Home⇨Undo (or press Ctrl+Z) to restore the deleted table heading. Then, click the Protect Sheet button on the Review tab (or press Alt+RPS) to re-open the Protect Sheet dialog box. This time, select the Format Cells check box, leave the default check boxes selected (don't bother to assign a password to unprotect this time), and then click OK.

    By selecting the Format Cells check and then turning on the worksheet protection, you enable formatting changes to locked cells in the worksheet, while at the same time denying the ability to make changes to their contents or delete them.

13. While the cell cursor is still located in cell B2, press Ctrl+I to italicize the Depreciation Table heading in this cell with italics. Then, press the Delete key.

    This time, Excel allows you to change the formatting of the heading in this cell while still preventing you from deleting its text.

14. Click OK and then position the cell cursor in cell A1. Then, save the protected version of the Depreciation worksheet in a new file named Depreciation Table – protected.xlsx in your Excel Practice folder before you close the workbook.

Doing Data Entry in a Protected Worksheet

When protecting a worksheet, you can easily set it up so that you and your users can jump right to the unlocked cells and avoid ever having to deal with the locked ones (that you can't change anyway) by using the Tab and Shift+Tab keys to navigate the worksheet. All you have to do is format the cells that need changing as unlocked and then deselect the Select Locked Cells check box in the Protect Sheet dialog box when you turn on the worksheet protection.

When you press the Tab key in such a protected worksheet, Excel moves the cell pointer to the next unlocked cell to the right of the current one in that same row. When you reach the last unlocked cell in that row, pressing Tab takes you to the first unlocked cell in the rows below. To move back to a previous unlocked cell, press Shift+Tab. When Excel reaches the last unlocked cell in the worksheet, pressing Tab takes you back to the first unlocked cell on the sheet.

REMEMBER

Provided that you haven't changed the After Pressing Enter, Move Selection direction of the Enter key in the Editing Options section of the Advanced tab in the Excel Options dialog box (Alt+FT), you can also use the Enter key to move down the columns instead of across the rows.

Try It

Exercise 18-3: Doing Data Entry in a Protected Worksheet

In Exercise 18-3, you practice doing data entry in a protected worksheet by first unlocking the cells that require data entry before turning on protection in the worksheet.

1. Open Exercise18-3.xlsx in your Chap18 folder in the Excel Workbook folder.

    This workbook contains a copy of the Spring Sale worksheet that is missing the furniture description and retail price information (all the other data is entered along with the formulas that determine the sale price). Use the sales table in this worksheet to practice doing data entry in a protected worksheet where your movements are restrained to just the unlocked cells in the sheet.

2. Select the cell range C4:D9 in the Spring Sale worksheet and then choose Home⇨Format⇨Lock Cell (or press Alt+HOL) to deactivate the Lock Cell command and unlock the selected cells.

   You unlock these cells because you still need to be able to make data entries in them after you turn on the worksheet protection.

3. Choose Review⇨Protect Sheet (or press Alt+RPS) to open the Protect Sheet dialog box. Then, deselect the Select Locked Cells check box, leave the other settings as is (don't bother to assign a password to unprotect the worksheet), and then click OK.

   After turning on worksheet protection with this check box unselected, Excel constrains the movement of the cell cursor to just the unlocked cell range C4:D9 in the worksheet.

4. Click cell C4 and then press the Tab key repeatedly until you've moved the cell cursor through each of the cells in the unlocked cell range, C4:D9.

   Excel now restrains the movement of the cell cursor to this range of unlocked cells in the worksheet.

5. Click cell A1 to attempt to locate the cell cursor in the Home cell of the Spring Sale worksheet.

   Note that clicking any cell outside of the unlocked cell range C4:D9 is no longer allowed as long as worksheet protection is in effect.

6. Position the cell cursor in cell C4 and then make the following data entries across the rows of the unlocked cell range in the designated cells by pressing Tab to complete each entry and, at the same time, move the cell cursor to the next cell in the same or next row:

   - **36-inch round table** in cell C4
   - **1250** in cell D4
   - **72-inch dining table** in cell C5
   - **1400** in cell D5
   - **Hutch** in cell C6
   - **2500** in cell D6

   Note that each time you press Tab to complete an entry in the Retail Price column and to move down to the next unlocked cell in the row below, Excel calculates the amount of the markdown and the new sales price for that item.

7. While the cell cursor is positioned in cell C7, make the following data entries down the columns of the unlocked cell range in the designated cells by pressing the Enter key to complete each entry and, at the same time, move the cell cursor to the next cell in the same or next column:

   - **Side chair** in cell C7
   - **Armchair** in cell C8

- **Armoire** in cell C9

- **350** in cell D7

- **500** in cell D8

- **1750** in cell D9

8. With the cell pointer back in cell C4, save the protected worksheet version with the completed Spring Sale Furniture Prices table in a new workbook named **Spring Furniture Sale – protectedentry.xlsx** in your Excel Practice folder and then close the workbook.

Protecting the Entire Workbook

You can apply one last level of protection to your Excel data and that is to protect the entire workbook. When you protect the workbook, you ensure that its users can't change the structure of the file by adding, deleting, or even moving and renaming any of its worksheets.

To protect your workbook, you open the Protect Structure and Windows dialog box (choose Review ⇨ Protect Workbook or press Alt+RPW). This dialog box contains two check boxes: Structure (which is automatically checked) and Windows (which is not selected and is also disabled). This dialog box also contains a Password (Optional) text box, where you can enter a password that must be supplied before you can unprotect the workbook.

When you protect a workbook with the Structure check box selected, Excel prevents you or your users from doing any of the following tasks to the file:

>> Insert new worksheets

>> Delete existing worksheets

>> Rename worksheets

>> Hide or view hidden worksheets

>> Move or copy worksheets to another workbook

>> Display the source data for a cell in a pivot table or display a table's page fields on separate worksheets (see Chapter 20)

>> Create a summary report with the Scenario Manager (see Chapter 19)

After you've enabled protection in a workbook, you can then turn it off by choosing Review ⇨ Protect Workbook (or pressing Alt+RPW). If you've assigned a password to unprotect the workbook, you must enter it in the Password text box in the Unprotect Workbook dialog box that then appears.

Exercise 18-4: Protecting the Entire Workbook

In Exercise 18-4, you practice protecting an entire workbook file while at the same time becoming familiar with the type of editing restrictions this protection entails.

1. Open Exercise18-4.xlsx in your Chap18 folder in the Excel Workbook folder.

   This workbook contains a copy of the Employee Data List, Salary Subset, and Department Subset you've worked with in earlier exercises. You use this file to practice protecting the workbook from further changes.

2. Choose Review⇨Protect Workbook (or press Alt+RPW).

   Excel opens the Protect Structure and Windows dialog box.

3. Leave the Structure check box selected.

4. Enter **letitbe** as the protect workbook password in the Password (Optional) text box and then click OK. Then, retype **letitbe** in the Reenter Password to Proceed text box in the Confirm Password dialog box that appears and then click OK.

   Now that you've protected the workbook, see what happens when you try making routine changes to it.

5. Double-click the sheet tab for the Employee Table worksheet as though you were going to rename it.

   Excel beeps at you and displays an alert box declaring, "Workbook is protected and cannot be changed."

6. Click OK in the alert dialog box and this time attempt to drag the sheet tab for the Employee Data List worksheet to reposition it as the last worksheet in the workbook.

   Excel now resists all attempts at reordering the sheets in a workbook: Any attempt to drag any sheet to a new position in the workbook only results in the displaying of the International No symbol (a circle with a backslash in it).

7. Right-click the Employee Table tab and note that the Insert, Delete, Rename, Move or Copy, Tab Color, Hide, and Unhide commands are all currently grayed out and unavailable.

   Now save this protected version of this sample workbook file under a new filename.

8. Save the protected workbook in a new file named **Employee List – protectedwrkbk. xlsx** in your Excel Practice folder and then close the workbook as you exit Excel.

5
Doing Data Analysis

» **Creating and playing with different scenarios**

» **Performing goal seeking**

» **Creating models with the Solver add-in**

Chapter **19**

Performing What-If Analysis

What-if analysis is a way of interrogating your worksheet data by playing around with different formula inputs to see how the formula result changes. This type of analysis is really a way of asking one or more "What if. . .?" questions: What if interest rates rise by one percentage point? What if they fall by two percentage points? What if I increase the down payment by $10,000? What if I increase it by $50,000?

Using what-if analysis in the worksheet to examine possible outcomes based on different inputs is one of Excel's fortes. Sure, you can build a model and plug in different formula input values by hand, but Excel offers a few data analysis tools that can make it much easier to interrogate your models. These tools include one- and two-variable data tables, Goal Seek, and Scenario Manager. And if these are not enough, it also includes the Solver add-in utility, which enables you to model more complex problems. In this chapter, you get a chance to practice performing what-if analysis using all these tools.

Performing What-If Analysis with Data Tables

In a normal Excel worksheet, you see the effect of changing an input value on the result returned by a formula as soon as you enter that new input: Each time you change this input value, Excel automatically recalculates the formula and shows you the new result based on the new value.

This method is fine for small models where you only need to test a few different values. This method is of limited use, however, when you're performing what-if analysis based on a large number of different input values and you want to easily compare all the results.

To perform this type of what-if analysis, you can use Excel's Data Table command. When creating a data table, you enter a series of input values in the worksheet, and Excel then uses each of them in the formula you specify. When Excel finishes computing the data table, you see the results produced by each change in the input values in a single range of the worksheet. You can then save the data table as part of the worksheet if you need to keep a record of the results of a series of input values.

Creating a single-variable data table

In a one-variable data table, Excel substitutes a series of different values for a single input value in a formula. To create a one-variable data table, you need to set up the master formula in your worksheet and then, in a separate range of the worksheet, enter the series of values that you want substituted for a single input operand in that formula.

Try It

Exercise 19-1: Constructing a Single-Variable Data Table in a Worksheet

In Exercise 19-1, you practice creating a data table with a single variable that changes with each what-if input value.

1. If Excel is not currently running, launch the program. If the program is already running and no workbook is displayed, create a new workbook (Ctrl+N). Leave the cell cursor in cell A1 of the first worksheet and then name this sheet as Data Table 1.

    You use this new blank worksheet to practice creating a single-variable data table that computes projected sales growth based on various growth rate percentages.

2. Enter the title, **Sales Projections**, in cell A1, choose Home ⇨ Cell Styles, and then apply the Title style from the gallery. Widen column A to display this entire title and make the following data entries in the designated cells:

    - **Sales** in cell A2

    - **Growth Rate** in cell A3

    - **Projected Sales** in cell A4

    - **$875,000** in cell B2

    - **2.75%** in cell B3

3. Name the cells in the cell range B2:B4 with the headings you entered in the cell range A2:A4.

HINT

    Select the entire range A2:B4 and then choose Formulas ⇨ Create from Selection button to open the Create Names from Selection dialog box. Be sure that only the Left Column check box is selected, and then click OK.

4. Position the cell cursor in the Projected_Sales cell (B4) and construct the following formula:

```
=Sales + (Sales * Growth_Rate)
```

Note that Excel automatically assigns the range name given to cell B2 rather than the cell address as you build the formula by pointing and selecting its references.

5. Format the cell with the Accounting format by choosing Home➪Accounting Number Format ($). Reduce the decimal places to zero by choosing Home➪Decrease Decimal two times. Copy this formatting by choosing Home➪Format Painter and then clicking the Sales cell (B2).

Now that you have the input values in place in the worksheet, you're ready to build the data table that will test different variables in the basic formula.

6. Paste a link to the Projected_Sales cell (B4) in cell C6 of the worksheet to bring its value forward to this cell.

HINT

Copy the contents of cell B4 into the Clipboard (choose Home➪Copy or press Ctrl+C) and then paste the link in cell C6 by choosing Home➪Paste➪Paste Link (or press Alt+HVN). Then, widen column C and press the Esc key to remove the marquee from the Projected_Sales cell (B4).

7. Enter the following potential growth rate percentages in the designated cells:

- **1.00%** in cell B7
- **1.50%** in cell B8

8. Use the fill handle to copy this series of half-percentage point increases down column B to the cell range B7:B17 so that the series ends with a 6.00% growth rate.

Be sure to select cell B7 and B8 as a range with the cell cursor before you drag the fill handle down to cell B17.

HINT

9. Select the cell range B6:C17. Choose Data➪What-If Analysis➪Data Table (or press Alt+AWT) to open the Data Table dialog box.

The Data Table dialog box contains two text boxes: Row Input Cell, where you indicate the variable from the top row of the data table that is to be substituted in the master formula, and Column Input Cell, where you indicate the variable that is to be substituted from its first column.

Because this one-variable input table contains the substitute values in a single column of the data table (cell range B7:B17), you only need to use the Column Input Cell text box in this case. And because the Growth_Rate cell (B3) contains the original value you want substituted in the master formula in cell B4, you need to enter this cell reference in this text box.

10. Position the cursor in the Column Input Cell text box, click the Growth_Rate cell (B3), and then click OK.

Excel then fills in the data table, substituting in succession the growth rate percentage entered in the cell range B7:B17 for the Growth_Rate cell in the master formula.

11. Click cell C6, choose Home⇨ Format Painter, and then drag the Format Painter through the range C7:C17. Check your results against those shown in Figure 19-1.

Next, examine the formula that Excel used in creating this single-variable data table.

| C7 | | ⌄ | : | × ✓ | *fx* | {=TABLE(,B3)} |

	A	B	C
1	Sales Projections		
2	Sales	$ 875,000	
3	Growth Rate	2.75%	
4	Projected Sales	$ 899,063	
5			
6			$899,063
7		1.00%	$883,750
8		1.50%	$888,125
9		2.00%	$892,500
10		2.50%	$896,875
11		3.00%	$901,250
12		3.50%	$905,625
13		4.00%	$910,000
14		4.50%	$914,375
15		5.00%	$918,750
16		5.50%	$923,125
17		6.00%	$927,500
18			

FIGURE 19-1: The completed one-variable data table.

12. Position the cell cursor in cell C7 and examine the contents of the formula on the Formula bar.

Excel inserts the following array formula (see Chapter 7) using the TABLE function in the cell range C7:C17 of the data table:

```
{=TABLE(,B3)}
```

The TABLE function can take two arguments, row_ref and column_ref, which represent the row input cell and column input cell for the data table, respectively. In this example, the data table uses only a column input cell, so B3 is the second and only argument of the TABLE function. Because Excel enters the results in a data table using an array formula, Excel won't allow you to clear individual result cells in its output range. If you try to delete a single result in the data table, Excel displays an alert dialog box telling you that you cannot change part of a data table.

13. Increase the value in the original Growth_Rate cell, B3, from **2.75%** to **2.875%** and the initial value in the range of variables from **1.00%** to **1.25%**.

The moment you enter the new 2.875% growth rate percentage in cell B3, Excel recalculates the values in cells B4 and C6, increasing them from $899,063 to $900,156. The moment you enter the new initial variable rate of 1.25%, the program recalculates the result in cell C7 of the data table and replaces the original value of $883,750 with $885,938.

You can, however, select the recalculation setting that automatically recalculates all formulas in the worksheet except those in data tables. That way, you can control exactly at what point Excel recalculates your data table using the new variables you've entered.

14. Choose Formulas ⇨ Calculation Options ⇨ Automatic Except for Data Tables (or press Alt+MXE).

    Now that you've put Excel in automatic recalculation except for data tables, see how the program responds when you modify the original growth rate percentage and the initial growth rate variable.

15. Reduce the value in the original Growth_Rate cell, B3 from 2.875% (displayed as 2.88%) to **2.50%** and the initial value in the range of variables from 1.25% to **0.875%** (displayed as 0.88%).

    As soon as you reduce the percentage in cell B3, Excel changes the values in cells B4 and C6 from $900,156 to $896,875. However, reducing the initial variable percentage in cell B7 from 1.25% to 0.875% has no immediate effect on the data table cell C7, whose calculated value relies upon this percentage.

WARNING

The Calculate indicator does not appear on the Status bar when you change variables used in the program's data tables after you switch the program's recalculation mode from Automatic to Manual or Automatic Except for Data Tables. This means that when operating in these two recalculation modes, it's entirely up to you to keep track of the changes you make to the variables in the table and whether the values in your data tables are up to date or are in sore need of manual recalculation before printing or publishing and sharing with your co-workers or clients.

16. Click the Calculate Now button on the Formulas tab or press F9.

    As soon as you select this button, Excel reduces the calculated amount in cell C7 from $885,938 to $882,656.

17. Reenter **2.75%** in Growth_Rate cell B3 and then select the Automatic option once again on the Formulas Tab's Calculation Options drop-down button. Save your data table on the Data Table 1 worksheet under the filename Data Table 1 Practice.xlsx in your Excel Practice folder. Leave the workbook open for the next exercise with a two-variable data table.

Creating a two-variable data table

In a two-variable data table, Excel substitutes a series of different values for two input values in a formula. When you create a two-variable data table, you enter two ranges of input values to be substituted in the master formula: a single-row range in the first row of the data table and a single-column range in the first column of the data table. When you create a two-variable data table, you place a copy of the master formula in the cell at the intersection of this row and column of input values.

Exercise 19-2: Constructing a Two-Variable Data Table in a Worksheet

In Exercise 19-2, you practice constructing a data table that changes two variables as it calculates the possible results for your various what-if scenarios.

1. Use the Data Table 1 worksheet in your Data Table 1 Practice.xlsx workbook containing the single-variable data table you constructed in the last exercise.

    You convert the original one-variable data table into a two-variable data table that not only uses a series of growth rate percentages but also a series of projected expenses to sales percentages in calculating possible projected incomes.

2. Select the cell range C6:C17 and then choose Home ⇨ Cells ⇨ Delete. Rename the Data Table 1 sheet to Data Table 2.

    Next, you need to insert blank cells between the ranges A3:B3 and A4:B4.

3. Select the cell range A4:B4 and then choose Home ⇨ Cells ⇨ Insert.

    Excel inserts two new blank cells in the range A4:B4, shifting down the existing entries (Projected Sales and the formula =Sales + (Sales * Growth_Rate) with the calculated result $899,063) to the range A5:B5.

4. Make the following data entries in the designated cells:

    - **Expense Rate** in cell A4

    - **3.00%** in cell B4

5. Assign the range name Expense_Rate to cell B4 containing the 3.00% rate of expenses to sales.

HINT

    You can assign this range name manually by typing Expense_Rate into the Name box of the Formula bar when cell B4 is selected or by choosing Formulas ⇨ Create From Selection when the cell range A4:B4 is selected.

6. Edit the formula in cell B5 as follows:

    ```
    =Sales + (Sales * Growth_Rate) - (Sales * Expense_Rate)
    ```

7. Paste a link to the Projected_Sales cell, B5, in cell B7 of the Data Table 2 worksheet.

    When creating a two-variable data table, you place the formula at the intersection of the row and column in the table that contains the series of input values.

8. Make the following data entries in the designated cells:

    - **2.00%** in cell C7

    - **2.50%** in cell D7

9. Format the cell range C7:D7 with Percent Style number format with 2 decimal places and then use the fill handle to copy this series of half-percentage point increases across row 7 to the cell range E7:G7 so that the series ends with a 4.00% expense/sales growth rate.

HINT

Be sure to select cells C7 and D7 as a range with the cell cursor before you drag the Fill handle across the row to cell G7.

10. Select the data table's cell range B7:G18 and then choose Data⇨What-If Analysis⇨Data Table (or press Alt+AWT) to open the Data Table dialog box.

To create a two-variable data table, you must specify both the Row Input Cell and the Column Input Cell in the Data Table dialog box.

11. Select the Expense_Rate cell (B4) as the Row Input Cell, the Growth_Rate cell (B3) as the Column Input Cell, and then click OK.

Excel then fills in the data table, substituting in succession the growth rate percentage entered in the cell range B8:B18 for the Growth_Rate cell in the master formula, and the expense rate percentage entered in the cell range C7:G7 for the Expense_Rate cell.

12. Use the Format Painter to format the cell range C8:G18 with the number formatting used in cell B7; widen the columns of the table with AutoFit as needed. Then, check your results in your data table against those shown in Figure 19-2.

C8		✕ ✓ *fx*	{=TABLE(B4,B3)}			
	A	B	C	D	E	F	G
1	Sales Projections						
2	Sales	$ 875,000					
3	Growth Rate	2.75%					
4	Expense Rate	3.00%					
5	Projected Sales	$ 872,813					
6							
7		$ 872,813	2.00%	2.50%	3.00%	3.50%	4.00%
8		1.00%	$866,250	$861,875	$857,500	$853,125	$848,750
9		1.50%	$870,625	$866,250	$861,875	$857,500	$853,125
10		2.00%	$875,000	$870,625	$866,250	$861,875	$857,500
11		2.50%	$879,375	$875,000	$870,625	$866,250	$861,875
12		3.00%	$883,750	$879,375	$875,000	$870,625	$866,250
13		3.50%	$888,125	$883,750	$879,375	$875,000	$870,625
14		4.00%	$892,500	$888,125	$883,750	$879,375	$875,000
15		4.50%	$896,875	$892,500	$888,125	$883,750	$879,375
16		5.00%	$901,250	$896,875	$892,500	$888,125	$883,750
17		5.50%	$905,625	$901,250	$896,875	$892,500	$888,125
18		6.00%	$910,000	$905,625	$901,250	$896,875	$892,500
19							

FIGURE 19-2: The completed two-variable data table.

13. Position the cell cursor in cell C8 and examine the contents of the formula on the Formula bar.

Excel inserts the following array formula in the cell range C8:G18 of the data table (note that the TABLE function in this formula uses both the row_ref and column_ref arguments):

```
{=TABLE(B4,B3)}
```

14. Save the Data Table 2 worksheet with your completed two-variable data table in a new workbook with the filename Data Table 2 Practice.xlsx in your Excel Practice folder and then close the workbook.

Analyzing Data with Scenarios

The data tables that I describe in the previous section enable you to perform what-if analysis based on varying the input in one or two so-called *changing cells*, which are cells referenced in a formula. However, it's not uncommon for a data model to have three or more changing cells. To perform what-if analysis on these more complex models, you can use Excel's Scenario Manager analysis tool.

A *scenario* consists of a group of formula input values to which you assign a name such as Best Case, Worst Case, Most Likely Case, and so on. Excel's Scenario Manager enables you to create and save scenarios and then apply all the input values at once by choosing the name of the scenario. This enables you to quickly view the results produced by each scenario in the worksheet. You can also use Scenario Manager to create a summary report showing you both the input values stored in each scenario as well as key results produced by each.

Try It

Exercise 19-3: Constructing Various Scenarios for a Worksheet

In Exercise 19-3, you practice using Scenario Manager to set up a most-likely, best-case, and worst-case scenario for projected sales. You also practice in creating a summary report that shows you the inputs and results used by each of these scenarios.

1. Open the Exercise19-3.xlsx workbook file in the Chap19 folder in your Excel Workbook folder.

    The Sales Forecast worksheet in this workbook contains the Sales Forecast table that you use to practice creating and using different growth scenarios using different rate of sales growth, COGS (cost of goods sold), and expenses.

2. Select the following changing cells for your scenarios as one cell selection (by holding down the Ctrl key as you click them):

    - Sales_Growth (H4)

    - COGS (H5)

    - Expenses (H7)

3. Choose Data⇨What-If Analysis⇨Scenario Manager (or press Alt+AWS) to open the Scenario Manager dialog box.

    The first time you open Scenario Manager in a worksheet, no scenarios are defined. You must use its controls to create the different scenarios that you want to apply to a data table.

4. Click Add to open the Add Scenario dialog box, type **Most Likely** in the Scenario Name text box, and then click OK.

The Scenario Values dialog box opens. Here, you indicate the values to be used by the changing cells in the Most Likely scenario you're building. Excel picks up the existing values 0.05, 0.2, and 0.28 for the Sales_Growth, COGS, and Expenses changing cells from the entries made in cells H4, H5, and H7, respectively.

5. Click OK to accept these values.

   The Scenario Manager dialog box reappears and you see the Most Likely scenario in the Scenarios list.

6. Click Add to open the Add Scenario dialog box, type **Worst Case** as the name for a second scenario, and then click OK.

   The Scenario Values dialog box appears again so that you can enter the values for this new scenario.

7. Change the values in the designated changing cells of the Scenario Values dialog box as follows:

   - **0.02** in Sales_Growth
   - **0.3** in COGS
   - **0.4** in Expenses

8. Click OK to return to the Scenario Manager dialog box.

   The Scenarios list now shows both the Most Likely and the Worst Case scenario.

9. Add a third scenario named **Best Case** on your own with the following changing values:

   - **0.1** in Sales_Growth
   - **0.05** in COGS
   - **0.1** in Expenses

   When you finish adding this last scenario, the Scenario Manager dialog box lists three scenarios: Most Likely, Worst Case, and Best Case.

10. With Best Case selected in the Scenario Manager dialog box, click the Show button at the bottom of the Scenario Manager dialog box.

    Excel plugs the Best Case scenario's values into the changing cells in the Sales Forecast table.

11. Take a look at the Worst Case scenario in the Sales Forecast table by double-clicking Worst Case in the Scenarios list box of the Scenario Manager dialog box.

    Note that you can use the Scenario Manager to quickly plug any number of different scenarios into your data table.

12. Display the Most Likely scenario in the Sales Forecast table and then close the Scenario Manager dialog box.

    Next, enter a series of values into the Sales_Growth, COGS, and Expenses cells in the Sales Forecast for table that are not used by any of your defined scenarios.

13. Enter the following values in the designated changing cells in the Sales Forecast for table:

   - **17%** in the Sales_Growth cell, H4
   - **25%** in the COGS cell, H5
   - **18%** in the Expenses cell, H7

14. Reopen the Scenario Manager dialog box and then click the Summary button in the Scenario Manager dialog box.

   Excel opens the Scenario Summary dialog box where you define the type of summary report to create (standard table or PivotTable) and range of cells containing the formulas into which the various scenario input values are to be applied.

15. Leave the Scenario Summary option selected, use the Result Cells range box to select the cell range B8:G8 in the worksheet table, and then click OK.

   As soon as you click OK, Excel inserts a Scenario Summary worksheet in front of the Sales Forecast worksheet in the Exercise19-3.xlsx workbook. This worksheet contains an outlined summary table that displays the total projected income for all four quarters along with the values of the Most Likely, Worst Case, and Best Case scenarios used to calculate these totals (as shown in Figure 19-3).

16. Move the Scenario Summary worksheet so that it follows the Sales Forecast worksheet, and then click cell A1 in the Sales Forecast worksheet. Then save your work in a new workbook file named Scenario Manager Practice.xlsx in your Excel Practice folder and close the workbook file.

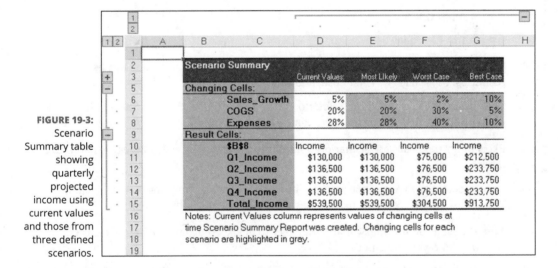

FIGURE 19-3: Scenario Summary table showing quarterly projected income using current values and those from three defined scenarios.

Goal Seeking in a Worksheet

Sometimes, you know the outcome that you want to realize in a worksheet and you need Excel to help you find the input values necessary to achieve those results. This procedure, which is just the opposite of the what-if analysis you've been doing so far, is referred to as goal seeking.

When you only need to find the value for a single variable that will give the desired result in a particular formula, you can perform this simple type of goal seeking with Excel's Goal Seek command. If you have charted the data and created a two-dimensional column, bar, or line chart, you can also perform the goal seeking by directly manipulating the appropriate marker on the chart.

To use the Goal Seek command, you select the cell containing the formula that will return the result you are seeking (referred to as the *set cell*), indicate what value you want this formula to return, and then select the cell that is the input value that Excel can change to return the desired result (referred to as the *changing cell*).

Try It

Exercise 19-4: Goal Seeking in a Worksheet

In Exercise 19-4, you practice using the Goal Seek feature to find out how much the projected sales have to change to reach a particular income target.

1. Open the Exercise19-4.xlsx workbook file in the Chap19 folder in your Excel Workbook folder.

    The workbook contains a version of the Sales Forecast table that you worked with in the previous exercise with an embedded Clustered Bar chart immediately below it. You will use this table and chart to practice doing goal seeking using both the Goal Seek command and direct manipulation of the data series in the Clustered Bar chart.

2. Position the cell cursor in cell C8 containing the forecasted income for the first quarter of the year and then choose Data➪What-If Analysis➪Goal Seek (or press Alt+AWG).

    Excel opens the Goal Seek dialog box with cell C8 entered in its Set Cell text box. The Goal Seek dialog box also contains a To Value text box, where you enter the target value you're seeking, and a By Changing Cell text box, where you indicate the cell whose value should be changed to reach the target value.

3. Type **500000** in the To Value text box. In the By Changing Cell text box, click cell C4 (which contains the Qtr 1 Sales figure in the worksheet). Click OK.

    Excel opens the Goal Seek Status dialog box. In this case, the dialog box indicates that the program has found a solution that increases the income in cell C8 to the target value, $500,000.

    Note that not only does Excel update the values in the Sales Forecast table to reach the target value but it also redraws the embedded Clustered Bar chart to suit as well.

4. Click OK to close the Goal Seek Status dialog box. Choose Home➪Undo (or press Ctrl+Z) to restore the original values to the Sales Forecast table and Clustered Bar chart.

    Excel restores the original values to the cell range C4:G8 and redraws the embedded clustered bar chart below to suit.

5. Choose Home⇨Redo (or press Ctrl+Y) to return to the values entered as the result of your goal seeking.

   You can switch between Undo and Redo to your heart's content to compare the two different goal-seeking scenarios.

6. Click cell A1 and save your work in a new workbook file named Goal Seek Practice.xlsx in your Excel Practice folder and then close the workbook file.

Creating Complex Models with Solver

Although the Data Table and Goal Seek commands work just fine for simple problems that require determining the direct relationship between the inputs and results in a formula, you need to use the Solver add-in when dealing with more complex problems. For example, you would use the Solver to find the best solution when you need to change multiple input values in your model and you need to impose constraints on these values or the output value.

REMEMBER

If you don't see the Solver button on the Data tab, you need to install the Solver add-in. Choose File⇨Options, click Add-Ins, make sure Excel Add-Ins appears in the Manage list, and then click Go. In the Add-Ins dialog box, select the Solver Add-In check box and then click OK.

The Solver works by applying iterative methods to find the "best" solution given the inputs, desired solution, and the constraints that you impose. During each iteration, the program applies a trial-and-error method (based on the use of linear or non-linear equations and inequalities) that attempts to get closer to the optimum solution.

When using the Solver, you need to remember that for many problems, especially the more complicated ones, there can be many solutions. Although the Solver returns the optimum solution, given the starting values, the variables that can change, and the constraints you define, this solution is often not the only one possible and, in fact, may not be the best solution for you. To be sure that you are finding the best solution, you may want to run the Solver more than once, adjusting the initial values each time you solve the problem.

When setting up the problem in your worksheet model to be solved by the Solver, you define the following items:

>> Target cell, which is the cell in your worksheet whose value is to be maximized, minimized, or made to reach a particular value

>> Changing cells, which are the cells in your worksheet whose values are to be adjusted until the answer is found

>> Constraints, which are the limits you impose on the changing values or the target cell

After you finish defining the problem with these parameters and you have the Solver solve the problem, the program returns the optimum solution by modifying the values in your worksheet. At that point, you can choose to retain the changes in the worksheet or restore the original values to the worksheet. You can also save the solution as a scenario to view later before you restore the original values.

You can use the Solver with the Scenario Manager to help set up a problem to solve or to save a solution so that you can view it later. The changing cells that you define for the Scenario Manager are automatically picked up and used by the Solver when you select this command, and vice versa. Also, you can save the Solver's solution to a problem as a scenario (by clicking the Save Scenario button in the Solver dialog box) that you can then view with the Scenario Manager.

Try It

Exercise 19-5: Using Solver to Modify Multiple Input Values in a Worksheet

In Exercise 19-5, you practice using the Solver add-in to modify multiple input values in a forecast table.

1. Open the Exercise19-5.xlsx workbook file in your Chap19 folder in the Excel Workbook folder.

   The workbook contains a copy of the Sales Forecast worksheet with the Sales Forecast table that you will use to practice using the Solver add-in to reach a target income based on changes to multiple parameters.

2. Choose Data ⇨ Solver (or press Alt+AY3 to open the Solver Parameters dialog box.

3. In the Set Objective text box, click cell G8 in the worksheet table to replace the default $A$1 value with $G$8.

   Next, you need to set the target equal to a new value and then indicate the changing cells.

4. Select the Value Of option button, and then type **650000** in the text box to the immediate right of the Value Of option button. In the By Changing Variable Cells text box, click the COGS cell (H5) and Ctrl+click the Expenses cell (H7).

   The By Changing Variable Cells text box now contains absolute references to the COGS cell ($H$5) and Expenses cell ($H$7) separated by a comma.

5. Click the Solve button in the Solver Parameters dialog box.

   Excel closes the Solver Parameters dialog box and then beeps before opening the Solver Results dialog box. In this case, Solver was able to find a solution to the problem by balancing changes to COGS and Expenses that would result in the desired target net income of $650,000.

   The Solver Results dialog box gives you a choice between retaining the adjusted values in the Sales Forecast table (the Keep Solver Solution option button) and returning to its original values (the Restore Original Values option button). You can also save the solution as a scenario.

6. Click the Save Scenario button to open the Save Scenario dialog box, type **Optimal** in the Scenario Name text box, and then click OK.

   Excel returns you to the Solver Results dialog box.

Because you saved the Solver's solution with the scenario name, Optimal, you can restore these values to the Sales Forecast table by opening the Scenario Manager dialog box, selecting the Optimal scenario, and then clicking Show.

7. Select the Restore Original Values option button, select the Return to Solver Parameters Dialog check box, and then click OK.

Excel returns you to the Solver Parameters dialog box, which retains your earlier settings for the target cell, value, and changing variable cells in their respective use in obtaining the first solution.

8. Click the Add button to the right of the Subject to the Constraints list box to open the Add Constraint dialog box and then click the COGS cell (H5) in the worksheet to insert $H$5 in the Cell Reference text box. Accept the default <= comparative operator. Use the Constraint text box to type **15%** and then click Add.

Excel clears the Cell Reference and Constraint text boxes so that you can define a new constraint.

9. This time, click the Expenses cell (H7) in the worksheet to insert $H$7 in the Cell Reference text box, leave the default <= comparative operator selected, use the Constraint text box to type **12%**, and then click OK.

Excel returns you to the Solver Parameters dialog box, where the following comparative expressions now appear in the Subject to the Constraints list box:

- COGS<=15%
- Expenses<=12%

10. Click Solve.

This time, when the Solver Results dialog box appears, it indicates that the Solver could not find a feasible solution. When the cost of goods sold and the expenses are kept down to these lower percentages, the projected net income must necessarily exceed the target of $650,000. (Note that the Solver has actually returned $757,375 to the Total_ Income cell, G8, using these percentages.)

11. In the Solver Results dialog box, select the Restore Original Values option button, deselect the Return to Solver Parameters Dialog check box, and then click OK.

Now save your forecast model under a new filename.

12. Position the cell cursor in cell A1 and then save your work in a new workbook named **Solver Practice.xlsx** in your Excel Practice folder. Close the workbook file as you exit Excel.

Chapter **20**

Generating PivotTables

Excel's PivotTables enable you to quickly summarize and play around with vast amounts of worksheet data. Many people consider PivotTables to be the most versatile of Excel's many data analysis features, if not its coolest and most powerful. In this chapter, you get the chance to practice creating and using PivotTables and their visual equivalent, PivotCharts, to see how they can help reveal complex relationships in your data that may otherwise go completely unnoticed.

Working with PivotTables

PivotTables are great for summarizing the data in a range, table, or external data source because they do their magic without requiring you to create formulas to perform their calculations. Unlike the Subtotals feature, another summarizing feature you encounter in Chapter 17, PivotTables let you play around with the arrangement of the summarized data, even after you generate the table. (The Subtotals feature only lets you hide and display different levels of totals in the list.) It's this capability to change the arrangement of the summarized data by rotating — or *pivoting* — row and column headings that gives the PivotTable its name.

PivotTables are also flexible in their ability to summarize data using a variety of summary functions (although totals created with the SUM function will probably remain your old standby).

When setting up the original PivotTable, you make several decisions: what summary function to use, which columns (fields) the summary function is applied to, and which columns (fields) these computations are tabulated with. You can also use PivotTables to cross-tabulate one set of data in your table with another. For example, you can use this feature to create a Pivot-Table from an employee database that totals the salaries for each job category cross-tabulated (arranged) by department or job site.

Try It

Exercise 20-1: Filtering an Existing PivotTable

In Exercise 20-1, you practice filtering the data in an existing PivotTable that summarizes the information maintained in an accompanying sample employee table.

1. If Excel is not currently running, launch the program. Then open the workbook Exercise20-1.xlsx in the Chap20 folder in the Excel Workbook folder.

   This workbook contains an Employee Table worksheet with a copy of the employee table followed by an Employee PivotTable worksheet that contains a PivotTable generated from the table. You use this PivotTable to practice filtering which data from the employee table are displayed in the table.

2. Click the Employee PivotTable sheet tab and then click B2. The PivotTable Analyze and Design contextual tabs are added to the Ribbon along with the PivotTable Fields task pane on the right side of the worksheet display.

   The PivotTable that appears on this worksheet uses the following fields from the Employee table:

   - Profit Sharing and Gender fields as the Filters fields (in cells B2 and B3, respectively)

   - Dept field as the only Columns field (in cell B5)

   - Location field as the only Rows field (in cell A6)

   - Salary field as the Values field for the data items in the body of the PivotTable (in the cell range B7:G13) using the SUM function (shown as Sum of Salary in A5)

REMEMBER

The PivotTable Analyze and Design contextual tabs and the PivotTable Fields task pane appear automatically whenever you position the cell cursor in any cell of the PivotTable. They disappear just as automatically when you move the cursor to a cell outside of the cells comprising the PivotTable.

3. Click the filter drop-down button attached to the Profit Sharing filter field in cell B2 and then click the Yes option on its drop-down list. Click OK to display the sum of the salaries in the various departments and locations where the employees do in fact par-ticipate in the profit-sharing plan.

   Excel then displays the sum of the salaries according to location and department for those employees who are part of the profit-sharing plan (as indicated by a Yes in the Profit Sharing field in their records within the Employee table).

4. Click the drop-down button attached to the Gender filter field in cell B3 and then select M on its drop-down list. Click OK.

   Now the body of the PivotTable displays the sum of the salaries in the various departments and locations only where the male employees participate in the profit-sharing plan.

5. Restore the (All) settings to both the Profit Sharing and Gender filter fields by selecting (All) on their respective drop-down lists.

   In addition to being able to filter the contents of the PivotTable by selecting particular criteria on a field's AutoFilter drop-down list (as you did in Steps 3 and 4), you can also filter the contents of your PivotTable with the Slicers feature. The great thing about using Slicers to do this filtering is that Slicers not only enable you to easily set up multiple filtering criteria but also graphically show you the criteria in effect and can be connected to more than one PivotTable.

6. Choose PivotTable Analyze ⟱ Insert Slicer.

   Excel displays the Insert Slicers dialog box containing a list of check boxes for all the fields in your PivotTable.

7. Select the Gender, Location, and Profit Sharing check boxes in the Insert Slicers dialog box and then click OK.

   Excel displays three Slicers — Gender, Location, and Profit Sharing — overlapping each other in the center of the worksheet, resting on top of part of the PivotTable. All the field buttons within each of the three Slicers are selected (indicated by their blue highlighting), signifying that all the items in these fields are displayed in the PivotTable (that is, there is no current filter applied). Excel also displays the Slicer contextual tab at the end of the Ribbon and temporarily hides the PivotTable Fields task pane.

   The Slicers you add to a PivotTable are actually graphic objects that you can resize, move around the worksheet, and position on different layers (see Chapter 16 for more on working with graphic objects) as well as filter the data you want displayed in connected PivotTables by selecting and deselecting their respective field buttons.

8. Use the mouse to drag the Profit Sharing, Location, and Gender Slicers to the right side of the worksheet so that they're side by side with all their buttons displayed. Then, click the M button in the Gender Slicer and the Yes button in the Profit Sharing Slicer. Finally, click the Atlanta button and then Ctrl-click the Boston and Chicago buttons in the Location Slicer.

   Excel redraws the PivotTable so that it now shows just the sum of the salaries for the male employees in the Atlanta, Boston, and Chicago offices who currently participate in the profit sharing plan. Note that these filtering criteria now in effect in the PivotTable are clearly indicated in the three Slicers by the highlighting of all the field buttons you selected.

9. Remove all the data filtering from the Employee List PivotTable by once again selecting all the field buttons in all three Slicers — Gender, Location, and Profit Sharing.

   There are two ways to remove filtering from a Slicer: Click the Clear Filter button in the Slicer's upper-right hand corner or hold down the Ctrl key as you click all the unselected field buttons.

You can also remove filtering from a PivotTable without manipulating the buttons in the Slicers. Simply, click the (All) or (Select All) option on the field's drop-down list in the connected PivotTable itself.

10. Reduce the height of the Gender and Profit Sharing Slicers so that not much more than their titles and respective field buttons are displayed and then position these Slicers side by side underneath the Employee List PivotTable. Next, reposition the Location Slicer so that it's displayed at the end of the PivotTable without overlaying any of the data in the final Grand Total field. Finally, click cell B2 in the Employee PivotTable worksheet to redisplay the PivotTable Fields task pane and the PivotTable Tools contextual tab on the Ribbon.

To resize a Slicer, click it to select it (indicated by the shaded border that appears around its perimeter) and then position the mouse pointer on the edge you want to make larger or smaller and drag once the mouse pointer changes to a white double-headed arrow. To reposition a Slicer in the worksheet, click somewhere in its title bar with the arrowhead pointing to a black cross with arrowheads and then drag the outline of the Slicer to its new location.

You can delete a Slicer as you would any other graphic object in Excel: Click it to select it and then press the Delete key.

Now save your changes to this PivotTable.

11. Select cell A1 on the Employee Table worksheet and then save your changes in a new workbook named PivotTable Filter Practice.xlsx in your Excel Practice folder before you close the workbook file.

Creating PivotTables

To create a new PivotTable, you position the cell cursor in one of the cells of the range or table whose data is to be summarized in the report and then choose Insert ⇨ PivotTable (or press Alt+NVT). Excel then selects all the data in the current list and displays the PivotTable from Table or Range dialog box, where you specify where to create the new PivotTable.

To set up the table, you use the PivotTable Fields task pane to assign fields in the table to the various parts of the PivotTable. You do this by dragging a field name shown in the Choose Fields to Add to Report section at the top of the PivotTable Fields task pane into one of the list boxes for the following areas displayed in the Drag Fields Between Areas Below section:

>> **Filters:** The fields you drag into this area appear at the top of the PivotTable. You use the values in these fields to filter the entire PivotTable report.

>> **Columns:** The fields you drag into this area appear in the top row of the PivotTable. They function as the column headings of the PivotTable.

>> **Rows:** The fields you drag into this area appear in the first column of the PivotTable. They function as the row headings of the PivotTable.

>> **Values:** The fields you drag into this area appear in the body of the PivotTable. The values in these cells are the ones summarized in the table using various statistical functions. Sum is the default, but you can also summarize your data by Count, Average, Max, Min, and so on.

Try It

Exercise 20-2: Creating a New PivotTable

In Exercise 20-2, you practice creating a new PivotTable from scratch using the data in a version of the now-familiar Employee table:

1. Open the workbook Exercise20-2.xlsx in the Chap20 folder in the Excel Workbook folder.

    This workbook contains a copy of the Employee Table worksheet with the table to create a new PivotTable.

2. Choose Insert ⇨ PivotTable (or press Alt+NVT).

    Excel opens the PivotTable from Table or Range dialog box while at the same time selecting the Employee table in the cell range A1:J33.

3. Select the Existing Worksheet option, click the Sheet2 worksheet tab followed by cell A1 so that the Location text box contains Sheet2!$A$1, and then click OK.

    Excel displays the blank PivotTable framework and opens the PivotTable Fields task pane on the right side of the worksheet area. Excel also adds the PivotTable Analyze and Design contextual tabs to the Ribbon (see Figure 20-1).

4. Drag the Profit Sharing field from the Choose Fields to Add to Report section of the PivotTable Fields and drop it into the Filters area in the PivotTable Fields pane. Then drag the following fields and drop them into the following areas on the same pane:

    - Dept field into the Columns area
    - Location field into Rows area
    - Salary field into the Values area

    Excel builds the basic PivotTable shown in Figure 20-2.

5. Rename Sheet2 of the workbook to Employee PivotTable. Then, save your changes to the Employee PivotTable worksheet in a new workbook named Employee List – PivotTable.xlsx in your Excel Practice folder and leave the file open for Exercise 20-3.

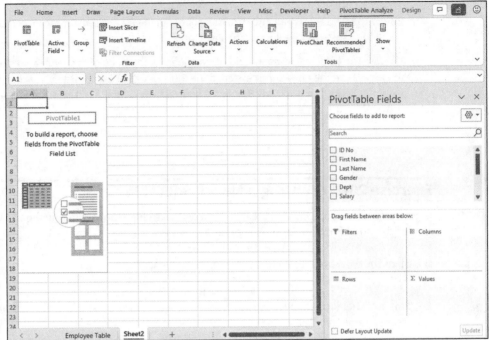

FIGURE 20-1:
Creating a new
PivotTable
using the
Employee table
on Sheet2 of
your practice
workbook.

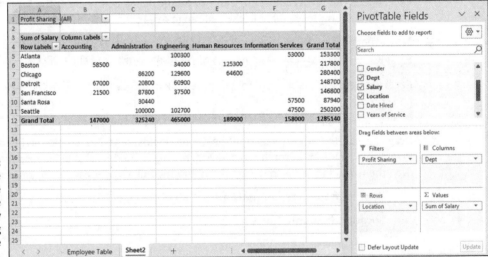

FIGURE 20-2:
The PivotTable
created for the
Employee table
immediately
after specifying
which table
fields to use.

Modifying the PivotTable

The fun just begins with the creation of the basic PivotTable. After that, you can refine its look by using the options on the PivotTable Analyze tab (as you did in Exercise 20-1) or the Design tab or by selecting different portions of the PivotTable and individually formatting them. You can also show and hide new levels of detail in the PivotTable. Perhaps most important, you can modify the structure of the PivotTable by pivoting its row, column, and filter fields. Finally, you can change the PivotTable's summary function as well as add your own calculated fields to the PivotTable.

Modifying the PivotTable formatting

You can modify the formatting of a new PivotTable with the tools available on the Design contextual tab. You can use the Layout options to change the basic layout of the PivotTable as well as the PivotTable Styles gallery and options to quickly transform its look.

Try It

Exercise 20-3: Modifying the Formatting of a PivotTable

In Exercise 20-3, you practice modifying the formatting of the basic PivotTable you created in Exercise 20-2.

1. Select a cell in the PivotTable you built on the Employee PivotTable sheet of the Employee List – PivotTable.xlsx workbook you created in the previous exercise.

    You use this PivotTable to get more practice formatting the table as well as changing what data it summarizes.

2. On the Design contextual tab, display the PivotTable Styles drop-down gallery and click the Light Blue, Pivot Style Medium 2 thumbnail (first row, second column of the Medium section). Then add borderlines to both the columns and rows of the table by selecting the Banded Rows and Banded Columns check boxes in the PivotTable Style Options group.

    Next, you need to format the values being summarized in the body of the table.

3. Click cell A3 (the label, Sum of Salary) and then choose PivotTable Analyze⇨ Field Settings (or press Alt+JTG) to open the Value Field Settings dialog box. Click the Number Format button to open the Format Cells dialog box. Next, click Currency in the Category list box, enter **0** in the Decimal Places text box, click OK to return to the Value Field Settings dialog box, and then click OK to return to the worksheet.

    Excel formats the summed salaries displayed in the body of the PivotTable using the Currency number format without any decimal places.

4. Click the drop-down button in cell B1 to the immediate right of the Profit Sharing field heading, click the Yes option on its drop-down menu, and then click OK.

    Excel updates the table to show the sum of the salaries for only those employees who are part of the profit-sharing plan.

5. Drag the Gender field from the Choose Fields to Add to Report section of the PivotTable Fields task pane and drop it into the Filters area below the Profit Sharing field.

    Excel adds the Gender field as a second field with which the report can be filtered.

6. Click the drop-down button in cell B2 to the immediate right of the Gender field heading, click the M option on its drop-down menu, and then click OK.

    Excel redraws the PivotTable, showing only the sum of the salaries for the male employees who are part of the profit-sharing plan.

7. Remove the filters from both the Profit Sharing and Gender filter fields by clicking the (All) option on their respective drop-down menus.

Now you're ready to save your changes.

8. Click cell B4 in the PivotTable containing the heading Column Labels and then save your changes to the workbook file (Ctrl+S) and leave the workbook file open for Exercise 20-4.

Pivoting the PivotTable's fields

As the name "pivot" implies, the fun of PivotTables is being able to rotate the data fields used as the rows and columns of tables as well as to change what fields are used and how they're presented. For example, suppose in the Employee Table PivotTable that, after making the Dept field the PivotTable's sole column field and the Location field the sole row field, you now want to see what the table looks like with the Location field as the column field and the Dept field as the row field.

No problem: All you have to do is drag the Dept field label in the PivotTable Fields task pane from the Columns area to the Rows area and the Location field label from the Rows area to the Columns area. Voila! Excel rearranges the totaled salaries so that the rows of the PivotTable show the departmental grand totals and the columns now show the location grand totals.

Try It

Exercise 20-4: Modifying the Structure of a PivotTable

In Exercise 20-4, you practice modifying the structure of the Employee able that you built in Exercise 20-2 and completed formatting in Exercise 20-3.

1. With the cell cursor in cell B4 of the Employee PivotTable worksheet of the Employee List – PivotTable.xlsx workbook file, pivot the Dept and Location fields in the table by doing the following:

   - Drag the Dept field label from the Columns area and drop it into the Rows area.
   - Drag the Location field label from the Rows area and drop it into the Columns area.

   Excel pivots the table so that the various office locations now form the columns of the PivotTable and the various departments its rows.

2. Drag the Gender field from the Filters area and drop it into the Rows area underneath the Dept field.

   Adding the Gender field in this manner as a second row field makes it into a subtotaling field so that the PivotTable can now display columns with subtotals of the men's and women's salaries as well as a column with their grand total.

   Note that Excel also adds Hide buttons (indicated by the minus signs) to each department name that you can click to hide the level of detail and show only the subtotals (after turning on the Subtotals option). These Hide buttons are then replaced with

Show buttons (indicated by plus signs) that you can click to display the salary totals for men and women in a particular department.

3. Drag the Profit Sharing field from the Filters area and drop it into the Columns area underneath the Location field.

   Excel makes the employee's profit-sharing status a subtotaling field for the columns of the PivotTable.

4. Drag the Years of Service field from the Choose Fields to Add to Report section of the PivotTable Fields task pane and drop it into the Filters area in the Drag Fields Between Areas Below section.

   Now you can filter the entire PivotTable on the seniority of the employees.

5. Choose Design ⇨ Subtotals ⇨ Show All Subtotals at Bottom of Group (or press Alt+JYTB).

   Excel adds a row of totals for each department and a column of totals for each location in the PivotTable.

6. Choose PivotTable Analyze ⇨ Field List (or press Alt+JTL) to close the PivotTable Fields task pane.

   Next, replace the generic Columns and Rows in the table with their actual field names.

7. Choose PivotTable Analyze ⇨ Options ⇨ Options (or press Alt+JTTT) to open the PivotTable Options dialog box. Click the Display tab, select the Classic PivotTable Layout (Enables Dragging of Fields in the Grid) check box, and then click OK.

   Excel now displays the field names Location and Profit Sharing on the top row of the PivotTable and the field names Dept and Gender in the first two columns.

8. Click cell C4 with the Location field heading and then choose PivotTable Analyze ⇨ Collapse Field button (or press Alt+JTP).

   Excel collapses the profit-sharing detail, showing only the totals of the salaries for each location.

9. Click A6 with the Dept field heading and then choose PivotTable Analyze ⇨ Collapse Field (or press Alt+JTP) again.

   Excel collapses the gender detail, showing only the totals of the salaries for both men and women in each department.

10. Position the cell cursor in cell A4 of the Employee PivotTable worksheet and then save your modifications to the PivotTable (Ctrl+S). Leave the workbook file open for Exercise 20-5.

Changing the PivotTable summary function and adding calculated fields

By default, Excel uses the Sum function to total the values in the numeric field(s) that you assign as the data items in the PivotTable. Some data summaries require the use of another summary function such as Average or Count. To change the summary function, either choose PivotTable Analyze ⇨ Field Settings or double-click the label of the value field (this label is located at the cell intersection of the first column and row field in a PivotTable that has only one data field and uses the default or classic table format). Select the Summarize Values By tab in the Value Field Settings dialog box and select any of the following summary functions in the Summarize Value Field By list box:

>> **Count:** Shows the count of the records for a particular category (note that Count is the default function if you use text data as the value field in a PivotTable).

>> **Average:** Calculates the average (that is, the arithmetic mean) for the values in the field for the current category and page filter.

>> **Max:** Displays the largest numeric value in that field for the current category and page filter.

>> **Min:** Displays the smallest numeric value in that field for the current category and page filter.

>> **Product:** Calculates the product of the numeric values in that field for the current category and page filter (all non-numeric entries are ignored).

>> **Count Numbers:** Displays the number of numeric values in that field for the current category and page filter (all non-numeric entries are ignored).

>> **StdDev:** Calculates the standard deviation for the sample in that field for the current category and page filter.

>> **StdDevp:** Calculates the standard deviation for the population in that field for the current category and page filter.

>> **Var:** Calculates the variance for the sample in that field for the current category and page filter.

>> **Varp:** Calculates the variance for the population in that field for the current category and page filter.

After you select the new summary function to use in the Summarize Value Field By list box in the Value Field Settings dialog box, click OK to have Excel apply the new function to the data presented in the body of the PivotTable.

Besides using various summary functions on the data presented in your PivotTable, you can create your own calculated fields for the PivotTable. Calculated fields are computed by assigning a formula using existing numeric fields in the data source.

After you finish defining a calculated field for a PivotTable, Excel automatically adds its name to the PivotTable Fields task pane and assigns it as a Values data item in the data area of the PivotTable. The program also adds a new data field and makes it the first column field in the PivotTable.

If you want to hide a calculated field from the body of the PivotTable, click the check box in front of the calculated data field's name in the Choose Fields to Add to Report section of the PivotTable Fields pane to remove the check mark. To add the calculated field back into the PivotTable, you click the same calculated field's check box again.

Exercise 20-5: Modifying the Summary Function and Adding a Calculated Field to a PivotTable

In Exercise 20-5, you practice changing the function used to summarize the data in your Employee List PivotTable as well as adding a calculated field to it.

1. With the cell cursor in cell A4 of the Employee PivotTable worksheet of the Employee List – PivotTable.xlsx workbook file, choose PivotTable Analyze ⇨ Field Settings to open the Value Field Settings dialog box. Click Average in the Summarize Value Field By list box on the Summarize Values By tab before, and then click OK.

    The body of your PivotTable now displays the average salary for each department and location in the company.

2. Open the Value Field Settings dialog box again, this time by double-clicking cell A4, and then use it to change the summary function from Average to Max.

    Excel redraws the PivotTable so that it shows you the highest salaries for each department and location in the company.

3. Restore Sum as the summary function in the table and then choose PivotTable Analyze ⇨ Fields, Items, & Sets ⇨ Calculated Field (or press Alt+JTJF).

    Excel opens the Insert Calculated Field dialog box where you define the parameters for a Bonus field that calculates bonuses as 2.5% of the employee's salary.

4. Type **Bonus** in the Name text box in the Insert Calculated Field dialog box and then press Tab to select the Formula text box. In this text box, delete the 0 (zero) after the = (equal) sign (which you want to retain), and then click Salary in the Fields list box followed by the Insert Field button.

    The Formula text box should now read

    ```
    =Salary
    ```

5. Type * (asterisk) followed by **0.025** in the Formula text box.

    The Formula text box should now contain the complete formula

    ```
    =Salary*0.025
    ```

6. Click the Add button and then click OK. Next, choose PivotTable Analyze ⇨ Field List (or press Alt+JTL) to redisplay the PivotTable Fields task pane.

    Note that Excel has added your Bonus field (as Sum of Bonus) as a data item to the body of the PivotTable. Also, note that Bonus appears at the very bottom of the list box in the PivotTable Fields task pane.

7. Position the cell cursor in cell A1 of the Employee PivotTable worksheet and then save your changes to the PivotTable (Ctrl+S) before you close the workbook file.

Creating PivotCharts

You can spice up your data summaries quite a bit by generating a PivotChart along with a supporting PivotTable. To do this, you follow the same procedure as you do when creating a sole PivotTable except that you choose Insert ⇨ PivotChart (or press Alt+NVC).

When creating a new PivotChart with a PivotTable, Excel embeds the PivotChart on the same worksheet that contains the PivotTable regardless of whether you place this table on the active worksheet or a new worksheet. After building the PivotTable (which simultaneously builds the PivotChart as a clustered column chart), you can use the Move Chart button on the Design contextual tab to move the chart to its own chart sheet.

Although Excel uses the clustered column chart as the default chart type for each new Pivot-Chart you generate, you can select another chart type for the PivotChart: Click the Design tab's Change Chart Type button and select the new chart type in the Change Chart Type dialog box as you would for any other chart you're creating.

Try It

Exercise 20-6: Creating a PivotChart

In Exercise 20-6, you practice generating a PivotChart to accompany a new PivotTable that you build for the Employee table that you've been using in the exercises in this chapter.

1. Open the workbook Exercise20-6.xlsx in the Chap20 folder in your Excel Workbook folder.

    This workbook contains a copy of the Employee Table worksheet with the table you use in creating a PivotTable along with a PivotChart.

2. Choose Insert ⇨ PivotChart (or press Alt+NVC).

    Excel opens the Create PivotTable dialog box. Here, you designate the data or table range to be used in creating the PivotTable and chart as well as their location in the workbook. Excel displays a marquee around the table range A1:J33 in the worksheet and displays the range name 'Employee Table'!$A$1:$J$33 in the Table/Range text box.

3. Select the Existing Worksheet option button, click the Sheet2 tab in the worksheet followed by cell A1 of this sheet so that the Location text field contains Sheet2!$A$1, and then click OK.

    Excel inserts two blank frameworks in Sheet2 of your Exercise20-6.xlsx workbook as shown in Figure 20-3. The program also displays the PivotChart Fields task pane on the right side of the worksheet area and the PivotChart Analyze and Design contextual tabs on the Ribbon.

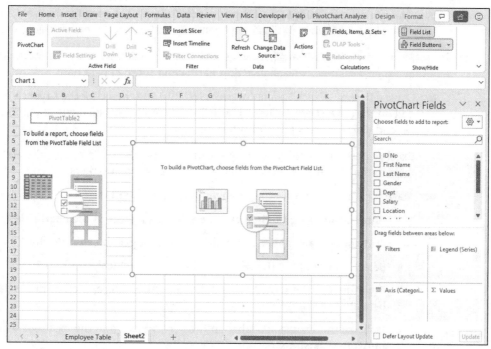

FIGURE 20-3:
Creating a
PivotChart for
the Employee
table.

4. Build the PivotTable by dragging these fields from the Choose Fields to Add to Report section of the PivotChart Fields task pane to the following areas in the Drag Fields Between Areas Below section:

- Dept field to the Filters area
- Gender field to the Legend (Series) area
- Location field to the Axis (Categories) area
- Salary field to the Values area

Excel generates an embedded clustered column chart whose columns compare the men's and women's salaries at the various company locations as it builds the underlying PivotTable.

This embedded chart is active in the worksheet as indicated by the appearance of the PivotChart Analyze contextual tab on the Ribbon.

5. Choose Design ⇨ Move Chart (or press Alt+JCM) to open the Move Chart dialog box. Select the New Sheet option, replace Chart1 with **Employee PivotChart**, and then click OK.

Excel moves the PivotChart to the new Employee PivotChart chart sheet that is inserted in between the Employee Table and Sheet2 worksheets.

6. Rename the Sheet2 tab Employee PivotTable and then reposition this tab so that it is inserted in between the Employee Table worksheet and the Employee PivotChart chart sheet and then click the Employee PivotChart tab to activate the PivotChart sheet.

Next, you change the type of chart used by your PivotChart and refine its formatting.

7. Choose Design⇨Change Chart Type (or press Alt+JCC) to open the Change Chart Type dialog box. Click the 3-D Clustered Column thumbnail and then click OK.

Excel redraws your PivotChart using 3-D clustered columns to represent the women's and men's salaries. Now change the chart layout for the PivotChart.

8. Choose Design⇨Quick Layout (or press Alt+JCL) and then click the Layout 1 thumbnail on the drop-down gallery. Choose Design⇨Add Chart Element⇨Data Table⇨With Legend Keys (or press Alt+JCABW).

Excel redraws the chart, adding a place for a chart title. The program also adds a data table to the bottom of the chart that includes the legend markers.

9. Make the following formatting changes to the PivotChart:

- Enter **Comparing Women and Men Companywide** as the chart title.
- Add horizontal and vertical major and minor gridlines to the chart.
- Select thousands as the display units for the vertical axis.
- Bold the text along the horizontal and vertical axis as well as in the data table beneath the chart.
- Italicize the Thousands label on the vertical axis and the locations along the horizontal axis.

Your PivotChart should now look like the one shown in Figure 20-4.

10. Click the Gender drop-down button above the PivotChart's legend, deselect the (Select All) and M check boxes (leaving only the F check box selected), and then click OK.

Excel redraws your PivotChart with only the blue cylinders representing the totals of the women's salaries displayed.

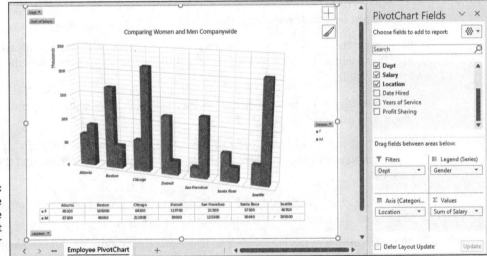

FIGURE 20-4:
The Employee
Table
PivotChart
after
formatting.

11. Click the Gender drop-down button again, select the Select All check box, and then click OK to restore the men's salaries to the PivotChart and then move the Dept field to the Axis (Categories) area and the Location field to the Filters area. Then remove the Sum of Salary field from the Values area and replace this with the Years of Service field.

HINT

To remove a field from a PivotChart, remove the check mark from its field name in the Choose Fields to Add to Report area of the PivotChart Fields pane.

Excel redraws the PivotChart so that it now shows the department names along the horizontal axis and at the top of the data table and compares the women's years of service with that of the men for all office locations.

12. Click the Location drop-down button and filter the clustered cylinder chart so that it represents the years of service for the men and women in only the Atlanta, Chicago, San Francisco, and Seattle office locations.

Select the Select Multiple Items check box on the Filters's drop-down menu, select the Atlanta, Chicago, San Francisco, and Seattle check boxes, and then click OK.

Excel redraws your PivotChart representing the years of service for women and men in just the Atlanta, Chicago, San Francisco, and Seattle offices.

13. Restore all the locations to the chart by selecting the Select All check box on the Locations drop-down menu and then clicking OK. Hide the PivotChart Fields task pane by clicking its Close (X) button.

Next, edit the chart title to reflect the data it now represents.

14. Modify the chart title so that it reads, **Comparing the Service of Women and Men Companywide**.

Now save your work in a new workbook file.

15. Select cell A1 on the Employee Table worksheet and then save your work in a new workbook file with the filename Employee List – PivotChart.xlsx in your Excel Practice folder. Close this workbook file as you exit Excel.

6

Macros and Visual Basic for Applications

Automate common worksheet procedures by recording them as macros.

Assign macros to the Quick Access toolbar and Ribbon.

Edit recorded macros with Excel's Visual Basic Editor.

Code custom Excel functions using the Visual Basic for Applications programming language.

Chapter **21**

Using Macros

D o you perform certain actions in Excel repeatedly? Perhaps you enter the same half dozen labels each time you start a new worksheet. Perhaps you apply the same formatting and options each time you create a new table or chart. These repetitive actions might not take up much time when you do them just once, but if you do them many times during the course of a day, they can add up to a significant chunk of your valuable time. To help you gain back most of that time, macros enable you to automate almost any task that you can undertake in Excel. By using Excel's macro recorder to record tasks that you perform routinely, you not only speed up your tasks considerably (because Excel can play back your keystrokes and mouse actions much faster than you perform them manually), but you're also assured that each step in the task is carried out the same way each time you perform the task.

In this chapter, you get a chance to practice recording, testing, and playing back macros that you use to automate repetitive tasks required when building and using your Excel worksheets and charts. You also practice assigning the macros you record to custom buttons on the Quick Access toolbar and the Ribbon.

Creating Macros

You can create macros for your Excel worksheets in one of two ways:

» Use Excel's macro recorder to record your actions as you undertake them in a worksheet

» Enter the instructions that you want followed in VBA code in the Visual Basic Editor

Either way, Excel creates a special module sheet that holds the actions and instructions in your macro. The macro instructions in a macro module (whether recorded by Excel or written by you) are written in the Visual Basic for Applications programming language. You can then study the VBA code that the macro recorder creates and edit this code in the Visual Basic Editor (see Chapter 22).

REMEMBER

It's helpful to display the Developer tab on the Ribbon if you plan to record macros regularly. The Developer tab contains all the command buttons that you need to record, play back, and edit the macros you create. To display the Developer tab, choose File ⇨ Options (or press Alt+FT) and then click the Customize Ribbon option. In the Customize the Ribbon panel, select the Developer check box and click OK. Excel adds the Developer tab to the Ribbon, between the View and Help tabs. The buttons on the Developer tab are divided into the following groups: Code, Add-Ins, Controls, and XML.

Recording and playing back macros

You can use the macro recorder to create many of the utility-type macros that perform the repetitive tasks necessary for creating and editing your worksheets and charts. When you turn on the macro recorder, it records all your actions in the active worksheet or chart sheet as you make them.

REMEMBER

Note that the macro recorder does not record the keystrokes or mouse actions you take to accomplish an action, but only the VBA code required to perform the action itself. This means that certain mistakes you make while taking an action are not recorded as part of the macro. If, for example, you make a typing error and then edit it while the macro recorder is on, only the corrected entry shows up in the macro without the original mistakes and steps taken to remedy it. However, Excel *does* record other types of errors. For example, if you click to activate the Home tab's Italics button by accident, and then correct your error by clicking to deactivate Italics, Excel records both actions.

The macros that you create with the macro recorder can be stored either as part of the current workbook, in a new workbook, or in a special, globally available Personal Macro Workbook named PERSONAL.XLSB that's stored in a folder called XLSTART on your hard disk. When you record a macro as part of your Personal Macro Workbook, you can run that macro from any workbook that you have open. (This is because the PERSONAL.XLSB workbook is secretly opened whenever you launch Excel and, although it remains hidden, its macros are always available.)

When you record macros as part of the current workbook or a new workbook, you can run those macros only when the workbook in which they were recorded is open in Excel. When that workbook is open, you can run its macros in any open workbook. Note, too, that if you store recorded macros in any workbook other than PERSONAL.XLSB, then you must save that workbook in a special file format that supports macros. Choose File ⇨ Save As, click Browse to open the Save As dialog box, use the Save as Type list to select Excel Macro-Enabled Workbook (*.xlsm), enter a filename, choose a location, and then click Save.

When you create a macro with the macro recorder, you decide not only the workbook in which to store the macro but also what name and shortcut keystrokes to assign to the macro you are creating. When assigning a name for your macro, you use the same guidelines as when assigning a standard range name to a cell range in your worksheet. When assigning a shortcut keystroke to run the macro, you can assign the Ctrl key plus a lowercase letter between a and z such as Ctrl+q (which is displayed as Ctrl+Q, although you press just Ctrl+q). Alternatively, you can press the Ctrl key plus an uppercase letter between A and Z as in Ctrl+Q (which appears as Ctrl+Shift+Q because you must press all three keys). You cannot, however, assign the Ctrl key plus a punctuation or number key (such as Ctrl+1 or Ctrl+/) to your macro, nor can you over-write any of Excel's built-in keyboard shortcuts, such as Ctrl+B (for bold) and Ctrl+P (for Print).

Try It

Exercise 21-1: Recording and Playing Back a New Macro

In Exercise 21-1, you practice using the macro recorder to record a macro that automatically enters and formats the company name in a cell whenever you play the macro back.

1. Launch Excel, click Blank Workbook, and leave the cell cursor in cell A1 of Sheet1 in the new Book1 workbook.

    You use Sheet1 of your new workbook to practice recording and playing back a new macro that enters the company name (Acme Coyote Supplies, in this case) in 12-point bold type and then centers the text across columns A through E with the Home tab's Merge & Center button.

2. Choose Developer ⇨ Record Macro (or press Alt+LR).

    If you elected not to display the Developer tab, you can still get a macro recording off the ground by choosing View ⇨ Macros ⇨ Record Macro (or by pressing Alt+WMR).

    Excel opens the Record Macro dialog box.

3. In the Macro Name text box, type **CompanyName**.

    Macro names use the same naming rules as when creating range names in a worksheet so that you cannot use spaces in their names or begin their names with numbers.

4. In the Shortcut Key text box, type uppercase **C** by pressing Shift+C.

    The Shortcut key appears in the Record Macro dialog box as Ctrl+Shift+C.

5. Use the Store Macro In drop-down list to select Personal Macro Workbook.

    If you store a macro in the current workbook or a new workbook, you can only use the macro while that workbook is open in Excel. When you save a macro in the Personal Macro Workbook, you can use the macro in any workbook you have open.

6. Select the Description text box, type **Enters company name in 12pt bold centered across 5 columns**, and then click OK.

    Excel closes the Record Macro dialog box and the Record Macro button on the Developer tab changes to a Stop Recording button.

7. Type **Acme Coyote Supplies** in cell A1 and then click the Enter button on the Formula bar.

   Don't press the Enter key here because in the next step you apply some formatting to the text you just entered, so you want to leave the cell cursor where it is.

   If you make a typing error while doing this entry, don't worry. Delete the incorrect characters and replace them with the correct ones.

8. Use the Home tab's Font Size button to increase the point size to 12 and then click the Bold button to add the boldface attribute to the text. Drag through the cell range A1:E1 to select it and then choose Home⇨Merge & Center.

   Now that you've finished taking the actions you want recorded in your new macro, you need to stop recording.

9. Click the Stop Recording button on the Developer tab of the Ribbon.

   No Developer tab? No problem: You can still stop a macro recording by choosing View⇨Macros⇨Stop Recording (or by pressing Alt+WMR).

10. Click New Sheet to add Sheet2 to the workbook, position the cell cursor in cell A1 of Sheet2, and then choose Developer⇨Macros (or press Alt+F8) to open the Macro dialog box.

    If you didn't add the Developer tab to the Ribbon. you can also open the Macro dialog box by choosing View⇨Macros⇨View Macros (or by pressing Alt+WMV).

    The Macro dialog box displays a list of all the macros that you defined in the PERSONAL.XLSB workbook as well any open workbook. You can use the controls in this dialog box to run or edit a macro, or even to play the macro back a step at a time. (The latter is especially helpful when a macro does something unintended and you want to find out where exactly it went off track.)

11. In the Macro Name list, click PERSONAL.XLSB!CompanyName and then click Run.

    Excel runs the CompanyName macro, which enters Acme Coyote Supplies in cell A1 of Sheet2 centered in 12-point bold text within a merged cell that includes the cell range A1:E1.

12. Click New Sheet to add Sheet3 to the workbook, select cell G1 in Sheet3, and then run the CompanyName macro using the shortcut key combination (Ctrl+Shift+C) you assigned to it.

    Excel runs the macro, but this time something unanticipated happens: The program enters the correctly formatted text in cell G1 while still creating the merged cell in the cell range A1:E1 instead of G1:K1 (which would then include the company name).

    Excel does this when you run the CompanyName macro in any cell other than A1 of a worksheet because the macro recorder automatically records the cell references in a macro as absolute rather than relative references (unlike when copying formulas). To fix this macro, you have to rerecord it with relative references, which you do in Exercise 21-2.

13. Exit Excel and select the Don't Save button when the alert dialog box appears asking you if you want to save your changes to Book1.

As soon as you select Don't Save in the first alert dialog box, Excel displays a second alert dialog box, this one prompting you to save changes to the Personal Macro Workbook, PERSONAL.XLSB, which contains your CompanyName macro. Normally, you would select the Yes button to save your macro for use in other workbooks during other work sessions. However, as you need to rerecord the CompanyName macro using relative references to make it run properly, click Don't Save.

14. Click the Don't Save button in the alert dialog box asking if you want to save your changes to the Personal Macro Workbook.

Recording macros with relative cell references

Now you understand why the Code group of the Developer tab contains a Use Relative References button. You need to use this button before you start recording any sequence in a macro that requires relative rather than absolute cell references. (If you forget the difference between relative and absolute references, see Chapter 7 for the details.) Try using this button when rerecording the CompanyName macro in Exercise 21-2 to see what difference it makes when playing back the macro in cells other than A1 in the worksheet.

Try It

Exercise 21-2: Recording a Macro Using Relative Cell References

In Exercise 21-2, you practice recording a macro using relative cell references so that it can be played back in cells of a worksheet other than those used in the original recording.

1. Launch Excel, click Blank Workbook, and then leave the cell cursor in cell A1 of Sheet1 in the new Book1 workbook.

You use this new workbook to practice rerecording the CompanyName macro, this time using relative cell references.

2. Choose Developer⇨Record Macro (or press Alt+LR) to open the Record Macro dialog box. Fill in its text boxes as follows and then click OK:

   - Enter **CompanyName** in the Macro Name text box.
   - Enter uppercase **C** in the Shortcut Key text box so that the shortcut appears as Ctrl+Shift+C.
   - Choose Personal Macro Workbook in the Store Macro In combo box.
   - Type **Enters company name in 12pt bold centered across five columns** in the Description text box.

3. Choose Developer⇨Use Relative References (or press Alt+LU).

Excel indicates that it is recording relative cell references by highlighting the background of the Use Relative References button on the Developer tab.

4. Rerecord the macro by typing **Acme Coyote Supplies** in cell A1 and then clicking the Enter button on the Formula bar. Then, use the Home tab's Font Size to increase the point size to 12 and click the Bold button to add the boldface attribute to the text. Finally, drag through the cell range A1:E1 to select it and then choose Home ⇨ Merge & Center.

   Now you're ready to stop recording the rerecorded macro.

5. Choose Developer ⇨ Stop Recording (or press Alt+LR).

   Now you can test your macro recorded with relative cell addresses.

6. Position the cell cursor in cell G1 in Sheet1 and then press Ctrl+Shift+C to test the rerecorded CompanyName macro with relative cell references.

   This time, thanks to relative cell references, the macro works as intended by entering the formatted company name, Acme Coyote Supplies, centered across the merged cell in the range G1:K1.

   Next, record another macro that enters all twelve months (from January to December) in a single row of the worksheet. This macro enters the names of the months, and then makes their names bold and italic, and widens their columns with the AutoFit feature. This TwelveMonths macro also requires relative references during recording to ensure that you can use it to successfully enter the months of the year in any columns of any worksheet.

7. Position the cell cursor in cell A4 of Sheet1 and then choose Developer ⇨ Record Macro (or press Alt+LR). Fill in the Record Macro dialog box text boxes as follows, then click OK:

   - Enter **TwelveMonths** in the Macro Name text box.
   - Enter uppercase **M** in the Shortcut Key text box so that the shortcut appears as Ctrl+Shift+M.
   - Choose Personal Macro Workbook in the Store Macro In combo box.
   - Type **Enters the 12 months from Jan to Dec in bold italic** in the Description text box.

8. Make sure that the Use Relative References button on the Developer tab is still highlighted (if not, press Alt+LU). Then, take the following actions:

   - Type **January** in cell A4 and then click the Enter button on the Formula bar.
   - Drag the fill handle to the right to extend the range to L4 so that all 12 months from January through December are entered in the range A4:L4.
   - Click the Home tab's Bold and Italic buttons.
   - Choose Home ⇨ Format ⇨ AutoFit Column Width.
   - Click cell A4 to deselect the range A4:L4.

   Now you're ready to stop recording the new macro.

9. Choose Developer⇨Stop Recording (or press Alt+LR).

Now you can test your new TwelveMonths macro.

10. Position the cell cursor in cell C8 of Sheet1 and then press Ctrl+Shift+M.

Excel correctly enters the twelve months of the year in the cell range C8:N8 while at the same time adjusting the widths of columns C to N to suit the length of the month each contains.

11. Exit Excel and select Don't Save in the first alert dialog box prompting you to save your changes to the Book1 workbook file. Select the Save button in the second alert dialog box when prompted to save your macros in the Personal Macro Workbook.

Assigning Macros to the Quick Access Toolbar

If you use the Quick Access toolbar (see Chapter 1 to find out how to display it) Excel enables you to assign macros you create to the custom buttons that you add to the Quick Access toolbar. When you assign a macro to a custom button on the Quick Access toolbar, you can then run the macro by clicking its custom button instead of having to open the Macro dialog box or typing its keystroke shortcut.

Try It

Exercise 21-3: Assigning a Macro to a Custom Button on the Quick Access Toolbar

In Exercise 21-3, you practice assigning your CompanyName and TwelveMonths macros to custom buttons on the Quick Access toolbar.

1. Launch Excel, click Blank Workbook, and leave the cell cursor in cell A1 of Sheet1 in the new Book1 workbook.

You use this new workbook to practice assigning the two macros that you created in Exercise 21-2 to the Quick Access toolbar.

2. Click the Customize Quick Access Toolbar button at the end of the Quick Access toolbar and then click More Commands to open the Excel Options dialog box with the Quick Access Toolbar tab selected.

To add your macros to custom buttons, you must choose Macros in the Choose Commands From list.

3. In the Choose Commands From drop-down list, click Macros.

Excel displays a list of macros in the list box below. Your own macros appear in this list, but you might see lots of other macros associated with some of the add-ins you've enabled in Excel (particularly the Analysis ToolPak).

4. Scroll down the list of macros (if necessary) until you locate your PERSONAL. XLSB!CompanyName and PERSONAL.XLSB!TwelveMonths macros. Then, click \<Separator\> at the top of the list followed by the Add button. Next, click PERSONAL. XLSB!CompanyName in the list followed by the Add button and then PERSONAL. XLSB!TwelveMonths followed by Add again.

    Your two macros now appear in the Customize Quick Access Toolbar list box on the right with a \<Separator\> appearing above PERSONAL.XLSB!CompanyName.

    By default, the name that Excel assigns to the command button is the macro name preceded by the name of the workbook in which the macro is stored, separated by an exclamation point (as in PERSONAL.XLSB!CompanyName). Excel also assigns a default "flowchart" icon to every macro command button. To make your Ribbon macro easier to differentiate and locate, you can customize both the button name and the button icon.

5. Click PERSONAL.XLSB!CompanyName in the Customize Quick Access Toolbar list and then click Modify.

    Excel opens the Modify Button dialog box.

6. Use the Symbol list to click the icon you want to assign to the macro command button, use the Display Name text box to rename the macro command button (note that you're just renaming the button, not the macro itself), and then click OK to return to the Excel Options dialog box.

    Repeat Steps 5 and 6 for the PERSONAL.XLSB!TwelveMonths macro.

7. Click OK.

    Your Quick Access toolbar now contains two new buttons.

8. Click the button that runs your CompanyName macro.

    Excel runs the company name macro by entering the Acme Coyote Supplies company name in bold in the merged A1:E1 super-cell.

9. Click cell G1 and then click the custom button that runs your TwelveMonths macro.

    Excel runs your TwelveMonths macro, which enters the names of the months January through December in bold italic in the cell range G1:R1 and adjusts their column widths using the AutoFit feature.

10. Exit Excel without saving your changes to the Book1 workbook.

Assigning Macros to the Ribbon

Excel also enables you to assign macros you create to custom tabs that you add to the Ribbon. When you assign a macro to a custom Ribbon tab, you can then run the macro by clicking its custom button instead of having to open the Macro dialog box or typing its keystroke shortcut.

Exercise 21-4: Assigning Macros to a New Group in a Custom Tab on the Ribbon

In Exercise 21-4, you practice assigning your CompanyName and TwelveMonths macros to a new Macros group on the custom Misc Ribbon tab that you created earlier in Chapter 1.

1. Launch Excel, click Blank Workbook, and leave the cell cursor in cell A1 of Sheet1 in the new Book1 workbook.

   You use this new workbook to practice assigning the two macros that you created in Exercise 21-2 to your Misc Ribbon tab.

2. Choose File⇨Options (or press Alt+FT) to open the Excel Options dialog box. Then, click the Customize Ribbon option to display the Customize the Ribbon panel in the Excel Options dialog box.

   Before you add your macros to the Misc custom tab you created in Chapter 1, you need to add a new custom group to the tab.

3. Click the Misc (Custom) tab in the Main Tabs list box on the right of the panel and then click the New Group button at the bottom.

   Excel expands the Misc (Custom) tab showing Data Form (Custom) followed by New Group (Custom) that's selected.

4. Click the Rename button and then type **Macros** in the Display Name text box of the Rename dialog box before you click OK.

   Excel replaces New Group (Custom) with Macros (Custom). Now, you're ready to add your macros to this new group.

5. Click the Macros option on the Choose Commands From drop-down menu.

   Excel displays your two macros PERSONAL.XLSB!CompanyName and PERSONAL. XLSB!TwelveMonths in the Choose Commands From list box as well as any other macros associated with the add-ins you've enabled in Excel (particularly the Analysis ToolPak).

6. Click PERSONAL.XLSB!CompanyName in the Choose Commands From list box and then click the Add button.

   Excel adds the PERSONAL.XLSB!CompanyName macro to the Macros (Custom) group in the Main Tabs list box.

7. Click PERSONAL.XLSB!TwelveMonths in the Choose Commands From list box and then click the Add button.

   Excel adds the PERSONAL.XLSB!TwelveMonths macro to the Macros (Custom) group in the Main Tabs list box immediately beneath the PERSONAL.XLSB!CompanyName macro.

8. Select the check box to the immediate left of Misc (Custom) to display this tab on the Excel Ribbon.

9. Click PERSONAL.XLSB!CompanyName in the Customize the Ribbon list and then click Rename.

    Excel opens the Rename dialog box.

10. Use the Symbol list to click the icon you want to assign to the macro command button, use the Display Name text box to rename the macro command button (note that you're just renaming the button, not the macro itself), and then click OK to return to the Excel Options dialog box.

    Repeat Steps 9 and 10 for the PERSONAL.XLSB!TwelveMonths macro.

11. Click OK to close the Excel Options dialog box.

    Excel adds the Misc custom tab to the Ribbon.

12. Click the Misc tab on the Ribbon and then with the cell cursor in cell A1, click the button that runs your CompanyName macro.

13. Click cell G1 and then click the custom button that runs your TwelveMonths macro.

14. Exit Excel without saving your changes to the Book1 workbook.

Chapter **22**

Using the Visual Basic Editor

Visual Basic for Applications (usually known simply as VBA) is the official programming language of Excel that you can use to edit as well as to write new macros. The key to editing and writing macros in Visual Basic for Applications is its editing program, the Visual Basic Editor (often abbreviated VBE). The Visual Basic Editor offers a rich environment for writing and debugging VBA.

In this chapter, you use the Visual Basic Editor to edit macros that you've recorded (see Chapter 21) as well as to enhance their basic functionality through the addition of interactivity. In addition, you use the VBE to create your own custom functions known as user-defined functions (often abbreviated UDF).

Using the Visual Basic Editor

You can open the Visual Basic Editor in one of three ways:

>> Choose Developer ⇨ Visual Basic (or press Alt+LV).

>> Press Alt+F11.

>> Choose View ⇨ Macros (or press Alt+F8) to open the Macro dialog box, select a macro, and then click the Edit button.

Figure 22-1 shows the arrangement of the typical components of the Visual Basic Editor when you first open it. As you can see, this window contains its own menu bar and beneath the menu bar, you find a Visual Basic Editor Standard toolbar, shown in Figure 22-2.

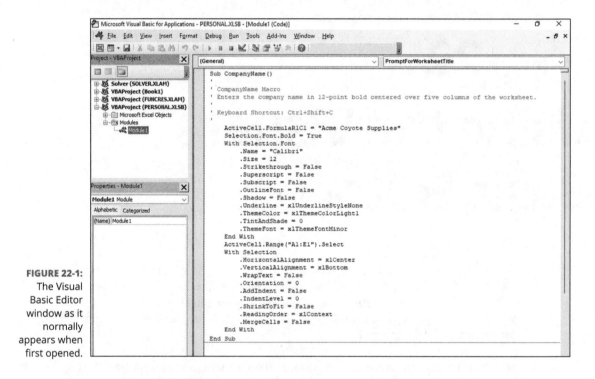

FIGURE 22-1:
The Visual Basic Editor window as it normally appears when first opened.

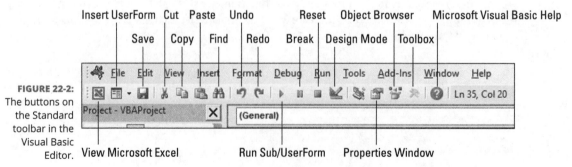

FIGURE 22-2:
The buttons on the Standard toolbar in the Visual Basic Editor.

Beneath the Standard toolbar in the Visual Basic Editor, you find several tiled windows of various sizes and shapes. Keep in mind that these are the default windows and their default arrangement. They are not the only windows that you can have open in the Visual Basic Editor (as though it weren't crowded and confusing enough), and this is not the only way that they can be arranged.

The two most important windows (at least, when you're first starting out using the Visual Basic Editor) are the Project Explorer and the Code window. The Project Explorer window, which is located near the upper-left corner of the Visual Basic Editor window, just under the toolbar, shows you all the projects you have open in the Visual Basic Editor and enables you to navigate their various parts. Note that in VBA, a project consists of all the code and user forms that belong to a particular workbook along with the sheets of the workbook itself.

Editing a recorded macro

The macros that you record in the workbook as well as any you write for it in the Visual Basic Editor are recorded on module sheets to which Excel assigns generic names such as Module1, Module2, and so forth. The actual lines of VBA programming code for the macro stored on a particular module sheet appear in the Code window when you select its module in the Project Explorer. (The Code window appears to the immediate right of the Project Explorer.)

To open a module in the Code window, double-click its module icon in the Project Explorer or right-click the module icon and select View Code at the top of its shortcut menu.

Although it's usually best to run your macros from the Macro dialog box in Excel, it's also possible to run any macro from within the Visual Basic Editor. In Excel, switch to the worksheet in which you want your macro to make its changes and select the starting cell. Switch back to the Visual Basic Editor, click anywhere inside the macro you want to run, and then use either of the following techniques to run the macro:

>> To run the entire macro, choose Run ⇨ Run Sub/UserForm. You can also either click the Standard toolbar's Run Sub/UserForm button (pointed out earlier in Figure 22-2) or press F5.

>> To step through the macro one line at a time (useful for testing your macro to see what effect each line has on your worksheet), choose Debug ⇨ Step Into (or press F8). Repeat this command (you'll probably want to use the F8 shortcut for this) to execute one line at a time. If at any point you want to run the rest of the macro without stopping, press F5; to stop the macro at any time, choose Run ⇨ Reset or click the Standard toolbar's Reset button.

TIP

If you want to rename a module in your VBA project to something a little more descriptive than Module1, Module2, and so on, you can do this in the Properties window that appears immediately below the Project Explorer. The Properties window shows the properties for the module or other item selected in the Project Explorer. In the Project Explorer, click the module you want to rename. In the Properties window, click the name (such as Module1) that appears after the (Name) label on the Alphabetic tab, type a more descriptive name, and press Enter. When renaming a module, remember that you must use the same naming guidelines as when naming a range name in a worksheet: Begin the module name with a letter, not a symbol or number, and don't put any spaces between words (use underscores instead).

After you've created a macro, you don't necessarily have to rerecord it to change the way it behaves. In many cases, it's easier to change the macro by editing its statements in the Visual Basic Editor. Note that if the macro you want to edit is stored in your Personal Macro Workbook (that PERSONAL.XLSB file in the XLSTART folder), it's much easier to edit the macro in the Visual Basic Editor by first un-hiding the Personal Macro Workbook file in Excel.

Exercise 22-1: Editing a Recorded Macro with the Visual Basic Editor

In Exercise 22-1, you practice making basic editing changes to the CompanyName macro that you created in your Personal Macro Workbook when doing the exercises in the previous chapter.

1. Launch Excel, choose View ⇨ Unhide (or press Alt+WU), to open the Unhide dialog box, click PERSONAL, and then click OK to unhide the PERSONAL.XLSB workbook containing your CompanyName macro.

   The Excel title bar now reads PERSONAL.

2. Choose Developer ⇨ Macros (or press Alt+F8) to open the Macro dialog box, click CompanyName in the Macro Name list, and then click Edit.

   Excel launches the Visual Basic Editor and opens Module1 from PERSONAL.XLSB, which contains your CompanyName macro. The Code window containing the statements in this macro appears to the right of the Project Explorer and Properties window.

3. If necessary, click the Maximize button on the upper-right of the Code window to maximize this window in the Visual Basic Editor.

   In the Code window, note that explanatory comments that are not executed as part of the macro are prefaced with apostrophes and appear in green text, whereas all the VBA commands and properties that are executed when you run the macro appear in blue and black text.

4. Locate the With Selection.Font statement in the CompanyName macro. Right below that statement, you see the .Name statement, which sets the font name to Calibri. Replace Calibri with Times New Roman. Make sure to retain the closed pair of double quotation marks around the font name, like so:

   ```
   .Name = "Times New Roman"
   ```

5. In the .Size statement, which sets the font size, change 12 to 14 (points):

   ```
   .Size = 14
   ```

6. Turn off the ThemeFont property by setting it equal to zero:

   ```
   .ThemeFont = 0
   ```

7. Click the View Microsoft Excel button on the Standard toolbar in the Visual Basic Editor (the very first one with the green XL logo).

   Excel returns you to the Personal Macro Workbook, PERSONAL.XLSB.

8. Hover your mouse over the Excel icon on the Windows taskbar, click the Book1 thumbnail to switch to that workbook, and then test the changes to the CompanyName macro by pressing Ctrl+Shift+C.

   This time, the macro inserts the Acme Coyote Supplies company name in the merged cell A1:E1 in 14-point bold using Times New Roman as the font.

9. Close the Book1.xlsx file without saving your changes, which should make the PERSONAL.XLSB workbook active (if not, switch to that workbook). Choose View ➪ Hide (or press Alt+WH) to hide the PERSONAL.XLSB workbook, and then exit Excel. Be sure to click the Save button this time when prompted to save your changes to the Personal Macro Workbook.

Adding a dialog box that processes user input

One of the biggest problems with recording macros is that any text or values that you have the macro enter for you in a worksheet or chart sheet can never vary thereafter. If you create a macro that enters the heading "Bob's Barbecue Pit" in the current cell of your worksheet, this heading is the only one you'll ever get out of that macro. However, you can get around this inflexibility by using the InputBox function. When you run the macro, this VBA function causes Excel to display an input dialog box where you can enter whatever title makes sense for the new worksheet. The macro then puts that text into the current cell and formats this text, if that's what you've trained your macro to do next.

To see how to use the InputBox function to add interactivity to an otherwise staid macro, follow along with the steps for converting the CompanyName macro that currently inputs the text "Acme Coyote Supplies" to one that prompts you for the name you want entered. Here's a simplified version of the InputBox function syntax:

```
InputBox(prompt[, title][, default])
```

Here's a rundown of the main arguments of the InputBox function:

>> *Prompt*: Specifies the message (up to 1024 characters) that appears inside the input dialog box, prompting the user to enter a new value (in this case, a new company name). To have the prompt message appear on different lines inside the dialog box, you include the VBA constant vbCrLf to insert a carriage return and a linefeed.

>> *Title*: Specifies what text to display in the input dialog box's title bar. If you don't specify a title argument, Excel displays the name of the application on the title bar.

>> *Default*: Specifies the default response that automatically appears in the text box at the bottom of the input dialog box. If you don't specify a default argument, the text box is empty in the input dialog box.

Exercise 22-2: Making a Recorded Macro Interactive by Adding an Input Dialog Box

In Exercise 22-2, you practice making your CompanyName macro interactive by adding an input dialog box that prompts the user to enter the name of the company to be inserted into the super-cell it creates.

1. Launch Excel and open a new Book1 workbook in the program. Then, working from Sheet1 of this workbook, unhide the PERSONAL.XLSB workbook and open the CompanyName macro that you edited in the previous exercise in the Visual Basic Editor.

   Now, you're ready to add the commands to the CompanyName macro that display a dialog box prompting the user for the worksheet title to enter each time the macro is run.

2. Position the insertion point in the Code window at the beginning of the ActiveCell. FormulaR1C1 statement on line 8 in column 5 and then press Enter to insert a new line. Then, press the ↑ key to move the insertion point up to the beginning of the new blank line 8 in column 5.

   Now you're ready to create the three variables — strPrompt, strTitle, and strDefault — that contain the values you want used as the Prompt, Title, and Default arguments of the InputBox function. You create all variables for the code at the beginning of the macro subroutine by declaring their names and setting them equal to the values you initially want used. Then, when you're ready to enter the InputBox function in the code, all you have to do is enter the variable names in the order of the InputBox arguments. Note that by using variables to supply the Prompt, Title, and Default arguments of the InputBox function, you avoid creating a long line of code that is not only hard to read, but hard to edit as well.

3. Type the following code on line 8 to create the strPrompt variable and then press the Enter key to start a new line 9:

   ```
   strPrompt = "Enter the company name or title for this worksheet in the
       text box below and then click OK:"
   ```

   You have now defined a variable called strPrompt that you use as the prompt argument of the InputBox function.

4. Type the following code on line 9 to create the strTitle variable and then press the Enter key to start a new line 10:

   ```
   strTitle = "Worksheet Title"
   ```

   You have now defined a variable called strTitle that you use as the optional Title argument of the InputBox function.

5. Type the following code on line 10 to create the strDefault variable and then press the Enter key to start a new line 11:

```
strDefault = "Acme Coyote Supplies"
```

You have now defined a variable called strDefault that you use as the optional Default argument of the InputBox function.

Next, you define a fourth variable, strWorksheetTitle. This variable receives the input returned by the InputBox function using the strPrompt, strTitle, and strDefault variables you just created as its prompt, title, and default arguments.

6. Type the following code on line 11 to create the strWorksheetTitle variable that receives the input returned by the InputBox function:

```
strWorksheetTitle = InputBox(strPrompt, strTitle, strDefault)
```

The last step is to replace the value, "Acme Coyote Supplies" in the ActiveCell. FormulaR1C1 property with the strWorksheetTitle variable (whose value is determined by whatever is input into the Worksheet Title input dialog box), thus effectively replacing this constant in the macro with the means for making this input truly interactive.

7. Select "Acme Coyote Supplies" in line 12 and replace it with the strWorksheetTitle variable (with no quotation marks) so that this line contains

```
ActiveCell.FormulaR1C1 = strWorksheetTitle
```

8. Carefully check your changes to the code of the CompanyName macro against those in the first five lines shown in Figure 22-3. Then, when everything checks out, choose File⇨ Save PERSONAL.XLSB on the Visual Basic Editor menu bar (or press Ctrl+S) to save your changes.

Now you're ready to test the interactive version of your CompanyName macro.

9. Click the View Microsoft Excel button on the Standard toolbar and then activate the Book1 workbook and test the interactive version of the CompanyName macro by pressing Ctrl+Shift+C.

A Worksheet Title dialog box appears, prompting you for the name of the worksheet.

10. Replace Acme Coyote Supplies in the Worksheet Title dialog box with ABC Corp. Sales and then click OK.

The macro now enters ABC Corp. Sales as the worksheet title in 14-point bold type centered over the merged cell A1:E1 in Sheet1 of Book1.

11. Close the Book1.xlsx file without saving your changes, and then hide the PERSONAL. XLSB workbook and exit Excel. Be sure that you click the Save button when prompted to save your changes to the Personal Macro Workbook.

```
Sub CompanyName()
'
' CompanyName Macro
' Enters the company name in 14-point bold centered over five columns of the worksheet.
'
' Keyboard Shortcut: Ctrl+Shift+C

    strPrompt = "Enter the company name or title for this worksheet in the text box below and
    strTitle = "Worksheet Title"
    strDefault = "Acme Coyote Supplies"
    strWorksheetTitle = InputBox(strPrompt, strTitle, strDefault)
    ActiveCell.FormulaR1C1 = strWorksheetTitle
    Selection.Font.Bold = True
    With Selection.Font
        .Name = "Times New Roman"
        .Size = 14
        .Strikethrough = False
        .Superscript = False
        .Subscript = False
        .OutlineFont = False
        .Shadow = False
        .Underline = xlUnderlineStyleNone
        .ThemeColor = xlThemeColorLight1
        .TintAndShade = 0
        .ThemeFont = 0
    End With
    ActiveCell.Range("A1:E1").Select
    With Selection
        .HorizontalAlignment = xlCenter
        .VerticalAlignment = xlBottom
        .WrapText = False
        .Orientation = 0
        .AddIndent = False
        .IndentLevel = 0
        .ShrinkToFit = False
        .ReadingOrder = xlContext
        .MergeCells = False
    End With
End Sub
```

FIGURE 22-3: The Visual Basic Editor Code window after adding new commands to make the macro interactive.

Creating User-Defined Functions

One of the best uses of Visual Basic for Applications in Excel is to create custom worksheet functions, also known as user-defined functions. User-defined functions are great because you don't have to access the Macro dialog box to run them. In fact, you enter them into your worksheets just like you do any of Excel's built-in worksheet functions, either with the Insert Function button on the Formula bar or by typing them directly into a cell.

To create a user-defined function, you must do the four following things:

>> Create a new module where the custom function is to be defined in the Visual Basic Editor by selecting its project in the Project Explorer and then choosing Insert ➪ Module.

>> Enter the Function keyword followed by the name of the custom function and specify, in parentheses, the names of the arguments that this function takes (if any) on the first line in the Code window. Note that you can't duplicate any built-in function names, such as SUM or AVERAGE, and so on, and you must list argument names in the order in which they are processed.

>> Enter the formula, or set of formulas, that tells Excel how to calculate the custom function's result using the argument names listed in the Function command with whatever arithmetic operators or built-in functions are required to get the calculation made on the line or lines below.

>> Indicate that you've finished defining the user-defined function by entering the End Function command on the last line.

To see how this procedure works in action, in the following exercise, you create a user-defined function that calculates the sales commissions for salespeople based on the number of sales they make in a month as well as the total amount of their monthly sales (they sell big-ticket items, such as RVs). Your custom Commission function has two arguments — totalSales and itemsSold — so that the first line of code on the module sheet in the Code window is as follows:

```
Function Commission(totalSales, itemsSold)
```

In determining how the commissions are calculated, you base the commission percentage on the number of sales made during the month. For five sales or fewer in a month, you pay a commission rate of 4.5 percent of the salesperson's total monthly sales; for sales of six or more, you pay a commission rate of 5 percent.

To define the formula section of the Commission custom function, you set up an If block. This If block is similar to the IF function you enter into a worksheet cell in that it uses an expression that returns either True or False, followed by the Then keyword. The statements immediately below the If *expression* Then statement get executed if the expression returns True. These statements are followed (usually) by the Else keyword, and the statements between Else and End If at the end of the block get executed if the expression returns false.

To set the custom function so that your salespeople get 4.5 percent of total sales for five or fewer items sold and 5 percent of total sales for more than five items sold, you enter the following lines of code underneath the line with the Function command:

```
If itemsSold <= 5 Then
    Commission = totalSales * 0.045
Else
    Commission = totalSales * 0.05
End If
```

Try It

Exercise 22-3: Constructing a Custom Function in the Visual Basic Editor

In Exercise 22-3, you practice using the Visual Basic Editor to create a custom function that you can then use in your Excel worksheets as you do the built-in functions.

1. Open the Exercise22-3.xlsx workbook file in the Chap22 folder in the Excel Workbook folder.

    This worksheet contains an RV Sales worksheet with the sales for three account representatives, Fred, Holly, and Jack, for which you will create the user-defined Commission function.

2. Unhide the PERSONAL.XLSB workbook and then choose Developer ⇨ Visual Basic (or press Alt+F11) to open the Visual Basic Editor window. Make sure that VBAProject (PERSONAL.XLSB) is selected in the Project Explorer window.

The Visual Basic Editor opens with the code in the last-accessed module selected.

3. Choose Insert ⇨ Module on the Visual Basic Editor's menu bar to insert a new module into the VBAProject component of the PERSONAL.XLSB workbook.

The new module named Module2 is selected in the Project Explorer and Properties windows.

4. Select Module2 following (Name) in the Properties window and then replace Module2 with CommissionUDF and press Enter.

Excel renames the Module2 sheet to CommissionUDF and this module name now appears above Module1 in the Modules list of the VBAProject component of the PERSONAL.XLSB workbook.

5. Click the insertion point in the Code window and then type the following code on Line1:

```
Function Commission(totalSales, itemsSold)
```

6. Press Enter to start a new line and Tab to indent; enter the following code on line 2 starting at column 5:

```
If itemsSold <= 5 Then
```

Excel automatically inserts the End Function command in Line 3.

7. Press Enter to start a new line and then Tab again to indent further, and then enter the following indented code on line 3 starting at column 9:

```
Commission = totalSales * 0.045
```

8. Press Enter to start a new line and then Shift+Tab to outdent; enter the following indented code on line 4 starting at column 5:

```
Else
```

9. Press Enter to start a new line and then Tab to indent; enter the following indented code on line 5 starting at column 9:

```
Commission = totalSales * 0.05
```

10. Press Enter to start a new line and then Shift+Tab to outdent; enter the following indented code on line 6 starting at column 5:

```
End If
```

Check the lines of code in your custom Commission function against those shown in Figure 22-4. When they check out, proceed to step 11.

11. Choose File ⇨ Save PERSONAL.XLSB on the Visual Basic Editor menu bar to save your custom function.

    Now you're ready to return to your Exercise22-3.xlsx workbook where, in the next exercise, you test your new user-defined Commission function.

12. Click the View Microsoft Excel button on the Standard toolbar in the Visual Basic Editor and then hide the Personal Macro Workbook PERSONAL.XLSB.

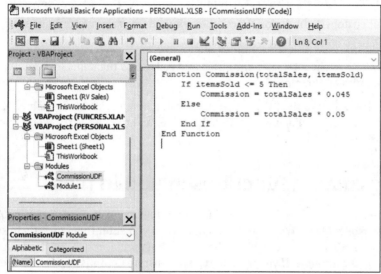

FIGURE 22-4: The Visual Basic Editor Code window after adding the lines of code for the user-defined Commission function.

Using a custom function in your worksheet

The great thing about custom functions is that they can be inserted into your worksheets with your old friend the Insert Function button on the Excel Formula bar. To find your custom function in the Insert Function dialog box, you just need to select User Defined as the function category.

Try It

Exercise 22-4: Using a Custom Function in a Worksheet Formula

In Exercise 22-4, you practice testing and using the custom Commission function you created in the previous exercise.

1. Make sure that the RV Sales worksheet in your Exercise22-3.xlsx workbook is active. Then click cell E5 in the RV Sales worksheet before you click the Insert Function button on the Formula Bar.

    The Insert Function dialog box appears. In the Or Select a Category drop-down list, select User Defined. Scroll down until you see the name of your custom function as PERSONAL.XLSB!Commission and click its name in the list. Then click OK.

The Function Arguments dialog box for your PERSONAL.XLSB!Commission function appears. This dialog box contains two argument text boxes: totalSales and itemsSold.

2. While the insertion point is in the totalSales argument text box, click cell C4 in the worksheet that contains Fred's total sales and then press Tab to select the itemsSold argument text box below. Select cell C5 in the worksheet that contains the count of Fred's sales and then click the OK button.

The custom commission function computes Fred's commission as $2,655 (using the 4.5% commission rate because the number of his sales is below five).

3. Use your custom Commission function to compute the sales commissions for Holly in cell E10.

Select cell C9 as the totalSales argument and cell C10 as the itemsSold argument for this Commission function.

HINT

4. Save your changes to the RV Sales worksheet in a new workbook file named RV Sales – commissionudf.xlsx in your Excel Practice folder and then leave the workbook open for Exercise 22-5.

Saving custom functions in add-in files

The only limitation to the user-defined functions that you save as part of a regular workbook file or the Personal Macro Workbook file is that when you enter them directly into a cell (without the use of the Insert Function dialog box), you must preface their function names with their filenames. So, for example, if you want to type the custom Commission function that's saved in the Personal Macro Workbook and you enter the following formula:

```
=Commission(C9, C10)
```

(assuming that cell C9 contains the total sales and cell C10 contains the number of items sold), Excel returns the #NAME? error value to the cell. If you then edit the function to include the Personal Macro Workbook's filename as follows:

```
=PERSONAL.XLSB!Commission(C9, C10)
```

Excel then calculates the sales commission based on the totalSales in C9 and the itemsSold in C10, returning this calculated value to the cell containing this user-defined function.

To be able to omit the filename from the custom functions you create when you enter them directly into a cell, you need to save the workbook file that contains them as an add-in file (with an .xlam filename extension). Then, after you've saved the workbook with your user-defined functions as an add-in file, you can start entering them into any worksheet without their filename qualifier after activating the add-in in the Add-Ins dialog box.

Exercise 22-5: Saving a Custom Function as an Excel Add-In

In Exercise 22-5, you practice saving your custom Commission function as an Excel add-in that you activate so that you can enter the function directly into a worksheet cell without having to preface the function name with the PERSONAL.XLSB designation.

1. With the RV Sales – commissionudf.xlsx workbook you created in Exercise 22-4 open, unhide your PERSONAL.XLSB workbook and then open the Visual Basic Editor window.

   Excel opens the Visual Basic Editor with your CommissionUDF module selected.

2. Choose Tools⇨VBAProject Properties.

   The Editor opens the VBAProject - Project Properties dialog box containing a General and a Protection tab.

3. Click the Protection tab and then select the Lock Project for Viewing check box.

   Putting a check mark in this check box prevents other users from viewing the custom functions so that they can't make any changes to them. Next, you add a password that prevents them from removing the view protection status.

4. Click the Password text box and enter **cerrado** (Spanish for closed) as the password. Then click the Confirm Password text box, reenter **cerrado** as the password exactly as you entered it in the first text box, and click OK.

   Now you're ready to return to the worksheet, where you can add a title and description for the new add-in file.

5. Click the View Microsoft Excel button on the Visual Basic Editor Standard toolbar.

   Before saving the PERSONAL.XLSB workbook as an add-in file, you should add a title and description of the user-defined Commission function it contains. (This information then appears in the Add-Ins dialog box whenever you select the add-in file.)

6. Activate the PERSONAL.XLSB workbook file and then choose File⇨Info.

   Excel displays the Info screen about the workbook in the Backstage view. Here you enter a brief name for the add-in in the Title field.

7. Type **Custom Commission Function** in the Title text box.

8. Choose Save As, and then click More Options to open the Save As dialog box. Then, scroll almost all the way to the bottom of the Save as Type drop-down list in the Save As dialog box and click the Excel Add-In (*.xlam) option.

   Doing this selects the AddIns folder in the Save In drop-down list box, showing the names of any add-in files that you've saved there.

9. Click the File Name combo box and change PERSONAL to **Commission** (without changing the .xlam filename extension), and then click Save.

   After saving your workbook as an add-in file, you're ready to activate the add-in so that you can enter its user-defined functions in any worksheet.

10. Restart Excel and then open your RV Sales worksheet in the RV Sales – commissionudf. xlsx workbook.

11. Open the Excel Options dialog box (Alt+FT), click the Add-ins tab, select Excel Add-Ins in the Manage drop-down list, and click Go.

    Excel opens the Add-Ins dialog box.

12. Select the Custom Commission Function check box and click OK.

    If the name of the Custom Commission Function doesn't automatically appear in the Add-Ins Available list box, click the Browse button. Next, click Commission.xlam file in the AddIns folder in the Browse dialog box and then click OK to add it to the list.

    Excel closes the Add-Ins dialog box and returns you to the RV Sales worksheet where you can test directly entering the custom Commission function into the formula you're constructing in a cell.

13. Click cell E18 and then type **=commission(**. Then click cell C17 with Jack's totals sales to make it the totalSales argument for the Commission function. Then, type a **,** (comma) to separate this argument from the next. Click cell C18 with the count of Jack's sales to make it the itemsSold argument for the Commission function and then type a **)** — close parenthesis.

    The formula in cell E18 and on the Formula bar should now read

    ```
    =commission(C17, C18)
    ```

14. Click the Enter button on the Formula bar.

    Excel accepts the formula =commission(C17, C18) — without the PERSONAL.XLSB filename designation — entering it into the Formula bar and returning the value $9,100 to the cell.

15. Enter a formula in cell E19 that sums the sales commissions in cells E5, E10, and E18.

    Create a formula that uses the SUM function with these three cell references as its number arguments.

HINT 16. Select cell A1 and then save your changes to the RV Sales worksheet (Ctrl+S). Exit Excel, being sure to save your changes to the hidden PERSONAL.XLSB workbook file when prompted to do so during the closing of the program.

7

The Part of Tens

IN THIS PART . . .

Learn the ten best features in Excel.

Explore ten tips on how to use Excel like a pro.

Chapter **23**

Top Ten Features in Excel

I f you're looking for a quick rundown on what's useful and what's cool in Excel, look no further! Here it is — my official Top Ten Features list. Just a cursory glance down the list tells you that the focus here is graphics, graphics, graphics!

The Excel Ribbon and Backstage View

The Ribbon is the heart of the Excel user interface. Based on a core of standard tabs, the Ribbon also displays various contextual tabs as needed when you select certain worksheet objects (such as tables, charts, PivotTables, and graphics). The Ribbon brings together almost every command you're going to need when performing tasks in Excel. See Chapter 1 for basic practice in locating and selecting commands on the Excel Ribbon. Excel also enables you to customize the Ribbon through the creation of your own custom tabs complete with whatever groups of buttons you need to get your work done.

Besides the Ribbon in the regular worksheet view, Excel also offers the Backstage View opened by clicking the File button that appears to the immediate left of the first tab of the Ribbon. In Backstage View, you find panels attached to ten File menu options: Home, New, Open, Info, Save, Save As, Print, Share, Export, and Publish. These panels bring together vital information and options pertaining to the particular menu option. For example, the Print panel (File ⇨ Print) not only displays a preview of the pages for your printed worksheet but contains controls that enable you to change common print settings before sending the report to your printer.

Conditional Formatting

Conditional formatting in Excel enables you to define formatting that Excel applies automatically when the cell values meet certain conditions. Most of these formats are background color that you specify, but you can also apply one of many different Data Bars, Color Scales, and Icon Sets to the cell selection by clicking the set's thumbnail in their respective pop-up palettes. When you apply a set of Data Bars to a cell range, the length of each bar in the cell represents its value relative to the others. When you apply a set of Color Scales, each shade of color in the cell represents its value relative to the others. And when you apply one of the Icon Sets, each icon in the cell represents its value relative to the others. See Chapter 3 for details on setting up conditional formatting in your worksheets.

Similarly, Excel offers a type of graphic representation for your worksheet data called Sparklines. Sparklines are charts that visualize some worksheet data, but they're small enough to fit snugly inside the cell in which they're created. You can use Sparklines to visually annotate data in a worksheet range and then, if you modify any of the data in that range, Excel automatically redraws the Sparkline chart to reflect your changes.

PivotTable Filtering with Slicers

Slicers are graphic objects that let you quickly and easily filter the data in a PivotTable on multiple criteria. Better yet, you can use Slicers to filter the data in more than one PivotTable created in the workbook by connecting the additional PivotTables to them.

Unlike filtering a PivotTable with AutoFilter buttons, Slicers show you exactly which filtering criteria are currently selected and in effect in the connected PivotTable(s). And because they're actual graphic objects, like images or drawn shapes, you can move, resize, and even temporarily hide them as needed in the worksheet. See Chapter 20 for practice using Slicers to filter the data in a PivotTable.

Home Tab Formatting and Editing

The Home tab of the Excel Ribbon brings home (pun intended) all the commonly used formatting and editing features. Whatever formatting or editing command you want to run, all you have to do is find the group that holds the command button you need and click it. What could be easier? See Chapter 3 for practice formatting data with command buttons in the Home tab's Font, Alignment, Number, Styles, and Cells groups on the Home tab. See Chapter 5 for practice using the editing commands in the Clipboard, Cells, and Editing groups on this tab.

Insert Tab Charting

Excel offers you direct access to all the major types of charts on the Insert tab of the Ribbon. Select the data to be charted, click the command button for the chart type on the Insert tab, and then select the style you want for that chart type. Presto! You have a professional chart that, thanks to the many command buttons and galleries on the Chart Design and Format contextual tabs, can be completed in no time at all! See Chapter 15 for practice creating and formatting charts with these Ribbon commands.

Format as Table

By formatting a range of data with one of the many table styles available on the Home tab's Format as Table drop-down gallery, you not only convert the range to a table in just a few clicks, but you're assured that all new entries made to the table are going to be formatted in exactly the same manner as others in similar positions in the table and are automatically considered as part of the table when it comes to sorting or filtering the data. (Filtering the data is made easy by the automatic addition of filter buttons to the top row of column headings.) See Chapter 3 for practice on converting a range into a table and then formatting its data using the Quick Styles gallery. See Chapter 17 for practice using these filtering buttons to sort the data in a table and to filter its data.

The Zoom Slider on the Status Bar

After you learn how to use it, you might wonder how you ever got along without the Zoom slider on the right side of the Excel Status bar? Instead of having to select a new magnification percentage for the worksheet from a drop-down menu on some obscure Zoom tool (something you can still do with the View tab's Zoom button, if you really want to), you can zoom in and out on the worksheet in the blink of an eye by dragging the Zoom slider right or left. See Chapter 5 for practice using the nifty Zoom slider in conjunction with frozen panes and custom views to keep all your worksheet data clearly in focus.

Page Layout View

Page Layout view in the Excel worksheet is just what the doctor ordered when it comes to visualizing the paging of printed reports. When you turn on this view by clicking the Page Layout button on the Status bar (or by choosing View ⇨ Page Layout), Excel doesn't just show the page breaks as measly dotted lines as in earlier versions but as actual page separations. The program also shows the margins for each page including headers and footers defined for the report (which you can both define and edit directly in the margin areas while the program is in this view) and as an extra nice touch throws in a pair of horizontal and vertical rulers to accompany the standard column and row headers. Couple this great feature with the Zoom slider and the Page Break Preview feature and you're going to actually enjoy getting the worksheet ready to print. See Chapter 4 for some hands-on practice using Page Layout view to check out pages and define headers and footers for your printed reports.

Style Galleries

Excel is jammed full of different style galleries that make it a snap to apply sophisticated (and, in many cases, very colorful) formatting to worksheet ranges, tables, charts, and graphics. Coupled with the Live Preview feature (discussed in the next section), Excel's style galleries go a long way towards encouraging you to create better-looking and more colorful and interesting worksheets. You get plenty of practice using style galleries in Chapter 3, Chapter 15, and Chapter 16.

Live Preview

You simply can't say enough about Live Preview and how much easier it makes formatting the worksheet. Live Preview works with all the style galleries as well as the Home tab's Font and Font Size pull-down menus. It enables you to see how the data in the current cell selection would look with a particular formatting, font, or font size before you apply the formatting to the range.

All you have to do is mouse over the thumbnails in the drop-down menu or gallery to see how each of its styles will look on your selected data. As an extra nice feature, many of the larger style galleries sport spinner buttons that enable you to bring new rows of thumbnails in the gallery into view so that you can preview their styles without obscuring any part of the cell selection (as would be the case if you actually open the gallery by clicking its More drop-down button). And when you finally do see the formatting that fits your data to a tee, click its thumbnail to apply the formatting immediately to the selected cell range.

Check out Chapter 3 for some practice using Live Preview to apply various font sizes to a table of data before selecting the one to use.

IN THIS CHAPTER

» Generating new workbooks from templates and organizing worksheet data

» Creating data series with AutoFill and using range names

» Freezing row and column headings and catching data entry gaffes

» Trapping error values and using array formulas

» Using outlines and displaying worksheets side by side

Chapter **24**

Top Ten Tips for Using Excel Like a Pro

Performing the exercises in this workbook gives you an opportunity to work with the most important features of Excel, especially those related to building and maintaining worksheets. To help you make the most of this hands-on experience, this chapter brings together ten of the most important ways to work efficiently and design the best possible worksheets as you start to work on your own.

Generating New Workbooks from Templates

Whenever possible, generate new workbooks or custom templates from the templates that are available for Excel. Don't forget that the program provides you with a host of useful online templates from meeting agendas to time sheets that you can start using right out of the box. Open the New panel in the Backstage View by choosing File ⇨ New (or pressing Alt+FN).

Besides the few templates displayed in the New panel, you can search Microsoft Office Online for other templates, which you can then download for use in Excel. Type a keyword or two in the Search for Online Templates text box and then click Start Searching (the magnifying glass icon; you can also press Enter).

If you can't find a readymade template online that comes close to generating the type of worksheet you need, you can create your own template from a sample worksheet that you build from scratch. In this workbook, you enter the default data, formulas, labels, and headings that you want to use in every workbook generated from your template. Format and secure the data as needed. Then you save the workbook as a template file by choosing File ➪ Save As, clicking Browse to open the Save As dialog box, using the Save as Type drop-down list to select Excel Template, entering a name in the File Name text box, and then clicking Save.

Excel automatically stores your custom-built templates in the Custom Office Templates folder. To access those templates, choose File ➪ New (or press Alt+FN) to open the New panel, click the Personal tab, and then click the custom template you want to use.

Organizing Data on Different Worksheets

Each new workbook that you open contains one blank worksheet into which you can enter the data required for your model. Unfortunately, rookie (and even some veteran) spreadsheet designers often restrict all data entry to just that one worksheet so they end up with a massive sheet that has its data spread far and wide. Although some models may require the single-sheet treatment, more often than not, the only reason that a worksheet designer puts everything on one sheet is because it's seems like the easier and faster option.

Sure, it probably is easier and faster to *enter* the data using just one worksheet but *finding* and *working with* all that data in one massive area is extremely inefficient and error-prone. By using two or more worksheets for your data, you can organize different parts of the overall model on separate sheets. This multi-sheet layout means that you not only end up with a more manageable spreadsheet model but you're far less likely to delete or overwrite crucial data.

In designing a worksheet that uses a multi-sheet layout, remember that you can add additional worksheets to the workbook — by clicking the Insert Worksheet button (it's to the right of the last visible tab in the workbook) or by pressing Shift+F11 — as needed. The only restriction to the total number of sheets in a workbook is the amount of computer memory available to keep the workbook open. You can also rearrange the sheets in a workbook by dragging their sheet tabs to the desired position in the workbook. You can also rename worksheets with more descriptive names by double-clicking their tabs.

REMEMBER

You can color-code the worksheet tabs in your workbook. To assign a new color to a sheet tab, right-click the tab and then click Tab Color on its shortcut menu. Next, click a color square in either of its two color palettes that appear on the menu's continuation menu to select a standard color or click the More Colors option to open the Custom tab of the Colors dialog box. In the Custom tab, you can assign a custom color by specifying its Red, Green, and Blue values or by dragging the color and intensity sliders before you click OK.

TIP

When creating a multi-sheet workbook, consider making the first worksheet a summary worksheet complete with hyperlinks that you or other users of the workbook can use to navigate quickly and directly to important tables and lists on the various worksheets. (To create a hyperlink in Excel, choose Insert ➪ Link ➪ Insert Link.)

Creating Data Series with AutoFill

One of the marks of a true Excel pro is their reliance on the AutoFill feature to quickly generate the data series needed in the worksheet. Remember that Excel is capable of creating many series such as months of the year, days of the week, and text with numbers (such as Item 100, Item 101, and the like) by entering the first entry in the series in a cell and then dragging the fill handle down the rows of its column or across the columns of its row to fill out the successive entries in that series (as indicated by the ScreenTip that appears beneath the fill handle).

Also keep in mind that you can use the fill handle to generate series that use increments other than 1 (which is the default assumed when you use the fill handle) or even decrements. All you have to do is make two data entries that indicate the increment that the series should use (such as Monday and Wednesday or 50 and 48), and then select both cells before you drag the fill handle down or across to create the series.

Further, you can define a non-incremental (or non-decremental) custom data series (such as a series of company locations such as Chicago, Pittsburgh, Dallas, and Boston) and then generate the custom series in a worksheet by entering its first item in a cell and then dragging the fill handle as you would with any incremental (or decremental) series.

To create the custom list, open the Excel Options dialog box (File ➪ Options or Alt+FT), click the Advanced tab, and then click the Edit Custom Lists button (scroll down to the General section) to open the Custom Lists dialog box. Use the List Entries box to type the individual items in the series (followed in each case by pressing Enter) in the order you want them to be generated with the fill handle; when your list is complete, click Add. Alternatively, if this custom series already exists in a cell range somewhere in the worksheet, click inside the Import List from Cells text box, select the range that contains the entries, and then click Import.

Using Range Names

Using range names in a worksheet provides several important benefits; perhaps the most important of which is that you can use the range name to both move to and simultaneously select the range in a flash no matter where this range appears in the workbook. After you've named a range, choose the name from the Formula bar's Name drop-down list and Excel immediately both navigates to and selects the range.

This method of selecting cell ranges can be a tremendous timesaver when you're dealing with a table or range of data that you find yourself referring to or editing regularly. This is especially true if the named range is located in a distant region of a worksheet.

The second important use for range names is to define and name a constant, such as a tax rate or interest percentage. Normally you'd enter such a constant in the worksheet as a separate cell entry. However, if the constant is one you want to use in multiple formulas throughout a workbook, repeating the cell entry where it's needed is too much work (especially if the constant changes value) and referencing just the one cell entry in all those formulas can be confusing.

A better way to go is to define a range name for the constant. Open the New Name dialog box (Formulas⇨ Define Name or Alt+MMD) and enter the name for the constant in the Name text box. If you'll be using this name throughout your workbook, be sure to leave the Scope value set to Workbook. In the Refers To text box, type an equal sign (=) and then type the value or formula you want to use. With all that done, click OK. To refer to the constant in a formula you're building, start typing the constant's range name, and then select the name from the menu that appears.

The final important use for range names is in documenting the functioning of the formulas in your worksheet ranges. You can do this by having Excel apply the range's row and column headings to the cells of the range. Select the range including the cells with the row and column headings, and then choose Formulas⇨ Create from Selection (or press Alt+MC) to open the Create Names from Selection dialog box. Select the appropriate check boxes (Top Row, Left Column, Bottom Row, or Right Column) that contain the range's row and column headings, and then click OK. To replace the cell addresses in the formulas in this table with the new range names, choose Formula⇨ DefineName⇨ Apply Names (or press Alt+MMA) to open the Apply Names dialog box. With the Use Row and Column Names check box selected, click OK.

Freezing Column and Row Headings

When it comes to the size of your monitor versus the size of your worksheet, your monitor loses hands down every time. This means that in all except the most concise range or table, the column and row headings that identify the entries in its cells soon disappear from the screen as you scroll down or to the right. To keep those headings onscreen at all times no matter how much you scroll the worksheet, you need to freeze the headings. To do this, position the cell cursor in the cell located immediately to the right of the column containing the row headings and immediately below the row with the column headings. Then choose View⇨ Freeze Panes⇨ Freeze Panes (or press Alt+WFF).

You can save the frozen panes you set up in a worksheet as part of a custom view for the worksheet that you can resume at any time simply by selecting its name in the Custom Views dialog box (View⇨ Custom Views or Alt+WC).

Preventing Data Entry Errors with Data Validation

Excel's Data Validation feature enables you to prevent users from entering the wrong type of data or invalid values in a specified range. You can also limit data entry errors by using Data Validation to compel the user to select the entry for a cell from only those values you display on the cell's drop-down list.

Choose Data⇨ Data Validation (or press Alt+AVV) to open the Data Validation dialog box with the Settings tab displayed. To restrict data entry for the selected cell, you use the Allow drop-down list to select the type of entry that's allowed in the cell: Whole Number, Decimal, List, Date,

Time, Text Length, or Custom. Depending on the type of entry you select, you then restrict the range of allowable values. For example, if you select Date as the allowed entry type, you then specify the start and end dates that determine the range of allowable dates.

If you select List as the entry type, you can create a cell drop-down list that contains the complete list of allowed entries. That way, the worksheet user doesn't have to type anything to make the cell entry. This type of cell data validation is perfect when its data entry is restricted to a relatively short list whose values must be consistent and spelled correctly (as when sorting or filtering data). You then specify the allowable entries for the cell drop-down list by selecting the Source text box on the Settings tab and then typing the entries, separated by commas. (Alternatively, if the entries are already in the worksheet, you can use the Source box to select the cell range containing the allowed entries in the worksheet).

When setting up Data Validation for a cell, you can use the Input Message tab to define a message that Excel displays when the user selects the cell. You can also use the Error Alert tab to define an alert message that Excel displays when the user makes an invalid data entry. The input message instructs the user on what range of values are allowed in the cell just as the error alert message informs the user why the entry they tried to complete was not allowed.

After setting up Data Validation for a single blank cell, you can then copy the validation settings to an entire range of cells in the worksheet using any of the standard copy methods (copy and paste, drag-and-drop, or AutoFill).

Trapping Error Values

Error values are not only unsightly but, because they spread so easily to other dependent formulas throughout the worksheet, they can be difficult to eradicate. The most professional spreadsheet designers therefore take steps whenever possible to prevent the spread of error values across the worksheet by trapping them at their source. The most famous example of where this kind of error trapping is needed occurs in division formulas where the divisor is a cell reference that at times can be blank. Blank cells as well as cells with text entries carry a zero (0) value as far as formula computations are concerned, so that if they serve as the divisor in a division calculation in a formula, that formula returns the #DIV/0! error value to the cell.

You can prevent Excel from returning this or any other kind of error value (including #N/A) to the cell by making the division calculation itself the value_if_false argument of an IF function that uses the ISERROR logical function in its logical_test argument to test for the return of an error value, and the value 0 (zero) as its value_if_true argument. See Chapter 13 for practice on error trapping.

So, for example, if cell K7 is the divisor and it could be blank at times (which would cause the division calculation to return #DIV/0!), you can prevent this and block its spread to other formulas dependent upon its result with the addition of the following IF function:

```
=IF(ISERROR(B7 / $K$7), 0, B7 / $K$7)
```

In this case, Excel returns zero (0) to the cell in place of any error value, performing the actual division only when it's safe to do so.

TIP

You can then use conditional formatting (see Chapter 3) to flag all error-trapping formulas that return zero (0) — instead of the desired calculated result — with a special type of color or font. Then, you can use the Find feature (see Chapter 5) to locate all the cells in the worksheet that now sport this special formatting when it comes time to fix their cell references so that their formulas return values other than zero.

Saving Memory by Using Array Formulas

In Chapter 7, you got some experience with constructing array formulas. An array formula is one that constructs the same type of calculation in an entire range of cells in a data table at the time you create it. As a result, you don't go through the normal process of first constructing a master formula and then copying to all the other cells in the table that need to perform the same type of calculation.

Array formulas offer two distinct advantages over normal formulas:

>> Array formulas enable you to create all the duplicate formulas needed in the table in a single operation

>> Array formulas require a lot less computer memory to store than individual copies of a single master formula

It is actually the latter, memory-related benefit that makes array formulas so useful. By building array formulas, you can save substantial amounts of computer memory. (Remember that Excel must be able to load every bit of data in a workbook into memory to be able to open the file at all. It doesn't perform like other programs that can load just parts of a document into memory, switching them out as you work.) This memory savings is important in large workbooks as it enables you to add more data to the worksheet as well as keeps Excel from completely bogging down when you open worksheets for editing or printing.

Using Outlines to Control the Display of Data

Many of the worksheets you create and maintain in Excel require more columns and rows than can possibly fit on a single screen (even with a huge monitor) unless you select a small zoom magnification percentage (which might be so small that it's impossible to read the data!). In some worksheets, such as the Regional Income and CG Media Sales tables that you worked with in several different exercises, you can easily reclaim some of this screen estate as well as maintain a great degree of flexibility in how much of the data to display by outlining the ranges.

When you outline a typical range (Data ⇨ Group ⇨ Auto Outline or Alt+AGA), Excel adds outline buttons to both the rows and columns of the range (that appear in the worksheet's row and column headers). You can then use these outline buttons to control how much of the data is displayed on screen (accomplished by hiding and unhiding particular rows and columns of the range).

Outlines are perfect for ranges such as the Regional Income and CG Media Sales tables, where the monthly income and sales data are naturally summarized by quarterly and annual totals for the various regions and products being tracked. With the help of the level outline buttons, you can quickly collapse the range down to the grand totals or quarterly totals and then just as easily completely expand it to display all the monthly income and sales data as well.

Outlining ranges like these makes it a snap to print and chart just a selected part of their data. For example, to create a chart using only the quarterly totals in the regional income table, use the level outline buttons to display only columns with totals in the data table, select the quarterly data, and then use the Insert tab's Charts group to select the desired chart type.

Using View Side by Side to Work with Two Workbooks

To be a true Excel pro, you need to be comfortable working not only with data on different sheets of the same workbook but on sheets of different workbooks as well. One way in which Excel facilitates this is through the program's ability to open side-by-side windows on two different workbooks that you have open at a time.

When you're only dealing with two open workbooks, you can create horizontal windows (one on top of the other), each displaying a part of a different workbook by choosing View ⇨ View Side by Side (or by pressing Alt+WB).

While the two workbook windows are open in Excel, you can select different worksheets and scroll to different regions in either one by using its sheet tabs and scroll bars that appear at the edge of the window when you make its workbook active (either by clicking the window's title bar or one of the cells of its worksheets).

To move or copy data between the open workbook files, you have a choice between using the drag-and-drop or copy-and-paste method. To use drag-and-drop, select the data to be moved or copied in the worksheet of one window and then drag the outline of the cell selection to the desired cell in the worksheet displayed in the other window. If you want to copy the cell selection, rather than move it, to the workbook in the other window, you must remember to hold down the Ctrl key as you drag its outline to its new position, releasing the Ctrl key only when you're in position and ready to drop the copied data into place.

Index

A

absolute references, 124–128

Access (Microsoft), 267–270

access keys, 12

Account button (Start screen), 21

Accounting (number format), 47, 48–49, 287

Accounting Number Format button (Number group), 44

Add button (Quick Access Toolbar), 18

Add Constraint dialog box, 298

Add Footer message/text, 64, 65

Add Header message/text, 64

Add Level button, 259

Add Scenario dialog box, 292

Add to Dictionary button (Spelling Checker), 97

Add-Ins dialog box, 296, 338, 340

AddIns folder, 339

Add-ins tab, 340

addition (+), 104

Adjust group (Picture Format), 237

alert dialog box, 24, 90, 96, 97, 109, 139, 141, 143, 200, 201, 215, 261, 263, 274, 281, 288, 321, 323

Align Text Right formatting, 46

alignment

  Excel as automatically left-aligning text entries, 30

  Excel as automatically right-aligning number entries, 30

  modifying of for labels in spreadsheets, 49–51

Alignment group (Home tab), 41, 46, 49, 50, 51, 243

Alignment tab, 46, 51

All (Paste Option), 89

All Border option, 44

All Except Borders (Paste Option), 89

All Using Source Theme (Paste Option), 89

Allow All Users of This Worksheet To box, 277

Allow drop-down button (Settings), 199

Alt+AGA (Auto Outline), 352

Alt+APNDC (Microsoft Access Database), 268

Alt+ASD (Sort Z to A option), 213

Alt+ASS (Sort), 259, 260, 262

Alt+AVV (Data Validation), 199, 201, 350

Alt+AWG (Goal Seek), 295

Alt+AWS (Scenario Manager), 292

Alt+AWT (Data Table), 287, 291

Alt+AY3 (Solver), 297

Alt+Enter (new line), 252

Alt+F (File menu), 120

Alt+F8 (Macros), 320, 330

Alt+FA (Save As), 36, 43, 45

Alt+FC (Close), 23, 36

Alt+FN (New), 24

Alt+FO (Backstage view's Open), 35

Alt+FS (Save), 36

Alt+FT (opens Excel Options dialog box), 11, 27, 125, 278

Alt+FT (Options), 143

Alt+HDC (Delete Sheet Columns), 86

Alt+HDD (Delete Cells), 86

Alt+HDR (Delete Sheet Rows), 86

Alt+HIC (Delete Sheet Rows), 86

Alt+HII (Insert Cells), 86

Alt+HIR (Insert Sheet Rows), 86

Alt+HJ (Cell Styles), 98

Alt+HOA (AutoFit Row Height), 38, 40

Alt+HOD (Default Width command), 37

Alt+HOE (Format Cells), 46

Alt+HOH (Row Height), 40

Alt+HOI (AutoFit Column Width), 38

Alt+HOL (Lock Cell), 276, 279

Alt+HOUC (Hide Columns), 56, 82

Alt+HOUL (Unhide Columns), 56

Alt+HOUO (Unhide Rows), 56

Alt+HOUR (Hide Rows), 56, 82

Alt+HOW (Column Width), 38

Alt+HT (Format As Table), 254

Alt+HVN (Paste Link), 118, 119, 238, 287

Alt+HVT (Transpose), 91

Alt+HVV (Paste Values), 90, 149, 153

Alt+JASE (Shape Effects), 230

Alt+JASF (Shape Fill), 230

Alt+JCABW (With Legend Keys), 312

Design tab, 42, 240

Developer check box, 318

Developer tab, 318, 319, 320, 321

dialog box, adding of that processes user input, 331–334

Different Odd & Even Pages check box (Header & Footer contextual tab's Options group), 65

digital ink entry, 30

direct precedents, 140

Directories list box, 269

Display Name text box, 14, 324, 325

division formula, 107

Documents Library, 52

dollar sign ($), 124, 126

double-declining balance, 162

double-headed arrow, 67, 222

Drag Fields Between Areas Below section, 302–303, 307

drag-and-drop, 88, 89, 91

Draw Borders command (Quick Access Toolbar), 18, 19

Draw tab, 11, 12

Drawing Tools contextual tab, 233

dynamic array formulas, 138–139

Dynamic Array Formulas worksheet, 139

dynamic arrays, 136

E

EDATE function, 150

Edit Custom Lists button, 349

Edit mode, 84, 85, 114

Edit Note command button, 93

editing

charts, 229–230

data entries, 84–86

finding and identifying the region that needs editing on worksheet, 79–82

formulas, 114–115

multiple worksheets, 97–99

recorded macro, 329–331

records in the data form, 255–257

selecting cell ranges for, 82–84

Editing group (Home tab), 41, 45, 87

embedded charts, 220, 221–223, 224–228

Enable Iterative Calculation check box, 143

Enter box (Formula bar), 31

Enter button (Formula bar), 85

EOMONTH function, 150

equal sign (=), 34, 103, 104

Equal To dialog box, 54

Error Alert, 199, 201

Error Checking dialog box, 141

Error Message text box, 201

error values

list of, 104

prevention of, 197

some as unavoidable, 205

tracing and eliminating formula errors, 140–142

trapping of, 351–352

working with in formulas, 109–110

Excel

getting familiar with interface of, 7–20

launching of, 7–8

top ten features of, 343–346

top ten tips for using Excel like a pro, 347–353

Excel Add-in (*.xlam) option, 339

Excel Add-Ins, 340

Excel Options dialog box, 13, 18, 19, 97, 323, 324, 325

Excel Template (*.xltx) (Save As Type), 23

Excel window, identifying parts of, 9–11

exclamation point (!), 118

Existing Worksheet option, 268

Expand button (+), 269

Expand Dialog Box button, 67

exponentiation formula, 107

Ext Ref sheet tab, 142

external references, 105, 118–120

External WrkBk Link button, 119

F

F2 (Edit mode), 114, 131

F2 (to place insertion point at end of current cell entry), 85, 86

F4, 128, 130

F7 (Spelling command button), 94

F9, 120, 121

F12, 36

FALSE (comparative formulas), 108–109, 175

FALSE function, 197, 198

Feedback button (Start screen), 21

file format, XML as default file format, 35

File Name text box, 35

filename extensions

.xlsx, 22

.xltx, 22

Fill Color button drop-down list, 51

Fill Color drop-down button (Font Group), 29–30, 41

Macros (Custom) group, 325

magnification, 29, 80, 81

Main Tabs list box, 13, 14, 15, 325

Manage drop-down list, 340

Margins tab (Page Setup dialog box), 63

Match Entire Cell Contents (Find and Replace dialog box), 95

match_mode argument, 189

Math & Trig category (Insert Function), 113, 167, 168–175

math functions, 167–177

MAX function, 179, 181–182, 262

Maximize button (Code window), 330

MEDIAN function, 180–181

Merge & Center button (Alignment group), 41, 46, 51, 320

Merge Cells (Text Control option), 50

Microsoft Access, 267–270

Microsoft Support web page, 143

Middle Align button (Alignment group), 50

MIN function, 179, 181–182, 262

Misc (Custom) tab, 14, 15, 325

Misc tab (Ribbon), 256

mixed references, 128–132

Modify Button dialog box, 324

More button (Table Styles gallery), 43

Most Likely scenario, 293

mouse pointer

  black-cross mouse pointer, 242, 243

  as double-headed arrow, 67, 222

  four-headed arrow, 234

  I-beam cursor, 84, 85, 205, 207

  moving of, 24–26

  white-cross mouse pointer, 24, 84, 85, 89, 124

Move Chart button, 310

Move Chart dialog box, 223, 311

Move Down button (Customize Quick Access Toolbar), 18, 19

Move Up button (Customize Quick Access Toolbar), 18, 19

MS Access Database option, 269

multiplication, 34, 104, 169

multiplication formula, 107

My Table Has Headers check box, 42

N

NA function, 207

Name box (Formula bar), 72, 84, 90

Name drop-down box, 103

Name Manager button, 109

Name Manager dialog box, 140

Navigator dialog box, 268

nesting IF functions, 203–205

NETWORKDAYS function, 150

New button (Start screen), 21

New File button, 18

New File command button, 19

New Group button, 325

New Group (Custom), 13, 14, 15, 325

New Name dialog box, 133

New Sheet icon (+), 28

New Sheet option button, 223

New Tab (Custom), 13

Next Page button, 61, 63

No Fill option (Fill Color button drop-down list), 51

No Glow thumbnail, 230

NOT functions, 197

Note cell style, 52

Notes (Paste Option), 89

notes, adding of to worksheet, 92–93

Notes group (Review tab), 92

NOW function, 111, 148–149, 152

nper argument, 130, 131, 156

NPER function, 156, 157–158

Nper text box, 130

NPV (Net Present Value) function, 155, 156, 159–162

Number (number format), 46

Number Filters (criteria option), 265, 266

Number Format button, 305

Number Format (Cell Styles gallery), 52

Number Format drop-down button, 49

Number Format (Home tab), 147, 152

number formats, 46–47

Number Formats sheet, 48

Number group (Home tab), 41, 44, 49

Number of Pages button (Header & Footer Elements group), 65

Number tab, 46, 47, 49, 56

Number1 argument, 113

Number2 argument, 113

Number3 argument, 113

numeric (value), as one of two types of cell entries, 30

numeric entries, making of, 30

O

Odd Page Header indicator, 65

Omit Column Name If Same Column check box, 135

R

V

Validation (Paste Option), 89

Value Field Settings dialog box, 305, 308, 309

Value Of option button, 297

value_if_false argument, 198

value_if_true argument, 198

values

applying conditional formatting to range of, 54–56

choosing between alternate values, 198–201

formatting various values with Format Cells dialog box, 48–49

using Solver to modify multiple input values in worksheet, 297–298

Values (Paste Option), 89

Values and Number Formats (Paste Option), 89

Values data item, 308

VBA (Visual Basic for Applications) code, 317, 318, 327

VBAProject - Project Properties dialog box, 339

Vertical (Category) Axis option, 230

Vertical (Value) Axis option (Format tab), 228

vertical ruler, 60

view buttons, 9

View Microsoft Excel button, 331, 333

View Side by Side feature, 32, 45, 134, 353

View tab, 11, 12, 13, 81

Visual Basic Editor Standard toolbar, 328, 331

Visual Basic Editor (VBE), 317, 318, 327–340

Visual Basic for Applications (VBA) code, 317, 318, 327

VLOOKUP function, 188, 189, 190, 191, 193–195, 199, 200, 201

voice entry, 30

W

WEEKDAY function, 150, 151–152

WEEKNUM function, 150, 151–152

what-if analysis, 285–298

white-cross mouse pointer, 24, 84, 85, 89, 124

Width drop-down button, 70

wildcard characters

asterisk (*), 94, 255, 257, 265

question mark (?), 94, 255, 265

window (of Excel), identifying parts of, 9–11

Windows Start Menu and Taskbar, pinning Excel to, 8

With Selection.Font statement, 330

WordArt, 234, 235, 243–245

workbook filename, 9

workbooks

generating new ones from templates, 347–348

moving and copying cells in, 89–91

moving around in, 24–28

moving to different sheet in, 27–28

opening new one, 21–23

opening new one from template file, 24

password-protecting of, 272–274

printing all or part of, 71–77

printing entire one, 72–74

protecting data in, 271–274, 280–281

protecting entire workbook, 280–281

saving spreadsheet data in workbook file, 35–36

using View Side by Side to work with two workbooks, 353

WORKDAY function, 150

worksheet area, 9

worksheet tab, 9

Worksheet Title dialog box, 333

worksheets

adding first worksheet column as Print Title for report, 66–67

adding graphics to, 231–248

adding notes to, 92–93

changing name of, 106

charting worksheet data, 219–230

color-coding worksheet tabs, 348

deleting and inserting cells in, 87–88

doing data entry in protected worksheet, 278–280

editing formulas in, 114–115

editing multiple ones, 97–99

entering data in, 21–36

finding source of error values in, 140–142

formatting of, 37–57

goal seeking in, 294–296

grouping worksheets together, 106

making first worksheet summary worksheet, 348

modification of, 79–99

moving cell cursor to new area of, 25

moving cell cursor to unseen parts of, 26

moving cell cursor using Ctrl and arrow keys, 26–27

moving to different sheet in workbook, 27–28

organizing data on different worksheets, 348

previewing pages in, 59–61

printing charts in, 74–75

printing worksheet formulas, 76–77

printing worksheet reports, 59–77

protecting data in, 274–280

renaming of, 27, 28

using custom function in, 337–338

Worst Case scenario, 293

Wrap Text (Text Control option), 50

X

XLOOKUP function, 188–190

XML (eXtensible Markup Language), as default file format, 35

Y

YEARFRAC function, 150–152

Your Text Here placeholder, 245

Z

Zip Code format, 49

zoom control, 9

Zoom dialog box, 80–81

Zoom feature, 80

Zoom In button, 80

Zoom Level button, 80

Zoom slider, 29, 345

Zoom to Page button, 67, 68

About the Authors

Paul McFedries has been a technical writer for 30 years (no, that is not a typo). He has been messing around with spreadsheet software since installing Lotus 1-2-3 on an IBM PC clone in 1986. He has written more than 100 books (nope, not a typo) that have sold more than four million copies worldwide (again, not a typo). Paul's books include the Wiley titles *Excel All-in-One For Dummies, Excel Data Analysis For Dummies, Teach Yourself VISUALLY Excel,* and *Teach Yourself VISUALLY Windows 11.* Paul invites everyone to drop by his personal website (https://paulmcfedries.com) and to follow him on Twitter (@paulmcf) and Facebook (https://www.facebook.com/PaulMcFedries/).

Greg Harvey authored tons of computer books, the most recent being *Excel 2019 For Dummies.* He started out training business users on how to use IBM personal computers and their attendant computer software in the rough-and tumble days of DOS, WordStar, and Lotus 1-2-3 in the mid-80s of the last century.

After working for a number of independent training firms, he went on to teach semester-long courses in spreadsheet and database management software at Golden Gate University in San Francisco.

Greg's love of teaching translated into his equal love of writing. *For Dummies* books were, of course, his all-time favorites to write because they enabled him to write to his favorite audience, the beginner. They also enabled him to use humor (a key element to success in the training room) and, most delightful of all, to express an opinion or two about the subject matter at hand.

Greg passed away January 2020 after a multi-decade battle with cancer. This edition of *Excel Workbook For Dummies,* and all subsequent editions of this work, are dedicated to his memory.

Dedication

To Karen and Chase, the best beings in the world.

Author's Acknowledgments

If we're ever at the same cocktail party and you overhear me saying something like "I wrote a book," I hereby give you permission to wag your finger at me and say "Tsk, tsk." Why the scolding? Because although I did write this book's text and take its screenshots, that represents only a part of what constitutes a "book." The rest of it is brought to you by the dedication and professionalism of Wiley's editorial and production teams, who toiled long and hard to turn my text and images into an actual book.

I offer my sincere gratitude to everyone at Wiley who made this book possible, but I'd like to extend a special "Thanks a bunch!" to the folks I worked with directly: Executive Editor Steve Hayes, Project Editor Rebecca Senninger and Technical Editor Guy Hart-Davis.

Publisher's Acknowledgments

Development Editor: Rebecca Senninger

Executive Editor: Steven Hayes

Technical Editor: Guy Hart-Davis

Production Editor: Mohammed Zafar Ali

Cover Image: © one photo/Shutterstock